AveofAutism.com

W9-BLI-776

THE AGE
OF
AUTISM

THE AGE

OF

AUTISM

MERCURY, MEDICINE, AND A MAN-MADE EPIDEMIC

Dan Olmsted and Mark Blaxill

Thomas Dunne Books
St. Martin's Press
New York

THOMAS DUNNE BOOKS.
An imprint of St. Martin's Press.

Quotations from the article by Kanner and Adams reprinted with permission from the *American Journal of Psychiatry* (Copyright © 1926), American Psychiatric Association.

THE AGE OF AUTISM. Copyright © 2010 by Dan Olmsted and Mark Blaxill. Foreword copyright © 2010 by David Kirby. All rights reserved. Printed in the United States of America. For information, address St. Martin's Press, 175 Fifth Avenue, New York, N.Y. 10010.

www.thomasdunnebooks.com
www.stmartins.com

ISBN 978-0-312-54562-8

Book design by Mspace/Maura Fadden Rosenthal

First Edition: September 2010

10 9 8 7 6 5 4 3 2 1

FROM DAN: *To Mark, Mark, and Mark—in that order*

FROM MARK: *To Michaela, Sydney, and Elise—
and all the other families affected by the tragedy of autism*

CONTENTS

FOREWORD

When it came to collecting quicksilver, the ancient Romans would send condemned criminals and slaves into the mercury mines to extract the poisonous metal from the earth's crust. The work, so gruesome and hazardous the miners would soon die a crazed and anguished death, was considered unsuitable for even the lowest classes of Romans.

But once it was mined, the Romans had no qualms about using the powerful neurotoxin for medicine and other purposes.

They would have been far better off leaving the stuff in the ground.

Humans have always been exposed to limited amounts of naturally occurring mercury from, say, volcanic eruptions, springwater, or fish. Over the millennia, these low-level exposures have spurred the development of natural defenses (called "mercaptans," from the Latin for "capturing mercury") that bind with heavy metals and eliminate them from the body.

But then humankind began to mine mercury, drawing it up from the rocks below and using it for all sorts of strange purposes. Mercury, the second deadliest element on earth after plutonium, of course does not break down, dissolve, or turn into something else. Instead, it accumulates—in our food, air, and water.

And though we may laugh at the Romans for being so ignorant as to use mercury in medicine (and lead in water pipes), the risky and unnecessary practice continues to this day.

Worldwide mercury exposures have been skyrocketing in the last decade or so, and dwarf anything seen in the time of Dickens and the industrial revolution. American lakebeds reveal astronomical levels of the metal in recently settled sediment. Small fish and even songbirds are turning up with high levels of mercury contamination, which was hitherto the sole province of top-of-the-food-chain predators. Mercury deposition rates rise each year, much of the mercury coming from coal burning in the Far East, whose metal-laden emissions cross the Pacific and settle onto North America in the form of rain fallout, only to be kicked up again into the atmosphere by raging wildfires near increasingly populated areas.

All of this "background" mercury means that our own personal levels are rising as well. People might poke fun at the actor Jeremy Piven and his claims of quicksilver toxicity (via a diet heavy in sushi), but consider this: A new study has shown that inorganic mercury was detected in the blood of 30 percent of U.S. women in the Centers for Disease Control and Prevention (CDC)'s most recent National Health and Nutrition Examination Survey (NHANES). That figure was 1,500 percent higher than what was reported in the 1999–2000 survey, when only 2 percent of women had inorganic mercury in their blood.

No one knows the exact effect of these rising mercury exposures in people, and especially in pregnant women and their unborn children. But we do have some idea. Mercury can ravage the immune system, trigger autoimmunity, attack mitochondria (the "batteries" inside cells), increase oxidative stress, activate brain cells called microglia, spark chronic neuro-inflammation and block production of glutathione—the body's most powerful mercaptan that protects us from mercury in the first place. And all of these problems can be found in at least some children with autism.

Today, one in six American children is born with mercury levels in their blood that are high enough to cause neurodevelopmental deficiencies later on in life. Perhaps coincidentally—or perhaps not—the same number of American children will go on to develop a learning disability, and one in one hundred will develop an autism spectrum disorder (ASD).

These poor kids are born already set up for neurological failure. Many of them are already at the exact toxic tipping point when it comes to prenatal and neonatal exposures to toxic metals. So why on earth would we inject them with vaccines containing organic ethylmercury and aluminum salts beginning on day one, and repeated at regular intervals over the next couple of years?

There is now ample science to tie mercury toxicity to autism, just as there are historical examples to tie mercury exposure to what appears to be mental illness. After all, mad hatters' disease was an affliction of the felt trade, which used copious amounts of mercury in its production. And just outside Phoenix you will find the defunct cluster of Dreamy Draw mercury mines, so called because of the mildly psychotic state in which the miners emerged from their shafts. (Today it is the site of the Mercury Mine School.)

In the following pages, Dan Olmsted and Mark Blaxill—two men I consider friends, colleagues, and patriots—walk us through humankind's disastrous dalliances with mercury over the centuries, leading us inexorably toward our own new and unsettling Age of Autism.

One very disturbing trend emerges in this book, and that is the ignorance and arrogance of medical professionals, who have insisted over the years that mercurials in medicine could treat or prevent the onset of horrible, disfiguring diseases, while utterly ignoring or dismissing the evidence that their "medicine" was often doing more harm than the diseases it was designed to fight.

Whether the problem was syphilis or teething pain, doctors often prescribed mercury. As Olmsted and Blaxill so eloquently describe, this blind belief in a known poison was misguided, immoral, and in some cases, patently criminal.

Mercury, they argue forcefully and convincingly, is found at the root of many "plagues" of the industrialized world—from the "lunacy" of Dickens's coal-choked England, to Freud's "hysterical" Viennese women, to the collection of symptoms we now call autism spectrum disorders. In each case, the metal left behind its insidious footprints. Olmsted and Blaxill have done a masterful job of retracing these clues through an encyclopedic history of metal-induced madness.

Can toxins trigger plagues? They can. Autism is a man-made disease, Olmsted and Blaxill warn us. But that is cause for hope. By cracking autism's code and revealing its underpinnings, we may solve the mysteries lurking behind many modern-day scourges, including Alzheimer's, Parkinson's, and Lou Gehrig's disease. Anyone concerned with environmental health owes it to him- or herself (and to the world) to read this revolutionary book.

—DAVID KIRBY

Where observation is concerned,

chance favors only the prepared mind.

Dans les champs de l'observation

le hasard ne favorise que les esprits préparés.

—Louis Pasteur, 1854[1]

THE AGE
OF
AUTISM

INTRODUCTION: THE SEED

You are not to expect visible proofs in a work of darkness. You are to collect the truth from circumstances, and little collateral facts, which taken singly afford no proof, yet put together, so tally with, and confirm each other, that they are as strong and convincing evidence, as facts that appear in the broad face of the day.

—JUDGE FRANCIS BULLER TO THE JURY IN A MURDER TRIAL, 1781[1]

When we decided to investigate the natural history of autism, we never meant to dig so deep.

We simply wanted to trace the rise of the disorder beginning with a landmark 1943 report by Johns Hopkins psychiatrist Leo Kanner on eleven anonymous children born in the 1930s.[2] But right from the start, we discovered more than we bargained for. No one, it seems, ever tried to identify those original children and their families. No one looked past the patterns recited over and over: Those first parents were highly educated; they were atypically affluent; many of them had medical and scientific backgrounds, mothers included. From those observations based on limited data, it was just a wrong turn or two to the idea that something was wrong with these families. The fathers and mothers were labeled aloof and career-obsessed; they were "refrigerator parents"; their cold indifference to each other and their own offspring drove these children into the "empty fortress" of autism. In Kanner's words:

> Most of the fathers are, in a sense, bigamists. They are wedded to their jobs at least as much as they are married to their wives. The job, in fact, has priority.[3]

Once the idea that parental coldness had promoted autism in their children was abandoned, scientists turned to their genes. "Autism is one of the most heritable complex genetic disorders in psychiatry," reported a respected academic journal in 2003.[4]

But we unearthed something different—something that did not point to mutant genes or malignant parenting. We decided, instead of taking Kanner's word for it, to learn about these previously anonymous families ourselves. We took clues from his extensive case descriptions and started uncovering the identities of the original families. Time and again, we connected the occupations of the parents to plausible toxic exposures and especially to a new mercury compound first used in the 1930s as a disinfectant for seeds, a treatment for lumber, and a preservative in vaccines. Yes, the parents' professions were clues—but not to their obsessions or their marriages or their parenting or their genetic oddities; instead, they pointed to a strikingly consistent pattern of *familial exposures to the same toxic substance.*

This discovery is something entirely new. While debate has raged—inconclusively—over whether mercury in vaccines was responsible for the explosion in autism diagnoses beginning in 1990, we saw the seeds of autism planted one by one, family by family, six decades earlier.

This led to a deeper question than the one we'd originally sought to answer: namely, were clues like this missed before? Was mercury the buried seed that gave rise to other disorders, disorders that seem different but fit into the same pattern of misdiagnosed mercury exposure? Once again, the answer our investigation supports is yes. Different kinds of mercury and different exposures can cause a variety of disorders, often delayed and disguised. "We need to assign mercury to the illnesses it causes," Eric Gladen of the World Mercury Project told us. "That hasn't happened, and I don't know why."[5]

Our research uncovered a hidden history of mercury poisoning—a history that needs to be exposed before it can be put to an end. For centuries, mercury use was widespread in medicine, and the consequences were disastrous. The greatest plague of Europe and America, spanning five hundred years, was syphilis, and the standard of care (the generally accepted medical treatment of the time) before penicillin was mercury. Our investigation has led us to believe that a man-made mercury compound, interacting with syphilis itself, caused the horrendous affliction called general paralysis of the insane. This illness, also called GPI, is a classic instance of the synergistic dangers of metals, microbes, and man. Tens if not hundreds of thousands of people in medically "advanced" countries suffered and died as a direct result, while doctors ducked or missed the truth, clearing the way for subsequent catastrophes. In nineteenth-century Vienna several of the key cases of so-called hysteria seen by Sigmund Freud were actually instances of mercury poisoning, we argue. Young women of this time were expected to care for sick relatives, often treating their own fathers with mercury for syphilis. Men, too, succumbed to mercurial medicine or workplace exposure and were also labeled mentally ill. These erroneous diagnoses sent psychiatry off on several tangents—blaming parents for all kinds of mental disorders and concocting elaborate psychosexual theories of mental illness. The Freudian tendency to link "hysterical" mental disorders to childhood psychic trauma may have been one reason medical experts later missed the environmental cause of autism.

In acrodynia (or pink disease), an illness that would foreshadow autism, teething powders and other over-the-counter nostrums containing mercury poisoned untold thousands of children. Hundreds died. The cause remained a mystery for decades. In addition, the "heroic" use of mercury in the United States may have given rise to all kinds of chronic health problems including a nineteenth-century collection of symptoms called neurasthenia.

Medicine was not the only source of mercury exposure. England's coal-fired Industrial Revolution spewed tons of mercury, lead, and arsenic into the atmosphere for the first time in history, a surge that correlates with a baffling explosion of severe mental illness. As manufacturers stepped up the use of mercury compounds, accidents and excesses led to environmental catastrophes like Minamata disease in Japan, and to a spike in autism cases in a district next door.

We suspect today's ever-expanding coal pollution, combined with thousands of new environmental contaminants, continues to fuel mental, physical, and neurological problems that no one can figure out, let alone cure. (Studies suggest American children have a higher risk of autism the closer they live to coal-fired plants.)

We believe that autism was newly discovered in the 1930s for the simple reason that it *was* new. The organic chemicals industry that grew out of chemical warfare research during World War I led to new commercial uses for mercury, including the introduction of some extraordinarily toxic compounds made from ethylmercury. This, our research suggests, led directly to the first cases of autism. Among the parents of those first eleven cases described in 1943, you will meet a plant pathologist experimenting with ethylmercury fungicides in Maryland; a pediatrician in Boston who was an early champion of mass vaccinations containing ethylmercury; and a stenographer in a pathology lab in Washington, D.C., who spent her workday exposed to mercury fumes while her future husband, a psychiatrist, treated syphilis with mercury just as Freud had done decades earlier. Several other families cluster around the medical profession, agriculture, and forestry—the three biggest risk factors for exposure to mercury in its newest and most toxic form. Leo Kanner provided some clues to the backgrounds of these early parents—such as their professions—but our investigation uncovered dramatic new details about what the parents were doing when each child was born and in the critical years before that.

By the time our five-year journey was done, we had worked our way through newspaper clippings, professional archives, city directories, cemetery records, ancestry searches, last-known addresses, and libraries from Washington, D.C., to Moscow, Idaho. We found and interviewed family members of several of the first eleven children; most memorably, we met two of those "cases" ourselves. At the end of our search, we talked with "Case 1: Donald T." around the kitchen table in his lifelong home in the small lumber town of Forest, Mississippi. By any measure, he has fared astonishingly well. President of his college fraternity and later the Forest Kiwanis Club, a pillar of his Presbyterian church, he had a long career at the local bank, plays a competitive game of golf, and regularly travels the world. We learned how "Donald T." went from being the first unmistakable case of autism to the first unmistakable case of *recovery*. He also reminds us how recent autism is—the space of one man's lifetime: "Donald T." turned seventy-seven in September 2010.

Leo Kanner's original cases, linked only by this overlooked association with mercury, suggest that from the very beginning autism was an environmentally induced illness—a toxic injury rather than something inherited or inculcated. Certainly, some children were more susceptible to mercury exposure—and that may implicate genetic vulnerabilities. This is very different, however, from saying that autism is an inherited genetic disorder.

Tragically, the best and the brightest in science and medicine have missed these clues from the start, blinded first by the belief the parents were responsible and then by their ongoing pursuit of the "autism gene." The Great Autism Gene Hunt has come up empty—but continues to drain off millions of dollars and thousands of hours that should go to more promising environmental research.

Having thoroughly failed to solve the autism puzzle, the medical industry is putting forth a new wave of epidemic deniers to claim autism isn't really increasing after all. Simply put, this idea is nonsense; and sadly, it prolongs the epidemic and prevents the urgent response this public health crisis demands.

In tracing the history of autism, we cannot avoid discussion of what we have already acknowledged as a controversial topic: vaccines. Some critics have labeled us antivaccine for even broaching the subject. But our interest has more to do with vaccination as a risk factor, perhaps one of several. We want to state explicitly that we *support* vaccines as long as they are individually and collectively tested for safety, and not deployed excessively, as part of an overall policy to promote childhood health. We are not antifungicide or antivaccine or anti- anything but autism. We support progress and innovation. (Mercury was removed from fungicides in the 1970s for safety reasons after several episodes of mass poisoning.) We don't want crops to wither, or houses to rot, or children to die of vaccine-preventable illnesses. We simply want to stop an autism epidemic whose origin we believe can be discerned from a careful examination of its environmental history.

Vaccines have played an important role in public health, from the eradication of smallpox to the near-eradication of the rubella virus that can cause fetal harm (as we outline in chapter 7). But too many vaccines too early may be a part of the toxic picture, which almost certainly argues for fewer vaccines delivered with careful attention to the potential for adverse reactions.

We do not pretend to know precisely which exposures, in which combination, may have played a role in the current rise in autism rates. Possible suspects include sources of mercury from power plants and fish consumption, and other toxins as well, from chemicals in plastic baby bottles to those that are found in pajamas. But we do believe mercury—and that certainly includes the ethylmercury in vaccines—was present at the creation, when the disease first emerged, and continues to be a major player as autism rates have surged over the last two decades. And we believe uncovering autism's historical roots leaves no doubt as to its origin and nature: Autism is man-made. Informed by this simple truth, we can stop triggering autism and start treating it for what it is. And we can learn lessons that may help crack the code of other modern plagues from Alzheimer's and Parkinson's to asthma and Lou Gehrig's disease.

We believe these possibilities are cause for hope.

—

Doctors have been using mercury in an attempt to heal since antiquity. The Egyptians, Greeks, Romans, Arabs, and Chinese put it to a whole range of uses; in Western medicine it was used mainly to treat the skin lesions of lepers and balance the humors. The demand for mercury in medicine, as a pigment, and in alchemy spurred a mining industry that stretches back to the Roman Empire and the mines of Almaden in Spain and Idrija in Slovenia. For just as long, miners have been getting poisoned; in fact, the Romans sent convict laborers into the mines as a death sentence.

Mercury use became more widespread with the epidemic of syphilis in Europe, but even then little changed in the commonly prescribed forms for centuries. Doctors worked with mercury mostly in its metallic form, in rubs and vapors and applied it to the skin, where it had undeniable effects in killing both the syphilis and leprosy bacteria. Convinced that mercury was the essential weapon in the armory of any practicing physician, enterprising apothecaries soon began experimenting with new mercury compounds and ways to deliver them—not just on the surface. Chloride compounds of mercury, mercurous and mercuric, were easiest to synthesize from the base metal and became the most widely used formulations. Also, starting in the eighteenth century, Viennese physicians began experimenting with internal administration. The idea was simple: Deliver a more powerful form of the poison more directly to the source of the disease process; instead of the skin, go straight to the diseased organ; instead of an ointment that requires absorption and evaporation, develop a more targeted, toxic dose of a manufactured compound. This made mercury compounds the original chemotherapy, the first synthesized pharmaceutical substance with a specific chemical mission—to reach and eliminate the source of disease.

During all this innovation, concern about mercury's impact on human health was never far from the surface. But its use in medicine continued to spread. In 1807 *The New Encyclopaedia* reported a case that echoes the infamous Vietnam-era statement about destroying a village in order to save it: "The particulars of this case we need not quote, as the patient, a child at the breast, aged 7 months, though cured of the hydrocephalus, by a mercurial course of 7 days, died on the 8th about 8 P.M." The article cites a Dr. Percival as blaming "the powerful action of the mercury."[6]

While mercury intoxication is often linked in the popular imagination to the stereotypical tremors and distorted thinking of mad hatters' disease, symptoms can vary from subtle personality changes to vision problems to muscle contractions and paralyses to unbearable intestinal pains euphemistically labeled as "gastric crises" . . . to death. Mercury is the Great Pretender, mimicking many diseases and their symptoms: the tremors of Parkinson's, the hallucinations of schizophrenia, the paralyses and contractures of stroke, the gastrointestinal pain of ulcers and cancers.

Even when patients are given the same dose of the same mercury compound, the effects in different cases can be totally idiosyncratic and unpredictable. In pink disease, for instance, only one in five hundred children treated with teething powders succumbed to the illness. No wonder it took decades, and the development of new instruments to measure (supposedly) trace amounts of mercury, to connect the two.

But the heart of the problem in recognizing mercury poisoning is latency. For reasons still unknown, there can be a long time lag—days, weeks, months, even decades—between a mercury exposure and the manifestation of its ill effects. The benefits of mercury were always clear: When it was rubbed on a skin lesion, the sore would disappear. The risks of the medicine were often far subtler and almost always delayed. For the physician, dedicated to his mission of combating disease, the temptation to ignore the delayed effects of the favored therapeutic was often overwhelming. The negative consequences were mysterious, difficult to trace, and easy to pin on other factors, especially the illness itself. This skewed combination of risk and benefit has made mercury controversial throughout the history of modern medicine.

In August 1996 Dartmouth chemistry professor Karen Wetterhahn, a toxicologist who was working on understanding how chemicals like mercury and chromium might cause cancer, had donned goggles, lab coat, and gloves to work with a small vial of dimethylmercury.

Dimethylmercury was invented in 1854 as part of the ongoing quest for more potent forms of mercurial medicine that could be delivered at smaller concentrations.

Wetterhahn, a star of the chemistry department at Dartmouth and recipient of many prestigious grants from the National Institutes of Health, thought she knew the risks. She used state-of-the-art protection: She wore latex gloves and carefully handled the vial underneath a chemical fume hood that blew vapors away from her. But the contents of the vial—three or four drops, about the weight of a small paper clip—accidentally spilled, and within seconds they had penetrated the protective layer of latex and begun working their way through her skin.

For many weeks thereafter it was as if nothing had happened. She continued with her normal duties and soon forgot the accident under the lab hood. Then, slowly, she began to notice subtle signs of illness that she still did not connect to the incident. Eventually the symptoms became progressively more serious. A full five months later, she was finally admitted to the hospital suffering from mental confusion, balance problems, and loss of appetite. It was only then, after doctors ran a standard panel of tests, that a surprising result jumped off the page: mercury levels that were off the chart. Despite efforts to remove the mercury chemically through a process called chelation *(key-LAY-shun)*, her symptoms evolved quickly and she was in a coma when she died in June 1997, ten months after the exposure.[7]

Luckily, dimethylmercury is secured behind locked doors in no more than one hundred laboratories around the world, but the mercury we need to pay attention to right now faces no such barriers. It beats four main paths to our door:

1. **Natural emissions.** These predate human civilization and include natural events such as volcanoes and forest fires. These emissions are part of the background level of mercury that has always been with us. As humans we've developed methods to detoxify these low levels of exposure—the body has built-in defenses, molecules like glutathione and other natural chelators that filter out the mercury reaching us in our water, air, and food.

These defenses usually permit us to deal with natural mercury exposures just fine.

2. **Industrial emissions.** With the Industrial Revolution has come an onslaught of new forms of mercury. These include emissions from specialized industrial processes used in chlorine plants, mirror- and hat-making facilities, and cement factories. But the single largest source of mercury is from coal and thus integrally linked to the fossil-fuel-based economy that has led to climate change concerns and widespread alarms over rising carbon dioxide levels.

   As this new wave of man-made, or anthropogenic, mercury is released in the environment it finds its way into the food chain through numerous paths, most prominently when bacteria in marshes and rivers convert inorganic mercury from these emissions into a more neurotoxic form called methylmercury. As the toxin passes from prey to predator up the food chain, its concentration is magnified. By the time we eat tuna we're ingesting one of the most concentrated storehouses of mercury in the world.

3. **Manufactured chemicals.** The active properties of mercury have long made it an attractive element for chemical companies in synthesizing commercial products, especially pesticides. Mercury exposure from these sources has been at the root of some of the most infamous disasters in the history of twentieth-century industrial manufacturing. Although much has been done to reduce or eliminate these exposures, mercury is still in demand for targeted applications from fluorescent lightbulbs to computer screens.

4. **Medicinal sources.** While we've removed the gross, high-volume, low-toxicity forms of mercury from medicine, the "march of progress" has led to its use as an antibacterial agent in many medicines, and as fillings in teeth. The controversy continues; ethylmercury was removed from some vaccines beginning in 1999 after federal officials became alarmed at the total amount an infant could receive by the age of two.[8]

But the economic advantages of mercury still propel its use. Dentists around the world regularly place "silver" fillings—which are actually amalgams of mercury, tin, and nickel—into the mouths of millions. And

all over the globe, ethylmercury remains in regular childhood immunizations for diphtheria, tetanus, pertussis, hepatitis B, and influenza. In
the United States, the much-publicized fear of bird and swine flu epidemics has been used to excuse the continued presence of mercury in
millions of doses of influenza vaccine administered to pregnant women
and infant children. As influenza vaccine coverage has risen, the toxic
effect of these early exposures has increased even as the doses from other
vaccines have fallen. And in the meantime, substitute chemicals have
emerged to perform part of ethylmercury's function in vaccines, including new preservatives to prevent bacterial growth in multidose vials, and
new adjuvants (or immune stimulants) such as aluminum, another highly
toxic metal.

———

Understanding the composition of mercury, as well as what makes it different from other substances, will help make sense of what follows. Mercury is an atom: number 80 out of the 118 currently displayed on the
periodic table of elements. Designated Hg, it is a relatively heavy atom,
lying close to gold, lead, and platinum on the sixth row of the periodic
table.[9] This gives it some strange and not always wonderful properties,
properties that are captured in the colloquial usage of the word "mercurial" to mean "volatile, erratic, unstable . . . or changeable in temperament."[10] Although we may be tempted to think of mercury as a singular
element, in fact its behavior and properties vary quite widely depending
on the specific chemical form it takes.

    In its most basic form, mercury is described as elemental or metallic
mercury. This type is stable and doesn't react much with surrounding
molecules. For anyone who remembers playing with a broken thermometer, the mercury you then encountered displayed some of the element's
unusual properties. Metallic mercury is liquid at room temperature. A
relatively stable configuration of electrons discourages it from binding or
dissolving into other substances, which explains why some people are
capable of swallowing even large amounts of metallic mercury without
suffering ill effects. Miners who refine liquid mercury are often known to
play parlor games with outsiders; a *National Geographic* article from 1972
entitled "Quicksilver and Slow Death" shows a veteran miner in street
clothes floating with no part of his body below the surface on top of a vat

of pure liquid mercury, its density—13.5 times that of water—so great that it can support the weight of a fully grown man.[11]

Writers have long commented on quicksilver's peculiarities. "And then there is mercury, arguably the barmiest of all the elements," writes Natalie Angier in *The Canon,* a layman's guide to science. "Mercury is liquid at room temperature, and it conducts heat and electricity so poorly that it barely merits inclusion in metaldom. Behind mercury's unusual behavior are its massive nucleus and the strong pull of its 80 protons. The positive packet at mercury's core keeps such a powerful lock on all the surrounding electrons that, even though the element theoretically has two negative particles to share in an electron sea, those electrons prefer staying close to their nuclear family, leaving the metallic bonds linking one mercury atom to another weak and easily disrupted."[12]

Because of its weight[13] and well-known reputation for toxicity, mercury has helped define a common term for toxic substances: "heavy metals," a category that strikes fear into the hearts of many, and also includes lead, arsenic, and cadmium. But the fact that mercury is heavy[14] and "barely" a metal actually provides little guidance as to its toxic effects. Many heavy elements are nontoxic. Bismuth, the heaviest stable element, heavier than mercury, is the active ingredient in Pepto-Bismol. And since the vast majority of elements on the periodic table are classified as metals or "metalloids," it's hard to see what being a heavy metal has to do with anything.

Toxicologist John Duffus has argued that it's time to get rid of the term "heavy metal," a phrase he derides as a "meaningless term."[15] But understanding why mercury is so highly toxic requires some explanation of why mercury interacts in the way it does with other atoms, in molecular combinations, and in living things. According to Duffus, getting closer to an understanding of the toxic properties of certain metals requires us to go deeper into the intrinsic character of these substances. Duffus doesn't formalize such a classification, but he offers some suggestions on how to do so. And his reasoning leads us away from the properties of metallic mercury—the least interesting form of mercury in terms of toxicity—and instead toward considering mercury in its reactive, positively charged form, what is typically described as inorganic mercury. (Inorganic mercury is perhaps best defined in contrast to its opposite, organic mercury, which is any mercury compound that contains carbon atoms. By definition, neither metallic mercury nor inorganic mercury compounds contain carbon.) When one or two of the outermost electrons orbiting a mercury atom are stripped off, mercury enters its reactive form Hg^+ or Hg^{++}. In this state, it becomes capable of accepting electrons from other "donor atoms," and forming larger molecular combinations. And in such combinations lie mercury's particular toxicity.

Mercury has long been known to react selectively with certain substances, such as sulfur and iodine. University of California chemist Ralph Pearson, observing mercury's binding propensities, developed a chemical theory around it, one that relied on the natural affinity of acids (electron donors) and bases (electron acceptors).[16] Specifically, he suggested that some substances were chemically "soft" while others were "hard." Mercury species like Hg^{++} are, according to Pearson, the classic soft acid.

What makes mercury chemically soft? In its reactive states, mercury has a large atomic radius, one that is easily distorted by the electrical fields of nearby molecules. That tendency for distortion (what chemists call polarizability) is basically what makes it soft, and attractive to its necessary partners in reactions, the soft bases such as sulfur and chlorine. And those bonds between soft acids and soft bases, observed Pearson, wind up being particularly strong.

What seems certain from Pearson's analysis is that soft is dangerous, at least as far as mercury goes, because it's not only inorganic mercury that's soft, it's also the organic mercury forms—most prominently methylmercury—that react strongly with soft bases as well. (As we noted above, organic compounds, such as ethyl- and methylmercury, are defined by the presence of one or more carbon atoms in the molecule.) And both play a role in the chemical reactions that make mercury especially dangerous, those that take place in living organisms. The ability of both inorganic and organic mercury to bind to sulfur groups means that they find ways to bind in vivo to the amino acid known as cysteine, an important structural and functional component of many proteins and enzymes.

As machines are to a factory, so enzymes are to the metabolism—they cut up chemical compounds, assemble them, twist and bind them. And while biologists speak of these enzymes as strings of amino acids (the outputs of the code in our DNA), they are more than strings in real life; in a living cell, they're actually nanoscopic, three-dimensional machinery. In building that machinery, the sulfur atom plays a special role. In a long amino acid chain, sulfur atoms connect at different points to one another, building disulfide bridges that give certain enzymes their three-dimensional shape. Interfering with those bridges is like throwing sand in the gears of a machine; they won't work the way they're supposed to. Of all the toxic substances you can throw into the body, the reactive forms of mercury have a specific capacity to disrupt these disulfide bridges.

———

Based on our research, autism is only the latest "mystery illness" with a not-so-mysterious link to mercury. While mainstream medical groups and public health officials remain resolutely baffled, even questioning whether the disorder is increasing, autism has become a modern plague. In the United States, the estimates of the number of affected children rise continually, going from one in ten thousand in the 1960s and 1970s to one in one hundred today; in some states the rate has risen to more than 1 percent of children and nearly 2 percent of boys.[17] (Autism affects boys at about four times the rate of girls.) Contrary to the calming assurances of some who see autism as a natural part of the human condition, most families affected by autism experience the disease as serious and disabling. Children affected with autism will require special services and in most cases lifelong care. While rarely fatal itself, an autistic condition puts children at far greater risk of accidental death, most frequently in the form of drowning; autistic children have an affinity for the water even when they can't swim.[18]

When faced with the prospects of dealing with a lifetime of daily disruption and duties, parents often get overwhelmed and look to a future with no relief in sight. For those who find a way to adapt their lives and purpose to support their disabled son or daughter, the greatest fear is their child's inability to live independently. "What will happen when I die?" worries every parent of an autistic child.

Within the larger picture, we have come to see autism as a leading indicator. As we increasingly saturate our environment and food supply with mercury and other toxins and run uncontrolled medical experiments on children including but not limited to the injection of mercury, the latest generation born in the developed world may be the sickest in our memory.

They are not sick in the sense of the infectious-disease epidemics of the great cities such as cholera, typhoid, and diphtheria, but sick in ways the modern medical profession has been slow to recognize and unable to explain—one child in six with a developmental disorder ranging from ADD to autism;[19] children dropping dead with even the slightest exposure to peanuts; nearly one in ten with asthma,[20] leading to schools filled with special-ed classes, epi-pens, and inhalers. Summer camp, which used to be a break from (and for) the parents, is now an experience accompanied by professional staff to administer multiple medications; the rise of deficits in attention, hyperactivity, depression, and bipolar illness has made children a new target for psychotropic drugs, all of them palliative and none of them addressing the root question: Why are so many children sick?

We contend that to answer this question medical science needs to embrace a new model of disease. The first convincing formulations of germ theory by Robert Koch and Louis Pasteur ushered medicine out of the dark ages, providing a deeper understanding for a whole range of illnesses caused by microorganisms that had previously been "explained" through the superstitious theory of the humors. James D. Watson and Francis Crick's discovery of DNA sparked a new wave of hope for understanding illness according to an inheritance model of disease. Unfortunately, as analyses of the genetic profiles of victims of autism and other chronic diseases have shown, genetics alone has failed to provide a comparably satisfying answer for this latest wave of chronic diseases of advanced civilization.

In what follows, we describe a range of potential disease models. Could some autism cases be a simple matter of undiagnosed mercury poisoning, like acrodynia or some cases of hysteria? Or the outcome of well-meaning but dangerous medical treatments, perhaps the interaction between mercury and a microbe? Or is the situation worse than that, a complex mix of genetic susceptibility, toxic chemistry, and poorly understood events in childhood? We offer a series of new explanations for specific diseases, each of which we have traced to common roots in the use of medicinal mercury and industrial mercury exposure.

We do not provide a definitive answer to the autism puzzle. We do, however, believe we are pointing in the right direction.

It has no doubt occurred to you: Who are these authors, and what is the research they refer to?

One of us, a father of a child with autism, is a business professional skilled in statistical analysis who has contributed peer-reviewed scientific articles on the prevalence of autism and its association with mercury exposure. The other is a journalist who has written widely on autism, mental health issues, and the dangerous side effects of prescription drugs. Our ideas and discoveries have grown out of several years of collaboration, each of us contributing to a bigger picture than either saw alone.

Aspects of our argument have been proposed before: David Kirby's award-winning book *Evidence of Harm* chronicled how parents themselves first connected the rise in mercury exposure via vaccines with the explosion of autism cases starting in 1990.[21] But our historical sweep and geographic scope is both more ambitious and inevitably more speculative. We are seeking to "collect the truth from circumstances, and little collateral facts," as Judge Buller advised in 1781, and let you render a verdict. Historical epidemiology, another term for this approach, may be one of the few fields of science open to all: We set out to establish a fresh reading of the medical literature (and it really is literature, an epic narrative with great characters and high drama), uninfluenced by received wisdom, conflicts of interest, or fear of ridicule.

We also possess a sense of urgency and purpose, and a belief that our discoveries can help reshape the public discussion of autism and other environmental illnesses. Such a discussion is long overdue. Nearly one hundred forty years before Karen Wetterhahn's death at Dartmouth, a Scottish woman named Elizabeth Storie wrote about her own mercury poisoning at the hands of a doctor. Storie was treated for a minor childhood skin ailment, nettle rush, which today would probably be diagnosed as hives, an allergic reaction.

The doctor, a friend of the family who had just begun practicing medicine, stopped by and found Elizabeth ill; he offered to "send up a few powders that would do me good." This concoction contained calomel—mercurous chloride—according to her later book, *The Autobiography of Elizabeth Storie*.[22] "My head began to swell to a great extent, and saliva to flow in large quantities from my mouth." Salivation is a sure sign of an overdose, though often it was considered beneficial under the theory of humors.

As the doctor kept "helping," Elizabeth just got worse. Her gums turned to mush, her teeth fell out, her jaws fused; her health never recovered. For the rest of her life she had to take nourishment, such as it was, through a straw. The medical establishment of the time denied responsibility for this blatant malpractice, and judges refused to enforce the thousand-pound verdict she won against her doctor. But she remained undaunted:

> The facts which will be brought to light may also serve to warn those in high power of the danger of doing injustice or injury to any, trusting that through the insignificance of their victims the world may never know how much they have made others to suffer. . . . I can offer nothing attractive to the reader of this book except the truthfulness of the statements made therein."[23]

The victims of disease are more than just statistics on paper: They have names and faces; their suffering is real and should never be lost in the search for scientific proof. Truth matters, and denial of an injury that produces suffering, whether direct or indirect, dishonors the victims and puts future generations at risk. Our discoveries, we hope, will honor the suffering that has gone before as it helps the truth emerge.

PART ONE

THE ROOTS

Primum non nocere.

(First do no harm.)

—Attributed to Hippocrates but coined in 1860[1]

CHAPTER ONE

THE AGE OF SYPHILIS

A night with Venus, a lifetime with mercury.

—ADAGE DESCRIBING THE CONSEQUENCE OF CATCHING
SYPHILIS FROM A SEXUAL ENCOUNTER.
{MERCURY WAS THE MAIN TREATMENT FOR FOUR CENTURIES.}

The Reversed Loop

Epidemics have beginnings in both time and place. Determining when
and where they start, where they come from, and how they spread is the
work of epidemiology. To take a close analogy, AIDS first appeared in
the United States in two deadly disguises, skin cancer and pneumonia in
gay men, and in two different places, Los Angeles and New York. The
only thing the patients seemed to share was sexual orientation and immune suppression, but as CDC epidemiologists connected the dots, they
came to a startling realization: "[AIDS] appeared to be caused by an
infectious, sexually transmitted agent, probably a virus. As in a reversed
loop of film, the whole tumbling cascade of cards suddenly—and surprisingly—re-formed into a neat deck."[2]

Ultimately, AIDS was traced back to Africa, although exactly how and
when it migrated to America has been impossible to determine. Randy
Shilts, in *And the Band Played On*, envisioned one possible vector—the arrival

of the tall ships in New York Harbor for the bicentennial celebration in July 1976: "Ships from fifty-five nations had poured sailors into Manhattan to join the throngs. . . . This was the part the epidemiologists would later note."[3]

The trajectory of syphilis was also a reversed loop. One speculation: When the *Pinta, Niña,* and *Santa Maria* sailed back into port in Spain from the Americas, their crews and captives were carrying the bacteria. (The syphilis bacterium belongs to the *Treponema pallidum* species of the spirochete order; spirochetes—pronounced *spy-roh-keets*—are so named because of their spiral, coiled shape. Under a microscope, they wriggle like living corkscrews.)

Whether syphilis was part of the so-called Columbian Exchange— when diseases like measles and mumps arrived from the Old World to decimate huge swaths of the Americas—has been debated for centuries. Some scientists have argued that the syphilis bacterium was always present in Europe, and the timing of the epidemic in 1495 was a coincidence. But a consensus slowly has formed that syphilis was indeed among the "gifts" exchanged—Columbus brought syphilis to Europe along with tomatoes, gold, peppers, tobacco, chocolate, and many other wonders never before seen.[4]

They had left behind similar gifts in the Americas. The dramatic toll of new diseases in the New World has only recently been appreciated, most notably the idea that some 95 percent of its population died off without any direct contact with European civilization—fatal diseases like measles and smallpox spread like wildfire through these virgin populations. "This wild oscillation of the balance of nature happens again whenever an area previously isolated is opened to the rest of the world. But possibly it will never be repeated in as spectacular a fashion as in the Americas in the first post-Columbian century, not unless there is, one day, an exchange of life forms between planets."[5]

If the toll of the Columbian Exchange was lower in the Old World than the New, it was a heavy toll nevertheless. And the onset of the syphilis epidemic in Europe can be dated much more precisely than AIDS in America: "History records a specific event, the invasion of Naples by the French army of Charles VIII in 1495, as the natal moment (22 February 1495 at 4:00 P.M.) of the worldwide syphilis epidemic," writes Deborah Hayden in her superb blend of science and speculation, *Pox: Genius, Madness, and the Mysteries of Syphilis.*[6] French soldiers in retreat from Naples found themselves besieged by a very different enemy: Because the signs were so immediate and so much worse than even the dreaded smallpox, it soon gained the nickname of the great pox, or simply the pox.

From there syphilis spread unchecked. Many of the French army's soldiers were mercenaries (and, significantly, many of those were from Columbus's Spain). Dispersing to their home countries, they planted syphilis like so many malignant seeds, in a much more virulent form than we know today. Doctors seemed to compete in describing its horrors. Benedetto, a Venetian doctor writing in 1497, was one of the first: "Through sexual contact, an ailment which is new, or at least unknown to previous doctors, the French sickness, has worked its way in from the West to this spot as I write. The entire body is so repulsive to look at and the suffering is so great, especially at night, that this sickness is even more horrifying than incurable leprosy or elephantiasis, and it can be fatal."[7]

As Jared Diamond outlines in *Guns, Germs, and Steel,* "Today, our two immediate associations to syphilis are genital sores and a very slowly developing disease, leading to the death of many untreated victims only after many years. However, when syphilis was first definitely recorded in Europe in 1495, its pustules often covered the body from the head to the knees, caused flesh to fall off people's faces, and led to death within a few months. By 1546, syphilis had evolved into the disease with the symptoms well known to us today. . . . Those syphilis spirochetes that evolved so as to keep their victims alive for longer were thereby able to transmit the spirochete offspring into more victims."[8] Following the principle that microbes invariably adapt to their host, the virulence with which syphilis attacked Europe before subsiding into a more chronic affliction argues for its more recent arrival on the continent of Europe.

Neurosyphilis

As ferocious as syphilis could be when the disease first broke out, perhaps equally frightening was a related condition, general paresis of the insane, which came to light in the early 1800s. "Paresis" is an antiquated term for paralysis, or, more precisely, impaired movement; so the words imply some of its horrors. Before penicillin put an end to the Age of Syphilis in the mid-twentieth century, a small, highly variable percentage of syphilitics succumbed to the physical and mental ravages of a lethal condition: general paralysis of the insane, or GPI, as it was widely known. GPI could sneak up on its victims, provoking uncharacteristic outbursts and memory lapses, headaches, weakness and tremors in the limbs. Less frequently it announced itself in an instant; Friedrich Nietzsche collapsed on a street in Turin in 1889, suffering a massive breakdown, and spent years in an asylum before dying in 1897.[9]

However it presented, general paralysis of the insane was one of the most cruelly debilitating diseases ever described—GPI before penicillin was akin to AIDS before retroviral therapy, both in mode of transmission and in its relentlessly grim consequences, leaving many of its victims incontinent, insane, and immobilized.

We owe some of the most detailed descriptions of this condition to the German psychiatrist Emil Kraepelin (1856–1926), widely considered the father of modern scientific psychiatry. Kraepelin was convinced that mental illness was an organic, biological process, and that treatment required science, technology, and a combined understanding of biology and the brain. His clear delineation between affective disorders like depression and mania and psychotic disorders like schizophrenia remains the foundation of twenty-first-century psychiatry.

"The usual clinical picture of general paresis . . . is a progressive deterioration leading to complete undermining of the whole mental and physical personality, accompanied by peculiar irritative and paralytic phenomena," Kraepelin wrote in "General Paresis," a two-hundred-page chapter in his monumental and authoritative *Textbook of Psychiatry*, which was translated into English in 1913. "The termination of paresis is regularly death."[10]

In writing about GPI, Kraepelin identified an Alzheimer's-like decline. "The patient is absent-minded, inattentive, does not grasp events transpiring about him with accustomed clearness. . . . He mistakes persons and objects, overlooks important circumstances or changes . . . loses himself among familiar surroundings."[11] In addition, he noted a marked change in disposition: "The patient is capricious, easily angered and surly, thrown into transitory states of emotional excitement by trivial causes, at which times he completely loses control of himself and flies into a violent passion."[12]

The physical side of the condition was also progressive: Symptoms included impaired movement coordination, sight impairment, and sensations of numbness in varying areas of the body. "The motor symptoms are especially prominent in paresis. The patient cannot catch a quickly moving object, button the coat, thread a needle or knit." The condition spared few faculties, attacking also the senses: "On the *sensory* side, there are similar attacks . . . defects in the visual fields; a hand 'goes to sleep'; the fingers get numb; one side seems to the patient to be swollen . . . an arm becomes dead and is useless for half a day."[13] Another common symptom was digestive problems.

Typically, over the course of two to four more years, the physical debilities evolved into paralysis and the mental disturbances into insanity. Then, to shorten Kraepelin's phraseology, you died. The only good thing to be said about GPI was that the wreckage was so complete you often didn't know you had it. "Paretics seldom have a true realization of their condition," Kraepelin wrote. "On the contrary, the patients frequently feel healthier than previously or, at least, they do not appreciate they have lost all their mental powers."[14]

General paralysis was not the only neurological condition associated with syphilis—there were two other major categories and many variations, including meningovascular syphilis and tabes dorsalis, which affected the spinal cord and the peripheral nervous system; all went under the general category of neurosyphilis, meaning involvement of the brain, the nervous system, or both. But one sign made GPI stand out: Some of the most grandiose delusions ever recorded in the psychiatric literature. Here, Kraepelin catalogs just a few (note that these were being experienced by early twentieth-century Germans):

The patient thinks he possesses extraordinary physical strength, can lift 10 elephants, is 800 years old, 9 feet tall, the most beautiful Adonis in the world, weighs 400 pounds, increases 25 pounds every week, has an iron chest, sinews like a man-eater, an arm of silver, a head of pure gold, travels a thousand miles a minute, can fly. He is infinite, has died and again come to life, can have intercourse with 100 women, has 1,000 million boys and girls, a compressed brain, has run a race with the grand duke. His urine is Rhine wine; his evacuations are gold. Ten years ago he had an enormous chancre, his sexual organs and fingers are constantly getting larger; his brain is still growing; he has an immense movement of the bowels. He has studied all sciences, speaks all the languages in the world, plays Wagner at sight, impersonates Don Carlos like a God.[15]

There was no shortage of spectacularly delusional statements to report; this was just one paragraph from pages and pages of such descriptions. And GPI was as baffling as it was bizarre. Although the syphilis epidemic hit Europe like a tidal wave in 1495, GPI and its unmistakable manifestations were not observed until three hundred years later. One of its first widely accepted descriptions is from 1809, when John Haslam of Bethlem asylum (also known as Bedlam) in England wrote, "Persons this disordered are in general not at all sensible of being so affected. When so feeble, as scarcely to be able to stand, they commonly say that they feel perfectly strong, and capable of great exertions."[16]

A further complication was that once a person was infected with syphilis, it usually took years for GPI to show up—typically twelve to fifteen years, though sometimes as few as three or four, and sometimes far longer. For that reason, the best medical minds in Europe were slow to realize that everyone with GPI had syphilis, though not everyone with syphilis developed GPI. Indeed, GPI affected a relatively small percentage of all those with syphilis. No one knew for sure what the GPI rate among syphilitics was; estimates varied from 5 to more than 20 percent. All they knew was that—like syphilis itself centuries before—GPI seemed to come out of nowhere and it was on the rise, filling the hospitals and asylums of Europe.

A Meeting at Hiawatha

In April 1925 sixty-nine-year-old Emil Kraepelin came all the way from the University of Munich Hospital to the Hiawatha Asylum for Insane Indians in Canton, South Dakota; he was in search of Native Americans with syphilis. More specifically, he was looking for general paralysis of the insane, and the federal government's sole mental hospital for Native Americans seemed like a good place to find it.

Another doctor, Leo Kanner, had also come to Hiawatha to meet the great Kraepelin in order to help him overcome the language barrier with the locals and to tell him that he had found what he was looking for—a Native American with general paralysis of the insane. At the time, Leo Kanner was a psychiatrist at South Dakota's state mental hospital in

Yankton. Yet in a sense, Kanner had come as far as Kraepelin. An Austrian by birth, Kanner had been living in Berlin only the year before when he accepted an offer to join the staff of the Yankton State Hospital.

"Serendipity" was one of Kanner's favorite words. "I do not hesitate to say that I seem to be endowed with serendipity, or 'the gift of finding unsought treasures,'" he wrote near the end of his long career.[17] Leaving Germany before Hitler's ascent was "clear serendipity," and connecting with Kraepelin was, too: it would help lead to his appointment at a great teaching hospital; to establishing the first childhood psychiatric clinic; to writing the first American textbook on the subject; and to becoming, like Kraepelin, a patriarch in his own right, the father of child psychiatry. Kanner played a key role in several of the medical sagas described in this book, including, as we noted in the introduction, the discovery of autism.

Kraepelin had a theory—one that led him to North America and ultimately to Hiawatha. He believed that alcohol made syphilis worse and was probably the cause of GPI. Sounding a bit like a Prohibitionist (the Eighteenth Amendment was in effect by the time Kraepelin arrived at Hiawatha in 1925), he wrote that "peoples who are not susceptible to paresis [GPI] are entirely or nearly free from alcoholic influence, either because they have no alcohol industries to flood the country with their products or because legal or religious precepts demand abstinence." He made it clear that freed slaves and "the North American Indians, who are well supplied with whiskey in their reservations," had especially succumbed to both alcohol and GPI.[18]

This was no passing reference. Again and again he put forward the assertion. He wrote that Native Americans with syphilis "suffer severely from paresis," and he emphasized: "It is remarkable . . . with what extraordinary rapidity paresis has spread among the negroes and Indians of North America."[19] There was one problem. Kraepelin had no evidence. So early in 1925, Kraepelin set off on what would be his last field investigation, a three-month journey through the United States, Mexico, and Cuba to investigate the incidence of GPI in blacks and Native Americans. Assuming alcohol triggered GPI in syphilitics, the evidence would not be hard to find.

The evidence was not hard to find—it was *impossible* to find. By the time Kraepelin got to Canton, he had not encountered a single case of GPI among Native Americans with syphilis. Nor were there any at the Hiawatha Asylum for Insane Indians. The scarcity of GPI stood in stark contrast to the high prevalence of syphilis on Native American reservations.[20]

This large population of Native Americans with syphilis did not "suffer greatly" from GPI, as Kraepelin had asserted; quite the opposite, they didn't seem to suffer from it at all.

Enter serendipity. Kanner had learned from the Sioux City newspaper that Kraepelin would be nearby looking for GPI among North American blacks and Native Americans and managed to persuade his boss, G. S. Adams, the Yankton superintendent, to get invitations to meet both Kraepelin and Felix Plaut, one of his assistants, at Hiawatha. Kanner wasted no time in connecting with the great man. "Their curiosity was aroused when I told them that we had at Yankton a paretic Indian. In all their travels they had not been able to lay eyes on one. Kraepelin was excited and, regretting that arrangements had been made for him to leave for Mexico the following morning, made me promise that I mail the data to him and that I publish the case in detail."[21]

But the case Kanner mentioned was hardly a typical Native American. The patient was a farmer named Thomas T. Robertson. In photos taken at Yankton, he wore a coat and tie. His great-grandfather was a Scotsman of the same name who had joined the Sioux Nation in South Dakota's early days as a territory. While the rest of his ancestors were Sioux (though all the men kept the Tom Robertson name), his delusions as well as his pedigree reflected a European influence:

Mental state: When last examined in April, 1925, he was partially oriented as to the place. He knew that this was Yankton, but did not realize what kind of a place he was living in. As the date he gave the second and third months of 1924. His memory is very poor now, his answers often irrelevant. He has several delusions of grandeur. He has two million dollars in a bank. He "takes care of all the houses, all the horses, all the cattle, all the farms, and everything." He is to be married to a young "preacheress" of a very good family. He is the best man in the world next to Jesus Christ. When he marries that girl he will be able to make people very rich; he is going to be a powerful man; he will become President of the United States. The Lord has appeared to him several times in dreams and he is proud of these visions and attaches great importance to them. On the ward he behaves quite well, is fairly clean in his habits. His insight into his condition is extremely poor and so is his judgement about his fellow patients. He is always happy and when asked to do so, he will gladly sing some of his Indian songs and dance some of his tribal dances. He runs a floor polisher on the ward and does other coarse work possible with his incoordinate movements.

Diagnosis: Dementia paralytica [GPI]. Mesaortitis syphilitica.
Volumen pulmonum auctum [Heart and lung problems].[22]

This Native American obviously had a foot in the Western world. A Sioux named Robertson who imagined millions in the bank, who wanted to be Jesus Christ and the president of the United States, was not representative, and Kanner knew it even at the time: "It appears furthermore of the greatest importance not that an Indian has been found affected with general paralysis, but that such a case is so rare that it is really regarded as a curiosity, a fact that very decidedly calls for explanation."[23] By contrast, in Europe and most parts of the United States you could find GPI effortlessly; it represented one of the largest single patient populations in any mental hospital, as many as 25 percent of men. Still, to find even one instance among Native Americans was considered a publishable accomplishment.

"To my knowledge, Thomas T. Robertson has remained to this day the only paretic Indian to be fully studied and reported," Kanner wrote years later.[24] He certainly looked hard, getting in touch with every hospital that could conceivably have an Indian paretic as a patient, and checking with Dr. Hubert Work, secretary of the interior who was also a leading neurologist. Work told Kanner that the department was about halfway through a census of general paresis among Native Americans—and so far had found none: "It may be said that general paralysis is extremely rare, even in tribes that are known to be more or less syphilitic."[25] The U.S. Census listed a grand total of one, whom Kanner tried in vain to locate (he may well have died).

The evidence was convincing. GPI was practically nonexistent in Native American populations. So what was going on?

Kanner and Adams observed that after syphilis first hit Europe, its initial and outward manifestations gradually became less severe, though it remained a deadly chronic affliction. They cited the likelihood that syphilis originated in the Americas—that it had been endemic here thousands of years longer. Then they put the two ideas together to form their own theory: that the longer syphilis resided in a people, the milder an affliction it became; in that case, Native Americans, having been exposed to syphilis for centuries longer than Europeans, would display less GPI. They called attention to the fact that Tom Robertson was one-sixteenth Scot, implying a sliver of European heritage could have made him more susceptible.

This was an imaginative speculation, but not particularly plausible:

Syphilis would have to enter a new population without causing GPI;
then, in a spontaneous event several centuries later, suddenly mutate into
a neurotoxic strain (as in Europe); and then at a later date, for reasons
unknown, the neurotoxic strain would spontaneously disappear (as in
Native Americans).

Why would this occur? There was also no evidence that once GPI
emerged after centuries of syphilis's circulation in European populations, it had begun to decline; quite the opposite. It was the seventh-
leading cause of death in New York State in 1914, tied with typhoid fever
and claiming about one thousand lives a year. One in nine New York
males who died between ages forty and sixty died of GPI, far more than
all other complications of syphilis combined.[26]

If only by process of elimination, the question of treatment must arise.
Europeans and European Americans used mercury to treat syphilis while
Native Americans, and many other less "advanced" cultures, largely did
not. Now, read these observations by Kanner and Adams in that light:

> It has been agreed upon, it is true, that the disease occurs most frequently
> in the civilized countries and that natives of regions where there is a lower
> civilization and where the struggle for existence is less exhaustive, are
> comparatively free from it, and it has been stated that members of such
> races or tribes found to be affected with general paralysis have either
> brought it back from their sojourn in Europe or else have become "Euro-
> peanized" in their habits of life.[27]

Others were making global comparisons as well, Kraepelin among
them. Note the similar findings and the interesting anomalies:

> Of much greater significance for the understanding of paresis are the
> extraordinary differences in its frequency in different countries. While in
> France, England, Italy, Austria, the Netherlands, Switzerland, in Western
> Russia and the Eastern United States almost the same relations [i.e., high
> prevalence rates] obtain as in Germany . . . [i]n Norway, according to
> Vogt's personal observations, paresis is so rare that sometimes there is not

a single case in the institution of 330 beds at Gaustad. . . . [GPI] is
apparently unknown in British East Africa, Uganda, Zanzibar, Kamerun,
Togo, Samoa, the Marschall Islands and in Nicaragua.[28]

One can sympathize with Kraepelin's difficulty in sorting out this data:
GPI seemed to be European yet, according to Ragnar Vogt, one of the
leading Norwegian experts on neurosyphilis,[29] in Norway it was absent.
It may have been caused by consumption of alcohol, but then alcoholic
Indians with syphilis didn't get it. It seemed to be racial/genetic, but
then race didn't offer protection when individuals changed their environment. Kraepelin concluded that "one may consider first the habits
of life which indeed have a profound effect on the people's health."[30]

But the notion that medicine might have been that habit just didn't
occur to Kraepelin, nor to Kanner, nor Adams—perhaps because it
could only mean doctors were causing the worst manifestation of syphilis. And that was simply inconceivable. Yet as we'll see, by then there
was plenty of controversy about exactly what side effects medicinal mercury was triggering. And we have found contemporary evidence that
Indians treated syphilis differently. Here is an account from 1812: "We
have been told, that the natives of America cure the venereal disease, in
every stage, by a decoction of the root of a plant called the Lobelia. It is
used either fresh or dried; but we have no certain accounts with regard
to the proportion." A footnote adds: "Though we are still very much in
the dark with regard to the method of curing this disease among the
natives of America, nothing is more certain than that they do cure it
with speed, safety, and success, and that without the least knowledge of
mercury."[31]

A second source also notes the different way Native Americans dealt
with syphilis. In the journals of Lewis and Clark on their voyage west-
ward two decades later, Meriwether Lewis discusses treating a member of
the expedition with mercury for syphilis, and also how Indians treated it
with Lobelia.[32]

Although Indians in the Southwest and California made war paint
from cinnabar, we have found no evidence they used mercury internally,
for syphilis or for any other purpose. According to John N. Low, a visiting assitant professor in the American Indian Studies Program at the
University of Illinois, medicinal uses of mercury would have required
mining and transport—a greater degree of industrialization than Indian

culture possessed. And there was relatively little trade between Western and American Indian civilizations, according to Low.[33]

This pattern—of finding no instances of GPI in populations that had not been treated with mercury—continued. In 1938, just a few years before penicillin rendered mercury obsolete, researchers observed: "Several authorities have expressed the opinion that cerebral and neurological lesions due to syphilis are extremely rare among Indians in North America. . . . The scarcity of characteristic signs of syphilis in the Indian groups studied in Yucatan and in Guatemala, is the more significant because the disease had not been checked by the use of recognized forms of treatment."[34]

Not using "recognized forms of treatment"—which by 1938 included mercury and arsenic, but not yet penicillin—may have spared the American Indians the brain lesions symptomatic of neurosyphilis.

―

Kanner and Adams's paper, "General Paralysis among the North American Indians—A Contribution to Racial Psychiatry," appeared in the July 1926 issue of the prestigious *American Journal of Psychiatry*. Along with a follow-up and several other papers in medical journals, Kanner's work at Yankton won him a fellowship at Johns Hopkins University School of Medicine in Baltimore, where he stayed for the rest of his working life.

Kraepelin died the same year the Kanner-Adams paper appeared, while at work on the 2,700-page ninth edition of his *Textbook of Psychiatry*. Eight years after their visit, the federal government was shamed into closing Hiawatha. The site where Kanner and Kraepelin crossed paths is now a golf course; a graveyard for more than one hundred Indians who died at Hiawatha is between the fourth and fifth fairways.[35]

"The Disease of the Remedy"

Mercury had long been used as a treatment for the scabs of leprosy and other conditions, because its toxic properties killed bacteria by contact.

So when faced with the horrific lesions of syphilis, doctors reached for the element they already knew could relieve skin disorders. In fact, lesions did diminish, leading to the seemingly obvious conclusion that syphilis could be "cured" with adequate treatment—immediate, vigorous, and prolonged application of mercury.

But from the start, treatment came with delayed effects and a disturbing question: Mercury was killing the superficial spirochetes, yes, but what else was it destroying? Giacomo Berengario da Carpi used mercury on hundreds of patients in Italy in 1495 but had to leave town in a hurry because the cure frequently proved worse than the disease. "He did wisely to get out of Rome," according to one account. "For not many months afterwards, all the patients he had treated grew so ill that they were a hundred times worse off than before he came; he would certainly have been murdered if he had stopped."[36]

As syphilis spread throughout Europe and around the globe, killing millions as it went, treatments became more ambitious, elaborate, and, inevitably, dangerous. Patients coated in mercury often stayed wrapped in bedclothes for weeks or sweated in overheated rooms next to hot fires—treatments believed to hasten mercury's work of expelling toxins. They sat in baths saturated with mercury or squatted on stools above a steaming cauldron of it inside makeshift tents. They salivated quarts of liquid; their teeth loosened and fell out. And while they might have gotten some relief from the immediate outward manifestations of syphilis, in the long run they got no better.

There were many besides da Carpi who learned that mercury made things worse. By 1811 British surgeon Andrew Mathias summed up three centuries of controversy: "Another effect of mercury is that debility which it produces after it has been employed for a great length of time, and in excessive doses," he wrote. "Mercury appears to destroy the energy of the nervous system, producing weakness, tremors, palsies . . . epilepsy, and mania, the most dreadful of all its consequences."[37] The reference to epilepsy and to mania as the most dreadful effect, coming in 1810, could have been an early observation of GPI.

Mathias freely acknowledged he was not the first to point this out. "I pretend not to the discovery of a new complaint," he said. Rather, he wanted to show "that mercury, in some instances, ceases to act as a remedy, and produces a specific action in the system, differing entirely from all its other operations, having in itself a power of suppressing, but not of curing, the venereal action. . . . When mercury begins to disagree with the constitution, and ceases to act in removing the venereal virus, this disagreement is constantly to be accounted for from this morbid specific action taking place; which, if the expression may be allowed, I would wish to call the disease of the remedy."[38]

Despite the antiquated language, this was a useful set of observations: Mercury could suppress, but did not cure, syphilis; its use over a long period in people with syphilis had uniquely damaging effects; and the nervous system seemed especially at risk.

Mercury was even dangerous to those who provided the treatment. Inunctions of mercury mixed with lard and other emollients to create rubs were sometimes performed with a spatula—at what practitioners hoped was a safe distance. It was not. As early as 1713, in *Diseases of Workers,* Bernardino Ramazzini observed: "Mercury nowadays is no less dangerous for surgeons and others who administer mercurial inunction in the worst cases of *lues venera* which every other remedy has failed to cure. . . . At present, those who anoint with mercurial ointment persons afflicted with [syphilis] belong to the lowest class of surgeons who carry on for the money to be made; for the better sort of surgeons avoid a service so disagreeable and a task so full of danger and hazard. Though they wear a glove when so engaged, it is impossible for them to prevent the mercurial atoms from penetrating the leather. . . . Moreover, since this work is done before a blazing fire, it is inevitable that noxious exhalations taken in by the mouth and nose should reach the internal organs, so that they rub this dire mischief in their brains and nerves."[39]

But given the terrors of the epidemic, critics of mercury remained on the margins. Despite all the evidence and concern, the heart of the medical profession remained committed to mercury treatment, and mainstream physicians rose strongly to its defense. "Although in the 16th century there was vehement opposition to the mercurial treatment of syphilis," wrote French physician Henri Dujardin-Beaumetz in 1885, "the war against the hydrargyrate [mercury] treatment has been waged with the greatest violence in this present century." He fumed that some doctors "have gone so far as to affirm that the accidents [effects] observed in syphilis are due to mercury."[40]

Speaking out against the treatment was viewed as heresy not to be tolerated, especially not by the mainstream medical establishment of the day battling a gruesome disease, armed with almost no weaponry. Mercury was used everywhere and intensively, from the beginning and for a very long time. And while every city experienced the ravages of syphilis and the risks inherent in using mercury as a mainstay, one European capital was especially hard hit and became the center of treatment innovation.

Inventing the Vienna Treatment

For the capital of a small country (8.3 million people), Vienna is incongruously magnificent: Ornate apartments are bathed in light at evening; exquisite public buildings and fountain-splashed plazas crowd together within the Ringstrasse, the broad boulevard that encircles the central city, built on the fortifications that once surrounded it. The immense St. Stephens Cathedral, blackened with soot except for the restored tile roof, rises from the center, brooding, ancient, and overpowering.

All this grandeur makes sense when you consider that Vienna was once capital of the mighty Austro-Hungarian Empire, an epoch that includes some of the defining figures in all world history: Mozart, Strauss, Klimt, Wittgenstein, Popper, Asperger, Bettelheim, Hitler, Freud, Kafka. There was no grander moment than that of the Habsburg empress Maria Theresia (1717–1780). A builder of institutions as well as grand architecture, Maria Theresia used the vast wealth of her realm to redesign the city, reform the army and the economy, and turn Vienna into one of the great capitals of the world. And she was determined to bring it to the forefront of European medical practice as well.

In this pursuit she stepped outside both her country and its Catholic religion, recruiting one of medicine's up-and-coming names from Protestant Holland, one Gerard van Swieten. She commissioned him to overhaul the fragmented and nepotistic medical establishment of the day and run it with a hierarchical and systematic model. The Viennese school would soon rival Paris and London, and all three cities developed what has been called a "spiritual connection" as the world's most advanced centers of medical practice and education.

Van Swieten is an iconic figure in Viennese medical history—he has a street named after him that runs alongside the massive military hospital and medical school. The empress built him a luxurious house on the edge of the Schönbrunn Gardens. As her personal doctor, he had Maria Theresia's ear and could do things that might have gotten another courtier decapitated; on one occasion he plopped food equivalent to the meal the plump monarch was eating into a pail to demonstrate her overindulgence.

But like other cities in Europe, there was a dark side to Vienna. It was rife with prostitution, and syphilis was the great scourge of the army garrisoned there that maintained the far-flung patchwork empire. Maria Theresia took decisive action: She outlawed prostitution and shipped its practitioners out of town, in large part to keep them away from the troops. Van Swieten himself had a keen interest in the health of the military, and soon the Garnisonspital (garrison hospital) became the leading institution of syphilis treatment and mercury therapeutics for all of Europe.

Van Swieten was an effective administrator, and a medical innovator as well. Concerned about the long-term internal consequences of syphilis infection, including bone disease, cardiovascular problems, and gummatous lesions (spongy masses that slowly grow inside the body), he decided doctors needed to do more than just rub mercury on the skin. They needed a way of internally administering mercurial medicine that would deliver it more directly to the spirochetes that lurked deep in the tissues of the body. This was not an easy task. In the wrong amounts or the wrong form, mercury could either poison its host or fail to reach its target. His solution was a liquid form of mercuric chloride that became known as Van Swieten's liquor.

Mercuric chloride (also called mercury chloride II, mercury bichloride or corrosive sublimate) had been synthesized many years previously and was known to be many times more toxic than mercur*ous* chloride (the calomel Elizabeth Storie received that destroyed her teeth and jaw). It was even used as a poison: In the early 1800s in England, Mary Bateman, also known as the Yorkshire Witch, was a fortune-teller and swindler who got her clients to give her everything they had. She tried to hasten the demise of one recalcitrant couple with mercuric chloride, only managing to kill the wife. Mary Bateman probably should have picked a quicker and less obvious poison; she died on the gallows in March 1809.[41]

Van Swieten explored smaller dosing. And because mercuric chloride was soluble in water, he came up with the idea of oral administration. Its appeal was obvious. According to D. R. de Horne, a French specialist during the era of Louis XVI: "Using corrosive sublimate [mercuric chloride] one can treat, in secret, even in the very bosom of the family, a young man who has mistakenly erred or a husband whose misfortune will make him wiser and more careful, and with it one can bring about that return to duty which the public revelation of their licentiousness sometimes causes men to abandon irrevocably."[42]

Given this advantage, Van Swieten's influence, and the importance of syphilis treatment, mercuric chloride became the standard of care throughout Europe by the end of the eighteenth century, and Swietini's liquor, as it was also called, was his lasting legacy.

With the Vienna medical establishment in place and officially sanctioned methods of treatment widely accepted, a new age of Viennese public health emerged, not necessarily improved in terms of its outcome, but certainly better organized. Prostitutes were accepted back into the city as long as they registered. A department of syphilis—the world's first—emerged at the University of Vienna. But mercury, no matter how it was deployed in or on the human body, did not vanquish syphilis or prevent its transmission, and syphilis rates—most notably among the elites and the upper classes of Vienna—remained epidemic. In fact, fear of the disease may have led to overprescribing of mercury—and subsequent mercury poisoning—for other ailments that mimicked syphilis.

Because mercury and syphilis exposures in Vienna were so widespread, it is likely that many of its citizens, prostitutes, and military officers—as well as many of its most elite—were affected by this poisoning. In this light, one case study of a man whose death in 1791 has remained the subject of widespread speculation caught our notice; a man many consider the greatest musician who ever lived.

Genius Interrupted

Wolfgang Amadeus Mozart knew syphilis. It scared him to death. That's why he put off seeing his friend, fellow composer Josef Mysliveçek, as long as he could. But in 1777 Mozart was in Munich rustling up musical commissions, and Mysliveçek was being treated at a hospital there. Mozart arranged to meet him in the hospital garden, where his friend strolled from eleven to noon. He knew part of Mysliveçek's nose had been cut off to counter the ravages of the disease, but the actual encounter still shocked him almost speechless.

"When he came up to me," Mozart wrote his father shortly afterward,

"I took him by his hand and he took mine, in friendship. Just look, he said, how unfortunate I am! His words and his appearance, which Papa knows already from earlier descriptions, touched me so deeply that I couldn't say anything, except, half-crying: my dear friend, I feel for you with all my heart."[43]

In 1777 Maria Theresia may have ruled the empire, but Mozart ruled Vienna. The man whose bust now occupies the centermost spot in the city's central cultural institution, the opera house, was the superstar of his day. Adept at composing not only opera but concertos and symphonies as well, he dazzled the court with his presence and the prospect of decades more of his wonderful music.

In his private life, too, the stars seemed to shine on Mozart. At nineteen he married Constanze, with whom he had six children. By all accounts they remained passionately in love, and his frequent letters show his devotion in vivid language. While few question the depth of his love, there is little doubt that Mozart carried on affairs as well. Like a celebrity of any era, the temptations were enormous, and the times when his wife was pregnant—and as was the custom, often away at a spa to ensure a safe pregnancy—provided both means and opportunity.

Did he have such an opportunity in June 1791? Constanze, pregnant again, was at the Baden spa just outside Vienna. Her last pregnancy had ended with the baby's death during childbirth; with the summer heat bearing down, a rest cure seemed wise. Mozart wrote frequently: sixteen letters in six weeks. He also visited her, but stayed in the city and was busy professionally and quite possibly amorously. He was at work on the greatly anticipated *The Magic Flute,* due to be presented that fall at the opera house. Mozart's close collaborator was a man named Emanuel Schikaneder, his longtime librettist and an active member of the Viennese social scene. When it came to fidelity, Herr Schikaneder would not have been a positive influence; he was widely recognized to be a libertine. His reputation as a ladies' man was so extreme that it even presented professional problems for him.

There's documentary evidence that in the summer of 1791 Mozart was socializing with Schikaneder and women who were not his wife. On June 6, he wrote his first letter to Constanze in Baden: "I am going to be here [at a friend's house] this evening also, for now that I have given Leonore [the maid] notice, I would be all alone in the house, and that's not to my liking."[44] That same day, the *Wiener Zeitung* newspaper reported that "Mozart went to the Freihaus Theatre with Frau Anna von

Schwingenschuh to see Schikaneder's comic opera [*Anton at Court,* or *The Name Day.*]"[45] Mozart's companion was "the wife of an assistant at the Mint." If this was a dalliance, it was probably not his first with a married woman: One alleged mistress was a beautiful, married, twenty-three-year-old piano student of Mozart's, Magdalena Hofdemel.[46]

On July 26, Constanze gave birth to their sixth child, Franz Xaver Wolfgang. In the midst of this swirl of activity, Mozart already had busy plans for the fall. In September he was due in Prague to write a score celebrating the coronation of King Leopold II. On August 25 he and Constanze left on a three-day journey from Vienna to Prague.

We know from historical sources that Mozart's mood—despite the safe birth of Franz—had turned dark. In Prague he was depressed and concerned about illness. One possibility, although never confirmed, is that sometime in the previous weeks and months Mozart had discovered the first signs of a recently acquired case of syphilis. If he had, or even suspected that was the case, he would not have had to look very far to obtain the remedy; there is no question he could have relied on one of his closest friends.

One thing is certain: While in Prague his concern over some illness caused him to take aggressive action to treat himself; according to one translation, he "dosed himself ceaselessly" with medicine.[47]

Consider, then, the following scenario, one that combines motive, means, and opportunity: Mozart acquired, or believed he acquired, syphilis during a liaison that occurred in the summer of 1791. By the fall, as the signs became apparent to him, he began to treat himself with the remedy of the day—Van Swieten's liquor, developed by Gerard van Swieten in Vienna just a few decades earlier. And if he had questions about whether to use this powerful new cure, or how to get it, he would have had little difficulty obtaining a supply from a friend on whom he relied many other times—Gottfried van Swieten, Gerard's son.

Mercury as a poison generally did not act rapidly; it took days and weeks to take effect. In the days subsequent to Mozart's return to Vienna in October, his health began a rapid descent. On October 20 he spoke to Constanze about death. She commented on his declining health and told Mozart's first biographer, Franz Niemetschek, that he responded, "Certainly one has given me poison. *[Gewiss, man hat mir gift gegeben].*"[48]

Over the next few weeks Mozart's health became worse and worse; his systems seemed to be shutting down and he may have come down with a fever in addition to his general feelings of ill health. He died on December 5, 1791, and the presiding doctor gave the cause as *hitziges Frieselfieber,* or "acute miliary fever."[49] The *Oxford English Dictionary* defines this as "a specific disease characterized by the presence of a rash resembling measles, the spots of which exhibit in their centres minute vesicles of the form of millet seed."[50] Could that have been the rash of secondary syphilis?

Many theories have pointed to some medical problem, though the specifics vary. Speculations included rheumatic fever[51] and a rare disease called Henoch-Schönlein syndrome.[52] More recently, it's even been proposed that he had food poisoning from pork.[53] One of the most common medical theories is that he died of kidney disease.[54] This explanation would be consistent with self-medication with Van Swieten's liquor; kidney damage is one of the characteristic signs of mercury poisoning.

Another school of thought purports that Mozart was deliberately poisoned. Constanze later said he told her he thought the poison was arsenic, in the form of a deadly substance called *Aqua Tofana.*[55] Mercury has also been suggested as the poison,[56] and culprits from the Masons (he attended a lodge meeting the week he became ill) to Jews to Salieri have been (not very convincingly) implicated. Historians have widely condemned the mercury murder conspiracies, probably for good reason, but in the process have thrown out the idea of self-medication with mercury, potentially supplied by his friend Gottfried.

▬

The idea that Van Swieten's liquor, possibly interacting with a new syphilis infection, killed Mozart is a scenario, not a proof. Syphilis was clearly rampant in Vienna, and fear of syphilis was even more epidemic, as witnessed by Mozart's visit to his disfigured friend in Vienna. We are not the first to speculate that Mozart had affairs, that he had acquired syphilis, or that he suffered from poisoning. We are not even the first to question whether that poison was mercury. But we are connecting these ideas in a different way, and suggesting another link, his friendship with the son of the inventor of the Vienna Treatment.

"The Death-blow Is Struck from the First"

GPI surfaced not long after Mozart's death. But the syndrome took much longer to surface in America. One reason the disease may have been previously unknown in the United States is that Van Swieten's liquor was a European invention, to arrive later in the United States and supplant calomel, which had been the mainstay of American venereal treatment. The 1860 edition of an American medical handbook, *Gunn's Domestic Medicine*, refers to Van Swieten's as a French and British treatment and among "material remedies used in other countries."[57] Nonetheless, when GPI occurred in the United States it showed remarkably similar symptoms to the European manifestation, according to two American doctors.

"Men in the prime of life, intelligent and of active habits, have perhaps sustained a single attack of paralysis; a slight impairment of the mind, a slight faltering in the speech, and a little infirmity in the gait, only discovered by those who look for it, are the most prominent symptoms. Yet in all these cases the death-blow is struck from the first. . . . Their health, they say, was never so good, their mind never so clear, their prosperity never so secure. Fits of a convulsive character, sometimes decidedly epileptic, often supervene on this state; and each attack leaves the mind and body weaker, until a paroxysm more severe than common, proves fatal,"[58] wrote one doctor; another claimed, "The form of delusions has almost always born reference to immense amount of money, great power or some similar exultation. No recovery has occurred among them."[59]

These vivid accounts—so consistent with the observations of Kraepelin in Germany, Kanner in Yankton, and Haslam in England—show how identifiable the disease was. One Parisian doctor named E. Esquirol made an observation in 1845 that came excruciatingly close to the heart of the matter: "This complication [paralysis in the insane] is most frequently observed among that class of insane persons who have yielded to venereal excesses, or have been addicted to the use of alcoholic drinks; among those also, who have made an inordinate use of mercury, as well as those who, exercising the brain too vigorously, in mental strife, have, at the same time, abandoned themselves to errors of regimen."[60]

There are four possible clues to GPI in that one paragraph: alcohol, "mental strife" in advanced civilization, venereal disease, and mercury.

It is fascinating to see Emil Kraepelin nearly a century later pursuing the alcohol-induced GPI idea at Hiawatha, and puzzling over the risk to those in advanced cultures. But the real combination of clues in Esquirol's 1845 observation—mercury and syphilis coming together in advanced cultures—went unnoticed.

In the meantime the Viennese and their close research partners in Germany continued to work on improving treatments for syphilis. In the early 1860s, just across the border from the Austro-Hungarian Empire, George Lewin, working cooperatively with Carl Ludwig Sigmond's practice in Vienna, took Swietini's liquor to its next logical step. Instead of having patients swallow mercuric chloride, Lewin and Sigmund decided to deliver it more directly through injections. Writing in 1872, Lewin reported that public health authorities had immediately adopted his quick-and-easy treatment in their most at-risk population: prostitutes.[61]

While prostitutes suspected of having syphilis were forced to get mercuric chloride injections, Emil Kraepelin, also in Germany, observed that young women suffering from GPI were "strikingly often" prostitutes, noting that 11 percent of the women in a mental hospital in Berlin were prostitutes, while prostitutes comprised only 1.7 percent of Berlin's female population.[62] ("Paresis has apparently not yet been observed in nuns," he noted without comment.) In Paris Esquirol, too, noticed a connection between paralytic insanity and prostitution. He reported that although GPI was far more frequent among men than women, nevertheless one in twenty of the patients in Paris's famed Salpêtrière Hospital were female prostitutes and "they generally sink into the most profound misery and, as a consequence, into dementia of a paralytic form."[63]

All these observations point in the same direction—GPI arose with the internal use of mercuric chloride to treat syphilis. Groups that got intensive, frequent, and long-term treatment were much more likely to succumb to GPI, while in untreated populations it appeared exceedingly rarely.

As this new injection treatment took hold across Europe, the problem of GPI seemed to spread wildly. At the same time doctors were finally discovering that syphilis and GPI went together. In 1857 F. Esmarch and W. Jessen speculated that GPI was increasing and began to connect it with syphilis. Alfred Fournier, in 1876, first connected syphilis to tabes dorsalis, the affliction of the spinal cord, and over the next few years demonstrated conclusively that GPI occurred only in people infected with syphilis.[64] By the end of the nineteenth century it was clear that neurosyphilis in general and GPI in particular were part of the syphilis epidemic.

By then it was also clear that syphilis was far and away the most serious public health problem of the civilized world. Tomes of medical analysis and advice were written—more than on any other specific illness. GPI claimed the lives and minds of luminaries—besides Nietzsche there were Joyce, Maupassant, Baudelaire, Schuman, Schubert, and likely many more whose illnesses have been less clearly traced to the spirochete. Strangely, it was widely observed that no such celebrities appeared to have died in the eighteenth century from GPI—probably because Van Swieten's liquor did not come into wide use till around the turn of century.

In Vienna, the army garrison remained the focus of syphilis study, just as it had been in Van Swieten's day. Two army doctors named E. E. Mattauschek and Alexander Pilcz conducted the first systematic study of GPI rates among Austrian army officers. Published in 1913, their study examined the army officers treated according to the Viennese method between 1880 and 1910.[65] The two doctors hewed close to the practice guidelines of the day and remained convinced of the efficacy of current protocols. Indeed, their article made a point of celebrating the success of mercury treatments and continued to support its use in their own patients. But there was a crucial error in their analysis.

On average, GPI took about fifteen years to develop after the initial syphilis infection, so it was important to control for the effect of time since treatment. Evaluating GPI rates in patients who had only recently been treated would drastically understate the true rate, which could only be assessed in groups where the disease had had sufficient time to develop. And while on the surface, the GPI rates reported in the 1913 study looked modest enough, a rate of 4.7 percent, the sample of syphilitics included a wide range of treatment groups, some who had been treated thirty years before and others who had been treated only a few years previously. This approach resulted in misleading findings.

Later analysts would uncover Mattauschek and Pilcz's error. J. Aebley, writing from Zurich in 1920, estimated a higher rate: Between 9.75 and 13 percent of infected men would eventually develop GPI.[66] These subjects were followed for a period of twenty-five to thirty years, a time frame that could allow for full assessments of GPI rates. Most authors later accepted the validity of Aebley's recalculations.

Even less systematic studies tended to confirm the scourge of GPI— everywhere one looked there were high rates. At Johns Hopkins, close to 40 percent of white males with syphilis were afflicted with some form of neurosyphilis; close to 10 percent were paretics.[67] Neuropsychiatric wards all over the world saw GPI at rates of 5 to 35 percent of the entire caseload.[68]

But one part of Europe seemed exempt from this. As Ragnar Vogt had observed to Emil Kraepelin, there sometimes was not a single GPI patient in Norway's main psychiatric hospital. The head of the Oslo syphilis clinic, a doctor named Caesar Boeck, counted himself among the mercury skeptics. Based on years of clinical observation by his uncle Wilhelm, also a syphilologist, Caesar adopted his uncle's views on the adverse effects of mercury treatment. He decided as a matter of policy starting in 1890 that the Norwegian method would be different— patients would be strictly quarantined, kept in the hospital during infectious stages (as long as six months), and treated locally with potassium iodide along with topical treatments for skin rashes. Mercury was strictly forbidden. Speaking at the medical society in Oslo in 1909, Boeck elaborated on the perspective that he and his uncle had shared: "I wish to touch upon the remarkable fact . . . that in Denmark, where mercury therapy is in common use and, to the best of my knowledge, is as thoroughly conducted as in any other country, the relative number of paralytics in mental hospitals is more than twice as large as in Norway, where we have maintained an attitude of reservation as to the use of mercury in the treatment of syphilitics since the days of Wilhelm Boeck. . . . It will also have been noticed . . . that as compared with other countries general paralysis is, on the whole, relatively uncommon in Norway, whereas this cannot be said of mental disorders in general."[69]

From 1890 to 1910, Boeck emphasized the importance of keeping accurate statistics so patients could be followed up with. These records would become the basis for one of the most detailed studies ever on the effect of withholding mercury treatment.

The Beginning of the End

The end of the Age of Syphilis began, slowly, with the rise of another form of heavy metal injection as a treatment. This was Salvarsan, an arsenic compound that burst on the scene in 1911 as Formula 606. Paul Ehrlich's so-called magic bullet offered all the hopes once held for mercury treatment.

Ehrlich had received his medical education just a few years after George Lewin introduced mercury injections at the Charité hospital in Berlin. As he worked systematically through a large number of chemical formulations, the 606th—an arsenic-based molecule that he called arsphenamine—proved more effective than mercuric chloride against syphilis.

It also had the advantage of being less poisonous—the casualty-to-cure rate appeared to be more like one in ten in contrast to mercury's much higher mortality rate. "The ratio of 1:10 for mapharsen [an arsenic formulation] is the lowest of all the arsenical preparations used in the treatment of syphilis," wrote Joseph Earle Moore in *The Modern Treatment of Syphilis*.[70] Moore, one of the world's leading syphilis experts, went on to give a gruesome assessment for the risk-benefit calculus for mercury. "But with almost every [mercury] compound so far studied, the therapeutic ratio is 1:1 and never greater than 1:2, i.e., the curative dose and the minimal lethal dose are so nearly identical that although the infection is destroyed, so is the animal."[71] Still, mercury remained a part of the standard of care; mercury injections often went alongside arsenic injections, and mercury inunctions remained the dermatological treatment of choice.

The rise of Salvarsan had other unexpected consequences. In Norway, where Boeck had long resisted mercury injections, Salvarsan changed their approach; from 1911 forward, Norway joined the rest of Europe in its activist approach to the treatment of new syphilis cases. In the meantime, however, from 1890 to 1910 the Boeck cohort provided a fascinating test case for the effects or lack thereof of effectively untreated syphilis.

In 1929 E. Bruusgaard, one of Boeck's successors, organized a study that provided a counterpoint to the study of Austrian army officers, with accurate records on 2,181 syphilis cases.[72] Bruusgaard's study included a follow-up analysis for Boeck's original patients. In order to study the

conditions of health twenty to forty years later, he scoured the country-
side for former patients, looking for a wide range of outcomes, most notably GPI. This was not an entirely controlled study, because these
patients might have received some other form of therapy, including mercury, in the intervening years; private clinics in Norway and nearby
countries were using mercury treatments, and by 1929 arsenic treatments
were common. But while not as clean a study as, say, the study of cultur-
ally separate Native Americans, the effect of Boeck's approach would be
evident nevertheless.

Bruusgaard was able to obtain detailed reports on 473 of the original
2,000-plus patients, but still believed he had found every case of GPI in
Norway. He found 13 cases, including patients who died, in a population
of 2.2 million—confirming Vogt's reports of the virtual absence of GPI
in the country.

It was Bruusgaard's study that finally shook the profession of syphilol-
ogy to its foundation. GPI, the most feared and fatal consequence of the
dreaded pox, present in 10 percent or more of the recipients of the Vienna
treatment, was virtually nonexistent among those who had received no
mercury treatment at all. What did that say about the centuries of effort
on the part of the European medical profession? Could doctors, in their
attempt to treat the surface symptoms of a hideous physical condition,
have planted the seed for a far greater mental and physical affliction?

Excavating documents and studies from decades and even centuries ago,
when diagnostic categories and data collection standards were far different, is no easy task. But neither is it impossible. Perhaps no single study
on its own is strong enough to definitively prove that GPI was a result of
treatment with mercury or other similar toxins. But the cumulative record makes the argument difficult to dismiss.

And the cumulative record on GPI and syphilis treatment includes
the most notorious study in American medical history. Any number of
contemporary observers had commented that neurosyphilis was hard to
find among blacks, and there was a belief that syphilis affected the races
differently, specifically that whites disproportionately had neurological
problems and blacks displayed cardiovascular symptoms. A study at Johns
Hopkins in 1922 found the rate of GPI among black men at 2 percent,

well below the rate for white men, 8.5 percent, which was attributed to a racial difference in disease risk.[73] But we also know the poor black population, like the Native American population, was less likely to receive the Vienna treatment than their more affluent and "Europeanized" white counterparts.

The ongoing syphilis epidemic in the United States spurred a number of efforts to measure the extent of the syphilis problem in the country. Some of the highest rates of the disease were among poor blacks in the rural South. Surveys in Macon County, Alabama, put the rate as high as 40 percent. "A considerable portion of the infected Negro population remained untreated during the entire course of syphilis," wrote U.S. public health officials. "Such individuals seemed to offer a unique opportunity to study the syphilitic illness from the beginning of the disease to the death of the infected person."[74]

Thus the Tuskegee experiment was born, formally named the "Study of Untreated Syphilis in the Male Negro." At the outset of the study in 1932, particularly in light of the Bruusgaard findings in Norway, the idea of withholding treatment from the local population would have included the absence of arsenic and mercury injections and mercury rubs. Some could argue that, in hindsight, this offered the population a greater opportunity for a healthy life since it removed any possibility of complications from these treatments. But truly, the ethics of this study were compromised from the start. First, the treatments withheld were considered at the time (at least by mainstream medicine) to be beneficial and were received by the majority of the population. Above and beyond this injustice, participants were not given informed consent and generally were viewed as laboratory animals rather than as a disadvantaged group deserving high-quality government care. They were not told they had syphilis but that they had "bad blood" that the public health system promised to help them control.

To entice participants, the federal government provided physical examinations and "incidental medications such as tonics and analgesics." The Milbank Memorial Fund's offer of burial assistance to indigent families made possible a higher degree of post-mortem examinations. Free medication (though not to treat syphilis), free hot meals, free rides to the doctor's (which included the opportunity to stop in town to shop or visit with their friends on the streets)—all helped encourage the men to enlist and kept them coming back.

Macon County, home of the Tuskegee Institute, lies in Alabama's

Black Belt, named for its rich soil. The lives of its poor blacks were little changed from post–Civil War sharecropper days: More than three thousand blacks were eking out a living on depleted land in the middle of the Depression; they plowed with mules, and roads to town were often too rudimentary and rutted to reach in an automobile. There were ten physicians in the county, only one of them black, and none accessible to blacks in southern and southwestern portions of the county. The county was more than 80 percent black at the time.[75]

The project managers of the Tuskegee experiment recruited 600 study participants—399 of whom had syphilis determined by two positive test results, and 201 who were uninfected—with the aim of following all of them on through to death. An early publication noted that the incidence and character of syphilis among African Americans had been a controversial topic for many years. The authors noted two camps: one group who believed that GPI and tabes dorsalis were not common in African Americans, and a second that believed their frequency was essentially the same as in whites.[76]

Although the authors emphasized the common occurrence of central nervous system symptoms in their 399 untreated cases—and even invented a category called the benign parenchymatous type, meaning there was evidence of syphilis in the spinal fluid but absolutely no symptoms of neurosyphilis—they nevertheless had to admit that serious neurosyphilis was rare in this study group: "With regard to the benign parenchymatous type, such cases did not appear to run the usual classic course of dementia paralytica [GPI] or of tabes dorsalis. . . . No typical cases of dementia paralytica or tabes dorsalis were noted but one case of simple dementia was found. In order to be certain that there was no selection of cases through loss to institutions for the insane, it was learned that not a single male Negro over 25 years of age was confined with syphilis of the central nervous system in the Searcy hospital at Mt. Vernon, Alabama, where the Negro insane in this State are hospitalized."[77]

It's worth emphasizing the statement buried in the middle of this article. In the American population with the highest rate of syphilis ever measured, where the "benefits" of modern European civilization were just a few miles, or in some cases a few years, away, the most dreaded form of syphilis—general paralysis of the insane, not to mention its close cousin tabes dorsalis—was nowhere to be found. GPI was not found in the study population that the researchers had selected, nor anywhere that it might have been expected to show up, such as the state mental hospital. Unlike the Boeck/Bruusgaard study in Norway, which was a follow-up of a previously identified population, this first study in Tuskegee simply provided a snapshot in time, a look at the entire disease burden at a given moment in a given population and including residents ranging from the age of twenty-five into their sixties and seventies.

As the years passed, the study continued. Following this first examination in 1932–33, five subsequent surveys were performed over the next thirty years, in 1939, 1948, 1952, 1954, and 1962. Each round of surveys and examinations stimulated a new round of scientific analysis and publications, of which there were a dozen in all before public outrage finally brought the study to an abrupt end in 1972.

Although observers have tended to lump the whole Tuskegee project into one sordid episode, it's worth considering the project in two periods, before and after the invention of penicillin. Before penicillin, the untreated Tuskegee patients were being investigated in the context of the Bruusgaard Oslo challenge, in which patients with untreated syphilis, in hindsight, may have had advantages over those treated with mercury and arsenic. Following the introduction of penicillin, however, every day in which treatment was withheld was another day of effective treatment denied.

The way this unfolded is charted in these two tables.

In the 1932 study none of the patients had received treatment of any kind. But over the next two survey rounds, well over half of the study population were found to have received some form of treatment on their own: By 1938, 115 of the 270 surviving patients reported receiving treatment, which at that time would have always been in the form of mercury or arsenic injections. In 1948 nearly three-quarters (72 percent) of the study group had received treatment. Since mercury and arsenic were still considered viable treatments, these individuals had to be removed from the study group. The removal of these participants was always disappointing to those running the experiment, as it was considered a clear weakness of the study. In those early follow-ups, although, not surprisingly, the authors found evidence that having syphilis seemed to increase the risk of negative neurological effects in infected subjects as compared to subjects with no infection at all, they were still unable to locate any cases of GPI.

All that started to change by the early 1950s as a series of remarkable developments took the study down a darker path. Into the late 1940s, there were legitimate questions about the true efficacy of penicillin as a

THE FIRST PHASE OF THE TUSKEGEE STUDY: 1932–48

Stage of the Project	Males Infected with Syphilis			GPI cases	Uninfected Controls		
	Study group (untreated/treated)	Mortality rate	Neurological status (%)		Study group	Mortality rate	Neurological status (%)
1932–33 population/ prevalence survey and examination	399 (399/0)	—	"Syphilis of the central nervous system" • Clinical—31 (7.7%) • CSF only—73 (18.3%)	0	201	—	N/A
Changes Recruited Deaths* Lost to follow-up	+11 −101 −39				— −28 −20		
1938–39 follow-up survey and examination	270 (155/115)	24.6%*	"Condition of the nervous system" • 21 (13.6%)	0?	153	13.9%*	"Condition of the nervous system" • 13 (8.5%)
Changes Deaths Infected Lost to follow-up	— — −22				−12 −9 −47		
1948 follow-up survey and examination	248 (70/178)	24.6%	"Psychosis" • 14 (20.0%)**	0?	85	19.9%	"Psychosis" • 9 (10.6%)

*First mortality survey was conducted in 1944.

**Only untreated cases were included in the analysis of clinical status.

Note: See Appendix A for further notes and explanations.

THE SECOND PHASE OF THE TUSKEGEE STUDY: 1952–1963

Stage of the Project	Males Infected with Syphilis				Uninfected Controls
	Study group	Cases of non GPI neurosyphilis	Cases with GPI or paretic symptoms	Treatment status	Study group
Starting population	408*				192*
1952 follow-up surveys					
Died (% of population)	165 (40%)				51 (27%)
Autopsy performed (Brain autopsy)	92 (46)	8 (1)	2–3 (1)		32 (13)
Living and examined	159	6 (tabes dorsalis, related diagnosis)	1	4 of 7 (including 1 paretic) "inadequately treated"	92
1954 follow-up survey					
Serological tests done	299			261 (87%) "inadequately treated"	
1962 follow-up survey					
Living and examined	90			86 treated (96%) • 11 had Hg injections	65
Living with neurosyphilis		3	0	2 received Hg injections 1 unknown 1934 treatment	

*Most second-phase studies described a starting population of 600 with 408 infected cases and 192 controls, presumably moving 9 infected controls into the study group. This is probably an oversimplification, since as many as 438 infected individuals may have been active in the study at one time or another.
Note: See Appendix B for further notes and explanations.

syphilis treatment. But by the 1950s, the benefits of penicillin had become compellingly clear. In the second table some new dimensions of the study are apparent. First, as the curative powers of the new wonder drug became obvious, the Tuskegee scientists decided to take all the patients they had previously bemoaned as lost from the study group because they had received treatment, and returned them to the study sample, grouping together an "inadequately treated" subset with cases who had never received treatment. Most of this new subset were deemed "inadequately treated" because they hadn't received enough arsenic injections—patients who received full arsenic treatment were still excluded—but a sizable minority had received mercury injections sometime along the way. None had received penicillin, the new standard of care—and GPI, which had remained undetected during the first three surveys, had begun to make an appearance in this population: 3 of the 92 patients receiving an autopsy by 1952 were reported to have died with GPI.

At this point, the researchers concluded that if they could make sure none of the participants got the new "adequate treatment" (penicillin), they could resume the study with a much larger population. Sidney Olansky, the director of the project on behalf of the Public Health Service, commented that "medical progress has not been so great nor medical care so widespread among our patients in Macon County as to defeat the project as a study of untreated syphilis; despite the present prevalent use of antibiotics with their known anti-syphilitic potency, the study group remains untreated."[78]

This specific choice to deny penicillin treatment to these men was the worst decision these researchers made. That these men were exploited from the outset as lab rats rather than cared for as human beings is a terrible tragedy. But widespread revulsion about the project as a whole (which is deserved) has also obscured the additional outrage of this moment. Along with the decision to undertake the experiment in the first place, it was just as great a moral failure on the part of the Public Health Service to insist on continuing its prospective epidemiology study after the historic introduction of penicillin should have overtaken it and shut it down.

Instead of the kind of introspection that might have produced a change in course, the investigators seemed instead never to have considered it. Rather, they praised themselves for their selfless contributions to medical knowledge: "It seems appropriate, after 20 years of experience, to comment upon some of the operational aspects of the study, which, to our knowledge, is the first prospective longitudinal long-term study involving the ideal of 100 percent observation of a large group of diseased and control patients through life to autopsy. . . . A quality of dedication to the ideal of a long-term study based upon love of and respect for the dignity of the individual within the group, and upon the satisfaction of making a single, valuable contribution to the increment of knowledge, without concern for credit, is fundamental."[79]

The beginning of this survey in 1952 coincided with a visit to the United States of Trygve Gjestland of Norway, the chief worker in a contemporary reexamination and reevaluation of the survivors of the Boeck-Bruusgaard study. "At the invitation of the Division of Venereal Disease, he visited Tuskegee and observed the first group of patients as they were examined. He saw, firsthand, the remarkable socioeconomic and racial difference between the rural Alabama Negro farmers and the fair-skinned Norwegians he has been studying.

"As the first aged men trooped into the hospital for re-examination, Dr. Gjestland and the examiners felt as if they were witnessing a strange and historic procession. Their feelings were similar to those of Bruusgaard in Oslo, who wrote in 1929: 'It produced a curious impression to see these patients after so many years . . . several of them over 70 . . . A strikingly large percent of the cases were free of clinical symptoms. . . . Many of these patients had apparently tried to undermine their health by an unreasonable mode of life, but had not succeeded.'"[80]

The Fine Art of Burying Your Mistakes

During the shift (roughly from 1911 to 1943) from the use of mercury injections to penicillin, two drastically different standards of care, a flurry of treatments developed, further complicating the distinction between adequate and inadequate treatment. Most notable was arsenic-based Salvarsan, for which Paul Ehrlich won the Nobel Prize in 1908. Another Nobel winner for syphilis treatment was Viennese Dr. Julius Wagner-Jauregg in 1927; he pioneered the idea of treating syphilis with fever therapy, induced by infecting patients with malaria.

The idea was that the high fevers could actually kill the spirochete. As penicillin later proved, regardless of the toxic background, if the spirochete could be killed, GPI would be stopped in its tracks. The disadvantages of malaria therapy, however, were manifold, including a mortality rate of around 5 percent.[81]

Thus, it is hard to know the exact toll of mercury treatments for syphilis in the first half of the twentieth century, and what the rate of GPI was—though in Europe's hospitals the toll was clearly large. Perhaps the most reliable estimate is Aebley's recalculation of the Austrian army officer treatment grouping, in which roughly 10 percent or more of men treated with mercuric chloride injections for syphilis developed GPI. On the other side of the coin, the untreated populations—from the Native Americans that Kanner and Kraepelin inquired about to Boeck and Bruusgaard's Oslo cohort—GPI in untreated syphilitic patients was nearly nonexistent, quite possibly zero.

Salvarsan, while less toxic, seemed not to eliminate the risk of GPI in the treatment group; indeed, arsenic might have had a similar though less toxic effect as mercury. One study in Denmark showed the long-term rate of GPI in Salvarsan patients at 3 to 4 percent.[82] The accompanying table summarizes the evidence.

Up to the very last moment before the arrival of penicillin, syphilis experts claimed extraordinary progress with ever more sophisticated application of heavy metals (mercury very much included) and fever therapy. At Johns Hopkins, Dr. Joseph Earle Moore's *Modern Treatment of Syphilis* included a chapter on the virtues of mercury treatment with numerous unattributed statistics and extravagant claims about the benefits of heavy metals and the dangers of leaving syphilis untreated.

With the advent of penicillin by the end of the decade, however, this kind of "modern treatment" instantly became a quaint concept. Still, it continued to pose an interesting dilemma for professional syphilologists even as they embraced the first medicine that offered unambiguous benefits. How would history treat their efforts? Kraepelin's and Kanner's investigations into obscure populations were more easily dismissed, but the Oslo study with its modern prospective design and its convincing critique of "inadequate treatment" in the form of mercury offered a sour endnote to the Age of Syphilis. To be sure, the Tuskegee study showed that having syphilis wasn't good for you even if it remained untreated—it had long-term effects on cardiovascular health and generally reduced life expectancy. But the question remained: Did mercury have benefits for the patient, or would the world have been better off without the Vienna treatment and its successors?

Dr. Moore decided to take action. He enlisted a young, ambitious

FREQUENCY OF GENERAL PARESIS OF THE INSANE (GPI) AMONG MEN INFECTED WITH SYPHILIS: SELECTED STUDIES

Population (publication by)	Mode of Treatment	Study Type	Treatment Period	Syphilis Cases (male)	GPI Cases (males)	GPI Rate (%)
Austrian army officers (Aebley, 1920)	Mercuric chloride injections	Follow-up (29–33 years)	1880–1884	617	60	9.72%
Danish syphilis registry (Nielsen, 1950)	Salvarsan injections	Follow-up (30–40 years)	1913–1920	467	20	4.28%
Oslo residents (Bruusgaard, 1929)	Untreated	Follow-up (up to 40 years)	1890–1910	793	4	0.50%
Tuskegee Study of Untreated Syphilis in the Male Negro (Vonderlehr et al., 1936)	Untreated	Population prevalence in 1932	Pre-1932	399	0	0%
Native Americans (Adams & Kanner, 1928)	Untreated	Case finding survey	Pre-1925	many	1	~0%

Norwegian, Trygve Gjestland—the same doctor who had watched the parade of elderly patients into the Tuskegee clinic—to undertake an exhaustive reexamination of Bruusgaard's influential 1920 Oslo study.

On its face, "The Oslo Study of Untreated Syphilis" was an odd exercise.[83] It was published in 1955, after penicillin carried the day, and at 329 dense, chart-filled pages it was fourteen times longer than Bruusgaard's original paper. But behind the scenes, the project mattered a lot. In his preface, Gjestland notes that Moore had visited Oslo, and that he and J. R. Heller, then chief of the Venereal Disease Division of the U.S. Public Health Service (and a key player in the Tuskegee study), used their "influence in securing funds to finance the study." American syphilis doctors, in effect, helped initiate and fund a study in Scandinavia to vindicate their own medical practices in the United States.

If the concept of "inadequate treatment" in syphilis studies was an exercise in moving goalposts, the Gjestland study was an exercise in lowering the denominator. Bruusgaard had calculated the rate of GPI—a minuscule 0.6 percent—by dividing GPI cases by the entire population of male participants (793) in Boeck's mercury-free treatment regimen. Gjestland instead divided cases by the smaller number of participants who could be tracked down in 1928. He also failed to separate out those who had subsequently been treated with arsenic. That gave him a rate of 2.9 percent with GPI, still a relatively small number but enough to obscure the virtual nonexistence of the disease.

Still, what took 329 pages? A big enough barrage of statistics and digressions for its sponsors to get what they were paying for—the manufacture of doubt. What's breathtaking here is the lack of a reality check: Vogt, the psychiatrist quoted by Kraepelin, had said there were times the big mental hospital in Norway had no cases of GPI at all; Bruusgard had managed to find records for just thirteen men, alive and dead, in the whole country; elsewhere in Europe, the asylums were bulging with them. But the mercury apologists sowed enough confusion to avoid acknowledging one of the most catastrophic medical treatments in history, one that went on for centuries.

Gjestland's prodigiously muddled verdict was for all intents and purposes the last word on the Age of Syphilis. There were a few dissensions; one

Danish author reminded readers in a diplomatically worded review that Gjestland had lost the point of Bruusgaard's original concern in his 329 pages, which was that mercury treatments were worse than the disease.[84]

In today's medical texts, the Age of Syphilis is marked by the singular triumph of penicillin and some discussion of the American origins—or not—of *T. pallidum*. The centuries of poisoning with mercury and the iatrogenic horrors of GPI play no role in these histories, which are reserved for the progress of medical innovation.

But we take a different set of lessons from this history. Syphilis had a beginning, a middle, and an end. It had an age. And so did general paralysis of the insane; the first reports started trickling in at the end of the eighteenth century; then clusters of cases were noted; then the incidence rate soared until penicillin was used to kill the bacteria.

As we saw in the case of Karen Wetterhahn, the scientist at Dartmouth, even fatal doses can take months to show their first signs; the latency between first exposure to mercury and first symptoms of illness can be remarkably long. Likewise, the long trajectory of GPI made it hard to connect it to syphilis, let alone to mercury treatments.

But once the syphilis spirochete dies off, neurosyphilis stops. So what exactly was the role of mercury? We don't know. But multiple streams of evidence suggest that internal use of mercury drove the microbe mad— that without the ingestion or injection of mercuric chloride as a treatment, there was essentially no general paralysis of the insane. Medicine created a hideous manifestation of the disease it was designed to treat, then performed more twists and turns than the spirochete itself in order to avoid the stark reality of cause and effect.

CHAPTER TWO

THE AGE OF HYSTERIA

*In more than half of the severe cases of hysteria, obsessional neurosis, etc.,
which I have treated psychotherapeutically, I have been able to prove with
certainty that the patient's father suffered from syphilis before marriage. . . .
I am . . . of opinion that the coincidence I have observed is neither accidental
nor unimportant.*

—SIGMUND FREUD, *THREE ESSAYS ON THE THEORY OF SEXUALITY,* 1905[1]

The Clue in Footnote 6

In the early 1890s a prominent and wealthy Viennese manufacturer
named Philipp Bauer was referred to a neuropathologist after suffering
an attack of confusion, "followed by symptoms of paralysis and slight
mental disturbances."[2]

It didn't take long for the specialist, Sigmund Freud, to recognize the
signs of syphilis, which Bauer acknowledged acquiring before marriage.
While Freud is remembered for founding psychoanalysis, his academic
training was in neurology and anatomy. As an intern at the Vienna
General Hospital, he regularly saw male patients with syphilis in the
dermatology ward; "PP"—for progressive paralysis or GPI—is written
in his own hand in the hospital's admission rolls.

Freud prescribed Bauer "an energetic course of anti-luetic (syphilitic) treatment, as a result of which all the remaining disturbances passed off."[3] In that era, such treatment could only have been mercury, and its "energetic" application probably involved both mercury inunctions (rubs) and injections of mercuric chloride.

"This fortunate intervention of mine," as Freud put it, so impressed Bauer that he brought his daughter, Ida, "who had meanwhile grown unmistakably neurotic," and introduced her to Freud four years later.[4] That visit did not lead to ongoing treatment, but two years after that, her condition had further deteriorated; she had become despondent and wrote a note that her parents interpreted as suicidal. So in 1900 when Ida was almost eighteen, her father brought her back for psychothera-peutic treatment. She stuck with it for three months, a treatment course that became a turning point in the history of psychiatry.

Freud changed her name to Dora and wrote about her in a case study formally titled "Fragment of an Analysis of a Case of Hysteria," one of the foundational works of psychoanalysis and modern psychiatry. "After 'Dora,'" writes Freud biographer Peter Gay, "psychoanalytic technique was never the same."[5]

Freud attributed Dora's symptoms to emotional and sexual conflicts triggered by improper advances from Herr K., the family friend who ac-companied her father on his initial visit to Freud. Also stirring the plot was Dora's belief (probably correct) that her father was having an affair with Herr K.'s wife. And Freud was more than a little suspicious that Dora had sexual feelings for the wife as well.

But Freud may have missed something more important—the real reason for Dora's decline. The clue is in the epigraph at the top of the chapter, and in footnote 6 to "Dora": "Now a *strikingly high* [emphasis in original] percentage of patients I have treated psychoanalytically come of fathers who have suffered from tabes or general paralysis [GPI]. In consequence of the novelty of my method, I see only the severest cases."[6]

Sometimes in medicine the truth can be found in a footnote, and this is a remarkable example. In that footnote Freud describes "the conclusion to which I have been driven by my experience as a neuro-pathologist—namely, that syphilis in the male parent is a very relevant factor in the aetiology of the neuropathic constitution of children."[7]

But why? Syphilis is not inherited, though it can be contracted from the mother during birth (just like HIV). And while having a father with syphi-lis certainly could create psychological problems, and counseling could help resolve them, this does not seem to be Freud's argument. Furthermore, the symptoms these offspring developed go way beyond what Freud in another case called "commonplace emotional upheavals."[8]

On this, however, we agree with Freud: The connection was neither accidental nor unimportant.

─────

In the popular imagination, Victorian-era hysteria is perceived as the convenient fainting spells and histrionic behavior of upper-crust women. Most cultural historians believe that hysteria was triggered by the emerging conflict between female self-empowerment and traditional roles. ("'Hysterical' is what men call women they can't control," says one scholar of German literature, and in modern parlance that's a good definition.[9]) But as we shall see, both the mental and physical symptoms of clinically diagnosed hysteria were severe, and they were precisely defined.

Dora had these symptoms, although not to the totally disabling extent of some other patients. According to Freud, "When she was about twelve she began to suffer from hemicranial headaches in the nature of a migraine, and from attacks of nervous coughing. . . . The most troublesome symptom during the first half of an attack of this kind, at all events in the last few years, used to be a complete loss of voice."[10] Other signs and symptoms included "piercing gastric pains" and sometimes dragging her right foot.

Now let's look at the timing of Dora's troubles and her father's treatment for syphilis: Dora was "about 12" when her father saw Freud for neurosyphilis and was given "an energetic course" of what was undoubtedly mercury.[11] Who tended him? Dora. "The nature of her disposition has always drawn her towards her father," Freud wrote, "and his numerous illnesses were bound to have increased her affection for him. In some of these illnesses he would allow no one but her to discharge the lighter duties of nursing."[12]

It gives an entirely new meaning to "transference" if the treatment Freud prescribed for the father inadvertently poisoned Dora as she nursed him in his sickbed. All her symptoms—headaches, persistent cough, trouble walking and talking, gastric crises, depression—are also symptoms of mercury poisoning (and reminiscent of Kraepelin's description of GPI itself). And their appearance entirely coincides with her involvement with her father's treatment.

Rereading Freud with this in mind, his psychosexual explanations for Dora's symptoms seem even less plausible. Consider her persistent cough, or *tussis nervosa*, as Freud called it. He believed it represented her obsession with her father's probable affair with Frau K. and the thought of them having oral sex. "The conclusion was inevitable. . . . She pictured to herself a scene of sexual gratification *per os* [by mouth] between the two people whose love-affair occupied her mind so incessantly."[13] She also felt the residual trauma of Herr K.'s attempt to molest her and, according to Freud:

> declared that she could still feel upon the upper part of her body the pressure of Herr K.'s embrace. . . . I believe that during the man's passionate embrace she felt not merely his kiss upon her lips but also the pressure of his erect member against her body. This perception was revolting to her; it was dismissed from her memory, repressed, and replaced by the innocent sensation of pressure upon her thorax, which in turn derived an excessive intensity from its repressed source. Once more, therefore, we find a displacement from the lower part of the body to the upper.[14]

Dora may well have been revolted by Herr K.'s behavior and distressed by images of her father's possible affair, but the constellation of severe physical and mental symptoms Freud attributes to that distress seems unlikely. We are hardly the first to take issue with the good doctor; poking holes in Freudian theory has become sport. Under relentless attack for decades, many of its theoretical foundations have since crumbled. But while we propose that mercury poisoning may have caused some of Freud's most formative cases, we do not mean to dismiss everything that has followed as folly. Recent research has begun to suggest quantifiable benefits from intensive and long-term psychodynamic therapy, as psychoanalysis is now known.[15]

Nor is the idea of toxic exposures among Freud's cases a "fringe" proposition. Another patient, Anna O., whose symptoms were similar to but much more pronounced than Dora's, is considered the very first case in psychoanalytic literature. In the 1984 anthology *Anna O.: 14 Contemporary Reinterpretations,* one essayist wrote: "In considering a speculative, retrospective diagnosis, I believe one cannot exclude the possibility of a toxic psychosis—perhaps based on a morphine-opium addiction."[16] Anna had used these drugs to overcome severe facial pain, and this conjecture came from the director of the Chicago Institute for Psychoanalysis, a past president of the American Psychoanalytic Association (nothing "fringe" about him).

Once you begin looking, clues to possible mercury toxicity are everywhere in Freud's cases. Take Frau K., who was probably having an affair with Dora's father: "Their acquaintance with the K.'s had begun before her father's serious illness; but it had not become intimate until the young woman [Frau K.] had officially taken on the position of nurse during that illness, while Dora's mother had kept away from the sick room," Freud recounts.[17] But as the families became friends, the nurse-patient role ended. "And, while previously Frau K. had been an invalid and had even been obliged to spend months in a sanatorium for nervous disorders because she had been unable to walk, she had now become a healthy and lively woman."[18]

While the chronology is not precisely detailed, Frau K.'s involvement in nursing, her severe mental and physical problems—and her remarkable recovery when her nursing role ended—may be clues to the cause of Dora's problems as well.

The idea that mercury could have triggered the clinical symptoms of "hysteria" in his patients was not a connection Freud ever seems to have made, even though "toxic hysteria" had been written about since the mid-1800s. Five years before Freud saw Dora, *Intoxications et Hystérie* by Camille-Henry Hischmann included a specific account about what was believed to be the relation of hysteria to chronic poisoning by lead, alcohol and mercury.[19]

Freud had the book in his personal library.[20] It is strange that he could miss the possibility when he himself almost certainly prescribed mercury to Dora's father and noted that she took care of him. But by the time Freud was treating her father, his mind was focused on other possibilities that soon came to dominate his thinking.

The Stigmata

Almost forty years before Freud treated Philipp Bauer, Louis Pasteur's germ theory of 1862 heralded the beginning of modern medicine and led to the discovery of penicillin in the 1920s. The stunning insight: that microorganisms were responsible for much of human illness. The decisive use of penicillin against syphilis in the 1940s was followed by many other antibiotics, medicines, and medical techniques. But the most immediate application of germ theory was in antisepsis—preventing infection in wounds created by injury or surgery.

In England Joseph Lister read Pasteur and had the insight to apply his ideas to surgery. The first antiseptic treatment was carbolic acid, first used in 1867; it saved the life of the first surgical patient Lister used it on. Lister wrote about its success in the prestigious medical journal *The Lancet* in 1867,[21] and carbolic acid was soon in wide use. This was a revolution in surgery and saved the lives of countless people. Antiseptic treatment competes with penicillin as one of the great accomplishments of medicine.

Lister and others were soon looking for better antiseptics, and they quickly found that mercury did a great job in preventing bacterial growth. So as antiseptic use spread like wildfire across European hospitals in the 1870s, so did an entirely new application for mercuric chloride (the inorganic, water-soluble mercury salt also known as corrosive sublimate and Van Swieten's liquor). While it had previously been used for treating syphilis, it was now widely adopted in surgery, for dressing of bandages, as a spray in the operating room, and even for household use as a cleaning agent and disinfectant.

In 1881 Robert Koch reported that low concentrations of mercuric chloride were effective as an antiseptic and gave the stamp of approval to mercuric chloride solutions such as Van Swieten's liquor.[22] One commentator described its adoption as "universal"; Lister himself wrote an enthusiastic review in 1884.[23]

With Koch's and Lister's endorsements, the use of mercury in Europe multiplied greatly from the 1870s on. Doctors and nurses slathered on mercury-based creams to treat skin conditions, including the sores of syphilis. Injections of mercuric chloride were used in syphilis wards. Physicians and nurses dipped their hands in it to kill germs; so did housewives and cleaning staff. Inevitably, many people simply came into contact with too much of a toxic chemical—in other words, they got poisoned by the exposure to so much mercuric chloride, the most toxic form of mercury yet known, far more toxic than simple rubs or elemental mercury and calomel, the other common mercury formulation. In effect, Van Swieten's liquor, the most popular solution containing mercuric chloride, had spilled from the bottle marked FOR SYPHILIS ONLY into a much wider population of patients, not to mention those who treated and cared for them. The law of unintended (and unseen) consequences was about to be applied on a tragic scale.

▬

In October 1885, seven years before his sessions with Dora, Freud arrived in Paris to study with the greatest neurologist of his day: the father of modern neurology, Jean-Martin Charcot. Charcot presided over the Salpêtrière, the vast combination of poorhouse, madhouse, and hospital rolled into one. Freud came to Paris on the heels of what might have been a career-ending disaster for a less resilient professional. In "Über Coca," published earlier the same year, Freud had extolled the virtues of cocaine while completely missing its addictive and toxic effects. He even thought it could wean someone safely off a morphine addiction (in truth, it simply led to a potentially fatal double addiction). Ultimately, he missed co-caine's one useful property, as a local anesthetic for eye surgery.[24]

Freud desperately wanted to be famous. To that end, he seemed to have a weakness for medical figures who already were; perhaps he took their very prominence as evidence of perfection. Witness Freud's report on Charcot:

> The man who is at the head of all these resources and auxiliary services is now 60 years of age. He exhibits the liveliness, cheerfulness, and formal perfection of speech which we are in the habit of attributing to the French national character; while at the same time he displays the patience and love of work which we usually claim for our own nation. The attraction of such a personality soon led me to restrict my visits to one single hospital and to seek instruction from one single man.[25]

Significantly, Charcot had also treated general paralysis of the insane and was starting to study another group: patients whose symptoms mimicked those of GPI—coughs, paralysis, and other baffling problems—but who did not have syphilis. These, we suspect, were examples of mercury expo-sure or other toxic effects without the synergistic, and fatal, involvement of the syphilis bacterium.

Charcot changed Freud's life. The six months he spent in Paris were one of the pivotal experiences of Freud's career, and set him on the path to fame and glory—toward the "great, great nimbus" of admiration he acknowledged seeking. That made Charcot's influence crucial not just to neurology, but to psychiatry as well.

Charcot had become a medical intern at the Salpêtrière in 1848. The immense complex, capped by a dome, was built in 1634 to store saltpeter—an element in the making of gunpowder. In 1656 Louis XIV had turned it into the female branch of the Paris Hôpital Général, where it also housed many of the poor and indigent of the city. It soon became the largest charitable center of its kind in Europe. In Charcot's heydey, it housed some five thousand patients and developed an equally busy outpatient practice.[26]

This was a gold mine for a researcher interested in neurology: Inmates and patients presented all kinds of ailments, and because they lived in the facility, they died there, too; thus their brains were then available to be autopsied. A well-known sketch shows Charcot in profile, wearing a top hat and holding a brain in his hands.

Charcot ultimately returned in 1862 to become a professor of pathological anatomy at the hospital. Building on that specialty, his pioneering approach was described as "anatomo-clinical," a method that consisted of describing and classifying signs of individual disorders and then, on autopsy, connecting those symptoms to particular parts of the brain that showed lesions or anomalies. And he was brilliant at it. Over the next two decades, Charcot discovered Parkinson's, multiple sclerosis, and many other maladies and presided over a cadre of gifted physicians who lent their names to other crucial discoveries, Tourette and Babinski among them.

In 1870 the hospital was reorganized and Charcot became responsible for outpatients as well as those who lived at the Salpêtrière. This opened his eyes to a disorder that until then he had paid almost no heed; in his numerous publications before 1870, he showed little interest in it. Then, on October 12, 1878, he gave his first lecture on what he called hystero-epilepsy.

Hysteria ended up as an impossibly vast diagnostic catchall for diseases that nobody could figure out, but as Peter D. Kramer writes in *Freud: Invention of The Modern Mind,* "The term first referred to patients who showed neurological symptoms, such as epileptic seizures or paralysis of a limb, without having the underlying brain or nerve damage that would explain the symptom."[27] But mood disorders, hallucinations, and simply eccentric behavior, especially by women, could also be deemed hysterical. Charcot considered a number of hypotheses: a hereditary neurological weakness that could be triggered by a physical trauma; unconscious ideas (hypnosis seemed to confirm they contributed to the expression of hysteria); even sexual problems. Charcot is reputed to have told Freud at a dinner party that one woman's hysteria was due to her husband's sexual inadequacy and that it is *"la chose génital, toujours, toujours, toujours."*

In 1880 Charcot had begun taking pictures of his hysteria patients, perhaps the first systematic depiction in photographs of a clinical syndrome. The photos were fascinating, the symptoms were bizarre, and his lectures soon drew large crowds.

Indeed, by the time Freud arrived, Charcot had established himself as a showman as well as a precise medical practitioner. His showcase was the weekly Tuesday lecture in which he exhibited his hysteria patients. These collectively came to be known as his Salles des Hystériques. "The huge amphitheatre was filled to the last place with a multicoloured audience drawn from tout Paris, authors, journalists, leading actors and actresses, fashionable demi-mondaines," wrote an author who was frequently present.[28]

The show began as, one by one, patients were brought on stage and discussed. Mostly women, some had strange contractures, while others went into fits on command. There were patients who shook, made strange noises, and adopted seemingly impossible positions—their heads on one chair, their feet on another, their torsos suspended in air but stiff as a board. Others formed the *arc de cercle,* in which their heads and feet touched the ground and their bodies made a semicircle like a performer from Cirque du Soleil. Charcot induced some of these bizarre effects on command through hypnosis, then in vogue and believed to reveal a deep hidden layer of the psyche.

Ever the clinician, Charcot carefully described and diagrammed his patients' problems and formulated what he called the "stigmata" of hysteria. These were the central cluster of symptoms—contractures, visual-field constriction, and loss of feeling in various parts of the body, often on one side, a condition known as hemianesthesia. The word "stigmata" was meant to refer to the permanent symptoms of hysteria as opposed to the seizures and trances that came and went.

Charcot was a popular figure, so in order to give his Tuesday lectures a broader audience, they were compiled into multivolume texts that were translated from the original French language and sold all over the world. In one such text,[29] the third volume contains references to hysteria everywhere. Perhaps the most striking impression one gets in paging through the volume, however, is a visual one: Charcot's discussions of hysteria are anchored by a notably large number of charts (what the publishers called woodcuts) documenting the "hysterical stigmata": ophthalmic charts showing the restricted visual fields of his hysteria cases;[30] full-body charts highlighting "zones of anesthesia" where patients experienced a loss of sensation;[31] and drawings of palsied and contracted limbs.[32]

Charcot clearly believed that the stigmata were so unique and distinctive in terms of defining the core of the disease that he took great pains to illustrate them visually. The overall impression of a modern observer not wedded to any preconceptions is that something quite real was wrong with most of these patients. The problem with Charcot's theory of hysteria was his assumption that simply because nineteenth-century neurologists couldn't pinpoint an organic cause, one did not exist.

———

The classic case of Charcot's hysteria was a man Charcot called Le Log——.[33] In October 1885, the same month Freud came to Paris, Le Log——, a florist's deliveryman, was knocked unconscious by a carriage while pushing his wheelbarrow. Taken to a hospital, he remained in a coma for several days. Six months later he was transferred to the Salpêtrière, his legs nearly paralyzed, his memory impaired, the corner of his mouth twitching.

Charcot decided Le Log——, who also exhibited the so-called stigmata, was suffering from hysteria. He deduced that while the initial impact of the accident was real enough, the fact that he continued to experience symptoms was based on fear triggered by the incident.

Today, posttraumatic stress disorder is considered a credible psychiatric condition. Though a traumatic event may remain safely in the past, the patient's memory of it continues to elicit panic and anxiety, which may express itself in any number of ways. Charcot's hypothesis about Le Log—— seems a similar concept, a kind of posttraumatic *injury* disorder to explain the patient's continuing symptoms. But Charcot dismissed the fact that Le Log—— had sustained a physical injury, rather than simply an emotionally traumatic one. To conclude that continuing symptoms were merely emotional was an unjustified leap; it suggests a complete lack of understanding on the part of Charcot of what would now be readily diagnosed as a closed-head injury. This is additionally surprising given that Charcot had otherwise made astute neurological discoveries based on physical investigations of the brain.

"From this," Freud scholar Richard Webster writes, "we may derive a conclusion which is both simple and terrible in its implications: Le

Log——, the classic example of a patient who supposedly suffered from traumatic hysteria, did not forget [amnesia was one of his major symptoms] because he was frightened. He forgot because he was concussed. His various symptoms were not produced by an unconscious idea. They were the result of brain damage."[34]

While anyone who looks at the Le Log—— case today can clearly see the error of Charcot's ways, we believe similar clues have remained hidden in many of Charcot's other cases, for much the same reason they have stayed submerged in Freud's "Dora." The physical trauma of being hit by a carriage is plain to see—and allows us to draw new and very different conclusions based on modern understanding of the brain—but the impact of a toxic exposure was, and remains, less obvious. Mercury and other toxins often left the victim every bit as disabled but with no eyewitness to identify the culprit.

Perhaps Charcot's most famous female case was a nurse named Justine Etchevery, known as Etch—— in print. Before she became ill, Etch was a nurse at the main hospital in Bordeaux. She was nearly raped, and her subsequent descent into a "nervous state" and then a convulsive attack, one year later at the age of twenty-five, were attributed to the sexual assualt. Afterward, she worked at a children's hospital in Paris, but suffered "repeated and more frequent convulsions, urinary retention, paralyses, and other complications"—again, symptoms entirely compatible with occupational mercury exposure.[35]

It seems logical that harmful effects of mercury were as much a hazard of nursing in the later nineteenth century as being hit by a carriage was a hazard of working as a deliveryman. The arm and hand contractures mirror earlier accounts of "palsy of the hands" in those who rubbed on mercurial ointment, even when wearing gloves.

Many other patients of Charcot had backgrounds that obviously implicated mercury as the culprit. But once the theory of hysteria had taken hold of the confident and accomplished neurologist, this explanation was continuously ignored or overlooked. Charcot describes a hospital attendant treated "for abdominal pains, a right hemianesthesia, [who] one morning on getting up he had fallen to the ground, without loss of consciousness, but had been unable to speak for forty-eight hours," but misses the fact that he was in the same line of work as Etch—— and had similar "hysterical" symptoms.[36]

Charcot wrote of another patient with clear evidence of mercury toxicity:

Gil—, 32 years old, a metal gilder, was admitted into the Salpêtrière in January, 1885 [early in the same year Freud studied with Charcot]. . . . His occupation, in which mercury is employed, has never produced any symptoms which can be connected with mercurial poisoning. There are no signs of alcoholism; no syphilis. His first attack [seizure] took place at the age of twenty without known cause. He was outside an omnibus when he felt the first warnings. He had time to descend and the convulsive attack took place on the street. After this, the attacks came on rather frequently. He reckoned about four or five a month.[37]

Charcot assumed that routine mercury exposure under the rudimentary precautions of the day couldn't possibly be toxic, absent some calamitous accident. Yet Gil——'s job put him in direct contact with a substance known to cause the symptoms he experienced. In hindsight these seizures were likely the result.

It wasn't just mercury that Charcot missed or dismissed; he also misinterpreted the true cause of an analogous condition known as carbon disulfide hysteria, the result of workers' exposure to the toxin in rubber vulcanization factories. Its cause and symptoms, which were well known by the mid-1800s, included headaches, muscle weakness, body numbness, and insomnia as well as deficits of memory, confusion, and even mania.

But Charcot was having none of it when he presented a glaring case of carbon disulfide poisoning on November 6, 1888. The patient, a worker in one of the vulcanization plants, was knocked out by fumes, comatose for half an hour, and in bed for two days; afterward he continued to exhibit classic symptoms of decreased sensation, twitching, and vision loss. What did Freud's mentor deduce from all this? A doctor recently observed: "To Charcot all this could only mean one thing; they had before them an unfortunate victim with all of the classic manifestations of hysteria. . . . [Here] Charcot's clinical misinterpretation of carbon disulfide intoxication becomes most clearly illuminated, highlighting profound flaws in the presumptions of hysteria. . . . Instead of considering the evidence at hand, Charcot's observations bent reality to make it conform to the preset demands of the diagnosis he needed to make."[38]

By the end of his life, Charcot had become even more extreme. His approach could be described as "überhysteria." In *A Text-book on Nervous Diseases* by Francis Xavier Dercum, published in 1895, the author, reflecting medical consensus, states that "the toxic tremors are those caused by arsenic, mercury, lead, copper, and alcohol."[39] But not so according to

Charcot: "Shortly before his death, [he] began to teach very positively that mercurial tremor was always hysterical, and he based his conclusions on the sudden recoveries and the frequent presence of his so-called hysterical stigmata, namely, concentric limitation of the field of vision, an emotional condition, and seemingly erratic impairments of sensation."[40]

But the reverse is true: Mercury tremors and the characteristic constriction of the visual field are always *not* hysterical. The core symptoms of Charcot's so-called stigmata that he ascribed to hysteria, along with seizures and mental disturbances, were actually evidence of poisoning, most often by mercury.

The tragedy for Charcot, as well as for Freud and many more who followed, is that he was observant, and he correctly interpreted hysteria as a disease of the nerves. But despite the great contribution he made to neurology, he was deeply confused both about the origins of the disease and its treatment. In the midst of the most widespread daily exposure to mercury in human history, he dealt with its victims on a daily basis—and missed its impact entirely.

—

Freud returned to Vienna on a contact high from his few months with Charcot, and on October 15, 1886, presented his mentor's theories on male hysteria at a meeting of the Vienna Society of Medicine. By all accounts the event was not the epoch-making triumph he envisioned. Freud felt he was met with rejection by the hidebound Viennese medical establishment. In truth, the concept (that men as well as women could be hysterics) was nothing new at the time, and what Freud took to be contempt was actually indifference.

Regardless, Freud set out to find an actual case that matched Charcot's criteria. Freud found him through a laryngologist; the patient was a twenty-nine-year-old man he called August P.[41] Three years before, August P. had begun suffering from a panoply of symptoms including ringing in the ears, left-sided headaches, pressure inside his cranium, violent heart palpitations, convulsions, and loss of sensation on one side of his body—hemianesthesia.

In addition to penning his own case study, Freud had an opthamologist friend, Leopold Königstein, write up a separate piece on August P.'s vision problems. Freud's and Königstein's papers were published in consecutive issues of the *Wiener Medizinische Wochenschrift,* a Viennese medical journal, in December 1886.

Both articles exist in a bound volume in Freud's archive in London, where he fled following Germany's annexation of Austria in 1938 (and died the next year). The contents of the volume are written in Freud's own hand on the first blank page. When we visited the archive, the director, Michael Molnar, turned the pages of the rare text for us—and when he came to Königstein's article, we were suddenly staring at the same type of visual-field constriction chart we had seen so many times in Charcot's cases. August P. had been an engraver, which suggests he experienced the same kind of occupational exposure to mercury and/or other metals seen in many of the hysteria patients Charcot diagrammed. Freud, it seems, had learned so well from his mentor he was doomed to repeat his mistake.

Tunnel Vision

Josef Breuer, despite being credited by Freud for originating psychoanalysis, is perhaps the most forgotten person in the history of psychiatry.

In July 1880 a young woman named Bertha Pappenheim (Breuer called her Anna O., using initial letters that preceded those of her real name) fell sick while tending her father during a sudden illness. Her symptoms were both bizarre and diverse, from severe visual-field constriction, tremors, contractures, and hallucinations—including "hallucinations of absence" in which only Breuer would be visible to her in a room full of people—to inexplicable speech disruptions.

Although the family was Jewish and anti-Semitism was on the rise, the Pappenheims had acculturated to the point that they spent summers at the same Austrian spa village as Prince Leopold of Bavaria. During the summer of 1880, the family vacation turned into a nightmare when Anna's father, a grain merchant, fell ill with what was described as a peripleuritic abscess—probably a pulmonary complication of the tuberculosis then sweeping Vienna. A surgeon was called from the capital, and as Anna waited for him, sitting at her father's bedside, she had the first of her symptoms—her right arm became paralyzed and she hallucinated snakes coming out of her fingernails.[42]

Her father's health never recovered, and she faithfully attended him upon the family's return to Vienna. But her symptoms worsened and were joined by a relentless cough. During the last few months of his illness, she herself was barred from the sickroom and sometimes confined to bed. Breuer was called in to treat the cough (he may also have been the family physician), and, given her florid mental symptoms, he diagnosed the cough as hysterical—a *tussis nervosa*, the same symptom Freud later diagnosed in Dora.

After that, "a series of severe disorders that were *apparently* [emphasis in original] quite new developed in quick succession: pains at the back of her head . . . a complaint that the walls are falling in . . . paresis of the front neck muscles. . . . contracture and anaesthesia of the right upper, and, after some time, of the right lower extremity."[43]

There were also problems with speech, similar to Dora's but worse. "For as the contractures developed, a deep functional disorganization of speech set in. The first thing that became noticeable was that she could not find words and gradually this became worse. Then her speech lost all grammatical structure, the syntax was missing, as was the conjugation of verbs, so that in the end she was using only infinitives that were incorrectly formed from a weak past participle, and no articles. As the disorder developed she could find almost no words at all."[44]

Most remarkable perhaps were the ways in which her sight was affected. "There was high-degree restriction of the field of vision. Looking—with delight—at a bunch of flowers she could only ever see one flower at a time. She complained that she could not recognize people; that she used to be able to recognize faces without having to think about it and work at it."[45]

Breuer treated Anna O. with hypnosis and also began to interview her deeply. Over the next few months, Anna's symptoms worsened dramatically till she was unable to eat. But as Breuer talked with her about her problems—and spent several hours a week with her—he thought he noticed something. When they hit on what appeared to be an association between a symptom and some event in the past, the symptom seemed to diminish and even disappear. The first and most dramatic example was that despite her thirst, Anna had stopped drinking water, getting liquid only by sucking on fruit. But one day she mentioned her disgust that someone had let a dog drink from a glass of water intended for humans, and soon after that she took her first sip of water.

This has been described as the moment when psychoanalysis—or, as Anna called it, the talking cure—began. It was also around the time when mercuric chloride began coming into use as an antiseptic. The onset of Anna's symptoms—on the evening when she waited by her father's bed for the surgeon to arrive and treat an abscess that was possibly mercuric-chloride-soaked—may be far more meaningful than their apparent improvement when she mentioned a dog drinking out of a water glass.

One problem with Breuer's approach is that despite the fact he and Freud declared the Anna O. case a "complete success," it was no such thing. Anna stayed in a sanitarium for two years and continued having evening hallucinations for several years more.

Toxic Relationships

It is remarkable how closely the symptoms of hysteria fit mercury poisoning in particular and toxic exposures more broadly. For example, the product label for thimerosal, the ethylmercury preservative still in use in medical products, is a virtual summary of hysterical stigmata: "Early signs of mercury poisoning in adults are nervous system effects, including narrowing of the visual field and numbness in the extremities."[46]

These effects and many more, as we've noted, were well described by the time Charcot, Freud, and Breuer overlooked or ignored them in pursuit of grand unified psychiatric theories. But the focus had almost always been on the patient receiving mercury treatments, not on the caregiver. Intermittent reports did arise of hazards common in caregiving professions. A twentieth-century survey of mercury exposure noted, "Chronic mercury intoxication remained an occupational hazard for physicians who treated syphilis by rubbing mercury inunctions on their skin."[47] The 1925 report *Industrial Poisons in the United States* ran through a wide range of mercury's exposures and described its effect on a physician who had to resort to applying a mercurial rub without gloves: "Not long after he began this he had three violent attacks of abdominal pain closely resembling lead colic."[48]

Almost as striking as these words—a description that sounds like Dora's gastric pains—are their placement: in the middle of a discussion of occupational mercury exposures of workers ranging from hatters to miners to dentists. Caregivers fit right in. They breathed the fumes, changed the bedding and bandages, washed their hands in mercuric chloride solutions, and rubbed on mercury. Yet these exposures went largely unnoticed because in so many cases those caregivers were unpaid and unpedigreed—and they were women; they were Dora and Anna O., the daughters of the affluent taking care of their ailing parents. This was part of the job description for young women of their station and their day.

Other mercury-exposure symptoms described in *Industrial Poisons* are worth noting as well: "delirium with hallucinations, intense tremor, clonic spasms, followed by paresis, mental torpor, and loss of memory . . . Sometimes insomnia is the chief complaint, or bad dreams, or depression. . . . Despondency, loss of memory, melancholia with suicidal tendency, even manic-depressive insanity."[49] Given this virtual cheat sheet of hysteria symptoms, why didn't the medical profession pick up on the adverse consequences of this "caregiver effect"? As we saw in chapter 1, mainstream doctors were in denial over the consequences for the very patients they were *treating* with mercury. Deducing in 1900 that Dora, for example, might be suffering secondhand effects of the same toxin that was causing symptoms in her father would be like expecting tobacco companies in the 1930s to have acknowledged the dangers of secondhand smoke.

Yet such denials were a subject of controversy even in the heyday of mercury treatments. We found one searing indictment of the abuse of mercury in an 1847 essay in England's *Provincial Journal* by "Robert Storrs, Esq., Surgeon, Doncaster":

Mercury has long been known to be an active and frequent cause of paralysis in its various employment in arts and manufactures, or in the working of mines from which it is obtained; but its power of producing remotely paralytic diseases has been seldom alluded to. We often flatter ourselves with the supposition of having been able to shorten the course of this or that disease by the promptitude of our treatment, frequently including in that treatment the exhibition of this drug; but we might moderate our exultation were we able to look back upon the ruined constitutions, the disabled limbs, or the shortened lives, which a rash, prolonged, or sometimes even uncalled-for use of this active mineral has produced. . . . These are painful reflections, but they must have occurred to almost every conscientious practitioner, in the solitude of the closet, or in the silence of the night, when we are but too apt to magnify our errors, or to exalt the successes of others. We will, however, dismiss this unwelcome train of thought, satisfied that such reflections are often productive of beneficial warnings.[50]

About the same time Freud prescribed his "energetic" treatment to Dora's father, Dr. H. H. Hoppe published an article in the *Cincinnati Lancet-Clinic*.[51] He wrote: "In the female, hysteria is found more frequently in the so-called better classes, in the wealthy, the cultured, the refined, those who occupy comfortable and easy positions in life. In men it is the opposite; its more frequent subject is the working man, the hard toiler."

That's a pretty good description of Dora and Anna O., of August P. and Gil——.

▬

Sigmund Freud and Josef Breuer were friends and colleagues in the medical milieu of Vienna in the 1880s, and Breuer told Freud about his "talking cure" of Anna O. Freud described the case and its seemingly successful outcome to Charcot in 1885, but, wedded to hypnosis and his anatomical approach to hysteria, the Parisian neurologist was uninterested. Still, Freud saw in Breuer's radical treatment a new path, and he took up the talking cure with a passion.

Together Breuer and Freud wrote a "preliminary communication" in 1893.[52] They proposed an ambitious theory of hysteria: From now on, courtesy of Anna O. and her amazing response, the hysterical stigmata designated by Charcot would have a "psychogenic" basis. Hysteria was triggered by a strong idea; a traumatic moment; a conversion in which the unwanted thought, emotion, or instinct was submerged, and physical and mental symptoms emerged in their place. Resurrecting the trauma and its associated emotions under the skillful guidance of the psychoanalyst would eliminate the symptoms and restore the patient's health.

In 1895 Breuer and Freud published *Studies in Hysteria*, which began with the story of "Fräulein Anna O." These are the case histories that launched Freud and the whole of psychoanalysis, as well as the ideas that came to dominate not just psychiatry, but intellectual discourse, the arts, and our understanding of sexuality. (Breuer soon parted company with

Freud; he thought Freud's belief in the early sexual roots of most adult problems was ridiculous.)

If Pasteur began the modern age of medicine, Freud launched the modern age of culture. And there may have been far more of a connection between their discoveries than anybody has realized.

"Commonplace Emotional Upheavals"

Among the five case histories in *Studies in Hysteria*, "Elisabeth von R." stands out for exhibiting absolutely no emotional problems. Her legs just hurt.

"In autumn 1892 a colleague and friend of mind asked me to examine a young lady who had suffered from pains in her legs for more than two years and had difficulties walking," Freud begins. "On making this request he added that he thought that this was a case of hysteria, even though none of the usual signs of neurosis could be found. . . . [Elisabeth told Freud] a fairly large, ill-defined area on the front of the right thigh was indicated as the focus of the pains. . . . The affliction had developed gradually over the last two years and varied greatly in intensity."[53]

It turned out that Elisabeth was also nursing a loved one. "Their father had hidden, or perhaps overlooked, a chronic heart complaint. One day he was brought home unconscious after his first attack of pulmonary oedema. He was nursed for the next 18 months, and throughout this time Elisabeth made sure that she had first place at his bedside. She slept in her father's room, woke at night when he called, watched over him by day. . . . This period of nursing had to be connected with the beginning of her illness, for she could remember that during the last six months of the nursing she had been confined to bed for a day and a half because her right leg was so painful. . . . In fact it was not until two years after the death of her father that she felt ill and that her pains prevented her from walking."[54]

Although the doctor who referred her believed the pains were hysterical, he could not pinpoint their psychological cause. "For the doctor, the patient's confession [description of her life] was at first a great disappointment. It was, after all, a case history made up of commonplace emotional upheavals, which explained neither why the person concerned should necessarily fall ill with hysteria, nor why the hysteria had assumed precisely this form."[55]

Undaunted, Freud pressed ahead. When he got nothing through an attempt at hypnosis, he used "the trick of applying pressure to her head. . . . This I implemented by demanding that the patient tell me, without fail, what appeared to her inner eye or drifted through her memory at the moment of pressure. She was silent for a long time, then, at my insistence, confessed that she had thought of an evening on which a young man had accompanied her home after a party, of the conversations that had occurred between the two of them, and of the feelings with which she then returned home to care for her father."[56]

And the painful legs? At last, Elisabeth recalled something that immediately suggested the explanation to him: "This was, in fact, the place where her father's leg rested every morning while she replaced the bandages which bound up his severely swollen leg. This must have happened a hundred times, and yet strangely enough she had not thought of this connection until today."[57]

Finally, Freud had linked a somatic symptom to its presumed source in her emotional conflict. Elisabeth could not, figuratively speaking, get up and walk away from her obligation to her father, as much as her libido might be telling her to do so; the sensation embodying that reality was her father's bandages touching her thigh as she changed them.

Freud concluded:

> In this way the painful area had, first, grown by apposition, in that each new theme which had a pathogenic effect occupied a new region of the legs; secondly, each of these scenes that made a powerful impression left behind a trace by establishing a permanent and constantly increasing 'cathexis' of the various functions of the legs, a linking of these functions with the sensation of pain; but yet a third mechanism had unmistakeably been collaborating in the formation of the astasia-abasia.[58]

As a literary device, this works beautifully (and some have wisely pointed out that psychoanalysis has more in common with literature than with science). In the nonfiction world of 1892, however, those bandages Elisabeth must have changed "a hundred times" would likely have been soaked, and the father's wounds cleansed, with the "universal" antiseptic of the day, mercuric chloride. Repeated exposure is very probably why her pains radiated from there.

Freud did pause to muse about the connection between nursing and hysteria, puzzling over its frequency. "Experience shows that nursing [ill family members] and strong sexual feelings also play the main role in most of the more closely analysed case histories of hysterics," he and Breuer write.[59] Why?

"There are good reasons why nursing should play such a significant role in the prehistory of hysterias," Freud said. "Indeed, there is clear evidence of a series of factors that are operative in this: disturbance of one's physical state by interrupted sleep, neglect of one's physical well-being, and the repercussions of continually gnawing anxiety on the vegetative functions."[60]

But that, he went on to say, was a little too obvious. "What is most important lies elsewhere." Anyone nursing a loved one needs to suppress his or her own emotions and best interests. "The nurse, then, stores up within himself a wealth of impressions that could be intensely emotional. . . . He is providing himself with the material for a retention hysteria."[61]

———

So far we've offered a surprising hypothesis: Charcot and Freud frequently misdiagnosed mercury poisoning as hysteria—so frequently, in fact, that the theories based on those cases simply aren't credible. Freud himself observed that most severe hysterics had fathers with syphilis, which was treated with mercury; we also noted Freud's remark that most severe hysterics shared a history of nursing sick relatives, and we've seen the scattered reports over four centuries of mercury's effects on caregivers as well as patients. Of a dozen major case studies, in fact, such exposure is plausible in most of them.

These seem to overlap in an unexamined way: secondhand exposure to mercury as syphilis treatment and as antiseptic. And the similarity of severe, clinically defined hysteria to mercury poisoning is striking: from visual-field constriction to gastric pains to numbness and paralysis and mental disturbances. Even the *tussis nervosa* and chest pressure shared by Anna O. and Dora look to us like mislabeling of a known effect of mercury exposure, pneumonitis.[62]

To be sure, symptoms of mercury poisoning could be signs of other conditions as well. But if a patient came to a modern-day doctor with the stigmata of hysteria, for example, would mercury poisoning be one of many possible causes or in fact the presumptive cause itself? We can

FREUD'S HYSTERIA CASES AND THEIR SYMPTOMS

Case Order	Case Name	Real Name	Case Date	Family/Occupational Risk	Hysterical Stigmata	Other Symptoms
1	Anna O.	Bertha Pappenheim	1880	Father had surgery	Visual-field disturbances Paralysis/contractures Anesthesia	*Tussis nervosa* Paraphasia Somnambulism
2	August P.	unknown	1886	Engraver, brother died of neurosyphilis	Visual-field constriction Paralysis/contractures Anesthesia	Headaches Tremor Stomach pains
3	Emmy von N.	Fanny Moser	1889	unknown	Paralysis (right leg) Anesthesia (right leg)	Tics/stammering Gastric pains
4	Caecilie M.	Anna von Lieben	1889	unknown	Facial neuralgia	Foot pain
5	Elisabeth von R.	Ilona Weiss	1892	Surgery in both parents	Hyperalgesia	Leg pain
6	Lucy R.	unknown	1892	Governess	Analgesia/paresthesia	Olfactory issues
7	Katharina	Aurelia Kronich	1890s	unknown	Epilepsy/seizures?	Anxiety
8	Dora	Ida Bauer	1899	Father treated for syphilis	Epilepsy/seizures?	*Tussis nervosa* Dyspnea
9	Little Hans	Herbert Graf	1909	unknown	—	Anxiety
10	Rat Man	Ernst Lanzer	1909	Father had syphilis	—	Obsessive compulsive
11	Wolf-Man	Sergei Pankejeff	1910	Took calomel; sister a suicide with $HgCl_2$	—	Diarrhea/constipation/worms

answer that with a fair amount of confidence: In the medical profession doctors make use of a process called differential diagnosis. Patients don't present to doctors with diseases, they present with symptoms, and it's a doctor's job to use those symptoms, and particularly the most distinctive, as a diagnostic tool to home in on the correct diagnosis. The hysterical stigmata have the virtue of being relatively specific, and some of the logic trees for doing differential diagnoses have been computerized and automated and made available publicly.[63]

If you enter each of the three stigmata separately—sensory neuropathy, tunnel vision, and spastic paralysis—mercury poisoning shows up as a possible cause of each of them, but it's one of a long list. So we asked the question: What if you put the two most common stigmata together? We started by typing "sensory neuropathy" into the search field, clicked on "possible causes," and forty-three possible diagnoses popped up, including "mercury chronic toxicity/poisoning." We then clicked "narrow findings" and typed "tunnel vision" into the search field. A single diagnosis was returned.

"Mercury chronic toxicity/poisoning."

This certainly strengthens a strong circumstantial hypothesis. Admittedly, it would be even more convincing if Freud actually misdiagnosed a documented case of mercury poisoning as hysteria.

And indeed he did.

"What Were Those Residues?"

In February 1910 Sergei Pankejeff had come to see Sigmund Freud. In time, he would come to be known in the psychiatric community as the Wolf-Man.

Pankejeff was the scion of a family that held vast tracts of land in Russia, and lived in not one, but two impossibly grand mansions down the road from each other, one for summer and the other for winter. Over the years preceding, Pankejeff had become increasingly incapacitated by depression, obsessions, compulsions, and physical dysfunction. A stay in a sanitarium, recommended by Emil Kraepelin, who examined him in Germany and pronounced him manic-depressive, did little to improve his condition.

The name Freud gave to Pankejeff, and the case study, conjures a more exotic image than the facts perhaps deserve: Sergei recalled a vivid childhood dream in which a tree with seven white wolves on the branches appeared outside his bedroom window. Through an elaborate series of associations, Freud deduced that Sergei had, as an infant, witnessed his parents having intercourse. This, Freud believed, led to problems in childhood. By Sergei's description, these problems do not sound particularly catastrophic: occasionally unruly behavior and fear of some animals. But those were the roots, Freud concluded, of the Wolf-Man's very real and debilitating adult difficulties.

The Wolf-Man was Freud's longest case study not only in duration (lasting four years, plus several more months in follow-up treatment) but in written length as well. Many Freud scholars consider it his most notable case, showcasing the mastery of his psychoanalytic technique.

Pankejeff's main physical problem was chronic and intractable constipation; essentially, Sergei's bowels did not move on their own. In fact, the assistant who was accompanying him in Vienna had two main tasks: to be the third player (along with Pankejeff's doctor) in a Russian card game similar to bridge, and to administer daily enemas. According to Freud, this physical symptom was a manifestation of hysteria. He wrote: "When, later, I come to describe the resolution of the patient's last symptoms, we shall see once again how his bowel disorder had placed itself at the service of the homosexual, expressing the feminine attitude towards the father."[64]

But here is an alternative explanation, and it comes from the Wolf-Man himself. In 1973, at the age of eighty-six, he began a series of conversations in Vienna with the writer and journalist Karen Obholzer; it is by far the greatest trove of relevant personal information ever provided by one of Freud's patients.[65] A key conflict between therapist and patient emerges from these overlooked conversations.

For his part, Freud attributed the immediate onset of Sergei's adult problems to a case of gonorrhea. But of course, mercury might well have been part of that disease's treatment, which Pankejeff describes as prolonged and unpleasant. By contrast, the Wolf-Man discusses with Obholzer his own beliefs about the constipation Freud diagnosed as a symptom of hysteria. She notes that after his four-year analysis, Pankejeff returned for several more months to clear up what Freud described in his case study as unresolved "residues" of his hysteria.

Q: Well, what were those residues?

A: It's unappetizing. . . . This is the way it was: I once had diarrhea, and Dr. Drosnes came to the estate [in Russia]. I tell him I have diarrhea. He takes a little bottle wrapped in paper from his pocket and says, "Take it." The result was that it got worse.

Q: The diarrhea?

A: The diarrhea. The next time, I tell him that it didn't help, it got worse. And he says, "I didn't give you enough."

Q: What was that medicine called?

A: Calomel. [Mercurous chloride]

Q: Never heard of it.

A: Later, a general practitioner told me that it is only given to horses, not humans. I am telling you that what happened was that I couldn't eat anything all winter long. I lived on tea, milk, things like that. Just a little tea, and I had to run to the toilet. It was terrible. All the mucous membranes were torn. And what happened as a consequence? The consequence was that these attacks of diarrhea stopped. But a new situation developed.

Q: Constipation, I imagine.

A: Yes, a constipation that nothing could be done about. When I took medicine, I got diarrhea again. I helped myself with those enemas that Freud then forbade.[66]

In the published case study of the Wolf-Man, Freud lays out a very different scenario, stating the bowel problem originated in childhood, continued into adulthood, and reflected early emotional conflicts: "In discussing these disruptions to the function of the bowel I have allowed my patient's later state of illness to take up more space than I had intended in a piece of work devoted to his childhood neurosis. There were two reasons for my decision: first, the fact that the bowel symptoms had remained virtually unchanged from the period of childhood neurosis to the later one, and, second, that they were enormously significant in bringing the treatment to an end."[67]

And how did these bowel symptoms help resolve the analysis? "Finally I recognized the significance of his bowel disorder for my intentions: it represented the touch of hysteria that is regularly found to underlie any obsessive compulsive neurosis. I promised the patient that his bowel activity would be fully restored. . . . I then had the satisfaction of watching his doubt disappear as his bowel began to 'add its voice' to the work, as if it were an hysterically affected organ, regaining its normal function, which had for so long been impaired, in the course of a few weeks."[68]

This does not comport, obviously, with the patient's own account—not even close. Surely Freud would have learned during the four-year analysis that Pankejeff himself believed his primary physical symptom was originally caused by calomel. (Furthermore, Freud prescribed him medicine for it and told him to stop using enemas, so the onset of the condition was doubtless discussed.) The patient also maintains that until being prescribed the calomel his gastrointestinal tract had been normal and that he didn't think talking with Freud for five years, including the last few months devoted solely to the "residues," had cured the problem: "I somehow got it to come by itself, a few times," Pankejeff says in the interview with Obholzer. "And he wrote, 'We've been successful!' No such thing!"[69]

We're left with two possibilities. Freud either did not believe Pankejeff's own assertion that mercurial medicine caused the symptom, or he chose to ignore it. His intent, clearly, was to connect the problem to a much earlier and much different point—the childhood witnessing of a primal scene followed by the dream that Freud placed at the heart of the Wolf-Man's diagnosis, treatment and "successful" outcome.

As with Anna O. and several others, Freud's claim that the Wolf-Man was cured by psychoanalysis was hardly substantiated by subsequent events. Quite the opposite: He continued to see psychoanalysts all his life for acute issues.

The Wolf-Man provided far more information about his personal life and his experience with Freud than any other analysand. It's hard not to wonder what similarly detailed medical and personal histories would turn up in other cases. The circumstantial evidence for mercury poisoning is much stronger in several (Dora, Anna, Elisabeth) about whom we know far less. And the Wolf-Man reminds us of the many ways people in the late 1800s were exposed to mercury. We would never have suspected it in his case if not for Obholzer's interviews.

Interestingly, as hysteria died out as a diagnosis, so did mercuric chloride as an antiseptic. In the 1920s and 1930s the toxic effects of mercurial antiseptics made them unpopular, and mercury ceased to be used as a syphilis treatment in the 1940s when penicillin replaced it. Most researchers attribute this demise of hysteria to what's called diagnostic substitution: Hysteria would now fall under conversion disorder, psychosomatic illness, or categories specific to the signs of mental illness the patient presented. But this attribution may very well be a misunderstanding of why "hysteria" really disappeared, based on a misdiagnosis of the true cause of many of its cases.

What were the real-life consequences of this fateful mistake? A psychiatrist we last encountered in South Dakota was about to enter the fray on behalf of those who were paying the price.

Mocking "the Great God Unconscious"

In 1940 Leo Kanner wrote an article for *The New York Times Magazine* titled "In Defense of the Parent."[70] By then, he'd been established at Johns Hopkins for a dozen years, his reputation rising as the dean of child psychiatry. The piece struck a chord, and inquiries from book publishers began arriving in Baltimore.

Why did parents, and particularly mothers, need defending? In two words, Sigmund Freud. The onslaught of Freudian theory in America was gaining momentum and mothers were assigned blame for almost every problem of their adult children: Oedipal conflict, oral and anal complexes, etc.

Kanner came to Hopkins in 1928, and in 1935 wrote the landmark textbook *Child Psychiatry*, a volume that deferred to Freud more often than not. But Kanner was a perceptive man, and he soon observed that Freud's influence had gone too far. As a child psychiatrist, Kanner frequently found himself in contact with mothers and fathers who felt themselves under assault. They could be blamed for everything bad that ever happened to their child: One misstep in a diaper change might arouse an infantile sexual urge that would echo for decades; one angry outburst during potty training might damage their child's psyche forever. Mothers in particular were on the defensive since Freud's disciples everywhere held mothers accountable for every unconscious thought. Inevitably, mothers were deemed responsible for even the most serious mental disorders in their children. In effect, the establishment was taking Freud even further than Freud went himself.

While he was certainly a mainstream psychiatrist, got along with his Freudian colleagues, and was influenced by Freudian ideas, Kanner found himself frustrated with this state of affairs. Judging by the interest from publishers following the *Times Magazine* article, he was not alone. The book that resulted—*In Defense of Mothers: How to Bring Up Children in Spite of the More Zealous Psychologists*—targets Freud head-on. One chapter, "The Great God Unconscious," turns Freudian child psychologists into a joke. Referring to the unconscious as G.G.U. or with a capitalized "Him," Kanner writes:

> The myth of the G.G.U. and his subdivisions has spread like wildfire. His religion is called psychoanalysis. His priests are people who have been initiated with long and elaborate rites. His altars are couches on which the worshippers, in recumbent position, are made to contemplate their spiritual navels, one hour each day or every other day, for a period of several years. Someday, when the G.G.U. will have changed His residence from the textbooks of psychology to those of mythology, parents will no longer be bothered about His mysterious vagaries.[71]

In going after Freud, Kanner had effectively chosen sides in the long-running debate over the origins of mental problems: namely, what roles organic factors and emotional factors played in mental illness. He was landing, definitely, in the camp of Emil Kraepelin (with whom he crossed paths at Hiawatha) and his scientific, biological approach to mental disorders. But Kanner was ahead of his time, and Freud was about to reach the height of his influence. (Dr. Spock wrote his first Freudian treatment of child psychiatry in 1938, and published his landmark volume *Common Sense Book of Baby and Child Care* in 1946, bracketing Kanner's defense of mothers.)

So while Kanner's common sense, empathy, and observational skills may have been right on the mark, the deeper truth skittered away like globules from a broken thermometer, ready to poison a whole new generation—this time, of children.

CHAPTER THREE

THE AGE OF ACRODYNIA

We would say the essential element present was some degree of emotional deprivation associated with the child's being unwanted.

—A Psychiatric Study of Six Cases of Infantile Acrodynia, 1952[1]

The ripple effects of mercury in medicine go far beyond the diseases we've described thus far. General paralysis of the insane and hysteria have common roots in mercury poisoning, but who knows how many deaths and other disorders have gone unrecorded and under the guise of treatment?

Mercuric chloride is the particular form of mercury that comes up in GPI and hysteria through the vehicles of Van Swieten's liquor and antiseptics, but even a cursory review of "chemotherapy" in medicine reveals that mercury use took an extraordinarily wide range of forms. Pick up any nineteenth-century catalog of medicines, and the section on mercury will be lengthy—mercury in pills, powders, and rubs along with a recommended set of uses for every ailment under the sun. Mercuric chloride was among the more common formulations, but perhaps the most widely used form of mercury was its cousin mercurous chloride, otherwise known as calomel.

The difference between the two may seem slight in both name and chemical formulation. Mercur*ic* chloride—also known as mercury bichloride or corrosive sublimate—is a single mercury atom bound to two chlorine atoms, designated $HgCl_2$. Mercur*ous* chloride is Hg_2Cl_2, meaning that each molecule has two mercury atoms bound to each other, and each bound in turn to a chlorine atom. Calomel was less toxic than its chemical cousin and more widely used by doctors for a range of problems. Doctors prescribed calomel for infants to help regulate their bowels and soften the gums during infancy in formulations marketed as "teething powders." This practice led to an ailment called acrodynia, an episode of medical malpractice that sickened thousands of children. Many died.

The history of acrodynia is now told as a heroic triumph of medical technology, and there is truth to this part of the story. But the Age of Acrodynia also shines a light on a range of other practices that characterize the medical industry. These practices—including direct-to-consumer advertising, lack of precaution with toxic formulations, and an eagerness to intervene even in the earliest months of life—remain object lessons to this day.

The medical industry promotes itself as a bastion of rigorous scientific objectivity, but the need for medical science often runs into conflict with the commercial imperatives of practicing entities—drug manufacturers, medical doctors, and the professional communities that set the standards of care. The heroic impulse to *do something* has more often embodied superstition and just plain bad medicine than the medical industry would care to admit.

The folklore that can accumulate over many years has remarkable staying power even when it's wrong. It's rare when insiders are courageous enough to call attention to these superstitions. One who did so was Leo Kanner, who, before he moved to the United States to study GPI and later take on Freud, started his career fascinated by superstitious beliefs that surrounded human teeth.

The Literary Bureau For Dentists

Leo Kanner was born Chaskel Leib Kanner in the small town of Klekotuv "at the easternmost tip of the Austro-Hungarian Monarchy, almost a stonethrow from the Russian border," as he wrote in his unpublished autobiography.[2] Kanner's nationality has generally been reported as Austrian, but the area was known in Kanner's time as Galicia, and, today, Kanner's birthplace lies in the sovereign nation of Ukraine. He grew up there and in a nearby community of Jews called Brody.

Before long he moved to Berlin, where he began medical studies, which he left in order to serve with the German army as a medical officer in World War I. After the war, Kanner settled back in Berlin to finish his degree and start a medical practice in the turbulent postwar Weimar Republic, which was beset from the beginning by social upheaval and staggering inflation.

Still, he was resourceful and found a way to augment his income. A government decree had offered dentists the chance to use the honorific "doctor" if they wrote a thesis after graduating from dental school. Suddenly, twenty thousand dentists from Vienna to Sarajevo were scrambling for original thesis topics. To one such acquaintance, Kanner suggested writing about superstitions and practices involving teeth among the peasants in the man's homeland of East Prussia.

The suggestion seemed to strike a chord, and word quickly spread that Kanner was a fountain of ideas. Soon dentists were besieging him for topics and commissioning him to prepare bibliographies and abstracts. He and a friend opened a "Literary Bureau For Dentists" in Kanner's small Berlin apartment. His wife, June, served as typist and wrote most of the abstracts.

Kanner was also teaching part-time in the medical school. Substituting for another professor one day, he struck up a friendship with Dr. Louis Holtz of Aberdeen, South Dakota, who was on a study tour of Europe to distract himself from the recent death of his wife. One day Holtz brought Kanner with him to the American consulate, saying he needed to deal with some small matter. Holtz disappeared into another room and emerged with a document for Kanner to sign: Holtz was pledging to sponsor the Kanners should they decide to emigrate from Berlin to America.

Although Kanner had no particular intention of moving, he signed the document and just two weeks later, Holtz told Kanner he had found him a job—at the Yankton State Hospital in South Dakota. The superintendent, George Adams, was a friend of Holtz's. In his autobiography, Kanner does not mention wrestling with this decision that would uproot his entire life; perhaps, combined with the endless specter of runaway inflation, Holtz made it so easy that it seemed almost inevitable.

On January 30, 1924, the Kanners (with their son Albert) left Berlin by train, took a boat across the Channel to England and boarded a vessel for New York City. In his autobiography, Kanner describes the voyage as serene and tranquil. But back in Germany, such tranquility was not on the horizon. Adolf Hitler was about to go on trial for the Beer

Hall Putsch. During the resulting prison sentence he wrote *Mein Kampf* and emerged a year later as a national force. Just a few years after that, Hitler's hatred would spill over into the shtetls; fifteen thousand people, nearly the entire population, were murdered in Brody alone. For Leo Kanner, serendipity had struck: the death of a doctor's wife in Aberdeen, South Dakota, spared Kanner from the Holocaust and put him on track to the top of his profession.

———

In Yankton, between poker games and learning to drive a Chevrolet, Kanner pursued his academic interests in medicine. His dental-thesis sideline in Berlin had left him with piles of research that he explored with growing fascination. Taking a cue from his first suggestion for a dental thesis, he decided to put all the pieces together and write a book: *Folklore of the Teeth*.[3]

This was a global anthropology of teeth, an in-depth analysis of cultural practices and superstitions all over the world. One remarkable aspect of Kanner's account is the detailed description of cultural practices with respect to infant teeth. The technical term is "dentition." Today we accept infant teething as a natural and trivial event. But for much of human history it was considered a passage of great importance. Kanner wrote:

> Dentition, according to the general belief, being one of the most important and also most dangerous processes in the life of an individual, it is easily understood that very great attention is paid by the baby's relatives to the eruption of the first deciduous tooth. Almost everywhere the mother or the father inspects the child's mouth very carefully each day to see if the eagerly expected little white spot has found its way through the gums.[4]

This heightened focus on dentition was not merely a charming old custom. Whereas today the happy arrival of the tooth fairy during the night is all that remains of the mystical dimension of teething, the focus through most of recorded history was laden with anxiety and, sometimes, downright dread:

> Nothing expresses the popular fear of dentition as well as the Spanish proverb: "When the child cuts its teeth, death is on the watch." The

Maronites of Mount Lebanon say: "If my mother only knew when my first teeth will come through, she would prepare a shroud for me." Therefore nothing should be omitted that, in the people's opinion, might help the child live through that perilous period safely. No expenses should be shunned; there exists a German adage that says: "When the child cuts its teeth, the mother should sell her skirt and buy wine for the baby."[5]

Kanner notes how concern for first dentition cut across cultures that had no contact with one another. Why that should be is hard to discern, but it might be a temporal association: maternal antibodies against diseases are passed to the infant through breast-feeding; when a child is weaned, those antibodies wane and he or she becomes susceptible to serious, sometimes fatal childhood illnesses. That is also about the time of first dentition.

However the fears arose, treatments inevitably evolved to ward off trouble. Kanner wrote about these treatments at some length. There were many approaches: topical ("One very common method consists in rubbing the baby's gums."), making use of different materials ("In ancient Greece either butter or honey was used for this purpose or the brain of a hare; in Rome hare's brain or sheep's brain or goat's milk."), and in a modern context they were downright odd ("In some of those regions the [hare's] brain is also eaten by the child. . . . The German inhabitants of Switzerland cut off the paws of a toad or of a water rat and rub with these the child's gums, both outside and inside; then, they hang the paws around its neck.").[6]

Another cross-cultural belief had a longer life: that keeping the child regular in its bowel habits could aid in teething. Again, exactly how these two very separate activities became conflated is uncertain, but it certainly led to strange practices:

Almost everywhere we find the opinion that the bad complications of dentition could be kept away by keeping the bowels open. . . . For this reason the Slovaks hate to check [prevent] diarrhea occurring in children at their teething age; if they do so, the babies will have difficulty in cutting their teeth. In Dalmatia the little ones are given castor-oil and enemata to facilitate dentition.[7]

To Kanner, a secular modernist, exposing these antiquated beliefs was part of putting them firmly in the past where they belonged. In the opening words of *Folkore of the Teeth,* Kanner declared himself a thoroughly modern medical man:

It has been one of the noblest endeavors of scientific progress of recent days to discredit superstition, to free the human mind from the oppressing clasp of mystical fears and apprehensions, to liberate the atmosphere from the fancied presence of spirits and ghosts, of demons and devils, projected into existence by the highly creative imagination of our bewildered ancestors.[8]

Writing in the 1920s, Kanner had reason for optimism, but he overstated the degree of progress in banishing superstition, a specter he was to grapple with later when he challenged Freud. Before taking on Freud, however, he had begun taking note of odd beliefs in his colleagues. He found another exemplar of weird science in his new boss, G. S. Adams, the Yankton superintendent. Kanner liked Adams, but was bemused by his beliefs, particularly his adherence to the "theory of focal infections," which ascribed all psychiatric troubles to the effect of bacteria lodged in some part of the body: "Patients were 'treated' by having their teeth, tonsils, gall bladders and appendices removed. A Chicago surgeon, Bayard Holmes, went about the country resecting parts of colons with the conviction that this would cure schizophrenia and with no other results than that, as Dr. Adolf Meyer punned, colons were changed to semicolons."[9]

What Kanner didn't know was that medical superstition was at that very moment proving more dangerous than any folkloric practice he had ever taken pains to criticize.

Bad Medicine

The connection between medicine and superstition is more pervasive than we often think. Ancient medical practices often involved witch doctors and shamans performing theatrical rituals that affected the mind of the patient as much as anything else. Most medical historians credit the Greeks with the transition away from superstition as a basis for medical treatment. But the rationality of the sort Kanner aspired to promote is more elusive than most of us recognize, and took longer to develop.

To be sure, a cumulative understanding of human anatomy and biology has grown over the centuries since the ancient Greeks. But even as a body of knowledge developed, the reasons people became sick remained

completely obscure and, as a result, the medical treatments that prevailed through much of human history remained correspondingly coun-
terproductive.

No one captures the hidden history of medical malpractice as much
as David Wootton in *Bad Medicine: Doctors Doing Harm Since Hippocrates.*
"I'm all in favour of good medicine," Wootton writes, "but the subject of
good medicine is inseparable from the subject of bad medicine . . . and
of the two subjects, bad medicine is by far the less explored and by far
the larger." In fact, he argues that before Lister applied Pasteur's germ
theory to surgery in 1865, "all medicine was bad medicine—that is to
say, it did far more harm than good."[10]

Underlying Wootton's critique is the dirty little secret of the Western
medical tradition. The medical treatments that the Greeks pioneered,
and that European doctors followed for centuries after the Renaissance,
were guided by a biological paradigm that now seems as magical and
superstitious as the incantations of witch doctors: the theory of the humors. Humoral medicine was based on the four supposed properties of
the body that in proper balance defined health; out of balance, they
were the source of disease. Though there were just four humors—blood,
black bile, yellow bile, and phlegm—their unsteady interaction yielded
endless permutations and numerous possibilities for unhealthy mischief
based on adverse combinations.

Medical ideas based on the humors go as far back as ancient Egypt,
but Hippocrates systematized them in the fourth century B.C. and Galen
popularized them a few hundred years later. This dubious march of diagnostic progress reached its next major milestone with Paracelsus in the
sixteenth century A.D.; often called the founder of modern pharmacology,
he was the first to propose specific chemical remedies based on his "superior" diagnoses of precise imbalances underlying specific illnesses.
Even today, despite his almost comically bizarre theorizing, Paracelsus is
sometimes credited with advancing the progress of medical thinking.
But even a cursory review of Paracelsus's writings shows that his theories
were more magical than Galen's, stirring astrology, religiosity, and alchemy into a witch's brew lacking only paw of toad.

Regarding these questionable advances in medicine, Wootton uses
an apt analogy: namely, the distinction between medieval astrology and
modern astronomy. Did the insights and revelations of Galileo and Coper-
nicus, Einstein and Hawking simply "update" the astrological worldview?
No, they relegated its practitioners to a corner of the comics page.

With medicine, in contrast, Wootton points out that "there was an almost wilful determination to pretend that modern medicine was a natural development from Hippocratic medicine, that Hippocrates could still be the doctor's daily companion."[11] A present-day echo: *The Lancet,* founded in 1823, is a prestigious English medical journal as well as the instrument used to open the veins of nineteenth-century English patients and bleed them in order to rebalance their humors.

———

The theory of the humors led to spectacular misconduct, including the use of leeches and bloodletting, and to unnecessary death. These ideas were not just damaging (and sometimes fatal) to individual patients. They placed major intellectual obstacles in the way of important progress. Wootton makes the point that the microscope, the technology necessary to discover penicillin, was available two centuries before a laboratory accident revealed that an extract of *Penicillium notatum* mold could kill bacteria. Perhaps the question is not how Alexander Fleming managed to discover it in 1928, but what took the medical industry so long.

"What we need in such cases as these is a history, not of progress, but of delay; not of events, but of non-events; not of an inflexible logic but of a sloppy logic," Wootton writes. "And these cases, it turns out, are in medicine (at least until very recently) the norm, not the exceptions."[12]

In all these mystical doctrines, from witch doctors' incantations to balancing of the humors to Paracelsus's hodgepodge, mercury's ability to produce a readily and rapidly observable physiological response made it an essential part of the medical tool kit for centuries. Mercury was also tailor-made to balance the humors. It caused a number of medically satisfying physiological effects—the disgorging of pints of saliva, the immediate loosening of the bowels, even the vomiting of last night's dinner as an "emetic." And for anxious mothers, it could speed the pace of dentition in infants by loosening the gums.

———

While mercuric chloride was used in treating syphilis and preventing bacterial infection in the operating room and the household, for everyday

medical applications, and in the early days of the pharmaceutical industry, mercuric chloride's chemical cousin calomel was by far the most
commonly used. Calomel was believed to be gentler than mercuric chloride and was known by such names as mercurius dulcus or beautiful
black (supposedly in honor of a black assistant who helped compound
the original formulation). But calomel was toxic, too—look what happened to Elizabeth Storie when she was treated for a minor ailment at
age four and her teeth fell out and her jaw fused; to the Wolf-Man when a
doctor gave it to him for diarrhea and it stopped his bowels from moving altogether. Such "side effects" were acknowledged but considered
by doctors a price worth paying for what they believed to be a virtual
cure-all. Besides, successive generations of doctors saw themselves as
"improving" on their predecessors' crude use of mercury, refining the
dose, the compound, and the usage in ways that made mercury, in their
hands at least, more helpful than harmful.

In 1860 Dr. Alfred Stille wrote *Therapeutics and Materia Medica: A Systematic Treatise on the Action and Use of Medicinal Agents, Including Their Description and History*. In it he agressively advocated the use of mercury in
medicine, though this didn't prevent him from working his way through a
catalog of its horrors. Numbering them as he went, Stille sounds a bit like
one of today's TV commercials reeling off the dangers of the drug it is
pitching: "1. Mercurial Fever . . . 2. Morbid Action on the Skin (The continued use of mercurial frictions irritates the skin, inducing at first redness
or tenderness, and afterwards . . . in some cases, a peculiar eruption, ery-
sipelas, or even fatal gangrene.) . . . 3. Ulceration . . . 4. Salivation . . . 5.
Mercurial Purging (evacuations become at first feculent, thin, and green-
ish, and afterwards watery or frothy, and pale in color. . . . There may be
ten or fifteen such stools in the course of twenty-four hours.) . . . 6. Affections of the Bones . . . 7. Affections of the Nervous System . . ."

The neurological and psychiatric details of number 7 will by now be
familiar: "Pains in the head and limbs . . . In other cases, the senses are
morbidly excited, or the perceptions are perverted; a moody melancholy
and fear of death may overtake the patient, who may sink into dementia;
or, more rarely, insanity of a maniacal form may be developed. In a few
cases, epilepsy results. The trembling palsey due to mercury has already
been described. In connection with, or independently of it, paralysis may
affect the limbs, involving only the upper or the lower limbs, or both at
once. . . . The same affection sometimes involves the laryngeal muscles,
producing aphonia [inability to speak]."[13]

Despite all this, over a period of about five centuries, some of the most prominent doctors in the major European medical centers were also the most fervent mercury advocates. Paracelsus elevated the element to his *tria prima* of mercury, sulfur, and salt; Van Swieten "perfected" its internal use against syphilis; Thomas Sydenham, who has often been described as the English Hippocrates, was a famous advocate of humoral practice who recommended purges with calomel as a necessary accompaniment to vigorous bloodletting. But while Sydenham favored the use of mercury, his primary treatment focus lay elsewhere. Many of his disciples, however, followed up on his treatment principles with more aggressive approaches. The most notorious of these was Thomas Dover, who has earned his name in history through his exuberant advocacy of mercury treatment: He is "the Quicksilver Doctor."

Dover is one of the most flamboyant characters in the history of medicine. Born in 1660 and educated at Cambridge, he began practicing medicine in Bristol. He interrupted his career for a while to become a pirate, or, to use the term preferred by those who plied the trade, a privateer. But he soon returned to Bristol to resume his medical practice. There, in 1742, he wrote an influential book, *The Ancient Physician's Legacy*, a paean to the benefits of mercury in treating his patients' illnesses.

Dover first used mercury therapy—oral doses of metallic mercury, the equivalent of making his patients drink from a thermometer—to treat "hysteria." In his book, he advocated it for almost everything under the sun including "the treatment of intestinal infestation, scrofula, ulcers, intestinal obstruction," for which he recommends: "You need to go no further for the cure of this fatal disease than take a pound, or a pound and a half of crude mercury."[14]

Dover prescribed two pounds of oral quicksilver to a leading British actor, Barton Booth, in 1733, and he died a week later. An autopsy showed the intestines had turned black and were lined with mercury, the rectum "so rotten and blackened with mercury" that it broke like tinder under examination.[15]

The essence of Dover's fatal error was to conclude that because mercury did *something*, these patients' seeming improvement in response to treatment meant it was curative. Side effects like salivation that pointed to its dangers were mistakenly seen as proof of efficacy. Today, discussions of mercury and its effects tend to focus on precisely matching each specific type of mercury to a set of specific (and distinctly different) effects. However, rereading the history of mercury treatments reveals a different pattern: Across its wide range of uses one generally also observes a wide range of adverse consequences, from vague neurological complaints to irritability to violent outbursts to frank psychosis, from salivation and diarrhea to constipation, from bad teeth to loose gums to fused jaws, from constriction of the visual field to blindness, from tremors to palsy to death. Over centuries of misuse, wide variations in formulation have generated a wide variety of symptoms, symptoms disparate enough to generate consistent controversy over whether they resulted from mercury exposure or something else. Anyone who believes he or she has isolated mercury's specific effects and pinned each one on an exact dose of a particular formulation is merely channeling Thomas Dover—showing a naive and inadequately respectful grasp of the dangers of quicksilver and its progeny.

In addition to the wide range of symptoms mercury could cause, there was also wide variation in susceptibility to its effects. But the reason for that was a mystery to Dover and his contemporaries and remains so today. Stille writes: "Some persons are so very susceptible to it that even the least dose of a mercurial medicine . . . will suffice to excite ptyalism," or salivation. "On the other hand, numerous cases have occurred of persons who appear to be quite insusceptible."[16]

Making America Sick

The use of calomel, purging, and other harmful practices reached a fever pitch in the United States under the doctrine of "heroic medicine," the American origins of which are most often attributed to the influential colonial physician Benjamin Rush. Heroic medicine aggressively upheld the theory of the humors and was notable in its focus on bloodletting, purging, and emetics. For the practitioners of this school, calomel was their drug of choice, and no one was a stronger advocate than Dr. Rush.

Rush was indisputably brilliant and passionately persuasive. He amplified the ideas of English predecessors like Dover and Sydenham, which he picked up in his own medical education. Because there were no established medical schools in the colonies, Rush went to study in Edinburgh with William Cullen, an ambitious theorist and influential teacher.

Cullen adopted a view of physical illness akin to Charcot's approach to hysteria, seeing illness as a disease of the nerves. From this followed the idea of "depletion therapy," which incorporated bleeding, restricted diets, purging, and calomel. Rush was an enthusiastic believer in depletion therapy and came up with his own variation on Cullen's theories, seeing all illness as excessive tension caused by disturbances of the blood vessels. Reduce the tension, drain the swamp of fetid substances afflicting the body, and health would surely be restored.

Not only was Rush a signer of the Declaration of Independence, he represented Philadelphia at the Continental Congress and soon became third in command of doctors in the Continental Army. A protégé of Benjamin Franklin, he grew to wield enormous influence in the young country based on the strength of his intellect, personality, and medical connections.

It was due largely to this influence that depletion therapy in general—and the use of bloodletting and calomel in particular—reached unprecedented and catastrophic levels in American medicine. Under his treatment, if ten grains of calomel didn't work or even made the patient sicker, the solution was simple—a higher dosage given more frequently.

The exact moment when this idea took hold of Rush is vividly described in his own words. Surrounded by disease and death during a yellow fever epidemic in Philadelphia in 1793, Rush was desperate to find an effective treatment. He came across an old manuscript describing the yellow fever epidemic of 1741, given to him by his friend and mentor Benjamin Franklin. He was struck by the comment that purging—expelling toxins via the bowels—"is more necessary in this than in most other fevers. . . . A new train of ideas suddenly broke in upon my mind. . . . I adopted [this] theory, and practice, and resolved to follow them."[17]

The purgative therapy he adopted was calomel. In hospitals during the Revolutionary War he had seen it given in ten-grain doses. Now, "I resolved after mature deliberation to prescribe [that] purge." He gave one patient "20 grains of calomel, at two doses [twice to four times as much as doctors were administering during the Revolutionary War fifteen years earlier]. They operated powerfully, upwards and downwards, and brought away a large quantity of bile. The effects of this medicine were such as I had wished. The next day he was out of danger. I prescribe the same medicine in many other cases with the same success."[18]

Success did have its side effects. "Now and then a salivation continued for weeks and months after the crisis of this fever, to the great distress of

the patient, an injury of the credit of mercury as a remedy in this disease." But Rush was not discouraged. He stepped up the dosage to 10
grains *four times* a day; one patient got 150 grains of calomel over a six-
day period. And, he concluded, it worked, "curing" the first four out of
five patients he tried it on. While mistaken, Rush's beliefs became self-
reinforcing. Rush dismissed his critics with the true-believer impatience
shown by Dover, the Quicksilver Doctor. And many grateful yellow
fever survivors backed him.

"There can be no question," wrote Robert North, retired professor of
medicine at the University of Texas in his essay "Benjamin Rush, MD:
Assassin or Beloved Healer?," "that Rush's mercury purges and copious
bloodletting were profoundly erroneous and sometimes fatal. How many
hundreds of deaths Rush watched during the [yellow fever] epidemic is
not known, but in each case he found some way to exonerate his 'remedies' as a cause. Many people that Rush should have respected, including most of his professional colleagues, pointed to their own observations
that Rush's treatment was often worse than the disease and murderous
in its consequences." Rush, however, answered to a higher authority:
"He truly believed," concluded North, "that he had been chosen by God
to save the people of Philadelphia and that opposition to his views was
heretical and sacrilegious."[19]

Rush's heroic model reached its peak during the Civil War and led to
one of the greatest showdowns in American medical history. In 1863
U.S. Surgeon General William Hammond ordered that calomel and
tartar emetic be taken off the approved list of medications for the army.
He had concluded calomel killed more patients than it helped. But this
triggered a vehement response from the medical community that came to
be known as the Calomel Rebellion. Union Army doctors, unwilling to
concede their treatment was worse than none at all, prevailed on the
secretary of war—already at odds with Hammond—to remove him.

Hammond would not go quietly, so he was court-martialed. Calomel
continued to be poured into soldiers suffering from everything from typhoid fever to constipation. And the medical conditions of Civil War
troops on both sides of the battle were simply terrible. Four hundred
thousand of the six hundred thousand soldiers who died in the Civil War
died from illness, not battlefield injury.[20]

While calomel was controversial on the battlefield, it was also ubiquitous in the general population; Americans consumed almost fourteen
thousand pounds of it in a twelve-month period in 1891–92.[21]

In the last half of the nineteenth century, as nearly every American took mercury for one reason or another (some in copious amounts), a condition called neurasthenia was first identified. Often compared to hysteria—"American nervousness," it was dubbed—neurasthenia comprised a cluster of physical symptoms that suggest a possible link to calomel.

Neurasthenia was first identified in 1869 by George Miller Beard, a neurologist; one of the chief proponents of neurasthenia as a clinically distinct disease was Giles Weir Mitchell, a Civil War surgeon who suffered from the condition (likely from his constant exposure to mercury in medicine). The symptoms included pain or numbness in parts of the body, anxiety, fainting, headache, stomach problems, what was called "hay fever" but now would probably be defined as allergy or asthma, and a bizarre affliction doctors called "movable kidney." This probably reflected swelling or tenderness in the kidney, the body's main organ for detoxification, which led doctors to believe it had changed position. But the idea that neurasthenia resulted from a toxic exposure was never part of the discussion; it was believed to result from the increasing urbanization and frantic pace of the times. "There is a large category of functional nervous disorders that are increasingly frequent among the indoor classes of civilized countries," Beard wrote in 1896, sounding like Emil Kraepelin discussing GPI in more "advanced" cultures.

> Neurasthenia is *an American disease* [emphasis in original] in this, that it is
> very much more common here than in any other part of the civilized
> world. . . . Neurasthenia, indeed, like the decay of the teeth, which in some
> cases is one of the symptoms of the neurasthenic tendency, was first made
> of special consequence in this country.[22]

But neurasthenia could have been "an American disease" because heroic medicine, with its gargantuan calomel purges, was an influential American movement. The condition was accompanied by another noteworthy symptom: "Sweating of the hands and feet, with redness."

> This phenomenon . . . is certainly more common in males than in
> females. . . . The milder phases are common enough, but there are severe
> manifestations that this syndrome may assume, which seem wellnigh

beyond belief. Thus a young man now under my care is so distressed
thereby that he threatens suicide unless he is permanently cured."[23]

Despite such severe physical symptoms, doctors defined and diagnosed
neurasthenia as a symptom of urban life and stress, just as Freud and
Breuer saw their patients as struggling with repressed emotions and unresolved childhood conflicts. Because neurasthenia, like hysteria, faded
as a diagnosis in the early twentieth century, today's historians of medicine and society have perceived it in much the same way, viewing the
whole episode in terms of late nineteenth-century social "discourse"—
and missing the truth entirely: These patients were real people who were
really sick.

From Teething to Teens

In 1931 a French doctor, Charles Rocaz, published a book titled *L'Acrodynie
Infantile* about a strange disorder afflicting children in increasing numbers.[24] Although most recovered, many died—official statistics reported a
total of thirty-three deaths of children in England and Wales that year, an
upward trend that started with one recorded death in 1923.[25]

The disorder's miseries become clear in the portrait of a three-and-
a-half-year-old child whose decline is depicted in the book. The child
had been sick for weeks, and while his parents treated him for "worms,"
strange symptoms accompanied his illness: "The hands and feet also
became red, swollen and moist. The child cried incessantly and was only
pacified when allowed to rub his hands together vigorously."

The child quit talking, tried to hit his parents, and "battered himself
against the bed. The parents sadly remarked that he resembled 'a raving
lunatic.'" He quit eating, refused to stand, became more lethargic and
apathetic and had difficulty swallowing. Three days after being taken
home, he died.[26]

In the English translation of Rocaz's book, the title was changed to
the disorder's more familiar name, *Pink Disease*. "Pink disease is one of
that group of diseases which appear intermittently in this world," Rocaz
begins. "Entering the realms of medical investigation afresh, they are

apt to be signaled as new diseases, the knowledge gleaned by our fore-fathers having been forgotten."[27]

Two decades later, when the cause of pink disease—mercury, the active ingredient in such popular childhood potions as teething pow-ders, worm treatments, and diaper rinses—was finally detected by a scientist in Cincinnati, Rocaz would be proven wrong. Pink disease was not newly rediscovered. Pink disease was *new*. Once again, the rem-edy was the disease and, once again, the clues were there—the worm treatment likely contained calomel and caused the child's suffering and death.

But for the first half of the century, doctors and scientists puzzled over this strange syndrome affecting infants. "There is not even the consensus of opinion as to the best name for the malady," Rocaz wrote. Among them: erythroedema, Feer's disease, Swift-Feer's disease, acro-erythroedema, neurosis of the vegetative system, trophodermatoneu-rose, dermato-polyneuritis.[28]

Acrodynia—the medical term that stuck—literally means "pain in the hands and feet" (from the Greek *acro-* for extremities, as in acrobats). Some of the first observations of the disease emerged in Australia around 1914. In 1920 a Melbourne doctor presented ninety-one cases in detail. One doctor suggested calling it "raw beef hands and feet," while Dr. Chubb of Sydney offered a shorter and more palatable name: pink disease.

"At about the same time the physicians of North America announced the pink disease had appeared in their midst," Rocaz reports—this in-cluded ten cases in Portland, Oregon, the first seen in 1914—it was also identified in the British Isles, Canada, and in parts of Europe.[29]

Although pink disease came to be named for its outward physical mani-festations and misery—"My hands are on fire! My hands are on fire!" one child wailed[30]—it was equally a neurological and psychiatric condition. Rocaz said "nervous symptoms" played the leading role in the entire course of the illness. The first reported affect was "the loss of the usual gay and happy disposition . . . The child ceases to display any affection and his fa-vorite amusements lose their charm. . . . The little patient conveys the im-pression of intense physical and mental suffering. At the same time he ceases to speak. A gay and talkative child may be completely mute."[31]

Rocaz goes on to describe even more extreme behaviors. These chil-dren were banging their heads against furniture, throwing themselves around at the risk of injury, tearing at their hair, and inflicting harm on themselves in any number of disturbing ways.

What on earth was happening? While Rocaz and others believed that better diagnosis was simply leading to the identification of more cases, many concluded it was too identifiable and bizarre to simply have escaped notice up until this point. Ideas of causation ran the gamut among medical professionals, including viruses, vitamin deficiency, exposures to toxins and poisons, or an allergic reaction. Some said it was psychosomatic, and some blamed parents.

On May 29, 1948, a paper just over a page long appeared in *The Lancet*.[32] Its authors were Josef Warkany, an assistant professor of pediatrics at the University of Cincinnati, and Donald M. Hubbard, an assistant professor of industrial hygiene there. These were not major players on the world's acrodynia research scene; Hubbard was not even an M.D. In that 1948 paper Warkany and Hubbard describe how, in 1945, a child aged fourteen months with severe acrodynia was brought to the Children's Hospital of Cincinnati. Running tests on a specimen of the child's urine, they discovered a high level of mercury but said, "The source of mercury could not be established in that child." Soon, however, they had examined a total of twenty children with acrodynia and found high mercury levels in eighteen.

As they attempted to determine the source of the mercury, the scientists found that the parents were not especially helpful; most of them didn't know which medications or creams might have contained mercury. Still, Warkany and Hubbard persisted and established that calomel had been an ingredient in a variety of products used on these children, whether by way of ointments applied to the skin or the ingestion of teething powders.

Ultimately they identified multiple sources of mercury (about a third of them teething powders), including diaper rinses that used mercuric chloride, and in one case possible exposure to thimerosal, a new mercury compound in medicine.[33]

The groundwork for this spectacular discovery was laid in the most prosaic way. Hubbard, the industrial hygiene researcher, had been working on technology that could detect minute amounts of mercury in urine, and in 1940 published a paper on "a photometric method using a new reagent, di-beta-naphthylthiocarbazone."[34] A follow-up paper in 1946, coauthored with Jacob Cholak, reported further refinement of the technique.[35]

After poring over endless papers about acrodynia (Rocaz's runs to 123 pages), reading Warkany and Hubbard's short, matter-of-fact report on mercury excretion in acrodynia patients is bracing—like coming upon Einstein's brief 1905 paper on special relativity: no footnotes, because there were simply no antecedents. Technology and toxicology enabled the breakthrough; Warkany credits Cholak, the coauthor of Hubbard's follow-up paper, with the suggestion that they look for a broad range of metals in the urine of the acrodynia patients.

Warkany wrote follow-up papers in 1948 and 1951 that definitively linked mercury poisoning to acrodynia, and he began moving on to the next logical step. "Awareness of the etiological relationship between acrodynia and mercury points the way toward prevention. Teething powders, the most frequent cause of acrodynia in our series, are apparently completely useless and should be abandoned."[36]

One would think that might be the end of it, but Warkany and Hubbard did not receive instant acceptance of their discovery. In 1953—five years after their finding of high mercury levels in children with acrodynia—the *Journal of Pediatrics* ran an article by Donald Cheek of Australia, who was unwilling to concede that the mystery had been solved. "It is sometimes dangerous to compare diseases of known etiology, such as mercury poisoning, with diseases of unknown origin. Although pink disease shows nearly all the features of mercury poisoning in its different phases, the same could be said of other agents."[37] He persisted with the idea that family dynamics could play a role, referring to a 1952 paper that claimed a striking frequency of stressful family situations in these cases, often more evident than in families of children attending psychiatric facilities.[38]

One reason for the lingering debate over acrodynia was that although Warkany and Hubbard found high levels of mercury in nearly every acrodynia patient, they could find the source of the exposure in only about two-thirds of them.

This does not suggest that a third of acrodynia cases were caused by something besides mercury—no one now disputes that mercury was the sole cause of acrodynia. Rather, it suggests how pervasive mercury compounds were through the first half of the twentieth century in the United States, Great Britain, and Australia.

WARKANY'S ACRODYNIA CASES AND THEIR EXPOSURE SOURCES

Case	Urinary mercury* (mcg/l)	Mercury source	Case	Urinary mercury (mcg/l)	Mercury source	Case	Urinary mercury (mcg/l)	Mercury source
	Mercurous chloride (calomel)							
7	80/60/120	Teething powders	28	58/85	Worm treatments	1	360/320	Unknown
8	430	"	29	230/200	"	2	100/20/180	Unknown
12	160	"	41	45	"	3	45/28	Unknown
15	300/360	"	32	80	Other calomel	4	6/0	Unknown
16	40	"	36	160/90	"	5	90/10	Unknown
19	70/80/20	"		Mercuric chloride in antiseptics		9	80/50/40	Unknown
21	17/30/40	"	27	120/20/10	Mercury bichloride diaper rinse	11	300/300	Unknown
22	280/140	"	31	10/30/100	"	13	300/300	Unknown
23	720/30	"	35	1680/1040	"	14	260/400	Unknown
24	330/210	"	39	90/300/100	"	17	0/0	Unknown
34	70/2430	"		Other mercury formulations		18	240	Unknown
38	40/45	"	10	14/72/40	Ammoniated mercury ointment	25	110/90	Unknown
6	100/130	Pinworms?	20	50/280/580	"	26	370/100	Unknown
			40	0/10	Thimerosal	30	40/80/110	Unknown
						33	25	Unknown

*Some cases had multiple urine samples.

It also signals the rise of a particularly modern institution: the first media-savvy pharmaceutical companies, who transformed the ancient craft of the apothecary with modern advertising techniques. These entrepreneurial innovators turned a backroom chemistry trade into a branded consumer-packaging business, offering treatments for everything from teething to constipation. These marketers grew prosperous through their skill in identifying profitable consumer markets and knowing how to make a sale: You'd have to be a bad mother if you didn't heed the call to use Steedman's "gentle powders."

While a number of companies peddled such products, Britain's John Steedman and Co. was the biggest, and it pioneered the kind of ubiquitous marketing that has reached its apogee in today's glut of TV pharmaceutical ads. One example we encountered is a postcard of a shoe full of kids crediting a Mother Hubbard character who "gave them all Steedman's from 'Teething To Teens'"—adapting the timeless nursery rhyme the way current advertisements pick up classic rock songs.

But why would *all* these children need Steedman's from infancy through the teen years? That is artfully explained in a palm-size pamphlet with a sturdy laminated cover titled "Hints to Mothers on the Treatment of Their Children—From Teething to Teens."[39] We found the undated eighteenth edition, suggesting a certain degree of popularity, in which was displayed a handy alphabetical list of the ailments to which children are prone—from Abscess, Adenoids, Backwardness and Bed Wetting to Warts, Whooping Cough, and Worms.

In this edition, teething is in the title to suggest infancy and the original use of the powder, but oddly, teething powders are not even mentioned. By this point, the firm's ambitions were much greater, and teething was merely a come-on. Echoing the superstitions observed by Kanner, the pamphlet notes: "The period of dentition is the longest, the most difficult, and the most critical operation through which a child must pass. . . . Teething may be accompanied by various rather alarming developments, such as child-crowing, convulsions, etc., which are discussed under these headings. The general health of the child requires particular attention if these troubles are to be avoided. The bowels must be kept regular."[40] For proper bowel regulation, the authors frequently urged use of a "gentle aperient"—meaning a laxative—and the phrase appears relentlessly in Steedman's promotions.

So perhaps the true cause of the rise of acrodynia was not just calomel, which had been around for a long time, but the marketing campaign to suggest it for all kinds of purposes and to prey on the fears of nervous mothers. This was a pioneering practice that also involved newspaper advertising. It offered an authentic-sounding source of authority—but a fatally toxic product.

As the economies of England, the United States, and Australia grew with mass transportation and sophisticated consumer marketing, mercury became big business and a leading product line for the nascent pharmaceutical industries. Companies like Merck sold arsenic and mercury compounds well into the 1940s,[41] and a teething product that began in an apothecary shop morphed into a remedy recommended for anything that might ail someone. As Britain's *Pharmaceutical Journal* reported in November 1939: "John Steedman was not only a good pharmacist—he also believed in bringing to the attention of the outside world the products of his pharmaceutical skill."[42]

The original Steedman was a founding member of the Royal Pharmaceutical Society of Great Britain, and his heirs married into another patent-medicine marketer founding family, the Hanburys, whose company after a series of mergers evolved into Glaxo Wellcome, Britian's leading drug company.[43]

The Calomel Legacy

Today the medical industry has set the acrodynia episode aside, just as the contribution of Warkany and Hubbard to genuine medical progress is largely overlooked. "There are a number of ways of being forgotten in science," Warkany's University of Cincinnati colleague Harold Kalter later wrote. "If you discover how to prevent a disease so successfully that it disappears and physicians do not remember it and students are not taught it, who will recall the name of the person that caused it to vanish?"[44] But as with syphilis and hysteria, there are lessons from the Age of Acrodynia that are crucial to absorb.

Chief among them is that new technology was required to solve the acrodynia puzzle. Mercury can be detected in urine, but it was only when new and more sophisticated technology arose in the 1940s that Warkany was able to consistently detect it at low levels in acrodynia cases.

Once again, two core problems—the latency of detecting exposures, and individual variations in susceptibility to mercury's adverse effects—confounded the efforts of those trying to understand acrodynia. It often set in weeks or months after parents first used teething powders, worm treatments, diaper rinses, or a "gentle aperient." And only a small proportion of children who received these exposures actually developed acrodynia, something on the order of one in five hundred. While some doctors continue to argue that children who succumbed to acrodynia were simply the ones who got the most mercury, that's not what Warkany believed. "The fact that after mercury medication children may excrete mercury in the urine in appreciable amounts without developing acrodynia suggests that an individual susceptibility . . . to mercury intoxication exists in the children who develop acrodynia."[45]

But children whose immune systems were weakened by viruses or bacteria may have been especially susceptible. Doctors noted that acrodynia seemed to occur more frequently during and after epidemics of influenza.[46] This might simply reflect confusion between the first signs of mercury poisoning and an apparent contagious illness, but it is worth considering in light of what we believe is a microbe-mercury connection in a variety of human disorders, most notably general paralysis of the insane.

———

Warkany and Hubbard's papers eventually won the day. Teething powders were banned. Acrodynia disappeared. Occasionally, the medical establishment refers to it, but the disorder is largely treated as an embarrassing episode of medical history to be swept under the rug. Today, mention acrodynia to a medical student and he or she will probably give you a blank stare.

But its legacy continues. A couple of decades after the high rates of acrodynia deaths were noticed in London during the 1940s, urologists began to observe an unusual pattern in men presenting with blockages in their sperm ducts. When operating on a broader set of patients with these blockages, doctors saw a specific course of illness in a subset of them. In 1970 an English doctor named Donald Young specified the syndrome, in which the effects of the blockage were uniquely painful.[47]

In addition to problems with sperm flow, Young's syndrome cases had other unusual symptoms: Chronic sinus and bronchial problems led researchers to suspect some form of damage to the delicate filaments that line the surface of sperm ducts, nasal passages, and the lungs. Most notable for our purposes, doctors recognized a relatively frequent history of acrodynia in their Young's patients. One study showed that a history of pink disease was unexpectedly common in Young's sufferers.[48] But as the birth cohorts of boys treated with calomel began to decline, so did the incidence of Young's syndrome. The conclusion? The toxic effects of calomel treatment had left a longer legacy to the generation of boys who grew up with Steedman's soothing powders, a wider swath than just those who showed symptoms of acrodynia. In this case the legacy was infertility: Only a tiny percentage of these men ever fathered a child.

Young's syndrome disappeared along with acrodynia and household mercury products, but other diseases have been connected to calomel in more indirect ways. One link that made news in 2009 is Kawasaki disease, a diagnosis given for Jett Travolta, the autistic child of actors John Travolta and Kelly Preston who died of a seizure. Kawasaki disease was first identified in Japan in 1967, where two notorious episodes of mercury poisoning took place and where mercury fungicides were also ubiquitous (mercury fungicides weren't banned in Japan until 1968).

Kawasaki disease is mostly known for its effect on the heart, but its symptoms closely resemble acrodynia. In a Japanese search for cases of Kawasaki disease before Kawasaki, a group of pediatricians from Tokyo University Hospital reported that the first case might have been identified as Feer disease (a synonym for acrodynia) in 1952.[49] As with Warkany's findings in the urine of acrodynia cases, practicing clinicians have observed elevated levels of mercury in the urine of children diagnosed with Kawasaki disease. One study reported that "six patients with diagnostic criteria for Kawasaki disease had abnormally high urinary excretions of mercury. . . . There are numerous clinical similarities between Acrodynia and Kawasaki disease and the appearance of . . . Kawasaki disease has been related temporally and geographically to environmental pollution with mercury."[50]

In 2008 an article noting the connections between Kawasaki disease, acrodynia, and mercury was published in the peer-reviewed journal *Current Medicinal Chemistry*. It noted the symptom overlap of "bright red, swollen hands, feet . . . Painful itching, burning sensations." The authors concluded: "Medical literature, epidemiological findings, and some case reports have suggested that mercury may play a pathogenic role. Several patients with Kawasaki's Disease have presented with elevated urine mercury levels compared with matched controls. Most symptoms and diagnostic criteria which are seen in children with acrodynia [are] known to be caused by mercury. . . . Since 1990, 88 cases of patients developing Kawasaki's Disease some days after vaccination have been reported to the Centers for Disease Control including 19% manifesting the same day."[51]

Despite the fact that one of the first recognized cases of Kawasaki disease may have had an acrodynia diagnosis, this disease does not seem to have disappeared in the same way as acrodynia and Young's syndrome. So while the calomel legacy has faded in some conditions, in others there may be other toxic agents that play a similar role to calomel in causing disease—and the impact is still being felt.

Perhaps the most affecting evidence of calomel's tragic legacy comes from the testimony of those who suffered from pink disease and are now adults, many of whom still suffer from severe after-effects. A high-profile survivor is Heather Thiele of Australia. She founded the Pink Disease Support Group in 1989.

She describes her life today: "In particular, I have a terrible sense of position of both my body and hands. For example, it takes me ages to line up a clothesline, the clothes and the pegs to hang out clothes. I have to have a rope hanging down from the ceiling of my carport to be able to have a guide to park the car in the correct place. I am hopeless with any locks, catches, car seat catches, etc. I go to open a door, but miss the catch by inches. I drift when walking and often bump into walls and doors. I cannot cope with verbal instructions at all and have to write 'everything' down. This is known as 'thinking in pictures' (Temple Grandin)."[52] Grandin is probably the most famous person in the world diagnosed with autism; *Thinking in Pictures* is the title of her best-known book.

We've focused here on a handful of the most compelling and significant episodes of mercury's broader use in medicine and especially on calomel, but these are likely just the tip of an iceberg. Below the surface are many more tragic medical and personal histories. While some are known or suspected, most are lost to history, the point Elisabeth Storie emphasized when she wrote about her own case to "warn those in high power of the danger of doing injustice or injury to any."

Acrodynia was the beginning of the end for calomel in medicine, which would soon give way to the carbon compounds of mercury. In fact, the cause of this illness was discovered almost simultaneously with the first application of penicillin, which ended the use of mercury to treat syphilis. Germ theory had killed off the philosophy of the humors that justified mercury's medicinal use. A new era of pharmacology was blossoming. If mercury killed children, and was connected to GPI *and* could be replaced as an antiseptic, why use it? But at the same time, why make a fuss? After all, the movement from mercury to penicillin could be chalked up not to a revolution in medicine, but rather to the march of progress of the medical profession.

But we'll give Warkany, who solved the riddle of acrodynia, the last word: "The fact that generations of physicians before us were well acquainted with the wide spectrum of adverse reactions to mercury whereas we were not, illustrates the dilemma. . . . One can go forward and yet go in circles."[53]

CHAPTER FOUR

POLLUTION

Three billion people—half of the world's population—now live in cities, many of which contain air that is unfit to breathe. Two hundred years ago, however, only one city on the planet used significant quantities of fossil fuels and experienced the pollution that such consumption entails.

—PETER THORSHEIM ON LONDON, IN *INVENTING POLLUTION*[1]

While superstition over teething had tragic consequences when infants were treated with mercury, in other circumstances teeth actually tell us a lot. As it turns out, teeth can store crucial evidence about what our environment is like. In one example, baby teeth unearthed from beneath the floor of a twelfth-century Norwegian church contained mercury levels ten times lower than those from a modern Norwegian sample collected in the 1970s. Researchers concluded that the teeth from the twelfth century reflected mercury uptake "from natural sources only" and that the increases since then were probably the result of industrial activity.[2]

Children's teeth, in fact, appear to be exquisitely sensitive mercury barometers. A study in Norway just twenty-five years after the 1970s sample was collected found mercury levels greatly reduced.[3] Why? The authors of the study noted the efforts on the part of Norwegian authorities during intervening years to ban the use or discharge of mercury, concluding that the reduction might have reflected a drop in environmental mercury in the area.

These intriguing studies are among the few ever done on mercury levels in human teeth. But another mammal at the top of the food chain has been studied much more extensively. The remains of whales, gathered in large volumes in the fishing centers of Canada, have been a recent focus of research. One study examined mercury in the teeth of beluga whales, an important food source for people living near the Arctic, and found levels from the late nineteenth century not much different from those dating up to about 1947. In the 1990s, however, teeth from the same species indicated much higher levels, exhibiting concentrations in twenty-year-old animals that were 7.7 times higher than samples from whales a century before. The studies also found that teeth from 1926 to 1947 were similar in mercury concentration to those of the late 1800s, suggesting that the increase had occurred sometime after the 1940s. The researchers cited industrial pollution as a plausible explanation for the apparent increase in mercury.[4]

Taken together, these studies imply a considerable rise in mercury exposure from the Industrial Revolution, with a post–World War II spike, and another big uptick in the 1990s. Six thousand tons of mercury pollution are introduced into our atmosphere worldwide each year; after general neglect of the issue during George W. Bush's administration,[5] in 2009 President Obama called for a treaty to reduce mercury pollution, labeling it (and properly so) the world's gravest chemical problem.

But where did all this mercury come from—and why, now that we know the havoc it can create, are we exposed to more of it than ever? The answer is inseparable from the substance that created the modern world: coal.

Up until now, we've focused on the direct connection between the medical administration of mercury and specific diseases. In this chapter we'll take a more speculative approach, looking at the modern emergence of a wide range of chronic disorders, while also placing a special emphasis on schizophrenia. And although we don't propose the same direct relationship between mercury and schizophrenia that we have suggested with other disorders, the history and trajectory of schizophrenia is a useful example to explore. The rise of schizophrenia resembles in many respects the sudden emergence of GPI, since the outbreak of "lunacy" in the nineteenth century caught most of Europe by surprise. Although GPI disappeared as the Age of Syphilis came to an end, nothing similar has happened with schizophrenia. Sadly, and unlike the case of Van Swieten's liquor, the environmental roots of schizophrenia are still with us. Nonetheless, the ongoing scourge provides an important model for the way the complex interactions between metals, microbes, and man can produce mental illness.

The main source of environmental mercury is coal, the original fossil fuel that fired the Industrial Revolution. The rising content of mercury in human and whale teeth gives us a running tally of these man-made mercury exposures. But mercury isn't the only toxin launched into the environment by coal burning; lead (perhaps an even more relevant risk factor in schizophrenia) and arsenic, not to mention greenhouse gases and acid rain, are also part of the emissions that rise from a coal-fired engine. Because the toxic footprint is so broad, when it comes to tracing the link from coal's many toxins to schizophrenia, we offer only a scenario rather than a proof. One thing is sure, however: Nothing good is coming from the rising background of anthropogenic mercury in our environment.

And while schizophrenia is our leading model, there are other conditions, newly discovered in the wake of Europe's Industrial Revolution, that we also believe are part and parcel of the effects of pollution. In a long list of conditions, diseases that were never previously described became epidemic in industrial Europe and have remained unexplained ever since. Beyond schizophrenia, disease scenarios we consider include conditions ranging from juvenile arthritis and attention deficit disorder to genetic mutations like Down and fragile X syndrome. We offer this longer list of scenarios as part of a broader theory about the relationship between man's industrial activities and the rise of a whole new class of diseases. In the context of the rise of autism, these scenarios are important to consider as we investigate the role of man-made chemicals and toxins in our environment.

Mercury Rising

London at the dawn of the Industrial Revolution was a sight to behold—if you could have seen either the city or the dawn.

The British capital was mired in dense black smoke, the result of the coal burning that powered England's world-conquering industry. England had turned to coal early on; in place of its denuded forests and exhausted supply of firewood, coal was easy to get, and seemingly inexhaustible.

Every home had its coal-fueled stove that provided both warmth and fuel for cooking, and the first factories didn't even have smokestacks— the residue of coal burning simply wafted across the city. As early as the seventeenth century, observers complained at length about the noxious effects of London's coal-burning frenzy. In 1661 John Evelyn wrote in arguably the first book on pollution, *Fumifugium:* "That this Glorious and Antient City . . . which commands the Proud Ocean to the *Indies,* and reaches the farthest *Antipodes,* should wrap her Stately Head in Clowds of Smoake and Sulphur, so full of Stink and Darknesse, I deplore with just Indignation. . . . [6]

"It is this horrid Smoake which obscures our Churches, and makes our Palaces look old, which fouls our Clothes, and corrupts the waters, so as the very Rain, and refreshing Dews which fall in the several Seasons, precipitate this impure vapor, which, with its black and tenacious quality, spots and contaminates whatever is exposed to it."[7]

It would be a long time before Evelyn's lone cry found a receptive audience—England was too busy to take note, spinning the textile trade and other coal-powered engines of commerce into the basis for its far-flung colonial empire. In fact, through the late 1800s people worried more about the health effects of what was known as miasma—bad air from decaying organic sources—and actually viewed coal smoke as benign.

But ultimately, the black cloud of coal pollution, as well as the miserable conditions in early industrial Manchester and London, created terrible health conditions and a pitiful life expectancy for the new working class. This, in turn, radicalized people with names like Marx and Engels and led to upheavals that shaped the modern history of the world.

———

Early Londoners referred to their black energy source as "Sea Coale" because coal would arrive in London in ships loaded in the north of England and following the eastern coastline down to the capital. At the center of the sea coal boom was Newcastle, where so much coal so readily accessible gave rise to the adage "Bringing coal to Newcastle," meaning any kind of superfluous effort (think: bringing coffee to Starbucks).

But how did coal come to be in Newcastle or anywhere else? Millions of years ago, England was actually at the equator. As giant primeval

plants died and decayed, an ever-deepening layer was matted down under increasing pressure. This process is called coalification: Deposits of
organic matter accumulate and only partially decompose. While the
water content—oxygen and hydrogen—diminishes, the matter left behind is largely composed of hydrogen and carbon: hydrocarbons, a synonym for fossil fuel. But this residue of ancient plant life also contains
other elements like nitrogen, sulfur, and heavy metals like mercury, the
residue of prehistoric geothermal activity, volcanic eruptions, and the
natural "degassing" of minerals from rocks and soils. When coal is burned,
these ancient storehouses of mercury accumulation are opened up to release their toxic inventories back into the atmosphere, all in a single moment of combustion.

For most of human history such coal reserves were an untapped re-
source. England was the main exception, with its large exposed seams.
But even in England, the ability to exploit coal reserves was limited for a
long time, largely because of the difficulty in reaching the supply farther
below the surface. All that changed with the invention of the steam
engine in the late eighteenth century.

It was a classic case of necessity as the mother of invention. As English
miners increasingly depleted the easy-access coal reserves, they began to
dig deeper pits, and eventually these pits became coal mines. As the
mines grew deeper, they grew wetter, creating the demand for pumps:
The original steam engines were primarily designed to help pump water
out of these deeper mines. Pumps led to the first steam device, called the
Newcomen engine, which actually used almost as much coal to power it
as could be extracted using the device. Soon James Watt figured out how
to increase its efficiency and turned the extraction of coal into a boom-
ing business. Before long, the steam engine became a general-purpose
technology using coal fuel to power mechanical operations of all kinds.
Watt's engine created a virtuous economic circle—it allowed for the
profitable extraction of coal, which enabled the steam engine to run ef-
ficiently elsewhere as a manufacturing workhorse. It launched the Industrial Revolution and spread like wildfire.

Steam engines powered looms that provided textiles for clothing.
They made possible the rise of ironwork and smelting and the use of

even more pure concentrations of coal as coke. Every element of the Industrial Revolution was powered by coal and created demand for more. This had large benefits, but simultaneously provided the first large-scale exploitation of fossil fuel, setting off a tidal wave of pollution that continues to roll over us.

Although we have some knowledge of where mercury is stored in coal, remarkably less is known about the environmental hazard produced by its emission. Far more is known about how mercury has been deposited around the earth, across different geographies and over time, but this knowledge has produced both understanding and controversy in its wake. As we've seen with the history of mercury in medicine, just about everything about mercury in the environment is controversial.

That said, there is one clear conclusion from all of the scientific research on mercury emissions. Unlike the once lethal coal-fired London Fog, which diminished and eventually disappeared with even the most rudimentary emissions control, the trend with mercury is the opposite: The rate of mercury entering the atmosphere and being deposited around the globe has increased many times since the Industrial Revolution. The studies all agree that the source of this increase is "anthropogenic," i.e., caused by the activities of man. The evidence from the teeth of humans and whales suggests just how much has built up in mammals; but the bulk of the evidence for the explosion of environmental mercury pollution comes from the land itself, sources like glacial ice cores, peat bogs, and lake bottoms. These archives are of the sedimentary kind, places where scientists are able to sample the residues of centuries of layered atmospheric deposits, as snow or rain falls to remain fixed in glaciers and wetlands and as each season's leafy remains and rainfall make their way to the bottom of freshwater lakes.

There is a massive and growing body of science focused on these land-based natural archives. The information gathered from these different sources is consistent in a general sense, but the specifics vary quite a bit, depending on the geographic location and exact nature of the archives being measured. The data from ice cores and peat bogs, for example, show higher levels of increase in mercury deposition compared to levels from the preindustrial period, anywhere between five to ninety times the amount deposited before the Industrial Revolution.[8] But studies like these that show the highest increases overall often exhibit a more pronounced fall-off in recent decades, perhaps the result of efforts to reduce the pollution from legislation like the Clean Air Act. By contrast, other data, most notably the studies of years of sediments from the bottom of freshwater lakes, show a lower increase since the Industrial Revolution, about three to five times the preindustrial rate. These technical differences can actually become important for policymakers. Peat-bog data suggest we're making progress in reducing mercury accumulation, but lake-sediment data suggest we should still be worried. In the words of one review, "Lake-sediment records generally indicate a peak in mercury deposition during the 1970s to 1990s. . . . In contrast several peat studies suggest a peak in deposition 10–20 years earlier."[9]

Given the stakes involved for the polluters looking to defend their activities and retain their right to burn as much coal as they can, one can readily see how the fine variations in these estimates can become subject to intense debate. The American coal industry, for example, argues vociferously that they burn "clean coal," that their mercury emissions have decreased substantially. They claim that domestic emissions are responsible for only a tiny fraction of worldwide anthropogenic emissions, that such emissions are also exaggerated and that they shouldn't have to spend as much money on emissions controls as environmentalists would like.

Who to believe? One systematic review says we should trust the bad news (the lake sediments) more than the good news (the peat bogs). "Although there are complications with both types of archives, it seems clear that lake sediments, as closed systems, are internally more consistent and less problematic than peat records."[10]

Regardless of the fine points of the trend argument, what is also clear is that mercury deposition doesn't respect state or national boundaries. Coal plants in the American Midwest throw out mercury that comes down in the Northeast. And coal burned in China can generate mercury emissions that make their way across the Pacific Ocean and come to earth in the continental United States. "As much as 25% of the air pollution in Los Angeles comes from China; at certain sites in California, as much as 40% of the air pollution comes from Asia," reported Laurie Garrett and Jane C. S. Long in the *Los Angeles Times* in 2007.[11]

And while mercury emissions may have decreased in some areas due to local efforts to clean the air, global consumption of coal, much of it driven by the massive and rapidly growing economies of Asia, has been hitting new heights. In 2006 alone, China added 102 gigawatts of predominantly coal-based electricity to its power grid, about as much as France generates in a year.[12]

This new surge in coal consumption has yielded disturbing results even in regions that have worked hard to limit mercury emissions, reversing trends where mercury monitors had held out hope for an improved and less toxic future. A recent study of fish in Minnesota (which, perhaps not coincidentally, has one of the highest reported autism rates in the United States) makes the point. "In a surprise development, mercury levels in Minnesota fish have been rising—likely due to coal burned in China and India," reported John Myers in the *Duluth News Tribune* in 2009.[13]

The Invisible Plague

The Industrial Revolution offers what is perhaps the first case study in how polluting the environment may have created conditions that could give rise to new disease. It certainly affected living conditions more rapidly and more profoundly than any other era in history. The rapid rise in productivity and incomes created a change in the human condition that was unprecedented. Most visibly, the effect was seen in the great industrial cities of England where Watt's steam engine was first deployed and where coal consumption rose first and fastest. English cities exploded in population, and London and Manchester reached sizes that had never been seen before. There were huge problems with garbage and sewage and generalized filth, along with the rise of industrial pollution as factories with few smokestacks and no emissions filters spewed coal smoke into the air. Coal residue was only one element of the pervasive filth. Progressive citizens also began to worry about the problem of hygiene.

This great shift in economic conditions produced intense reactions. Friedrich Engels (later of Marx and Engels) himself coined the term "the Industrial Revolution"; the son of a rich Manchester capitalist, in 1845, at age twenty-four, he wrote his famous book *The Condition of the Working Class in England* in an outrage over the conditions he observed up close (he had worked for two years in one of his father's cotton mills).[14] Engels's book was preceded a decade earlier by a book of observations by James Phillips Kay, which offers a glimpse of how quickly, and irrevocably, the Industrial Revolution had changed the human experience.

Beyond the power of the new commercial system, Kay found poverty and illness. He describes people "crowded into one dense mass, in cottages separated by narrow, unpaved, and almost pestilential streets; in an atmosphere loaded with the smoke and exhalations of a large manufacturing city. The operatives are congregated in rooms and workshops during twelve hours in the day, in an enervating, heated atmosphere, which is frequently loaded with dust or filaments of cotton, or impure from constant respiration, or from other causes."[15]

It was capitalism in its earliest and crudest form—both Darwinian and Dickensian. And as the century went on, it was the deaths of children in particular that galvanized both social and political action. Engels's 1845 portrait of the era's health conditions was even direr than Kay's of a decade earlier. On the east and northeast sides of Manchester where the working class lived, "ten or eleven months of the year the west and south-west wind drives the smoke of all the factories hither, and that the working class alone may breathe . . . the atmosphere is poisoned . . . and darkened with the smoke of a dozen tall factory chimneys."[16]

In a chapter titled "Results," he bore down on the human toll: "In Liverpool, in 1840, the average longevity of the upper class, gentry, professional men, etc., was 35 years." By today's standards that is appallingly brief, but the prospects for everyone else were even nastier, more brutish and much shorter. Businessmen and "better-placed handicraftsmen" lived twenty-two years on average; "operatives, day labourers, and serviceable class in general, but 15 years." And that was still not the worst of it.

"The death-rate is kept so high," Engels went on, "chiefly by the heavy mortality among young children in the working class. . . . No one need wonder that in Manchester . . . more than 57 percent of the children of the working class perish before the fifth year, while but 20 percent of the children of the higher classes, and not quite 32 percent of the children of all classes in the country die under 5 years of age."[17] Among children, "Epidemics in Manchester and Liverpool are three times more fatal than in country districts . . . affections of the nervous system are quintupled, and stomach troubles trebled, while deaths from affections of the lungs in cities are to those in the country as 2.5 to 1."[18]

If what the cosseted Engels saw was enough to radicalize him, imagine the impact on a father who lost several children in these conditions. That was the fate of Karl Marx, living in a cramped London apartment as he crafted the ideas that would become *Das Kapital*. Marx, himself afflicted with respiratory and other health issues, lost five of his six children, three in infancy and two to suicide.

The work of Marx and Engels has been remembered in history as the declaration of class war between industrialists and factory workers. To be sure, the great income disparities and oppressive conditions of the time were a major part of the outrage that sparked their *Communist Manifesto* in 1848. But the problems of the working class had as much (if not more) to do with their health as with their working conditions. Engels's most powerful writing describes the horrible lives of English factory workers. They suffered terrible health problems amid filth of all kinds, including new epidemics of infectious disease, from cholera to typhoid, tuberculosis, and respiratory disease.

But there were other kinds of health problems, more mysterious in origin, foreshadowed in Engels's remark that the risk of neurological disorders was five times greater in severely polluted industrial centers. The English population began to get sick in ways that mankind had never seen before.

Starting around 1750, more and more people simply went mad in England and Wales. Statistics in E. Fuller Torrey, M.D., and Judy Miller's book *The Invisible Plague*, on "Insane Persons in Psychiatric Hospitals, Workhouses and Under Care" tell the story. In 1807 the total was 5,500; by 1870 it was 54,713—a staggering tenfold increase over the 1807 figure.[19] Yet historical references to insanity are few and far between before the middle of the 1700s. The meager references to madness that do exist before this time don't usually reference any kind of early adult onset, a characteristic that often accompanied this emerging form of mental illness.

Insanity, as it was experienced in the majority of these cases, differed from the brief and fatal delusional period of a patient dying from GPI. GPI sufferers always had syphilis, acquired their condition late in life (an initial syphilis infection at age twenty-five would typically result in the onset of GPI fifteen years later), and died quickly. Schizophrenia, by contrast, came on earlier, often in adolescence, and produced a long-term state of mental illness marked by mania and auditory and visual hallucinations, but accompanied by otherwise good health. Contemporary physicians like Emil Kraepelin easily distinguished between the two.

The first major asylum was Bethlem. Its chief apothecary, John Haslam, wrote *Observations on Madness and Melancholy* in 1809 based on his experience with patients there; the first sentence reads: "The alarming increase of Insanity, as might naturally be expected, has incited many persons to an investigation of this disease."[20]

England seemed to be a particular hotbed for this frightening new plague. In 1733 George Cheyne published *The English Malady: Or, A Treatise of Nervous Diseases of All Kinds.* His preface offers a laundry list of possible causes that, however misguided, manages to allude to crowded, unhealthy cities and bad air:

> The Title I have chosen for this Treatise, is a Reproach universally thrown on this island by foreigners and all our Neighbours on the Continent, by whom nervous Distempers, Spleen, Vapours, and Lowness of Spirits, are in Derision, called the ENGLISH MALADY. And I wish there were not so good Grounds for this Reflection. The Moisture of our Air, the Variableness of our Weather, (from our Situation amidst the Ocean) the Rankness and Fertility of Our Soil, the Richness and Heaviness of our Food, the Wealth and Abundance of the Inhabitants (from their universal Trade) the Inactivity and sedentary Occupations of the better Sort (among whom this Evil mostly rages) and the Humour of living in great, populous and consequently unhealthy Towns, have brought forth a Class and Set of Distempers, with atrocious and frightful Symptoms, scarce known to our Ancestors, and never rising to such fatal Heights, nor afflicting such Numbers in any other known Nation.[21]

This sudden, sharp and inexplicable rise in "the invisible plague" of severe mental illness has been exhaustively and convincingly researched in Torrey and Miller's 2001 book. It tracks the rise in England of what we now call schizophrenia and bipolar disorder. Torrey, like Cheyne before him but with a great deal more scientific grounding, notes that the rise of this new plague was unique to England.

The English were forced to create a wide range of institutional accommodations of this new scourge. In 1828, responding to public outcry over the treatment of the rising number of "lunatics," Parliament created a system of county asylums. By the 1830s, Torrey points out, "The question of increasing insanity was being widely discussed in England."

While some of this rise was due to more humane approaches to the mentally ill and to the overcrowding of workhouses, according to another survey of "lunacy" prevalence: "A significant fact is that in both England and Wales the number of mentally infirm amounted to one in a hundred of the pauper population and the ratio was constant through the years until it became four in a hundred in the 1860s." Some of the rise in the population of "lunacy" may also have come from other causes. We know that GPI patients were also included in the asylum populations. However, only about 10 percent of the 1890 admissions to one asylum were under the category of GPI, and these patients would have died much faster than the rest of the "lunatic" population.[22]

Torrey also describes in vivid detail the literary preoccupation with madness in nineteenth-century England. By the mid-1800s, the "mania for madness" had infected a sizable portion of the literary establishment. The most famous of all the English writers with an interest in insanity

Figure 1—The Invisible Plague Reflected in the Increasing English Asylum Population

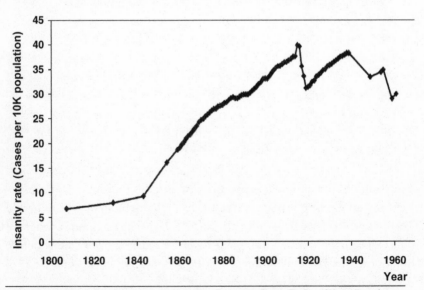

Source: Adapted from E. Fuller Torrey, M.D., and Judy Miller, *The Invisible Plague: The Rise of Mental Illness from 1750 to the Present* (New Brunswick, N.J.: Rutgers University Press, 2001) and verified using original data source.

was Lewis Carroll. Carroll's Mad Hatter was a famous model for mercury poisoning, and he also displayed a broader interest in the theme of insanity. Torrey argues that Carroll's enigmatic poem "The Hunting of the Snark" was actually an elaborate critique of England's so-called Lunacy Commission.

Torrey's documentation of the increase in the prevalence of lunatics is based on a painstaking collection of data on schizophrenia rates in England, obtained from scattered sources and over a long time span. They show a clear and steady rise starting in England in the early eighteenth century. Then the rates rise in Ireland and the United States, with a lag. Interestingly, the literary preoccupation with insanity followed. Notable Irish authors who took up the topic include playwright John Millington Synge; William Butler Yeats, whose sister Lollie was insane; and James Joyce, whose daughter Lucia descended into madness in her early twenties.[23] In American literature, writers as influential as Edgar Allan Poe and Nathaniel Hawthorne also were strongly influenced by the concept of insanity.

It's possible that the rise in mental disease wasn't limited to lunacy; it seems that there was a rise of "idiocy" or mental retardation, too. Isolated data show increases in idiocy as well, but less stable definitions make it hard to pin down.

What might have caused this spike in mental illness and perhaps retardation as well? Clearly, it was not a genetic change—genes don't mutate anywhere near fast enough to account for the epidemic rise. "If genes cannot explain the increase of insanity, then where should we look?" Torrey and Miller ask. "In reviewing the rise of insanity, one of the most striking aspects is its temporal correlation with the industrial revolution."[24]

All of the innovations of the Industrial Revolution sent enormous and unprecedented amounts of coal pollution into the air. And among other effluents like carbon (which produces carbon dioxide emissions), sulfur (which produces acid rain), and lead, coal contains mercury. Torrey does not directly link coal use and schizophrenia, but the correlation between coal production and insanity rates in England is quite strong, and similar results hold in Ireland and the United States. And although Torrey doesn't point to coal directly, the hypothesis is entirely consistent with his observation on the rise of insanity coinciding with the Industrial Revolution.

Torrey and Miller offer five possibilities for the epidemic increase: diet, which changed radically during the period and included far more gluten from wheat, which some have linked to schizophrenia; alcohol, for which (like Kraepelin's speculation on GPI) there is no evidence; industrial-age toxins such as insecticides to which people were newly exposed; some unintended consequence of increased medical care, perhaps in obstetrics; and infectious agents. In this category, Torrey includes GPI, "the polio model" (pointing out the similarity in the rise of paralytic polio and schizophrenia), vaccinations and "the pet cat model" (in which increasing cat ownership leads to new infections).[25]

Torrey's research shows his own strong interest in the pet cat theory and has suggested links between schizophrenia and several infectious agents, such as *Toxoplasma gondii* and cytomegalovirus.[26] Other research-

Figure 2—Asylum Populations in England Rose as Coal Production Increased, 1805–1961

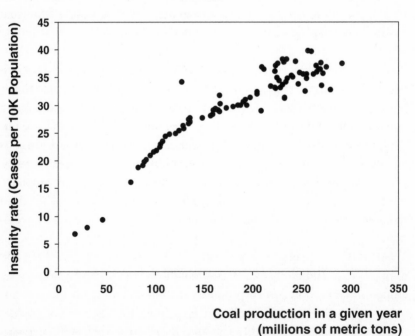

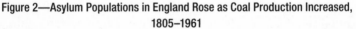

Source: Torrey and Miller; and B. R. Mitchell, *International Historical Statistics: Europe 1750–2000, 5th Edition* (New York: Palgrave Macmillan, 2003).

ers have shown a link between maternal influenza infection and schizo-phrenia, but the results are conflicting, and the most optimistic of the studies claims a causal link in no more than 14 percent of cases.[27]

Torrey has less to say for toxins, and far less research has been conducted here. And while there is nothing in modern medical literature about links between schizophrenia and mercury, there is recent evidence of a possible association with lead exposure, which along with mercury is highly related to coal emissions. A recent study on prenatal exposure to lead found a significant connection between maternal blood lead levels and schizophrenia risk. Children born to mothers with lead levels above a certain threshold are at almost double the risk of schizophrenia.[28]

A related correlation consistent with the idea of toxin exposure is that between city life and schizophrenia. One recent paper went by the marvelously exasperated title "Urban Birth and Risk of Schizophrenia: A Worrying Example of Epidemiology Where the Data Are Stronger Than the Hypotheses," and chided psychiatrists for failing to "have a sense of urgency in exploring the mechanisms linking urban birth and risk of schizophrenia."[29]

Overall, the body of evidence on the causes of schizophrenia, while slim, generally supports the idea that some combination of metals (coal products like lead and, conceivably, mercury) and microbes (including agents like *Toxoplasma gondii*, cytomegalovirus, and influenza) can enhance the risk of later illness in an unborn child. There are other pieces of evidence implicating specific factors in mother and child: Some research has looked at schizophrenia rates among children born during famine and implicated maternal starvation during pregnancy; other studies have implicated the body's detoxification system, the glutathione metabolism, as well as some genetic risk factors. But most likely the true cause of schizophrenia is some complex combination—of microbes, metals, and man.

The Plague of New Industrial-Age Diseases

Alongside schizophrenia, the nineteenth century witnessed the emergence of other neurological diseases and unexplained chronic illnesses. The Industrial Revolution saw the rise of great English diagnosticians:

men like James Parkinson, William John Little, John Langdon Haydon Down, and George Frederic Still.

Industrial England suffered from elevated mortality, particularly among the working classes, and much of this increased death rate was due to infectious diseases. Tuberculosis, always a dangerous disease, took a far higher toll in urban areas than in rural England. The spread of cholera requires someplace where the microbe can incubate, as John Snow famously showed by tracking a London cholera epidemic to a cesspit close by the Broad Street water pump. In many ways, it was a disease of congestion. When we think of these conditions of London, it is those industrial disease narratives we remember, in large part because they are the dominant narratives repeatedly told by the medical profession. And these stories are comforting because the threat of these diseases is largely gone; thus, the memory that has survived is that of the heroic physician, like John Snow, who sought the source of the disease and eliminated it.

The documented history of infectious diseases goes back in some cases to the pharaohs: Tuberculosis has been identified in Egyptian mummies, as has smallpox; Hippocrates first described the symptoms of mumps, diphtheria, and tetanus; whooping cough and measles were well described by the Middle Ages. Many of these illnesses have ancient histories because they entered human hosts as a result of a transfer from animals. Measles, a cousin of the cow disease known as rinderpest, probably made the species jump to humans when man began domesticating cattle. The bubonic plague arose in the Middle Ages as carrier rats began infesting medieval towns. Rabies often spread through dogs, one of the earliest animals domesticated by man. A large number of diseases were introduced to human civilization on the heels of a certain kind of human progress: the rise of farming and the domestication of the animals that enabled the transition from a hunter-gatherer lifestyle to life in the great cities sustained by an agricultural food supply.

This model of human disease is not particularly controversial, as historians from William McNeill *(Plagues and Peoples)* to Jared Diamond *(Guns, Germs, and Steel)* have explored the interactions between microbes and human civilization. But there's something missing in this perspective of human disease, namely, any mention of the kind of sickness that medicine cannot trace to a microbe. For alongside this list of familiar diseases that can be connected to their animal sources—e.g., measles (cattle), whooping cough (pigs), tuberculosis (goats)—there is a longer list that escapes easy explanation: a class of mental and chronic diseases, the bulk of which burst onto the scene in nineteenth-century Europe. This new class doesn't come with a heroic model of identification and conquest. Instead, the surviving narrative here is the diagnostic brilliance of the clinicians who saw a pattern in symptoms no one had ever seen. More often than not, a physician's reward for his discovery was a form of immortality as the condition he had recognized was given his name.

But were these men really seeing something that had been missed for centuries? Or did they happen to be in a position to observe a cluster of cases of chronic disease as it first appeared? We would argue, like Torrey in his view of schizophrenia, that many of these new diseases were indeed something new and not, as Rocaz incorrectly asserted in discussing acrodynia, "one of that group of diseases which appear intermittently in this world." What if they were diseases born of the newest phase of human civilization, children of coal combustion, distributed mechanical power, and the Industrial Revolution?

Run down a comparable list of today's well-known chronic diseases and one can't help but note that many of them were first described at the same time and place, during the rise of European industry in the nineteenth century. James Parkinson first described the "shaking palsy" in London in 1817; William John Little described Little's disease (now known as cerebral palsy) in 1861 and also in London; Charcot described a great number of neurological disorders in Paris's Salpêtrière that (unlike hysteria) remain with us, among them multiple sclerosis (1868) and amyotrophic lateral sclerosis, or Lou Gehrig's disease (1874); and Emil Kraepelin generally receives credit for formally describing both schizophrenia (1887) and bipolar disorder (1902).

We believe it's possible that just as the most common infectious diseases jumped the species barrier from animal to man as human progress put these animal species in close regular contact with large numbers of humans, industrial progress has similarly evoked a new set of human diseases: conditions that have their roots not in the microbes we shared with our animal companions but in the pollution we created as we began to unleash the power of fossil fuel, burning and releasing centuries of natural toxins that had settled in alongside the hydrocarbons.

Interestingly, most of these new conditions of the Industrial Revolution have causes that remain mysterious. There is no model like germ theory to guide the diagnosis of disease, no set of rules like Koch's postulates (a four-part test used for linking a single infectious agent to a specific disease) to show the path to prevention.

Most new illnesses were seen in adults, but there were also hints of new pediatric conditions. Some of them were ultimately traced to genetic defects, but some have remained of mysterious origin. Several conditions in children that were first described in nineteenth-century London, "the one city on the planet" that burned massive quantities of fossil fuels, deserve closer scrutiny.

George Still was credited with the first clinical description of juvenile rheumatoid arthritis, a sometimes fatal condition that not only swells and stiffens joints but causes spiking fevers and rash (alternately called Still's disease).[30] Still also first described a condition we would now call attention deficit hyperactivity disorder, using the phrase "defect of moral control" to describe children who were neither retarded nor mentally ill but could not govern their impulses or attention.[31]

In some of these newly observed childhood disorders an important question arises. Was the appearance of these newly observed conditions due to physician recognition of these disorders for the first time, or in fact the initial appearance of a novel syndrome, perhaps the first glimmers of the Age of Autism? John Haslam of Bethlem asylum describes four cases of childhood insanity in his 1809 *Observations on Madness and Melancholy*. Two are of particular interest because their early onset (before three years of age) meets the criteria for autism. "In the month of March, 1799, a female child, three years and a quarter old, was brought to the hospital. . . . The mother . . . related that her child, until the age of two years and a half, was perfectly well, of ordinary vivacity, and of promising talents; when she was inoculated for the small pox. Severe convulsions ushered in the disease, and a delirium continued during its course. The eruption was of the mild kind, and the child was not marked with the pustules. From the termination of the small-pox to the above date, (nine months) the child continued in an insane state." Previously able to "articulate many words," she lost language, she became violent and would "rake out the fire with her fingers" despite getting burned. She would "bite, or express her anger by kicking or striking," and tried to run away.[32]

This apparent first record of such behavior—early onset, loss of language, and sensory difficulties—seems striking for its similarity to autistic features.

A second case also involved an unusual response to inoculation with smallpox, combined with a case of the measles. "W.H., a boy, nearly seven years of age, was admitted into the hospital, June 8, 1799. . . . When a year old, he suffered much with the measles: and afterwards had a mild kind of inoculated smallpox." By age two, he was out of control. "There was a tardiness in the development of his mental powers. . . . He had arrived at his fourth year before he began to speak. . . . In a short time he acquired a striking talent for mimickry." His language improved, but regrettably "he had selected his expressions from those patients who were addicted to swearing and obscene conversation."[33]

When the patient was seen again at age fifteen, he continued to display atypical behavior. According to Haslam, he was able to whistle several melodies, but wasn't able to respond to ordinary questions, and the physicians reported he had a fixation on soldiers. This sounds like autism, and it is interesting to see both Still and Haslam attempt to describe a spectrum of inexplicable and inattentive behavior in otherwise typical children—in other words, children not obviously retarded or brain-injured in utero.

While autism was not a diagnostic term available to Haslam, it is worth considering whether two of the four "insane" children he described in fact represent the first descriptions of children with autistic features in the medical literature. Before the end of the century in England, however, there would be a more pronounced description of a cluster of cases with autistic characteristics.

A Classification of Idiots

While Haslam pioneered the observation of mental illness in children at the start of the 1800s, the causes remained mysterious. Still, some of the diagnostic efforts of the time ultimately led to a greater understanding of the disorders we've come to understand as genetic in origin. John Langdon Haydon Down was the century's premier diagnostician of developmental disorders in children and pioneered the observation of children we describe today as mentally retarded. The son of a pharmacist, Down showed precocious interest in science and planned to make that his career. He started out as an assistant to a surgeon and worked in the humoral tradition of bloodletting and purging, where he developed an obsession with dentition. Later, he worked in the laboratory at the Royal Pharmaceutical Society, focusing on the new field of organic chemistry, and was a research assistant to one of science's great figures, Michael Faraday. The death of his father detoured him into medical school for financial reasons and he proved to be an outstanding student. But rather than follow the road to riches and success, he became medical superintendant of Earlswood Asylum for Idiots in Surrey and began focusing on mentally retarded children.

This led to his original description, in an 1866 paper titled "Observations on an Ethnic Classification of Idiots,"[34] of what we now call Down syndrome. Down is considered a gross genetic defect, one in which the child carries three copies of chromosome 21—a "trisomy 21"—instead of the usual two. In about 90 percent of cases, a trisomy 21 occurs when the mother's egg forms with an extra copy of the twenty-first chromosome. This genetic defect wasn't identified until 1959 by Jérôme Lejeune, but Down was the first to recognize and describe the manifestations of the syndrome. In 1887 Down published a series of lectures and commented at several points that his work was based on "nearly thirty years of observation in London," which probably covered children born from the late 1850s to about 1885, and adults born earlier.[35]

But Down's observations also include some children with what might be described as autistic features. This point was made in 2004 by Darold A. Treffert, M.D., who has argued that Down not only discovered Down syndrome, he also first described autism.[36] In his 1887 collection of lectures, *On Some of the Mental Affections of Childhood and Youth*,[37] Down elaborated a broader theory of mental retardation, which he divided into several categories. A large part of the category that he named the "congenital" group was the famous "Mongoloid" syndrome we now call Down syndrome. But in two smaller categories, one he labeled "developmental" and the other "accidental," Down's descriptions of symptoms include many features that are consistent with autistic disorder. In his recent analysis of these two groups, Treffert claims to have found evidence that autism "is not a new disorder"[38] and that Down's narrative included autism in both its regressive form (the "developmental" group) and in children who were autistic from birth (the "accidental" group).

Although Treffert's observations are interesting, based on our reading of Down he also overstates his case. His strongest argument may lie in the group he spends the least time describing, the "accidental" group.

Here Down describes autistic symptoms in children whose physical appearance was perfectly normal yet who had no speech and displayed odd behaviors. "They are bright in their expression, often active in their movements, agile to a degree, mobile in their temperament, fearless as to danger, persevering in mischief, petulant to have their own way. Their language is one of gesture only, living in a world of their own they are regardless of the ordinary circumstances around them."[39] In one sentence, Down provides the most tantalizing glimpse of a child who might possibly have autism: "How the self-contained and self-absorbed little one cares not to be entertained other than in his own dreamland, and by automatic movements of his fingers or rhythmical movements of his body."[40] Unfortunately, none of these accidental cases are ever fully described and so it's impossible to distinguish between true autism cases or just the scattered presence of autistic behaviors.

Treffert focuses most of his attention on the developmental group, in which Down describes a clear pattern of regression at three stages of development: first dentition, second dentition, and puberty. Down's description of the earliest regression is interesting: "Their early months of babyhood were perfectly uneventful; there had been nothing to cause the slightest anxiety; intelligence had dawned in the accustomed way, when *first dentition proceeding* [emphasis added] a change had come over the aspect of the child. Its look had lost its wonted brightness; it took less notice of those around it; many of its movements became rhythmical and automatic, and with or without convulsions there was a cessation of the increasing intelligence which had marked its early career; anxiety was felt on account of the deferred speech, still more from the lessened responsiveness to the endearments of all its friends."[41]

The symptoms Down describes here might correspond with autism but also bear similarity to the symptoms of acrodynia. As for the other children in the developmental category, their later regressions at second dentition (which starts at age six) and puberty put them out of the range of an autism diagnosis.

In all of these "developmental" cases, however, Down was clearly describing a regressive condition, one that occurs relatively late in development. In making the case for Down as an early observer of autism, Treffert relies on his idiosyncratic willingness to set aside the timing of onset as a relevant marker for an autism diagnosis. Most of the cases he proposes as autistic wouldn't pass that bar for other observers. But besides overstating their similarity to autism, Treffert also overlooks the most prominent aspect of Down's case descriptions, an unusual head shape in the developmental group. Down reached for evocative language in describing these children's skulls: "These cases have usually character-istic crania; they are dolicocephalic [long-headed] and prow-shaped an-teriorly."[42]

Down doesn't seem to be describing just autism here, and goes on to say that the "prow-shaped cranium of the developmental class" is in fact the distinguishing feature of this group, a feature that makes them "al-most sure to break down at one or other of the developmental epochs."[43] This description raises an even more interesting association between Down's observations and this first cluster of cases, one that Treffert missed. And it suggests that retardation and autism could both result, in some instances, from environmental causes that arose at the same time in relatively recent history.

One focus of Down's discussion of his developmental class is headaches. Down observed that his "prow-shaped-head" children had headaches, often severe, quite possibly migraine headaches. Darold Treffert asserts that this finding supports the notion that these children were autistic; autistic children tend to experience a period of rapid brain growth and also tend to have a measurably larger head circumference than typically developing children. But as Treffert himself writes, "Down's observa-tions were not focused on head size but rather head shape."[44] And the head shape dimensions in question, "prow-shaped" and "dolicoce-phalic," sound remarkably similar to the head shapes in another genetic disorder called fragile X syndrome. A recent textbook provides the fol-lowing definition for fragile X: "Clinical Features: Moderate to severe mental retardation in 80% of males and 35% of females . . . Macro-cephaly, dolichocephaly, large squared forehead, prominent supraorbital ridges."[45]

What Down appears to be describing is the "characteristic crania" of fragile X cases. So in his observations of mentally retarded children, it's difficult to know whether Down found cases of autism. But it's quite likely that he may have observed autistic symptoms in cases involving the two most common genetic syndromes associated with autism: Down syndrome and fragile X syndrome. Fragile X syndrome is widely known as one of the first identified autism susceptibility conditions; roughly 20 percent of boys with fragile X are diagnosed with autism. And autism rates have been estimated as high as 7 percent in recent populations of Down syndrome children.[46] Both syndromes are the results of genetic defects: in the case of Down syndrome, an extra copy of the twenty-first chromosome in the mother's egg; and in the case of fragile X a mutation of a particular region on the X chromosome in which a sequence of DNA repeats itself dozens of times more frequently than it should.

But what could be causing these genetic defects? "Mongolian idiots," Down wrote, in an obvious error, "never result from accidents after uterine life. They are, for the most part, instances of degeneracy arising from tuberculosis in the parents."[47] "Tuberculosis" might be a proxy for the close living quarters, poor sanitation, and unbridled coal pollution that led to its endemic status in Manchester and London. Certainly, pollution is a possibility. Down also says: "My patients have come from all parts of the British dominions, and include every variety of societal rank, but still I am conscious that a very unfair proportion must have been drawn from this great city."[48]

<hr />

If pollution can increase the risk of genetic defects like Down syndrome and fragile X, one simple but overlooked question is this: Did Down syndrome even exist before the Industrial Revolution? The question was first raised in an unassuming way—via a short letter to *The Lancet* on July 13, 1968, by Arthur E. Mirkinson.[49]

"IS DOWN'S SYNDROME A MODERN DISEASE?" asked the letter's headline. Mirkinson mused that, given how common Down's is, it was "a source of wonder to me" that it had not been described until the mid-19th century. "Was the incidence less great until the advent of the 19th century with modern industrialization and living patterns evolving as we know them now?" he wondered, or did it reflect longer life spans and later maternal age?

All kinds of conditions and illnesses were portrayed for centuries, he noted, from polio on wall paintings in ancient Egypt to "the halt, the lame, and the syphilitic of Breughel. . . . Still, no mongoloid facies or figures." Mirkinson asked the journal's readers to identify early depictions if they could.

A small number of readers responded with selected early depictions of children purporting to show Down syndrome, but they were few, far between, not convincing, and even demonstrably wrong. One example was a child in a 1773 painting by Sir Joshua Reynolds, *Lady Cockburn and Her Three Eldest Sons*, the same child who grew up to be Sir George Cockburn, a British admiral who commanded the ship that carried Napoléon to exile on St. Helena in 1815.[50]

The question has continued to be raised. "Is Down Syndrome a Modern Disease?" asked E. Peter Volpe in 1986. "The last decade of the 19th century witnessed a flurry of clinical reports on Down syndrome, as if medical science took note for the first time of this rather conspicuous anomaly. . . . It is almost inconceivable that the existence of persons affected with Down syndrome was unknown prior to the last half of the nineteenth century. It seems that awareness of Down syndrome would predate the medical reports of the late 1800s by several centuries."[51]

Volpe comes down on the side of better diagnosis, speculating that the condition had been confused with cretinism, a distinct form of mental retardation that results from iodine deficiency in utero. But although children with cretinism and Down syndrome share a characteristically small head size, the highly distinctive facial features of a Down syndrome child make it difficult to believe they could be confused with another condition, cretinism or otherwise.

Down himself was so taken with the distinct features of his "Mongoloid" children that he developed a whole theory around it in his 1866 paper "Observation on an Ethnic Classification of Idiots": "I have for some time had my attention directed to the possibility of making a classification of the feeble-minded, by arranging them around various ethnic standards." And while he proposes Caucasian and Ethiopian facial traits for certain classification of "idiots," it is clear the Mongoloid children inspired his whole theory. "The great Mongolian family has numerous representatives, and it is to this division, I wish, in this paper, to call special attention. A very large number of congenital idiots are typical Mongols. So marked is this, that when placed side by side, it is difficult to believe that the specimens compared are not children of the same parents."[52] If children with Down syndrome were so distinctive even then that John Langdon Down was able to assign them an "ethnic" type and claim they appeared to be of a different lineage from their parents, then how was it possible that such unusual and recognizable features attracted no notice in earlier records or documents?

An Epidemic of Denial

The recorded rise of insanity, unique to England just as the Industrial Revolution was uniquely early and intense there, has provoked endless debate among historical epidemiologists—was it real, or were better provisions being made for the mentally ill?

In 1872 Henry Maudsley, a widely published medical authority, tried to debunk the increase as "not probable in itself and not supported by facts."[53] He argued the rise reflected better diagnosing, the gradual buildup of cases over time, and financial incentives for local governments to move the insane out of homes and into public institutions.

The issue was taken up in 1897 in a "Special Report of the Commissioners in Lunacy to the Lord Chancellor on the Alleged Increase of Insanity." Their report to Parliament: no problem.

> We have now to report to your Lordship, as the result of our investigation,
> that we have been unable to satisfy ourselves that there has been any
> important increase of occurring or fresh insanity. . . . We are well aware
> that there has been a very large and serious progressive increase in the
> number of officially-known persons of unsound mind; but . . . this has been
> chiefly due to accumulation, the result of the co-operation of the several
> causes . . . we have endeavored to describe.[54]

But front-line observers from Haslam to Cheyne were reporting that there *was* a problem—and what's more, they had been making those claims for decades. Haslam referred to "the alarming increase in insanity" in 1809, and *then* it rose tenfold in the next six decades. Modern experts, however, tend to accept that there was no real increase, just better diagnosis.

Torrey finds this denial bizarre. "Living amid an ongoing epidemic that nobody notices is surreal," he and Miller write. "It is like viewing a mighty river that has risen slowly over two centuries, imperceptibly claiming the surrounding land, millimeter by millimeter. . . . Humans adapt remarkably well to a disaster as long as the disaster occurs over a long period of time."[55]

So amid the rise of a novel and unmistakeable disease, it seems possible that a remarkable thing happened. Instead of raising the alarm, the medical profession decided that all of this was just the way things had always been. Instead of a mystery for which they had no explanation, the consensus cause of the plague instead became the rising competence of the medical profession: "better diagnosing."

So the claim of rising competence came from those who eventually took charge of monitoring the number of cases and delivering asylum services. With time, however, there also emerged a second camp to deny the epidemic: a more ideologically driven group who rejected the concept of insanity itself. Michel Foucault and Thomas Szasz argued that mental illness is actually a social construction and not real. They proposed that the construct was created during the Industrial Age, a consequence of our inability to accommodate forms of behavior that were once a normal part of the human experience.

But this theory of mental illness seems to have grown out of a concern for civil liberties. While asylums usually started out with good intentions, they became brutal places where inmates were neglected and abused, and Foucault and Szasz were reacting, in many ways, to the horrors of the asylums themselves. But despite their moral intentions, their theories of social construction were, like Freud's rickety edifice, untestable and unscientific. There was no evidence, no proof, just an elaborate exercise in anthropological speculation that was also at odds with the facts.

The simplest, most parsimonious explanation of the rise in schizophrenia got lost in the noise: There was a change in human circumstances that produced the conditions for a new kind of epidemic. Some did believe that this illness had something to do with the changing environment. But in the absence of any ability to specify the mechanism, these voices were lost, at least until Torrey's attempt to revive them. Still, Torrey's thesis has gone largely unheeded. Instead, over time, the modern science of psychiatry has reached a more benign view of schizophrenia, accepting its origins as a mystery but one that is likely genetic, and almost certainly a product of prenatal events like a maternal influenza infection or stress in the form of malnutrition. There is no sense of an inexplicable increase, an unacceptable prevalence, or a key role for environmental factors. Still, the search for genetic cause has proven fruitless. And even though there is modest evidence of infectious contribution, the microbial candidates fail Koch's postulates: one germ, one sickness.

In industrial England, an active movement worked to deal with the country's filth and develop solutions. What became known as "the hygiene and public health movement" focused on cleaning up cities, garbage, and sewers. New technologies were developed to enable the control of industrial emissions: Smokestacks were built higher, and eventually were equipped with electrostatic precipitators to filter out the most visible elements of the smoke, large black particles of unburned coal. This hygiene movement was a spectacular success. The life of cities got better. Walking around London or Manchester today, one can scarcely imagine the cesspool that so appalled Engels and killed Marx's children.

Alongside the field of hygiene a public health movement developed to deal with infectious disease. Quarantine and later vaccination were used to prevent the spread of dangerous germs. Clean water, indoor plumbing, clean underwear, and sanitation all combined to reduce both morbidity and the mortality rate of most major infectious diseases.

But beyond the general success in fighting infectious disease and finding solutions, there has been an odd acceptance of the new industrial diseases like schizophrenia, Parkinson's, and Still's disease: We have gained no understanding of their causes, nor investigated their origins in time and place. And perhaps the visible impression of less pollution has contributed to a sense that rising industrial production couldn't really have anything to do with these new diseases.

Still, a major aspect of the pollution problem was never actually solved, simply deferred. The old saying goes, "The solution to pollution is dilution." Smokestacks grew higher and pollutants like mercury were simply lofted into the upper atmosphere to come to earth with the rain in places like the U.S. Northeast, California, and Minnesota with its increasingly mercury-contaminated fish. And every day, the global cycle of mercury pollution simply gets worse.

———

Late in life, Leo Kanner, with one eye on his legacy as a great diagnostician, wrote about the history of mental retardation in a series of journal articles; implicitly, he placed himself in the long line of classifiers going back to Kraepelin. Almost a century after Down's 1866 paper, in 1964 Kanner wrote a short book titled *A History of the Care and Study of the Mentally Retarded*. His section on Mongolism reprinted, in full, Down's short "clinical lecture and report" from 1866. Kanner noted "there was no immediate reaction to Down's report."[56] But then a trickle of confirmatory reports turned into a tidal wave.

Kanner writes: "As is sometimes the case with new discoveries, retrospect shows that similar observations were made by others around the [same] time."[57] Still, Kanner leaves untouched the issue of why an initial observation of an obvious condition should lead so soon to so many more. For Kanner, a focus on classification trumped any real curiosity about causation—a combination we will soon recount in much greater detail.

CHAPTER FIVE

———

TARGETED TOXINS

New Improved Ceresan is poisonous, and instructions and precautions with all packages must be observed.

—FROM THE LABEL FOR AN ETHYLMERCURY FUNGICIDE
INTRODUCED IN THE 1930s[1]

Although miners have suffered the poisonous consequences of mercury exposure since Roman times, most early toxic exposures to mercury were medical. More recently, the general background level of mercury in our environment has been steadily increasing as well, as our growing industrial activities spew mercury into our atmosphere, where it circles the globe and falls to Earth in our oceans, fields, and waterways.

Those vectors would provide sufficient concern, but the dangers from mercury don't end there. In the late nineteenth century a new science emerged that discovered how to harness the toxic properties of mercury with more targeted formulations. Before long, mercury found its way into a whole new category of applications. In this chapter we trace three uses, all pioneered by the same inventor: seed disinfectants, lumber treatments, and vaccine preservatives. In our research, we have found sufficient association of each of these with the early cases of autism to warrant a closer look.

The new science of organic chemistry was extracted quite literally from the residue of an earlier technology. As coal continued to power industrial activity, the rising volume of coal burning left behind not only emissions but also ash and tar. The constituents of coal tar—conjoined rings of incompletely burned fossil fuel known as polycyclic aromatic hydrocarbons (PAHs)—provided the raw material for a whole new set of chemistry experiments.

The earliest application came from the accidental discovery of the coloring properties of one coal tar residue. William Henry Perkin famously discovered the first synthetic organic dye in 1856 in an experimental accident that created mauve pigments; when Queen Victoria wore mauve to her daughter's wedding in 1858, it sparked a whole new wave of European fashion. But before long these new technologies would be deployed in a far more sinister and lethal fashion as Europe went to war.

Better Dying Through Chemistry

A year after Leo Kanner was born in 1894 in Klekotuv, Morris Selig Kharasch was born in Kremenetz, just twenty miles away across the Austro-Hungarian border in Russia; now both towns are in Ukraine. Like nearby Brody, where Kanner moved as a boy, Kremenetz was a shtetl. It, too, was all but wiped out by the Nazis.

But Kharasch, like Kanner, escaped that fate, emigrating as a teenager to the United States, where his intellect and interest in science led him into chemical research. In the 1920s, while teaching at the University of Maryland in College Park, he began developing and patenting organic compounds. Not long before Kanner arrived at Johns Hopkins in Baltimore, Kharasch left Maryland for the faculty at the University of Chicago. Both men had found their academic homes. While Kanner became known as the dean of child psychiatry, Kharasch built a reputation as one of the American giants of the new field of organic chemistry.

Kharasch was thirteen when he came to the United States for educational opportunity, preceded by an older brother who took him under his wing. "Kharasch's life was largely devoted to his researches," according to a biographical memoir of Kharasch. Kharasch's contribution in a nutshell, the memoir explains, was the development of "free radical chemistry." "He discovered, or perhaps it would be better to say invented and explained—many new reactions. In most instances, these discoveries were the result of the application of a new set of principles, which postulated free radicals as transitory, unstable intermediates in chemical processes. . . . To the end of his career, he was seeking new and novel chemical reactions, and his most recent publications as well as his earlier ones bear the stamp of his originality." He died in 1957 in Copenhagen "while carrying out an assignment for the United States government."[2]

Kharasch's experiments would lead to the understanding of new and even more dangerous forms of mercury, designed to kill microbes that attacked seeds, lumber, and medical products, without harming either the environment or individuals. Given the lethal purpose of these new chemicals, it is not surprising that they were developed out of the same research programs that produced some of the first chemical weapons.

—

The collapse of the Austro-Hungarian Empire in 1914 plunged Europe into World War I. The new technology of war—machine guns, flamethrowers, and the first use of airplanes as weapons—led to massive casualties and great stalemates. Trench warfare and tunnels created standoffs with no apparent end in sight.

One solution that promised to break the stalemate was chemical weaponry. The Germans were the first to try it, in the form of a chlorine gas attack at Ypres, in Belgium. It killed thousands. But the chlorine gas was hard to control in combat—it had a tendency to waft back toward its originators and was easy to counter; later attacks used mustard gas.

The use of gas warfare was exploding in Europe just as the United States was mobilizing for war. So in 1917, U.S. Army leaders launched the Gas and Flame Service, a special operations unit that recruited great athletes like Ty Cobb and Christy Mathewson. Gas masks were needed and so a Gas Defense division was formed utilizing the expertise of the U.S. Bureau of Mines, which had long experience dealing with methane gas in mines. To build offensive stockpiles, the Edgewood Armory was created in Maryland to manufacture chlorine and mustard gas in high volumes. These separate efforts were consolidated in June 1918 into the U.S. Chemical Warfare Service.[3]

As the service gained momentum, America's research chemists mobilized for war alongside the troops. And as weapons research began in earnest, chemistry professors and their students were recruited from all over the country. E. E. Reid of the organic chemistry department at Johns Hopkins was in charge. He took in students from all over the country. One was a young University of Chicago undergraduate named Morris Kharasch.

Like many immigrants—American by choice—Kharasch had a strong sense of duty. So did his boss at the University of Chicago chemistry department, Julius Stieglitz, who also happened to be the head of the American Chemical Society. This was the man who made it the patriotic duty of all American chemists to dedicate themselves to the war effort. Stieglitz wrote President Wilson: "The American Chemical Society, with over eight thousand members, begs to place its services at your command, especially in matters facilitating preparations of munitions, supplies, medicinal remedies, and other chemical materials."[4]

The new research chemists worked on a wide range of ideas. Chlorine and mustard gases were by then known quantities and had many limitations in the field, so they worked on ways to kill the enemy more quickly. They experimented with hundreds of different compounds and poisons. Arsenic (the key ingredient in the revolutionary syphilis medicine of that time), produced the most remarkable breakthrough. Called Lewisite, this was the pride of the American chemical establishment.

Mercury was also a tool of the trade. Large amounts were used for production of other compounds (making chlorine, for example, requires mercury). Though mercury's own poisonous properties were well known, the problem was its latency: Mercury didn't kill quickly enough to make a difference on the battlefield.

Almost immediately, Kharasch emerged as a major talent in the Chemical Warfare Service. "Captain Ross, at the Edgewood Arsenal, said to me that of all the ten thousand enlisted men or officers, no one had made such a record or deserved such commendation as Kharasch of Chicago," reported a University of Chicago publication.[5]

But the mobilization for chemical warfare didn't last long—Americans never wound up launching a chemical attack (and never have). Almost as soon as they geared up, the war was over. Kharasch got his Ph.D. from Chicago early, in 1919. And then he needed a new project. The natural next step was to seek commercial applications for his wartime work.

And there was money available for the task.

———

Much of the previous research on mercury had been focused on its use as medicine, especially in treatments for syphilis. This application of a chemical familiar to Kharasch was a logical place for him to start, and one of his first papers, coauthored with Stieglitz (his department chair), proposed a possible combination of the two syphilis fighters, arsenic and mercury. "Although arsphenamine and neo-arsphenamine have proved very efficacious in the war on spirochaetes, it has been found most effective to alternate the administration of the arsenicals with mercury preparations," they wrote, repeating the scientific consensus of those prepenicillin days. "It was with this in mind that the preparation of an arsphenamine containing mercury was undertaken, a compound which would have the effects of both the mercury and the arsenic in the same molecule, and which should have both metals attached directly to carbon."[6]

Nothing came of this idea. But Kharasch was a one-man blizzard of scientific papers, most of them dealing with metals and how to combine them in new and useful ways with other atoms and molecules. In 1920 he mentioned his earlier wartime work on mercury, writing: "During the course of investigation of mercuri-organic derivatives . . . the amount of data has accumulated to such an extent that it has been deemed advisable to publish some of the results thus far obtained."[7]

Another paper he coauthored in 1920 stated, "Some time ago, one of us became interested in the mercurization of aromatic compounds and its relation to the various theories of substitution in the benzene nucleus." The one who became interested was clear: "This work was carried out under the direction of Kharasch, National Research Fellow in Organic Chemistry."[8]

"A Fair Start in Life"

Kharasch focused his mercury research on the organic mercury compounds and soon turned to the investigation of a class of organic molecules called alkyl mercury. These compounds—dimethyl-, ethyl-, and methylmercury—bore little resemblance in their properties to the relatively nonreactive mercury found in thermometers. They were deadly in minute amounts and, if properly harnessed, had great potential to kill unwanted microbes. Dimethylmercury (the compound that killed chemist

Karen Wetterhahn at Dartmouth) had proven too lethal for everyday use, but methyl- and ethylmercury seemed to balance a range of desirable commercial properties.

It was to the development of these properties that Kharasch turned his formidable skill. He worked on identifying ways to deliver alkyl mercury compounds by turning them into dusts or putting them together with salicylates (chemicals that naturally occur in plants) for solubility. The commercial potential of these efforts was obvious, and he quickly formed two key business relationships to fund the two distinct branches of his work, with the chemical company DuPont (on seed disinfectants and lumber treatments) and the pharmaceutical giant Eli Lilly (on antibacterials for medical products).

His dual focus on fungicides and pharmaceuticals is evident from multiple sources. In 1952 Kharasch won the Theodore William Richards Medal of the American Chemical Society, which cited him "particularly for his work on the 'organomercury' compounds, which are germicides and disinfectants. . . . Kharasch made pioneering studies on organomercurials important in agriculture (as seed disinfectants) and medicine (the antiseptic merthiolate)."[9] His obituary in *The New York Times* mentions that "he developed mercury compounds to disinfect grain seeds against fungus infections, providing savings for farmers."[10]

The first of his patents to be assigned to DuPont was filed in 1923; there would be eighteen more assigned to the Delaware company over the course of his career. The pattern of these patents in the 1920s accomplished a number of important goals—using the toxic properties of mercury to create effective fungicides; developing methods of delivery, including soil treatment in conjunction with fertilizer; creating powder preparations for plant dusting; developing materials for use with fungicides in spreading applications; and stabilizing the mercurial compound to reduce the danger of explosion. All of this, of course, required an eye on the bottom line: Farmers needed to be able to afford the products, and DuPont needed to make a profit.

Kharasch's efforts bore commercial fruit when DuPont filed a trademark application for an ethylmercury fungicide called Ceresan on May 13, 1929.[11] DuPont teamed with Bayer, a German company already in the mercury fungicide business, to market Ceresan and other organic mercury fungicides here and abroad under a joint venture named Bayer-Semesan. A German-born DuPont scientist, Max Engelmann, had been smuggled out of his homeland and also had been working on fungicides and filed several related patents. Together Kharasch and Engelmann provided the technology for this new mercury-based agricultural product.

━━━

When we open the freezer and pull out a bag of microwave-ready sugar snap peas, we are benefiting from a long, complicated, sometimes misbegotten series of trial and error in the applied science of plant pathology. Some historians trace the origins of the science to 1760, when a shipload of wheat sank at Bristol, England, and did more than survive its soaking in the seawater. Come harvest time, most of the rest of the wheat in England was damaged by a common fungus, but the seed soaked in seawater was fungus-free. Brine became the first fungicide.[12]

From there, the race for new and better treatments was on: copper sulfate (1761), hot water (1887), formaldehyde (1895), copper carbonate (1902), and, in 1915, an organic mercury compound created by Bayer in Germany called Uspulun. Dupont introduced a similar material in the United States in 1921 under the name Chlorophol. Soon other organic mercury disinfectants became available to plant pathologists. The most prominent of these was Ceresan, the product of Kharasch's research. Ceresan worked well and spread quickly, and plant pathologists greeted it with open arms.[13]

"The organic mercuries were used for years by many (including me) after they became available in the late '30s," Robert Aycock, retired chairman of the North Carolina State University Plant Pathology Department, told us.[14] "The arrival of these compounds and others were, in agriculture, almost akin to the discovery of the miracle drugs in medicine such as the sulfonamides and later the antibiotics.

"Up until that time plant pathologists had few chemicals that were effective against plant pathogens and that caused little or no phytotoxicity: Bordeaux mixture, sulfur, and a few other copper compounds, for example. Hence these highly effective mercuries were used widely."

Aycock went on: "It is probable that gloves or masks were rarely used. It would be difficult to estimate the huge number of plant pathologists who worked with these compounds during that period because they were so effective."

The new organic mercury compounds came in many flavors. There were dusts and liquids; there were phosphates, iodides, and chlorides. Most of all there were two types of active ingredients: ethyl- and methylmercury.

And while there were some subtle functional and economic differences between them, for much of the early commercial history of mercurial fungicides, the two were considered to be nearly identical.

The Ceresan brand was the commercial umbrella under which the alkyl mercury products were sold to farmers. Ceresan was marketed with pamphlets telling farmers how to get "Better Grain Yields with New Improved Ceresan." The marketing materials made the case for why farmers simply had to use the innovative new chemical: "You cannot tell by looking at a seed whether it carries disease organisms which will reduce yields and profits. This is why experts say, 'Treat seed every year—It pays!'"

Independent observers such as the New York Experiment Station provided added endorsements: "When applied to smutted or otherwise diseased grain, the gain in yield over untreated seed repaid the cost of treatment many times over." A farmers' organization from North Dakota gave Ceresan the ultimate compliment: "All seed should be treated with Ceresan to give the young plant all possible protection from root rots thus giving it a fair start in life as well as protection against bunt."

There was, though, a small warning: "New Improved Ceresan is poisonous, and instructions and precautions with all packages must be observed."[15] Still, researchers experimented with Ceresan to see how widely it could be applied, and by the end of the 1930s the new compound had been tried on everything from tobacco and cotton to tomatoes and cabbage.

Forests and Trees

To the lumber industry, trees are crops, harvested and "fed" to an economy hungry for fenceposts and telephone poles, houses and tables and chairs, the morning paper and the latest bestseller. Like agricultural produce, trees are threatened by microbes and insects, and, in the twentieth century, the technology to protect them became another target area for the science of organic chemistry. In the 1920s the main focus was not on seedlings but on the harvested result—lumber. Especially in the humid South, where pine forests stretch in a giant crescent from North Carolina to Mississippi and Texas, lumber is prone to a disease called sap stain, or blue stain, caused by a fungus that discolors and weakens it soon after it goes through the sawmill. This fungal infection sharply curtails its commercial value.

In 1921 the U.S. Department of Agriculture stepped into the arena and established eleven regional forestry research offices to support American foresters in their battle against pathogens. One of these was the Southern Forest Experiment Station in New Orleans.

Throughout the 1920s, when it came to forest pathology, the Southern Station's focus was on preventing sap stains and molds in the Deep South. For three summers, foresters with the experiment station tested more than one hundred chemicals on lumber to see which would ward off the dreaded blue stain. The first study enlisted three sawmills, two of them in southern Mississippi and one in Louisiana, all under the direction of forestry pathologist Ralph Lindgren.[16]

During 1928 Lindgren, also known by Lindy, treated matched billets of pine lumber and hardwood that he hoped might prevent blue stain. Most did little, but six of the chemicals showed good promise in controlling fungi. One of these six was ethylmercury chloride, provided by DuPont and called K-1, perhaps reflecting the name of its inventor, Morris Kharasch.

Shortly thereafter, according to one of his colleagues, Lindgren persuaded five companies in the region to test those chemicals on carload lots of green lumber. The untreated and ineffectively treated piles "turned practically black with sap stain, the lumber treated with some of the more promising chemicals stained pretty badly also. But the number treated with ethylmercury chloride remained consistently bright at all the cooperating mills.

"Lindy reported the results factually and undramatically in several trade journals. Apparently, though, word-of-mouth reports outstripped and overshadowed publication. Certainly industry—lumber and chemical— was keenly interested. Ethyl mercury chloride appeared on the market under the trade name of Lignasan."[17]

Kharasch held the patent. And his invention, first validated in Louisana and southern Mississippi in 1930, would spread quickly from this epicenter.

Years later, the connection between toxic environmental use of pesticides and chemical warfare was first made in the popular mind by envi-
ronmentalist Rachel Carson. Morris Kharasch's work is a striking example
of this original connection. In addition to his pioneering commercial
work, Kharasch remained active in chemical weapons research and was
appointed a consultant again in 1926. During World War II he returned
to the Chemical Warfare Service full-time.

"EXPERIMENTS WITH DEADLY WAR GASES RESULT IN COMPOUNDS THAT
WILL SAVE MANY LIVES," reported *The New York Times* on March 3, 1946.
"Fifteen hundred chemical compounds, many of them far deadlier than
those used in World War I, were tested in a secret 'Toxicity Laboratory'
at the University of Chicago. Of the 1,500 proposed chemical warfare
compounds, 300 or one-fifth were developed by Dr. Morris Kharasch,
noted organic chemist at the university."[18]

Most of the attention on dangerous environmental pesticides has
focused on post–World War II developments. In Carson's landmark
book, *Silent Spring,* she wrote about the herbicides and insecticides that
were being sprayed over wide areas. She traced DDT and other pesticides to World War II chemical weapons research, mentioning mercury
only in passing: "Marketed under trade names which give no hint of
their nature, many of these preparations contain such poisons as mercury, arsenic, and chlordane," she wrote.[19] Her real focus was on insecticides, their large-scale spraying and their roots in World War II.

Carson wrote: "All this has come about because of the sudden rise
and prodigious growth of an industry for the production of man-made
or synthetic chemicals with insecticidal properties. This industry is a
child of the Second World War. In the course of developing agents of
chemical warfare, some of the chemicals created in the laboratories were
found to be lethal to insects. The discovery did not come by chance: insects were widely used to test chemicals as agents of death for man." She
described the war as "a turning away from inorganic chemicals as pesticides into the wonder world of the carbon molecule."[20]

Carson's work has had an enormous impact, but her history was only
partly correct. The malignant "wonder world" she described and de-
cried had been created even earlier—by Morris Kharasch, as he developed organic mercury seed treatments on the foundation of World War
I chemical weapons research. Seed treatments like those developed by
Kharasch were much less visible than the spraying of insecticides, often

applied at the warehouse before being distributed to farmers or growers. But as would soon become apparent, they were just as deadly and, given mercury's peculiar properties, even more insidious. Chemical warfare against unwanted microbes ultimately proved to have significant collateral damage; it was the domestic equivalent of chlorine gas blowing back on those who launched it in World War I.

The War on Diphtheria

The third branch of Kharasch's research led him into medical products. In 1927 Kharasch filed the key patent for the development of thimerosal, the generic term for the ethylmercury compound that Eli Lilly gave the trade name Merthiolate.[21] In 1928, Eli Lilly filed the trademark for Merthiolate.

As the fruits of Pasteur's germ theory multiplied, the need for germicides in medicine coincided with an expansion in the use of new treatments called biologics—including vaccines and antitoxins prepared from natural sources such as blood that were sensitive to heat and microbial contamination. Those new formulations often required preservatives. The first disease conquered by advancements in germ theory was diphtheria; a vaccine worked for smallpox (Edward Jenner's serendipitous eighteenth-century discovery—that milkmaids did not generally get smallpox because their exposure to its close cousin, cowpox, protected them from the disease—led to the world's most successful vaccine product decades before Pasteur's insights), but its developers had no idea what the mechanism was. By contrast, a sustained R & D effort led to an effective vaccine against diphtheria.

Diphtheria symptoms develop when a toxin released by the diphtheria bacterium triggers dangerous respiratory distress and, on occasion, brain damage; the toxin also causes a membrane to grow across the throat that can ultimately choke its victim to death. Doctors were largely defenseless against the illness, which mostly attacked children and was called "childhood's deadly scourge."

The transformation from treatment to prevention occurred in 1913, when Emil von Behring altered the antidiphtheria serum he had invented in the late 1800s. Up until then, the serum had been used to halt the disease in progress, and was successful only when it was quickly administered after the outbreak. There had been no preventive measures. But von Behring had found a way to mix the actual toxin with an antitoxin—diphtheria antibodies extracted from the blood of immunized animals.[22] The French press proclaimed: "Diphtheria is vanquished."[23] Unfortunately that was premature; in the 1920s, diphtheria still struck one hundred thousand to two hundred thousand Americans and killed up to thirteen thousand a year.[24] Still, the toxin-antitoxin, as it became known, provided the basis for the first mass vaccination efforts, which were centered in New York and Baltimore.

In January 1929 New York City started a drive with the goal of ridding the city of diphtheria within two years. Urging parents to bring in their infant children for free immunizations, city officials planned a three-shot schedule.[25] But the three shots proved to be a problem, as children who showed any sign of a local or systemic reaction were unlikely to be brought back by their parents for the subsequent weekly shot. Diphtheria deaths continued to rise, and in 1932, eighty-seven children died in New York City. "The rise in diphtheria deaths is disappointing to the Department of Health," a city health official said, "in view of the fact that for three years it made an intensive drive against the disease."[26] But soon a new vaccination was introduced. Called the diphtheria toxoid, it cut the number of shots from three to two and reduced the number and severity of treatment reactions. The beginning of the 1930s saw the first distribution of these diphtheria toxoid packages, which quickly replaced the toxin-antitoxin treatments.[27]

In New York the toxin-antitoxin was discontinued in 1932 as the toxoid took over.[28] In Baltimore the first toxoid packages were distributed in 1930, the earliest direct reference we have found to its use. The city health department reported in 1931 that "during this year the Department began the distribution of diphtheria toxoid on a large scale."[29]

⸺

With the success of the new toxoid preparation, efforts intensified to vaccinate every child for diphtheria at six months or as soon as possible thereafter. Part and parcel with the vaccine, however, went the preservative thimerosal, or Merthiolate—the ethylmercury germicide invented by Kharasch and marketed by Eli Lilly.

Today, a toxic substance like ethylmercury could not be used in a medical product without rigorous testing. Ensuring its safety would entail a process that would start in a test tube and progress to animals; only after passing through several more stages could it win approval to be administered to humans. But before 1938, and the Food, Drug, and Cosmetic Act, drugmakers were not required to demonstrate the safety of their products in this manner before they were allowed on the market. The act spent most of the decade tied up in Congress, "stalled and gutted by the brawny proprietary-medicine lobby . . . with help from friends in the newspaper industry, which had become addicted to advertising revenue from wonder drugs such as Paw-Paw Pills and Cherry Pectoral," as *The Wall Street Journal* put it.[30] Instead, thimerosal was tested only on twenty-two meningitis patients in an Indianapolis hospital. They did not appear to show overt or immediate signs of mercury poisoning even though most of the patients subsequently died.

In a key scientific paper in 1930, "Merthiolate As a Germicide," two Eli Lilly scientists wrote: "During the past five years, the Lilly Research Laboratories, in collaboration with Dr. M.S. Kharasch of the University of Chicago, have synthesized twenty or more compounds" of mercury and an organic radical that can form a soluble salt. In the section "Toxicity in Man," they describe the Indianapolis experiment, making large claims for the safety of their new mercurial formulation: "These large doses did not produce any anaphylactoid or shock symptoms. Neither did these quantities in the repeated doses bring about any demonstrable later toxic effects. The toleration of such intravenous doses indicates a very low order of toxicity of Merthiolate in man."[31] On this basis, thimerosal became one of the most widely used commercial preservatives in the biologics field.

Using Merthiolate as a preservative enabled widespread efficiencies in vaccine production and helped spark the rapid spread of diphtheria toxoid vaccines. The New York State Health Department first noted making vaccines preserved with Merthiolate in 1931,[32] and by the mid-1930s, most American diphtheria vaccines were formulated using the tools developed by Kharasch and his partners at Eli Lilly. The modern age of mass vaccination had begun, and by the end of the decade, public health officials announced with justifiable pride that the war against diphtheria had been won.

Global Poisonings

Grossly toxic and unintended effects of alkyl mercury fungicides began to emerge quickly. In 1940 Donald Hunter, Richard R. Bomford, and Dorothy Russell published "Poisoning by Methyl Mercury Compounds."[33] The symptoms they described became known as Hunter-Russell syndrome. Hunter and colleagues described a Swedish factory where fungicidal dusts were produced that was the site of four cases of poisoning by inhalation of the mercury compounds used. Workers in the factory inhaled the fungicidal dusts and came down with serious health problems. The symptoms reported were loss of coordination, speech disorder, and constriction of the visual field. The report showed again how individual reactions to mercury ran the gamut—what felled one man was not even felt by another. Out of twelve coworkers who had the same exposure but did not become ill, eight had mercury in their urine.

The authors provide case reports on the four affected individuals. Typical was Case 1: "After about three months he complained that his whole body was going numb and tingling. He began to notice weakness in his arms and legs, and unsteadiness in his gait. . . . His speech became difficult and slurred, and it was noticed that he could sometimes not see objects put in front of his face."

He was described as a "thin, worried man of hysterical temperament." In fact, "The condition was thought to be hysterical until the other cases occurred." Just above this statement referencing hysteria is a diagram of visual-field constriction that recalls Charcot's "woodcuts" and the ophthalmalogical examination of Freud's first hysteria patient, Albert P.

Nor did things improve for Case 1: "Three years after the onset of symptoms there was little change in the physical signs. Visual fields constricted. . . . He was able to do light unskilled work." But the authors noted that the danger was heightened by being in an enclosed space with intense exposure and predicted farmers were "little likely to be affected."

The similarities of these organic mercury poisonings to the symptoms of hysteria and neurasthenia were repeatedly observed in subsequent reports. Another Swedish study in 1963 about poisoning from another kind of organic mercury notes that "unspecific neurasthenic symptoms may occur. . . . We have observed two cases with neurasthenic symptoms."[34]

Sweden was also the first to point to the problem with organic mercury fungicides in the environment: They noticed that bird populations were beginning to decline, primarily seed-eating birds. Scientists had a natural archive to work with: bird feathers and skins collected and preserved over many years. They compared the mercury content in the feathers and saw a sharp spike right after 1940 when organic mercury fungicides were first introduced to Sweden.

This was perhaps the first "silent spring." A definitive study by Swedish researchers found that "since the middle of the 1950s it became gradually evident that a more or less advanced mercury poisoning is widespread in Swedish wildlife, and the poisoning could soon be associated with the use of organic mercury compounds as seed disinfectants."[35] The report goes on to describe an increase in mercury concentrations ten to twenty times previous levels and notes the particular timing: "The appearance of increased mercury accumulations in birds mainly in the beginning of the 1940's, indicates that alkyl-Hg compounds used in seed dressings are chiefly responsible for that increase."

As a result of this work, mercury seed dressings were banned in Sweden in 1966. But three years later, scientists reported a deeply disturbing

Figure 3—Alkyl-Mercury-Treated Seed Dressings Were Consumed by Swedish Birds Starting in the 1940s. Example of Tail Feathers from Pheasants.

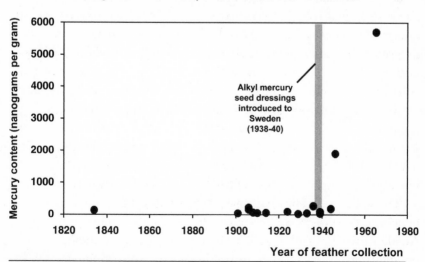

Source: Adapted from data in W. Berg, A. G. Johnels, B. Sjostrand et al., "Mercury Content in Feathers of Swedish Birds from the Past 100 Years," *Oikos* (1966) 17: 71-83.

finding. Inorganic mercury coming from such sources as power plants, pulp mills, and chlor-alkali plants could be methylated by microorganisms in rivers and lakebeds and converted to methylmercury.[36] This was very bad news; it meant that once released into the atmosphere these mercury compounds could become more toxic. Methylated mercury was particularly dangerous because once inside an organism, it was slow to leave the body and passed through the blood-brain barrier and the placenta, causing brain damage prenatally and postnatally.

Birds and factory workers were bad enough, but the catastrophes that put an end to the era of mercury fungicides were large-scale poisonings in human populations, many of which involved children.

In 1972 thousands of people in Iraq ate bread mistakenly made from grain that had been treated with methylmercury fungicide. These seeds were intended for planting, not human consumption. Hundreds died. A follow-up study on children whose mothers ate contaminated bread after giving birth and who were exposed only through their mothers' breast milk showed problems, including language delay, that led one parent to describe the children as "needles blunted by the poison."[37] Eating ethylmercury-treated grain led to similar poisonings in Ghana in 1967. Twenty people died. Of those who survived, children experienced earlier and more severe effects than adults. Speech disturbances in the children were particularly notable. The report added: "Of all the fungicides in modern use, the alkyl-mercury compounds [ethyl- and methylmercury] offer the most serious health hazards. . . . Serious concern has therefore been expressed about the necessary contamination of the environment with mercury, particularly from its use as fungicides in agriculture and in industry."[38]

Minamata, Niigata—and Autism

An industrial accident in Japan ultimately galvanized world attention over the dangers of industrial mercury usage. In 1956 wastewater from a

Chisso Corporation chemical plant spilled toxic levels of methylmercury into Minamata Bay. Children born to mothers who ingested methylmercury from the bay's contaminated fish while pregnant had profound physical and neurological problems even though their mothers did not show any impairment. Symptoms included crippled hands and feet and muscle weakness that resembled cerebral palsy, along with familiar signs of mercury poisoning including narrowing of the visual field, speech and auditory problems, and sensory neuropathy. Minamata disease, as it came to be known, was powerfully captured in a famed series of photographs; in one, a mother cradles her deformed adult child.

While less well known, a second incident took place less than a decade later in Niigata, a coastal city to the northwest of Tokyo, in 1965. The City of Niigata, located at the mouth of the Agano River, is the administrative center of Niigata Prefecture as well as a popular fishing location. Starting in August 1964, a number of patients living in or near Niigata began presenting with the characteristic symptoms of Minamata disease. Between August 1964 and July 1965, a total of twenty-six patients were diagnosed with the disease. Five of the patients died. Investigations into the cause of these illnesses determined that the patients were exposed to methylmercury through the consumption of contaminated fish from the river.[39]

An investigative team from the Niigata University School of Medicine set out to trace the source of the mercury. Based on previous experiences in Japan, they reasoned that the most likely source of the methylmercury in the contaminated fish was wastewater from an acetaldehyde manufacturing plant. Acetaldehyde is made with mercury catalysts, which can be unwittingly converted to methylmercury in the waste stream. The team located two acetaldehyde manufacturing facilities on the Agano River, and after eliminating the plant closest to Niigata, focused their study upstream.

The Kanose factory of the Showa Denko Company was located many miles up the Agano River, quite close to the source. By 1965 the aging facility had completed thirty years of service and was scheduled to be shut down later in the year. In order to build inventory for the transfer of production to a new location, the Kanose factory increased its output "above the production limit" for a number of years, starting in 1958. By 1964 the factory had reached peak production level, producing close to twenty thousand tons of acetaldehyde that year, a five-fold increase from the levels preceding the ramp-up. By pushing the production process so far beyond its designed limits, the managers of the Kanose factory created a dangerous hazardous-waste problem. Methylmercury compounds had accumulated in large amounts in solid production waste, which was routinely released into drainage pipes and then into the river untreated.

The investigators tested waste piles outside the factory and found methylmercury in high concentrations. They tested moss from the riverbank near the drainage pipes and found high methylmercury concentrations there. In a nearby village, they tested the remains of a cat that had reportedly "gone crazy" and died shortly after the outbreak of the disease around Niigata and found tenfold elevations of mercury in the cat's tissue. As a final bit of proof, they tested moss at several locations only a short distance upstream from the drainage pipes, including moss deposits that lay downstream from a nearby power plant. These moss samples all tested negative for methylmercury and had total mercury concentrations that registered less than 0.3 percent of the levels below the Kanose factory.[40]

The investigative team had found their mercury source. The company, despite denials, was found responsible, and victims were compensated.[41] But soon the episode would provide a clue to the cause of another disorder: autism.

—

Moving upriver from its mouth at Niigata, the Agano River winds its way into Fukushima Prefecture (or Fukushima-ken). Situated due east of Niigata Prefecture, the border of Fukushima-ken lies barely five miles away from Kanose, placing the Kanose factory within fifty miles of most of the population centers of the prefecture.

In 1977, about five years after publication of the Niigata University School of Medicine report, a team from Fukushima Medical College initiated an autism prevalence study in Fukushima-ken. The study was a massive effort, the largest of its kind that had ever been attempted, and it remains to this day the largest population ever screened for autism outside the United States.[42] Preliminary screening identified 397 children as autistic, 97 percent of whom were interviewed, as were their parents. From this group, a total of 142 children were diagnosed with autism. That yielded an overall prevalence rate of 2.33 per 10,000, not a particularly high number by current standards, though the researchers excluded 178 cases of children diagnosed with "autistic mental retardation," a diagnosis that might have been included in other studies. But the overall level was less interesting than the trend. The total number of autistic children born between 1960 and 1965 was very low, between zero and three per year. Starting with children born in 1966, however, the number rose rapidly into the teens, reaching a maximum of twenty-one in 1972, with children who would have been five years old at the time of screening.

Did this sharp rise have anything to do with the Kanose factory's mercury emissions that caused an outbreak of Minamata disease in 1965? Could women who became pregnant during or after 1965 have accumulated toxic levels of mercury in their own bodies that they then passed on to their fetuses? It seems to have been an idea that the study team considered and rejected, although there is no mention of the Niigata episode in the paper. Their interpretation of this sharp increase was outlined in the discussion section of the paper, in the first paragraph.

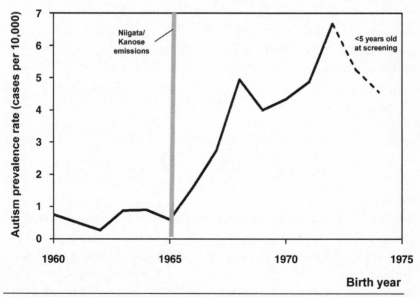

Figure 4—Autism Prevalence by Birth Cohort in Fukushima Prefecture 1960–1976

Source: Based on data from Y. Hoshino, H. Kumashiro, Y. Yashima, et al., "The Epidemiological Study of Autism in Fukushima-ken," *Folia Psychiatr Neurol Jpn* (1982) 36(2): 115-24.

The prevalence rates of autistic children differed from year to year in this
research, and the prevalence rates of children born between 1968 and 1974
were significantly higher than those of children born before 1968 and after
1975. The reason for the low prevalence rates before 1967 was probably
that autistic children had become older, lost the unique feature of young
autistic children and had been overlooked in the preliminary examination.
The reason for the low prevalence rates after 1975 was probably that
autistic children were too young to be suspected as autistic in the
preliminary examination.[43]

The trajectory of autism rates is shown in Figure 4.

Most studies of autism prevalence show a lower prevalence rate in
early age groups, in whom the suspicion of autism has not yet arisen,
so the post-1975 data are not surprising. Younger age cohorts are frequently left out of autism prevelance surveys. But this effect is most
strongly seen in children five years of age or younger; the CDC standard is eight years old. Experience has shown that by eight years ascertainment is relatively complete. It is highly unlikely that the ascertainment
of autism changed radically enough in Fukushima between the nine- and
twelve-year-old cohorts to explain an 88 percent decline in detection
and diagnosis rates.

This was a compelling association between alkyl mercury and an
otherwise unexplained spike in an autism rate. Were there similar connections to be found in the first case reports of autistic children in the
medical literature?

Planting the Seed

In 1936 a scientist named Frederick Lovejoy Wellman began working at
the U.S. Department of Agriculture's main research center, part of its
Bureau of Plant Industry. The bureau's sprawling mandate ranged from
fruits, vegetables, and cereals to cotton, tobacco, drugs, and rubber,
from the Division of Farm Machinery to the Division of Forest
Pathology—anything that grew and could be turned into products came
within its purview. The Beltsville Agricultural Research Center—

BARC, a nicely bucolic acronym—was sprawling, too. Its thousand acres of experimental farmland were dotted with dairy barns and laboratories and grazing animals, located just beyond the bustle of the nation's capital.

An environment that seemed more Wisconsin than Washington must have made Wellman feel at home—he earned his Ph.D. in plant pathology from the University of Wisconsin–Madison. This was the last big year of the Dust Bowl, which massively deepened the miseries of the Great Depression. The urgent need for better farming methods created opportunities for bright and idealistic young scientists like Wellman—and Congress had passed a law in 1935 mandating more basic agricultural research.

At Wisconsin, he had written his thesis on a type of cabbage fungus. Home to a large population of German immigrants, Wisconsin is the· nation's largest producer of cabbage intended for processing; lots of that ends up as sauerkraut served with bratwursts and beer. Handwritten notes show Wellman in 1922 summarizing research conducted by one of his teachers, a national pioneer in the field named J. C. Walker, on formaldehyde and mercuric chloride as fungicides: "Of these two treatments the mercuric chloride seems to be slightly superior in eradicating the fungus," Wellman wrote. "It is true, however, that many lots of seed will stand much more severe treatment, especially with mercuric chloride, but in event of such treatment preliminary tests should always be made."[44]

The first independent research paper in Wellman's extensive professional archive picks up on mercuric chloride (the kind used in Van Swieten's liquor to treat syphilis). It was a simple experiment to kill a common cabbage-seed fungus without killing off the seed, too, always a fine line in formulating targeted toxins. Notice the hands-on approach; it demonstrates why lab workers used to be called "bucket chemists":

> A number of infected seeds were counted out and divided into lots. These lots were treated with water at 50 degrees centigrade for 15 and 30 minutes. Lots were treated with Mercurid [sic] Chlorid. (1:500) solutions for 30, 60, and 120 minutes. Control was obtained by dipping the seeds in 50% alcohol for a few seconds (to remove the "bloom") and then into a 1:1000 mercuric chlorid solution for 1 minute and then rinsed twice in sterile water. The lots treated with mercuric chlorid were shaken vigorously at first to get thorough contact with the solution and at the end of the period of treatment the seeds were rinsed in sterile water at least twice.[45]

While at Wisconsin, Wellman met his future wife, a fellow student, Wisconsin native Dora U'Ren. After getting his Ph.D., he worked one year for the United Fruit Company in Honduras—the intense steaming heat, Wellman reported back to Madison, was not to his liking—then signed on with the Department of Agriculture. At the Beltsville research center, he attacked the same foes, now better armed with the new generation of far more toxic organic mercury fungicides. A résumé of his professional experience through 1940 noted eighteen years studying thirty-two different kinds of parasitic fungi. Elsewhere in the same document, he described experiments with "disinfection of cabbage, onion and tomato seeds."[46] Wellman knew he was handling highly toxic substances, and by the standards of the day he was being careful (a photo Wellman kept of himself standing in the lab of the United Fruit Company in Honduras, though, shows just how many dusts, fumes, and liquids surrounded the bucket chemists of the day).

Onion seed treatments he had personally experimented with included "organic mercury compounds. . . . Formaldehyde treatments with both dust and liquids and proprietary organic mercury dusts were found most satisfactory." Cabbage seed treatments included "proprietary organic mercury compounds." Again, organic mercury was among the "most satisfactory disinfecting agents." Tomato seed treatments included "mercury bichloride . . . and organic mercury compounds." Once again, "organic mercury dusts also gave good results."

Because Wellman described them as "proprietary," we know these were the patented, commercially available products and not his own laboratory concoctions. The memorabilia folder in his archives contains advertising pamphlets for them: dust and liquid formulations of Ceresan, the ethylmercury seed disinfectant patented by Morris Kharasch in the 1920s and introduced commercially by the DuPont-Bayer collaboration; and liquid Semesan, another of the firm's organic mercury compounds.[47] This places ethylmercury dusts in the hands of Frederick L. Wellman in a laboratory setting—and inevitably on his clothes, in his house, on his family. (According to the CDC's toxicological profile for mercury, "You can be exposed to mercury vapors from the use of fungicides that contain mercury. Excess use of these products may result in higher-than-average exposures. . . . Family members of workers who have been exposed to mercury may also be exposed to mercury if the worker's clothes are contaminated with mercury particles or liquid.")[48]

In the midst of this work, in May 1936, Dora Wellman gave birth to their first child. They named him Frederick Creighton Wellman III and called him Wikki as an infant, then Creighton.

Creighton's namesake, his grandfather, was an astonishing, larger-than-life character who titled his autobiography *Life Is Too Short*.[49] Even so, the first Frederick Creighton Wellman managed to lead medical missions to Africa, run a manganese mine in Brazil, and serve as the director of both the Denver Art Museum and the Tulane Medical School. He even had a bug named after him—*Wellmanius wellmani*, a parasite of Angolan antelopes. The patriarch's personal life was at least as eventful: He ran off to Europe with a novelist not his wife, changed his name to Cyril Kay-Scott, wrote three novels, and did not resurface as his former self for twenty-five years, after which he picked back up with his surprisingly indulgent adult children (no wonder it took two *Who's Who* entries, one under each name, to contain him).

Those five Wellman children were prismatic offspring of the charismatic patriarch, each a reflection of at least one of his many talents. The eldest was a newspaperman; next came a professional singer; then a writer for adventure magazines; a plant pathologist (Frederick Lovejoy Wellman, Creighton III's father), and last a painter/writer/radio commentator.

Frederick L. Wellman approached plant pathology with a passion befitting his peripatetic father. The first chapter in his 1971 book *Plant Diseases; An Introduction for the Layman* begins with a stark depiction of what can happen without the contributions of plant pathologists.

"There are many plant diseases that have destroyed important food crops causing poverty, misery, hunger, and, finally, the ugliest thing in all human experience: famine," he wrote. "I have seen and smelled villages in the last stages of famine. . . . To me, privileged, fed, and protected, the sight seemed an impossibility."[50]

Given his pedigree and his family's professional background, when Creighton was born in 1936, his parents had every reason to expect their child would make his mark. He did, but not in a way they could have imagined.

There were problems from the start. Before the birth, Dora Wellman had kidney trouble, a common symptom of mercury exposure, and the baby was delivered three weeks early by cesarean section. Creighton began exhibiting unusual behaviors very early on. He never offered the anticipatory response babies display when they are about to be picked up. He proved too unsociable to attend nursery school—either hiding in the corner or pushing his way to the middle of a group of children.[51]

By age six, he was obviously in his own world, and his parents de-cided to take action. They made an appointment at Johns Hopkins Hospital—about thirty miles up the Baltimore-Washington Road from the agricultural research center—to have Frederick evaluated by Leo Kanner, who had arrived at Hopkins in 1928 from the Yankton State Hospital in South Dakota and established an innovative psychiatric clinic for children. Frederick Creighton Wellman III would become the second case study in Kanner's landmark paper on autism.

PART TWO

THE RISE

Entia non sunt multiplicanda praeter necessitatem.

(Entities must not be multiplied unnecessarily.)

Given two theories, all else equal,
the simpler is preferred.

—The law of ontological parsimony, also known as Occam's razor
for philosopher-theologian William of Occam, c. 1288–1348

CHAPTER SIX

GERMINATION

Since 1938, there have come to our attention a number of children whose condition differs so markedly and uniquely from anything reported so far, that each case merits—and, I hope, will eventually receive—a detailed consideration of its fascinating peculiarities.

—Leo Kanner, Autistic Disturbances of Affective Contact, April 1943[1]

In 1943 Leo Kanner profiled eleven anonymous children in his study that introduced autism to the world, assigning each child a case number and a first name and last initial—"Case 1: Donald T.," "Case 2: Frederick W.," and so on. In a contribution to the history of autism that is markedly different from anything reported so far, we have identified seven of those eleven cases by matching details described in the paper with publicly available information. Some names yielded to simple Internet queries; others required months of trial and error and more than a little luck. We have so far been unable to find the remaining four.

In identifying the children, all born in the 1930s, we also came across a critical shared clue—exposure to the ethylmercury compounds introduced during that decade, compounds that had an uncanny proximity of time and place in the backgrounds of most of the families. For example, Frederick Wellman's experiments within the fungicide branch of Morris Kharasch's ethylmercury innovations is especially well documented; to find this father of Kanner's Case 2 working with the new ethylmercury fungicides at exactly the time his son was born ought to give any fair-minded observer pause. Were that the only association, it would be quite startling, but there is more. In another case, one mother's work as a public health pediatrician frequently brought her into contact with the ethylmercury-containing diphtheria vaccine, pointing to the presence of a pharmaceutical vector in the same small group of children. Other families' backgrounds signal the same two connections less directly—yet put together, they suggest this is no coincidence.

As we have throughout the book, we do not claim proof but offer patterns of evidence—patterns that place ethylmercury and vaccination in close proximity to the index cases of autism. They make it more difficult to dismiss the theory that autism is an environmental illness triggered by a toxic insult in vulnerable children, and they strengthen the argument that the Age of Autism began as another sad chapter in the long hidden history of mercury poisoning.

Before the Deluge

In the 1930s and 1940s, Johns Hopkins Hospital was a magnet for teaching, research, and cutting-edge treatment, rivaled by few big-city hospitals. Aerial shots from the period show a complex stretching for many city blocks around the original, ornate redbrick building. Even today, surrounded by modern glass-and-chrome buildings connected with elevated walkways and parking garages, the domed structure in downtown Baltimore resembles a beacon, like the Salpêtrière in Paris—a secular Lourdes, dedicated to healing, to medical miracles, offering a last hope for the desperate. People from around the country came to take advantage of its specialties, among them the syphilis treatment headed by the nation's acknowledged expert, Dr. Joseph Earle Moore; pioneering surgery for "blue babies" with congenital heart defects that saved tens of thousands; and the psychiatric service, launched by the legendary Adolf Meyer.

Meyer was at the front lines of American psychiatry in the twentieth century. And he was in the front row when Freud came to America (for the first and only time in 1909) and delivered the lectures at Clark University in Worcester, Massachusetts, that launched the Freudian frenzy in the United States. Meyer, however, was no Freudian. He was an empiricist with an eclectic approach he called psychobiology, which considered both biology and family dynamics as causal; he pioneered the use of detailed case reports in assessing psychiatric patients. One of his students, Wendell Muncie, wrote, "For almost half a century American psychiatry has been enriched by the work of Adolf Meyer."[2]

Psychobiology, according to Muncie in his book *Psychobiology and Psychiatry*, "is the study of those functions distinctively human, the things man is best known for, the mentally integrated performances. The study demands knowledge of the physical sciences and of anatomy and physiology, but those in no wise [way] explain the phenomena under observation. Their explanation must be in terms appropriate to the complexity of their level of integration: biological, but of a type operating with more or less consciousness, a hanging together in a flow with symbolization."[3] This description, with its mind-body integration and almost Eastern emphasis on consciousness as the mechanism through which human life is mediated, stands up quite well today (much better than classical Freudianism, as we outlined in chapter 2).

Adolf Meyer was the doctor to whom Leo Kanner wrote in 1928 from his position at the Yankton State Hospital, responding to the announcement of a psychiatric fellowship at Hopkins. Meyer interviewed Kanner at a conference both attended in Minnesota, and took note of the thirty-year-old's initiative—his papers on the rare incidence of general paralysis of the insane in Native Americans, as well as his original and comprehensive book *Folklore of the Teeth*, published the year before. But Meyer wondered whether Kanner was too research-oriented for the post, and although he responded with interest, he did not explicitly offer it to him.

Kanner, who had already navigated the considerably greater leap from Berlin to Yankton, seized the moment and simply announced when he would arrive at Hopkins. Once there, he never left; the fellowship turned into a faculty post and Kanner rose quickly. In 1930 Meyer and a famed Hopkins pediatrics professor, Edwards A. Park, put him in charge of the first children's psychiatric service within a pediatric department in the United States. By 1935 Kanner had published his groundbreaking textbook *Child Psychiatry*, a comprehensive diagnostic handbook for children's disorders. For the first time, every known childhood disorder was described in rich detail; Kanner had observed most of them firsthand among the many hundreds of children referred to Hopkins in his first years there, and his voracious reading and scholarly bent allowed him to develop a sweeping command of the field.

The textbook's 527 pages—with prefaces by Meyer and Park—apply the psychobiological approach to childhood disorders and catalog minor psychoses, including what was still known as hysteria; major psychoses like schizophrenia; organic disorders such as juvenile paresis—the tragic occurrence of general paralysis of the insane in children with congenital syphilis—and even Mongolism. "The present volume," Kanner wrote, "which is the first textbook of child psychiatry in the English language, is offered as an attempt to cover the entire field of children's personality disorders on a broad, objective, unbiased, practical basis. It has grown out of everyday contact with pediatricians, consultation work in a large pediatric clinic and dispensary, collaboration with private practitioners and with the various child-caring agencies of the community (schools, orphanages, hospitals, welfare groups, courts, custodial and correctional institutions), and teaching activities at the Johns Hopkins School of Medicine."[4]

Nothing remotely resembling autism appears in this "attempt to cover the entire field of children's personality disorders," so when Kanner described the autism cases he would soon encounter as different from anything ever reported, he deserves to be taken seriously. But it wasn't just the lack of earlier cases that we find so persuasive as evidence of an environmental risk for autism. It is the *kind* of families that started showing up in Leo Kanner's office.

Kanner's Discovery

The "well-baby visit" to the doctor for a checkup and vaccinations is the foundation of modern pediatric practice. Yet the concept is a relatively recent innovation. A pioneering program in the 1930s at the Harvard School of Public Health helped create the model.

"This Center was planned mainly to provide facilities for research upon well children equivalent to those of other departments concerned with the study of sick children," states a 1939 report by Harvard's experimental Center for Research in Child Health and Development. "The Center was also intended to afford an opportunity for students to become familiar with normal child development and preventive pediatrics."[5]

That opportunity included X-rays, dental observations, a detailed health history, dietary records and advice, even observations regarding the child's daily routine, from rest to exercise. "They also deal with the types of games indulged in and the mechanical toys available. They record progress toward walking and other accomplishments, evidence of emotional reactions to play, and evidence of fatigue."

Vaccines were a key part of the protocol. At nine months, the visits involved "routine examinations, routine interviews with mother, and diphtheria toxoid inoculation"; at twelve months, a Schick test to determine whether the diphtheria shot had taken effect, "and vaccination." By the late 1930s, the ethylmercury preservative called thimerosal had been widely adopted as part of mass vaccination with diphtheria toxoid; anyone receiving a diphtheria shot would have received an exposure to ethylmercury along with it. It is unclear whether the doctors and nurses who ran the program were also vaccinated, but it seems logical given the availability of the shots and the risk of infection that goes with dealing with susceptible children on a daily basis.

Seven pediatricians were part of the project. One of them, Elizabeth Peabody Trevett, was on a fellowship at Harvard after graduating from Johns Hopkins School of Medicine. She had three children in quick succession during this period.

By the time the fellowship ended, so had her marriage to Laurence Trevett, a neuropsychiatrist she met and married in 1931 when both were working on their medical degrees at Hopkins. Laurence Trevett, board certified in both neurology and psychiatry, had coauthored a 1945 paper on neurosyphilis—"Penicillin Treatment of Neurosyphilis"— which made clear that treatment of advanced forms like general paralysis of the insane was part of his practice and training.[6]

After the divorce, Elizabeth moved back to Maryland with her children, working a couple of years at Hopkins before settling in Annapolis, probably because of its proximity to her medical roots, and perhaps since a children's health program similar to the one she helped develop at Harvard was just getting under way there.[7]

Dr. Peabody—she sometimes used her maiden name professionally— continued to promote well-baby care for infants and children to stave off deadly illnesses, in the same way Frederick Wellman approached plant pathology as a weapon against famine, starvation, and death; it was her calling. "Dr. Elizabeth Peabody, well-known pediatrician in Annapolis, gave a timely talk yesterday at the monthly Parent-Teachers Association meeting of the Annapolis Grammar School held at the school," the Annapolis *Capitol* reported in April 1947:

> She spoke upon communicable diseases and outlined their prevention or control, a subject of vital interest to most parents. . . .
>
> Too many parents, said Dr. Peabody, have the proper shots given and then relax, forgetting that booster shots are needed and that immunization does wear off. Speaking specifically of some of the most prevalent ailments, she stated that a child cannot be vaccinated against smallpox too often and it should be done for the first time when a baby is between three months and one year of age. In the case of diphtheria, booster shots are extremely important.[8]

Meanwhile, children's welfare took on a poignant personal dimension for Elizabeth Peabody. Her son John, born in 1937 while she was part of Harvard's well-baby project, was never well, developmentally speaking. At first he appeared mentally retarded; she considered him "always slow and quiet." There was concern that he might be deaf because "he did not register any change of expression when spoken to or when in the presence of other people; also, he made no attempt to speak or to form words."[9]

John was the youngest of the three children; there were serious concerns as well with the oldest, a girl. She danced in circles, made strange noises, would say "you" when she meant "I," and ignored other people completely. But she seemed to "blossom out" after the divorce, her mother said.

John did not. His mother took him to see Leo Kanner in February 1941, and under the pseudonym "Herbert B.," he became Case 7 in Kanner's landmark series.

But the case that first alerted Kanner to the new syndrome he came to call autism was not a child from Maryland or a professional medical colleague. Instead, he was the son of a lawyer and a former schoolteacher who lived in the small lumber town of Forest, Mississippi. Kanner called him "Case 1: Donald T."

Donald T.'s full name was Donald Gray Triplett; his father was O. B.

Triplett, Jr., known by his middle name, Beaman. He was an attorney, "successful, meticulous, hard-working," who had earned his law degree with honors from Yale a decade earlier. If anything he might have been excessively conscientious—two "breakdowns" by age thirty-five were attributed to the strain of work; he also had asthma.[10]

The Tripletts were an old, affluent, and respected Forest family; Beaman's father was a lawyer, too, a pillar of Forest—he had served as mayor, as a school and church trustee, and as chancery clerk. Donald's mother, Mary McCravey Triplett, was a former schoolteacher with an impressive pedigree of her own—a graduate of Belhaven College in Jackson and daughter of the founder of the Bank of Forest, the most imposing building in town.

Beaman Triplett and Mary McCravey wed on June 19, 1930. Their circumstances were more fortunate than most in that first full Depression year, and they acquired seven acres on the edge of town where they built an unpretentious but comfortable wood house for their anticipated family, with a large screened porch and tall windows to look out on the flowers and the trees and the children who would play on the broad lawn. Donald was born September 8, 1933, full term, near seven pounds, the first child of this first family of Forest.

There were difficulties from the start. "Eating has always been a problem with him," his father wrote. "He has never shown a normal appetite. Seeing children eating candy and ice cream has never been a temptation to him." At age four he weighed no more than thirty pounds, a third underweight.

That was the least of it. Donald displayed a combination of startling gifts and strange behaviors—fascinating peculiarities, one might say.

First, the gifts: "He could hum and sing many tunes accurately" by age one—he possessed, in fact, the rare endowment of perfect pitch.[11] He had "an unusual memory for faces and names, knew the names of a great number of houses" in Forest. He knew the Twenty-third Psalm and the twenty-five questions and answers of the Presbyterian catechism. He knew the presidents from their pictures as well as "most of the pictures of his ancestors and kinfolk on both sides of the house." He could recite the alphabet backward and forward and count to one hundred.

When it came to relating to his parents or anyone else, though, Donald was markedly and uniquely different because of his *in*difference; he appeared to inhabit a universe of one. He was happiest when left alone, seldom went to his mother, failed to notice his father's comings and goings or anyone else's—even ignored Santa Claus. "He seems to be self-satisfied," his father wrote. "He seems almost to draw into his shell and live within himself."

What did interest him, starting in his second year, was "spinning blocks and pans and other round objects." His use of language was downright bizarre—he treated words as some kind of magic spell, as if summoning them in the right order could ward off unseen demons. If he wanted to get down from the crib after his nap, he would instruct his mother, whom he called Boo: "Boo say, 'Don, do you want to get down?'" After she complied, he would tell her, "Now say, 'All right.'"

He reversed pronouns as if he had no sense of self and other. When he stumbled but recovered, he said: "*You* did not fall down." Words took on idiosyncratic meanings that were fixed in place like quick-drying cement; Donald named each of his watercolor bottles for one of the Dionne quintuplets, who were then a media sensation—Annette for blue, Cecile for red, and so on. The word "yes" meant only one thing—he wanted his father to put him on his shoulders. This derived from Beaman's use of the activity to teach Donald "yes" and "no," but once "yes" came to stand for that, it stood for nothing else. When he was asked to subtract four from ten, he answered, "I'll draw a hexagram," a six-sided object that expressed the right answer in a language all his own.

His parents, naturally, were baffled and alarmed; they marshaled their considerable resources to try to help their firstborn. One summer they brought home from the local orphanage a boy Donald's age to try to draw him out, but "Donald has never asked him a question nor answered a question nor romped with him in play." They bought him a slide in the summer of 1937, hoping it might encourage playful interaction with other children, but he would only use it when no one else was around.

That August they placed him in a tuberculosis sanitarium to see if a change of environment would help; it did not. He gained weight, but developed a new habit of repeatedly shaking his head from side to side. The next year, their family doctor, stymied by this utterly typical-looking but completely unreachable child, suggested a consultation with the leading child psychiatrist in the United States.

So in October 1938, when Donald was five years old, the Tripletts set out from Forest by train to meet Leo Kanner. They traveled east across the pine forests of southern Mississippi, past the sawmills that hugged the tracks. The mills were mostly silent now, felled by the deepening Depression. The big lumber companies—Eastman-Gardiner, Bienville,

Marathon—were in financial distress. In their place, the New Deal was creating the Bienville National Forest around Forest in Scott County, putting thousands of unemployed young men to work in the Civilian Conservation Corps planting millions of seedlings.

Before Donald's arrival in Baltimore, Beaman Triplett sent Hopkins a thirty-three-page letter describing his son's behavior and background. But actually meeting Donald must have been electrifying for someone of Kanner's observational powers and professional ambition. Years later, he described this moment. "In 1938, five-year-old Donald T., brought to my clinic from Forest, Mississippi, made me aware of a behavior pattern not known to me or anyone else theretofore. When I saw a few more children presenting similar characteristics, I reported in 1943 eleven cases in some detail in a now extinct journal, *The Nervous Child*. This is the article so frequently cited ever since."[12]

No doubt influenced by Adolf Meyer's emphasis on detailed case histories, Kanner's accounts of those eleven original autistic children are as complete and compelling as any that have followed in the intervening decades. After a one-paragraph introduction ("Since 1938, there have come to our attention a number of children . . ."), he goes straight to "Case 1: Donald T.," who takes up five pages of observation and background. After that, the order in which the children appear in "Autistic Disturbances" seems idiosyncratic, following neither birth order nor the sequence in which they arrived. In fact, Donald was not the first case seen at Hopkins: In 1935 a three-and-a-half-year-old boy named David Speck was brought for evaluation by his mother, Miriam, a psychologist. She had separated from her husband, John, a chemist and attorney in the U.S. Patent Office in Washington, shortly after David's birth, and moved back in with her parents in Baltimore in the summer of 1932.

David's unusual behavior was duly noted in his Hopkins medical file. His mother reported: "Language developed slowly; he seemed to have no interest in it. He seldom tells experience. He still confuses pronouns. . . . Since he talked, there has been a tendency to repeat over and over one word or statement. . . . He is upset when the sun sets. He is upset because the moon does not always appear in the sky at night. He prefers to play alone; he will get down from a piece of apparatus as soon as another child approaches."[13]

In "Autistic Disturbances" Kanner made note of David Speck's 1935 visit to Hopkins (he calls him "Case 8: Alfred L."), so it is not clear why he would assert in later years that Donald, not David, was the very first, or sentinel, case—an important position in medical literature. Perhaps Kanner himself did not evaluate David on that initial visit in 1935. But *someone* apparently connected the dots: In August 1938, about the time Beaman Triplett's letter describing Donald arrived, the clinic asked David's mother for a follow-up report. They apparently were preparing for their exotic visitor from Forest.

Today, Baltimore is just a plane ride from almost anywhere in the world, but the effort and outreach it took to bring Donald from small-town Mississippi to the temple that Kanner once wryly called "the great Hopkins" should not be overlooked. It's nothing short of remarkable.

In order of arrival at Hopkins, then, David Speck in 1935 came first, followed by Donald Triplett in 1938. In 1939 came "Elaine C.," whom Kanner described as a daughter of a father who had studied at the Sorbonne and a magazine-editor mother; and in 1940 "John F.," whom we have identified as Lee Rosenberg, son of a Maryland psychiatrist. Then in close succession during an eighteen-month period between 1941 and 1942 came seven more: "Herbert B." (John Trevett, son of pediatrics pioneer Elizabeth Peabody Trevett), "Richard M." (son of William Dykstra Miller, a forestry professor in North Carolina), "Paul G.," "Barbara K." (real name: Bridget Muncie, daughter of Wendell Muncie, the colleague of Kanner and Meyer at Hopkins who wrote *Psychobiology and Psychiatry*), "Frederick W." (Frederick C. Wellman III, whose story we told in chapter 5), and the eldest child, "Virginia S." The last child seen was Charles N., in February 1943. So—eleven children, all born in the 1930s, arriving within eight years of each other.

Kanner quickly realized he was witnessing what any medical researcher hopes to encounter once in a lifetime—a new illness or clinical entity, in this case a distinctive developmental disorder. Fortunately, the opportunity to publish this discovery was close at hand: He had been invited to guest-edit an issue of a new medical journal, *The Nervous Child*, and he told Ernest Harms, a psychiatrist friend who was its editor, about his idea.

"As to the issue due early in 1943, I wonder what you think of the general topic, 'Affective Contact of Children'?" Kanner wrote Harms on January 19, 1942, showing that the pattern had formed in his mind at least a year and a half before publication, when he had seen eight of the eleven cases. "I might have [a] paper of my own on 'Autistic Disturbances of Affective Contact in Small Children.' I have followed a number of children who present a very interesting, unique and as yet

KANNER'S ORIGINAL 11 CASES

	Case Name	Real Name	Birth Date (referred)	Father's Name	Father's Occupation	Mother's Maiden Name	Mother's Occupation
1	Donald T.	Donald Gray Triplett	9/8/33 (10/38)	Oliver B. Triplett	Lawyer	Mary McCravey	English teacher
2	Frederick W.	Frederick Creighton Wellman III	5/23/36 (5/42)	Frederick L. Wellman	Plant pathologist	Dora U'Ren	History teacher and secretary
3	Richard M.	–	11/17/37 (2/41)	William D. Miller	Forestry professor	Catherine Ritchey	Organist/music teacher
4	Paul G.	–	1935 (3/41)		Mining engineer		
5	Barbara K.	Bridget Muncie	10/30/33 (2/42)	Wendell S. Muncie	Psychiatrist	Rachel Cary	Nurse
6	Virginia S.	–	9/13/31 (10/42)		Psychiatrist		
7	Herbert B.	John Trevett	11/18/37 (2/41)	Laurence D. Trevett	Psychiatrist	Elizabeth Peabody	Pediatrician
8	Alfred L.	David Newcomb Speck	6/20/32 (11/35)	John R. Speck	Patent examiner	Miriam Partridge	Psychologist
9	Charles N.	–	8/9/38 (2/43)		Clothing merchant		Theatrical booking agent
10	John F.	Lee Ruven Rosenberg	9/19/37 (2/40)	Seymour J. Rosenberg	Psychiatrist	Ruth Roman	Pathology lab stenographer
11	Elaine C.	–	2/3/32 (4/39)		Advertising copywriter		Magazine editorial work

unreported condition, which has both interested and fascinated me for quite some time. In fact, eventually I plan to use the material for a monographic presentation."[14]

And so, in April 1943, Kanner announced the disorder to the world in a journal whose archaic-sounding name he perceived as a minor drawback. (In later years he seemed to relish pointing out that while his discovery of autism stood the test of time, *The Nervous Child* was long gone.) As the guest editor for volume 2, number 2, Kanner wrote the introduction: "This symposium deals with the consideration of children's abilities to form affective contact with people. . . . This writer has encountered a number of children whose behavior from earliest infancy raises the question of the existence of an innate inability to form affective contact with people in the ordinary way to which the human species is biologically disposed."[15]

But what was on Kanner's mind as he assembled these cases into a series? Obviously, he wanted to create a clear and compelling narrative arc in which the children's behaviors emerged. So it made eminent sense to start with "Donald T.," the first case (at least in his own process of discovery) and the one whose savant qualities made him the most colorful. But we think the sequence of the eleven cases also points, perhaps inadvertently, to something else.

These cases are, we believe, in two distinct but connected clusters— three cases have links to agriculture or forestry ("Donald T.," "Frederick W.", and "Richard M."—Cases 1, 2, and 3), and in five of them the parents came from backgrounds in medicine, psychology, or psychiatry ("Barbara K.," "Virginia S.," "Alfred L.," "Herbert B.," and "John F."—Cases 5, 6, 7, 8, and 10). Another child—"Case 4: Paul G."—fits loosely with the first cluster that suggests an occupational risk. The other two children—"Case 11: Elaine C." and "Case 9: Charles N."—appear to have big-city Boston and New York backgrounds that could fit the second cluster.

The Fungicide Cluster

In the 1920s Madison, Wisconsin, was the place to be for a smart young agricultural scientist like Frederick Lovejoy Wellman—it was quickly becoming a locus for the emerging fields of plant and forest pathology. In addition to the university's pathology department, the U.S. Department of Agriculture's Forest Service had created the Forest Products Laboratory, the nation's leading wood research institute, in Madison in 1910.

In chapter 5 we described the universe of Morris Kharasch, his invention of an ethylmercury fungicide and the commercial products marketed by DuPont and Bayer. Those were launched into a world of practicing plant industry professionals, including government scientists, and moved from research chemists like Julius Steiglitz and Kharasch at the universities of Chicago and Maryland, to research chemists working inside DuPont, to clusters of research plant pathologists like Wellman, to the gardeners, farmers, and foresters who actually used these fungicides in their war on plant disease.

The 1930 edition of the University of Wisconsin plant pathology department's alumni newsletter, *Wisconsin Pathogen*, traces an unusually interesting subset of these close professional connections. In Figure 5 we show the central role of this department and how easy it is to connect the pioneers of ethylmercury fungicides (Kharasch, Engelmann, Lindgren) with the families of two of its first victims.

"Our family is increasing in size with each group of graduates, and everyone who leaves our circle has an interesting story to tell and always holds a warm place in his heart for the happenings around the laboratory."[16]

Figure 5—Plant Pathology Network

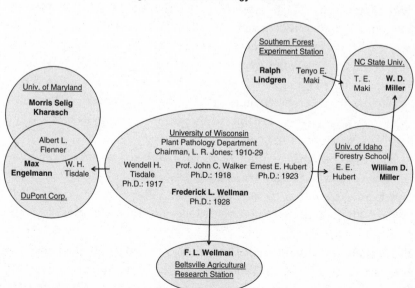

The *Pathogen* noted that recent graduate Wellman was "a pathologist for the United Fruit Company at Tela, Honduras Central America" (and that he hated the weather). Slightly older alumni were already reaching the top of the field. W. H. Tisdale, who earned his Ph.D. from Wisconsin in 1922, the year Wellman arrived, had just been named to a key post in private industry.

"W. H. Tisdale is Chief Pathologist for the recently organized Bayer Semesan Company, Inc.," the *Pathogen* reported. "The new Corporation has taken over the agricultural disinfectants divisions of the Bayer Company and the DuPont Company." Bayer Semesan is the joint venture we described earlier that marketed the organic mercury fungicide Semesan and was about to launch Ceresan.

Time magazine, in its inimitable style, caught up with Tisdale in April 1937. "Dr. Tisdale, a big, florid Alabaman of 45, is director of Du Pont's new anti-pest laboratory which was formally opened last week in the suburbs of Wilmington, and of which the formal name is Pest Control Research Section, Grasselli Chemicals Department, E. I. du Pont de Nemours & Co. A handful of newshawks assembled in the gleaming Nemours building, lunched with Lammot du Pont, who shook each one's hand, spent the afternoon in the battleship-grey laboratory, wound up at the Hotel du Pont bar. . . .

"On its staff are two plant pathologists, six entomologists, four chemists, some 20 assistants. With an initial investment of $100,000, the laboratory's operating cost is expected to be $125,000 a year. Object is to find new and better insecticides which Du Pont can sell to farmers, nurserymen, fishermen, manufacturers, housewives."[17]

Pest control was a family business for the Tisdales. W. H. Tisdale's brother, W.B., was a plant pathologist who spent time at the University of Wisconsin, where he coauthored a paper with Frederick Wellman's mentor, J. C. Walker, on cabbage fungus, "Fusarium Resistant Cabbage," in November 1920.[18]

Another Wisconsin alumnus leads us directly to Case 3, not only connecting Wisconsin to another original case but connecting the lumber preservative Lignasan to the case as well. The *Pathogen* noted: "E.E. Hubert, Moscow, Idaho, gave us a call recently on his way back to Idaho from conference in Washington." Hubert got his Ph.D. from Wisconsin and by 1930 was a major force in the School of Forestry at the University of Idaho in Moscow. At the time he joined the Idaho faculty, Hubert had launched a large research project on the best ways to protect jointed wood products from the fungi that caused decay and stain. The work was summarized in a 1934 special issue of *The University of Idaho Bulletin.* "Corners were sawed off and put in glass evaporating dishes, a shallow indentation was carved out of the center in which to put the toxic experimental chemicals to see which ones prevented decay and stain."[19]

In 1932 William Dykstra Miller, a newly minted Yale School of Forestry Ph.D., arrived in Idaho and joined Hubert on the faculty of the School of Forestry as an instructor. Miller, whose undergraduate degree was from Reed College in Portland, was returning to his Northwestern roots. In November 1931, just before Miller arrived, "a rot cellar was constructed for the purpose of subjecting entire window sashes and large pieces of wood and wood products to conditions which favored decay and stain. . . . The chemical dissolves and spreads through the surrounding wood, thus protecting it against fungi by poisoning the wood which furnishes the food for the attacking organisms."[20]

This is the kind of work Frederick Wellman was engaged in on the other side of the country; his focus was on plants, not trees, and his specialty was seeds, not processed lumber. But the basic idea—identify a problem caused by fungi and then try a series of toxic chemicals to see which ones solved the problem—was strikingly similar. So was one of the substances tested by Hubert and his colleagues: Lignasan, the ethylmercury fungicide invented by Morris Kharasch, who also developed Ceresan, the ethylmercury fungicide with which Wellman experimented.

"Other chemicals of a toxic nature which proved effective are Lignasan, an organic mercury compound," Hubert wrote. A photo of a window sash was captioned: "Contrast the clearness of the right hand corners, which were treated with Lignasan, with the stained and decay-infected left hand corners which were treated with pyridine." Another compound Hubert tried was called Borax plus K-1, described as "an organic mercury compound." K-1 was the same experimental compound that Ralph Lindgren first used to prevent sap stain in southern Mississippi.

Hubert's project summary acknowledges, as Wellman did, the razor's edge on which this kind of research perched: "The toxic chemicals must diffuse readily through the wood; and the compound should not be harmful to humans nor cause injury to the paint coating."[21] In a department comprised of only a half-dozen faculty members, William Miller was certainly either directly involved with this project or working in close proximity to these toxic chemicals in the forest pathology laboratory.

———

Three years later, in 1935, William Miller got a job as an associate professor at North Carolina State University, one of the country's oldest and biggest forestry schools, which had recently acquired more than eighty thousand acres called the Hofmann Forest. It would operate as an experimental commercial forest—a golden opportunity for a research-oriented academic like Miller. He and his wife, Catherine (née Ritchey), packed up and headed east.

Two years later, on November 17, 1937, they had a son who in 1943 became "Case 3: Richard M." in Kanner's "Autistic Disturbances of Affective Contact." "Richard" fit the familiar pattern when he was referred to Hopkins on February 5, 1941: "The child seems quite intelligent," an intern reported to Kanner, "playing with the toys in his bed and being adequately curious about instruments used in the examination. He seems quite self-sufficient in his play. It is difficult to tell definitely whether he hears, but it seems that he does. . . . He does not pay attention to conversation going on around him, and although he does make noises, he says no recognizable words."

In the examination room, he paid no attention to anyone "but was attracted to a small box that he threw as if it were a ball. . . . His first move in entering the office (or any other room) was to turn the lights on and off. . . . He did not communicate his wishes but went into a rage until his mother guessed and procured what he wanted. He had no contact with people, whom he definitely regarded as an interference when they talked to him or otherwise tried to gain his attention."[22]

"Richard's" father spent the rest of his career as an associate professor at North Carolina State; summers found him working with students at the research camp deep in the Hofmann Forest. He was promoted to full professor when he retired, in 1963. That same year, Frederick L. Wellman arrived at North Carolina State as a visiting professor, meaning the fathers of Cases 2 and 3 crossed paths in a way that demonstrated the close connections between the worlds of plant and forest pathology and autism. Miller left nowhere near the paper trail Wellman did—the latter's archives at North Carolina state fill sixteen tightly packed boxes.

But Miller did write the school's official history of the Hofmann Forest and a handful of research papers; one of them, "Planting Pines in Pocosins," appeared in the *Journal of Forestry* in 1955.[23] (Pocosins are upland bogs that make up a significant portion of the South's forestland.)

Miller's coauthor on that paper was a colleague at the North Carolina State School of Forestry who also had close connections to Lignasan. Tenyo Ewald Maki, known as Waldy or Tenyo, was Hofmann Distinguised Professor of Forest Management and head of the department of silvilculture in the School of Forestry. Earlier in his career, Maki had worked at the Southern Forest Experiment Station in New Orleans, where Ralph Lindgren did his experiments with ethylmercury in 1929, 1930, and 1931.[24]

One of the three lumber companies that participated in the Experiment Station tests from the beginning—Eastman-Gardiner, based in Laurel, Mississippi—owned timberlands that extended north till they virtually bumped into those of Bienville Lumber, which was headquartered in Forest, Mississippi. It seems logical that Bienville and other, smaller mills in the area would have been among the early adopters of Lignasan, whose use had quickly spread to more than two hundred mills.

Forest, of course, is where Donald Triplett's parents built their house in 1930. Their next-door neighbor, from whom they acquired the seven-acre site, worked for a lumber company,[25] most likely Bienville. (Lumber companies in those days took care of their employees and built their houses, gray for white workers, red for blacks.)[26]

Despite its promising start, by 1933 Lignasan was showing limitations as a treatment for pine lumber, "with Lignasan failing frequently, in contrast to more favorable results in former years. This is attributed to the tendency of this material to volatilize slowly and leave the lumber unprotected in cases where seasoning is prolonged."[27] The ethylmercury was evaporating, albeit slowly, out of the wood, leaving it less protected from blue stain. From the forest pathologists' perspective, that was an efficacy problem. But for a pregnant woman or an infant, in an enclosed space like a house, the exposure to ethylmercury would be a safety concern of the first magnitude.

It is impossible to know, of course, whether the Tripletts' house would have harbored such a hazard for Mary and Beaman's Triplett's child, but it is reasonable to point out the proximities of time and place, given Frederick L. Wellman's and William Dykstra Miller's backgrounds. It offers a possible explanation for an otherwise odd pattern: Why were the first

three autism cases a child from Forest, Mississippi; the son of a plant pathologist; and the son of "a forestry professor in a southern University"?

The Medical Cluster

The second cluster that we've identified is not associated with agricultural industry exposures to mercury, but was possibly associated with
mercury exposure nonetheless. This cluster is exemplified by Elizabeth
Peabody. Her work on vaccination revolved around the medical world of
the 1930s, especially the new effort to vaccinate every infant against
diphtheria with the new diphtheria toxoid shot preserved with thimerosal—or ethylmercury. We've already traced Peabody's route from Boston to Annapolis to Johns Hopkins with her son John (whom Kanner
called Herbert B., no doubt to mask the identity of a family in the same
profession). But the first family that suggested the medical connection
was that of David Speck, whose mother, Miriam Partridge Speck, moved
with him back to Baltimore from Washington just a few weeks after he
was born, in the summer of 1932, to live with her parents.

She returned to a city that was in full battle mode against diphtheria.
The war had begun in 1931, with a drive to immunize the city's children
by six months of age. This coincided with the rise of the diphtheria toxoid
vaccine outlined in chapter 5, a new treatment that was an improvement
on the toxin-antitoxin formulation because it was more effective, caused
fewer obvious reactions and required only two shots, not three (the use of
aluminum as an adjuvant reduced that to one shot by the mid-1930s—a
public health officer's dream).

The city's residents were bombarded. "In January 1932, the Commis-
sioner of Health sent a circular to the city's private physicians that included
a diphtheria inoculation certificate to be given to parents," stated the city
health department's annual report. The same month, a six-month greeting
card program was inaugurated. The purpose of the card was to call attention to the fact that "six months is the best age for the child to receive from
a physician toxoid inoculations for the prevention of diphtheria."[28]

The campaign was stepped up the following year. "In terms of children given two successive doses of toxoid the 1933 campaign was emi-

nently successful," the health department reported. By the end of 1933 health officials estimated that 31.3 percent of children under five had received the required inoculations, up from 24.1 percent at the close of 1932. The 1933 campaign featured a minute-and-a-half film (called a "toxoid talkie trailer") shown in thirty-one movie theaters in metropolitan Baltimore in the first half of May. Officials estimated that half the population saw the film.[29]

Did this campaign reach Miriam Speck and her infant son, David? That seems likely; when she returned to Baltimore she began studying psychology at Hopkins, which was in the middle of its drive to vaccinate every child. Just as the campaign was getting under way, the Eastern Health District of Baltimore was established in 1932 as a joint project of the city health department and Johns Hopkins. It operated very much along the lines of the well-baby clinic at Harvard, as doctors and nurses tried to promote health and prevent infectious illness through routine screenings, better sanitation and diet, and vaccination.

"Many district services concentrated on child health problems such as measles, hearing impairment and dental health," noted Elizabeth Fee, a Hopkins professor who wrote the definitive history of the effort. "The district provided prenatal clinics and well baby clinics; free smallpox vaccinations; diphtheria anti-toxin; medical, dental, and eye examinations; child care instruction; doctor and hospital referrals; and a constant stream of health advice distributed to anyone who would read or listen."[30] Fee continued that public health clinics provided fifty thousand medical exams each year, roughly one per inhabitant, with a special focus on newborn children.

The Baltimore Sun reported: "Every child in the district, and a good share of adults, comes sooner or later into the grasp of a health officer or nurse. No child can escape. Some of them are under the benevolent dictation before they are born."[31]

As with the fungicide cluster, the association between exposure and outcome rests not on one case alone, but in the way the evidence converges and overlaps. Elizabeth Peabody Trevett's work with the well-baby clinic and its diphtheria vaccination component at Harvard is the most direct sign of a connection to heightened risk of infant vaccination with a thimerosal-containing vaccine in the first cases. In addition, any mother employed in medicine would also have been more likely to vaccinate herself while pregnant. The way some of the early cases clustered around Baltimore and its active anti-diptheria campaign starting in the early 1930s is also noteworthy.

In 1927 Wendell Muncie completed his medical degree at Johns Hopkins. He spent one year at Henry Ford Hospital in Detroit, and another in the far more glamorous American Hospital of Paris, before settling into his psychiatric residency at the Henry Phipps clinic at Hopkins. Although later in life he was an office psychiatrist, early in his career he clearly spent a substantial amount of time doing laboratory work; in 1929 he co-authored a paper titled "Neuro-Epithelioma of the Cerebellum," a review of the tumors of the central nervous system that was based on the collection of brain pathology specimens at the Henry Ford Hospital.[32]

Shortly after the paper was published, he married a Hopkins nurse, Rachel Cary, in a union that brought together two medical professionals and their associated exposure risks. On October 30, 1933, they had a daughter, Bridget. Like the other children we have profiled, she had unusual problems from the beginning (suggesting a greater role for exposure during pregnancy) and soon became "Case 5: Barbara K." in Leo Kanner's landmark paper. Kanner no doubt chose a pseudonym to disguise Wendell Muncie's identity from his Hopkins colleagues, and perhaps because of that close relationship, he treated the family better than he did some others in print: "Barbara's father is a prominent psychiatrist," he wrote. "Her mother is a well educated, kindly woman."[33]

When Kanner saw Bridget Muncie in 1942, she followed the pattern with which he was by now familiar. "During the entire interview there was no indication of any kind of affective contact," he wrote. She could speak and knew the days of the week, but according to her father—a fine writer and trained observer, as evidenced by his *Psychobiology* text—she was never normal. "Repetitious as a baby, and obsessive now: holds things in hands, takes things to bed with her, repeats phrases, gets stuck on an idea, game, etc., and rides it hard, then goes to something else. She used to talk using 'you' for herself and 'I' for her mother or me, as if she were saying things as we would in talking to her."

Like Donald, she also had feeding problems: She nursed poorly and "quit taking any kind of nourishment at 3 months. She was tube-fed five times daily up to 1 year of age. She began to eat then, though there was much difficulty until she was about 18 months old."[34]

Feeding problems also plagued "Case 10: John F.," whose real name was Lee Ruven Rosenberg and whose father was Seymour Rosenberg, another psychiatrist with roots nearby. Rosenberg got his M.D. from George Washington University in 1927, the same year Wendell Muncie graduated from Hopkins. He interned at St. Elizabeth's Hospital, the big federal psychiatric facility in Washington, where in 1933 he published a paper on "The Diathermy Treatment of Dementia Paralytica" (GPI),[35] suggesting, like Laurence Trevett, a background in the contemporary standard of syphilis care, mercury and arsenic rubs and injections.

The Rosenbergs' first child, Lee, was born in 1937. By 1938 the father was doing research in neurophysiology at Hopkins and was an assistant dispensary physician; by 1939 he was an assistant psychiatrist. Given that neurosyphilis remained one of the chief causes of psychiatric hospitalization and that the arrival of penicillin was still a few years away, Rosenberg certainly had an occupational risk for exposure to mercury and other toxic substances, as did Trevett and Muncie. They were first and foremost neurologists—brain doctors. And Rosenberg's wife had an even more direct link, similar to Wendell Muncie's link of brain tumor research. Ruth Roman had been a stenographer in a pathology lab at the Gallinger Municipal Hospital in Washington.

In "Autistic Disturbances," Kanner calls her a *secretary* in a pathology lab, but the more precise job description is significant. In the days before recording devices, pathologists like Muncie dictated their findings as they hovered over dead bodies and preserved tissue specimens—and stenographers like Roman hovered nearby to record their observations.

Mercuric chloride, as we've seen, was once the medical antiseptic of choice; a related and longer use was as a fixative to preserve tissue specimens and prevent contamination. The risk of mercuric chloride exposure to pathology lab workers was very real, documented in a 1977 paper in the *British Journal of Industrial Medicine*. "The use of mercuric chloride as an histological fixative was associated with high environmental atmospheric concentrations of mercury vapour . . . as well as mercury compounds. . . . Technicians exposed to this environment showed increased urinary mercury . . . Contamination of histology laboratories by mercuric chloride should be minimized."[36] If this was a problem in 1977, one can only imagine the exposures half a century earlier at Gallinger Municipal Hospital where Ruth Roman worked, and the Henry Ford Hospital where Wendell Muncie did his research.

We propose that this combination of background exposure to mercury combined with the diphtheria shot provides the simplest explanation for the "medical cluster" apparent in the first case series. The vaccine was probably also given to the children in the fungicide cluster; Donald Triplett's brother, O. B. Triplett III, had a specific recollection of their family receiving diphtheria shots in his childhood,[37] and in 1939 the Millers' home state, North Carolina, became an early adopter of the vaccine and the first in the nation to require it by one year of age.[38] ("Richard" was born there in November 1937.)

When Seymour Rosenberg reached out to Kanner about his son Lee's problems, it was not behavior that he focused on. "The main thing that worries me is the difficulty in feeding. That is the essential thing, and secondly his slowness in development. During the first days of life he did not take the breast satisfactorily. After 15 days he was changed from breast to bottle but did not take the bottle satisfactorily. There is a long story of trying to get food down. We have tried everything under the sun."[39]

From the beginning, then, feeding and gastrointestinal issues plagued a significant number of children with autism—problems serious enough to be a major feature of the case descriptions. It is a topic that will loom larger as we bring the history of autism into the present day.

In summary, in addition to the three cases of the fungicide cluster, we have traced the family backgrounds of four more of Kanner's original eleven autism cases, all of them with medical connections, sometimes in both spouses. The children of these medical professionals echo (if more weakly) the exposure themes of the children of the fungicide cluster. In all cases, there is a plausible mercury connection. In addition, there is an association in time—one we concede is speculative—with the newly emerging availability of the first thimerosal-containing vaccine. We find it noteworthy that these two completely different sources of exposure were based on ethylmercury compounds synthesized by the same inventor; others will have to judge for themselves.

Of the remaining four children we have been unable to identify among the first eleven, this much can be said: They share similar attributes.

"Case 4: Paul G." fits the environmental exposure model if the mother and child had occupational exposures through the father; Paul

G's father worked as a mining engineer. Coal contains mercury; mercury is used to extract gold and silver from ore because of its strong chemical bond; mercury itself is mined and its hazards are legendary; and mining makes heavy use of blasting materials that are detonated by mercury fulminate. Some background exposure to mercury in one form or another would have been almost inevitable.

"Case 9: Charles N.," the son of a self-made clothing merchant father and a mother who was a theatrical booking agent in Manhattan, also fits. Charles was born in 1938, putting him in New York City after it had taken a leading role in adopting universal diphtheria toxoid vaccination. "Case 11: Elaine C." fits, too; she was born in February 1932 in what was no doubt a large city that would support her Sorbonne-educated father with a law degree and an ad-copywriting background, and her mother, "who had done editorial work for a magazine before marriage." Elaine had been evaluated by a psychiatrist in Boston, and as we have seen from Elizabeth Peabody, the well-baby vaccination regimen had roots there, too.

And finally, the eldest child fits—"Case 6: Virginia S." Her father was a psychiatrist, too. Kanner focused on his personal qualities—he clearly loathed the man. Perhaps he knew him, or the fact that his daughter had by then been "dumped" in an institution for half her life offended him. "I have never liked children," he quotes the father saying, "probably a reaction on my part to the restraint from movement (travel), the minor interruptions and commotions." Of Virginia's mother, her husband said: "She is not by any means the mother type. Her attitude [toward a child] is more like toward a doll or pet than anything.'"

Whatever the case, it is also true that Virginia was born just in time to be caught up in the early wave of diphtheria vaccination in Baltimore or New York or Boston or another early-adopter location. We continue to search for this eldest child of the Age of Autism and whatever clues her identity may hold.

"I Object"

Not surprisingly, "Autistic Disturbances of Affective Contact" attracted immediate attention in the profession. J. Louise Despert, another leading

child psychiatrist—and in marked contrast to Kanner, a committed
Freudian—wrote him from New York City not long after its appearance. "I take this opportunity to tell you how interested I was in your
article, 'Autistic Disturbances of Affective Contact,' which appeared in
The Nervous Child for 1943. In that article you certainly have clearly and
concisely defined a clinical entity which had baffled many observers."
That was faint praise, given Kanner's claim that the disorder was previously unknown to him *or anyone else*. Despert added more faint praise, conceding that his work "will do much to bring order and clarity in the
confused mass of mental illnesses of the earliest years." But she couched
her true opinion in the praise she withheld, commenting, "Whether or not
the similarities with the previously described schizophrenia in childhood
should be later established is an issue to be resolved after further study."[40]

Despert resolved that issue quickly in her own mind. On July 12, just
three months after "Autistic Disturbances" appeared, she wrote Kanner:

> It seems to me the greatest contribution this article is making is in its
> thorough, accurate and illuminating description of clinical cases. However,
> if you will permit me to say so, I object to the coining of new terminology
> for entities which, while perhaps not so carefully described, have been
> previously reported.

She cited accounts by herself and others of "early childhood schizophrenia with insidious onset, the symptomatology of which is in all respects
similar to the entity you describe. . . . Even you in your textbook have
given a general definition of schizophrenia—'withdrawal from the environmental realities, etc.'—which does not necessarily imply an initial
normal development."[41]

Kanner, confident in the originality of his observations, replied with
artful courtesy. "I thank you very much for your very thoughtful and
very helpful letter, and I want you to know that in principle I am in full
agreement with its contents," he wrote back three days later, suggesting
an eagerness to knock down this potentially serious objection without
making an enemy of a powerful peer. "I also want you to know that I am
thoroughly familiar with your own work, which in my opinion and that
of many others, represents a genuine contribution to our knowledge of
schizophrenia." And he noted, "I have, as is inevitable, seen typical
schizophrenic children at a very early age."[42]

Kanner was familiar with childhood schizophrenia, having described it in detail in his textbook *Child Psychiatry;* the vast majority of these cases experienced regression in childhood—the period between three years of age and puberty. In his letter to Despert, he outlined the difference between autism and the previous medical literature on mentally ill children that Despert claimed as antecedents. The eleven children in "Autistic Disturbances," he said, "singled themselves out by their very distinctive phenomenology":

> What strikes me in the group which I have discussed in my paper is the apparent disability from the beginning of life to form adequate affective contact rather than withdrawal from adequate or near adequate contact already established. This is the essential thing which, in my mind, sets the group off from other infantile schizophrenics of my acquaintance or those reported in the literature.[43]

Kanner's focus on this point—these children were *born* this way—was evident throughout his paper, which he closed by describing the eleven children rather antiseptically as "pure culture examples of *inborn autistic disturbances of affective contact* [emphasis in original]." "Autism" at that time had a precise meaning in psychiatry, defined in the 1934 edition of *Webster's New International Dictionary* as "absorption in phantasy to the exclusion of interest in external reality." (*Autos* is Greek for "self," as in autobiography.) So it was not autism—isolation from external reality—as an element of childhood mental illness that Kanner claimed as his discovery; that would be like a contemporary physicist breathlessly announcing that hydrogen was an element of water. It was the absence of emotional connection from the very beginning of life, an absence so complete it was autistic—*that* was new.

"First of all," he wrote in the paper, "even in cases with the earliest recorded onset of schizophrenia . . . the first observable manifestations were preceded by at least two years of essentially average development; the histories specifically emphasize a more or less gradual *change* in the patients' behavior. The children of our group have all shown their extreme aloneness from the beginning of life, not responding to anything that comes to them from the outside world."[44]

Of course, "autism" has long since come to stand for the specific disorder Kanner identified; he himself soon began to call it "early infantile autism," continuing to emphasize through repetition—early *and* infantile—its appearance from the beginning of life. In recent years, a subset called regressive autism has emerged, with onset usually apparent between the first and second birthdays after a period of normal development—but this is still *infantile* autism and also distinct from the well-recognized phenomenon of childhood schizophrenia that both Despert and Kanner discussed. Strictly speaking, the transition from infancy to childhood as a developmental phase does not take place till about age three, when the toddler begins walking and talking and is fully weaned from his mother.[45]

Autism Is Not Ancient

Childhood schizophrenia was well established as a diagnostic category long before Despert wrote Kanner about it. In 1938—the same year "Donald T." arrived at Johns Hopkins from Forest, Mississippi—a researcher named R. A. Q. Lay, at Guy's Hospital in London, published a thorough review in a twenty-eight-page paper titled "Schizophrenia-Like Psychoses in Young Children."[46] Such a survey would be expected to capture any case descriptions matching Kanner's striking syndrome. But none had the unique cluster of behaviors Kanner laid out in such meticulous detail.

Let's pause for emphasis here, because the lack of comparable cases in this contemporaneous survey of medical literature is a powerful counter to glib assertions that autism is ancient, that "surely autistic disorder, like mental retardation, has been one of man's medical maladies from earliest times,"[47] that "the history of autistic disorders stretches far back into the mists of time,"[48] that the "cluster of symptoms we now know as autism has probably been around for a long time, but no one really knows for sure."[49]

Severe mental illness of any kind was quite rare in children, Lay concluded. "Strecker (1921) was able to find 18 cases of psychosis in children among 5,000 admissions [to mental hospitals]; of these, 4 were dementia praecox, 10 manic-depressive and 4 of doubtful type. All, however were over 10 years of age." The few early-onset cases Lay does describe are not easy to confuse with autism. In a discussion of manic illnesses in children, he notes, "Bleuler stated that in 5% of his cases the subjects could be shown to have been predisposed from the very beginning." And in cases with arguably autistic features, the onset is obviously later. Lay cites two researchers, Willhem Weygandt and Theodor Heller, who described children in the early 1900s in Vienna and Germany with what was called dementia infantalis. "After a period of normal development, during the third or fourth year of life there appeared, in the cases he described, a change of behavior involving a marked degree of motor restlessness. These symptoms were always accompanied by serious disturbances of speech, leading eventually to its almost complete loss, and the whole process ending in complete dementia within a few months. [Weygandt] drew attention especially to the intelligent facial expression of the patient, and to the absence of any neurological lesion or convulsions."

The Weygandt and Heller cases would most likely be diagnosed today with childhood disintegrative disorder, under the grouping of pervasive developmental disorders described in the U.S. *Diagnostic and Statistical Manual of Mental Disorders (DSM)*; the rate is vanishingly low, as infrequent as one in ninety thousand children. Kanner was well aware of them by the time he wrote "Autistic Disturbances," and he later noted that Heller's cases were behaviorally similar to his, but with later onset.[50]

So neither Leo Kanner's own exhaustive 1935 *Childhood Psychiatry* textbook nor Lay's contemporaneous review of medical literature offered any indication that autism was ancient. Many capable observers over a long period of time had observed, recorded, and published papers on unusual behaviors in children and had not found anything of the kind. Excluding Down's analysis, which includes no case descriptions, we are left with a handful of scattered cases on which the entire argument against the novelty of Kanner's discovery rests. Each of these deserves detailed attention.

Kanner himself cited one pre-1930 child as autistic—a girl named Jane described in "Case Report Twenty-Eight Years After an Infantile Autistic Disorder" by George C. Darr and Frederic G. Worden.[51] "In 1921 a four-year-old girl was brought to the Henry Phipps Psychiatric Clinic of the Johns Hopkins Hospital," Kanner wrote in a preface to this republication of the case. "From the descriptions by Dr. Adolf Meyer and Dr. Esther Richards, who saw her, it is apparent that the child presented a syndrome now called early infantile autism."

Meyer, of course, was Kanner's mentor, and Richards was a colleague. While certain features of the case are consistent with autism—the child "does not look into people's eyes"; "nothing makes a great deal of difference"; she is "not much affected by stimuli"; "is afraid of certain objects, e.g., the stove"—other aspects are not. As a teenager she "had to be admitted to the disturbed ward of a mental hospital because of confused episodes, periods of excitement, threatening to jump out of the windows, feeling that she was being poisoned, that she was full of gas, and that there was no oxygen in her blood. . . . She explained at length in fairly friendly fashion that she had chemical poisons within her and that if she lit a match she would explode." Delusions, or any description of inner life, are simply not characteristic of children with autism.

An alternative explanation: Perhaps she *was* poisoned; one scenario is this was a case of acrodynia. There is detailed discussion in Meyer and Richards' case report of teething—"the first tooth erupted at six months . . . the second-year molars had not come in"; teething powders might well have been tried in her hometown of Philadelphia in the second decade of the century. We suspect there may have been another reason for Kanner's embrace of this single case—a nod to his mentor and his colleague: "No wonder that psychiatrists of the caliber of Drs. Meyer and Richards felt that they were dealing with something unique, with something they had not encountered before and for which they had no frame of diagnostic reference," Kanner wrote.[52] Even accepting the notion that "Jane" was a classically autistic child, Kanner's comment shows his continued emphasis on how rare and identifiable it was. Kanner never focused on this case again; it's possible that as the children in his own original case series began to grow into adulthood, he realized they bore little resemblance to Jane, the thirty-year-old adult.

Another case that is sometimes cited might also be acrodynia; it was titled "Don: A Curable Case of Arrested Development Due to a Fear Psychosis, the Result of a Shock in a Three-Year Old Infant," by Lightner Witmer, a Philadelphia psychologist. "I saw Donald for the first time when he was two years and seven months old [in 1919]," wrote Witmer. "His father carried him into the office, and deposited him, a soulless lump, upon the couch. He sat there with the stolidity of a Buddhist image, absorbed in the inspection of a card he held in his pudgy hands, as regardless of his father and mother as of the new objects around him."[53]

His overall physical development was profoundly delayed, Witmer recounted. "As the flower blooms, the fish swims or the bird flies, so the child crawls, walks and talks. It is the unfolding of his own instinctive impulses. But this child had to be taught to crawl and to walk, and even then he could only toddle around uncertainly. He never uttered a word spontaneously." These could well be autistic features; they might also be neurological signs we have seen described in acrodynia: mutism, "the loss of the usual gay and happy disposition," the failure to "display any affection" that Rocaz described in such children. It could also have been a postencephalitic condition: "He had an illness after birth," Witmer wrote of "Don," "which I now believe left his brain so devitalized that it permitted fear to gain the upper hand over desire."

Three more cases with plausibly autistic features were described in a retrospective analysis of case histories taken from the notes of Dr. William Howship Dickinson at London's Great Ormond Street Hospital for Children between 1869 and 1882.[54] The authors, Mitzi Waltz and Paul Shattock, examined 398 cases before identifying 3 that fit the criteria. These again could implicate some combination of the environmental factors we have already pointed to as raising the risk for autism—from the coal-saturated London atmosphere to the widespread use of teething powders. In fact, the authors mention the latter: "It should be noted that mercury chloride [*sic*—mercurous] came into popular use as a patent-medicine sedative for teething babies in the later years of the nineteenth century and was revealed several decades later to cause widespread developmental and physical health problems, including the condition known as pink disease."

But since these three are among the strongest of the plausibly pre-Kanner autism cases, let's treat them as evidence. It is worth noting a common feature: "Many of the children with autistic symptoms described by Dickinson also presented with serious bowel disturbances. In one of the three cases described in this article, senna syrup, calomel (mercury chloride), and cod liver oil were used to address the issue with some success."

Going farther back, among the first to cite childhood mental illness was John Haslam at Bethlem asylum, the same observer who gave one of the earliest descriptors of general paralysis of the insane among adults. As we described previously, one case in particular stands out. This child developed normally until she was two years of age, when she had an adverse reaction to Jenner's new smallpox vaccine. "From the termination of the small-pox to the above date, (nine months) the child continued in an insane state."

About the same time as Haslam was writing, a new phenomenon

emerged: the so-called feral child. A classic case was Kasper Hauser (who had smallpox "inoculation scars on both arms, usually a sign of high birth");[55] another was Victor, the so-called Wild Boy of Aveyron. These cases captured widespread popular attention, illustrating if nothing else their extreme rarity. The idea that such feral children were really autistic was first promulgated by Bruno Bettelheim, a twentieth-century Austrian transplant to Chicago. Bettelheim had become the leading advocate of the theory that neglectful parents, and especially mothers, were responsible for their child's autism.

As Nicole Simon writes, "Bettelheim (1959) proposed that the non-human behavior of children like Victor is the result of parental neglect suffered long before abandonment in the wild. He based this notion on his observations of autistic children and his conclusion that autism results from emotional rejection of the child by his parents."[56]

The argument that feral children were actually early cases of autism is now accepted by many in the medical profession, and given as evidence of its constant prevalence through human history. In his 1979 book *The Wild Boy of Aveyron*, Harlan Lane notes that "several contemporary authorities on child psychiatry have proposed that Victor suffered originally not from mental retardation but from a personality disorder unidentified [then], childhood psychosis or autism."[57] But Lane argues that "the similarities between Victor and autistic children seem to be exaggerated. . . . It is simply impossible to describe Victor as profoundly withdrawn from people; many passages . . . testify to his affection toward those who were kind to him, his desire to please, his sensitivity to reproach."[58]

And to the extent that he did have autistic characteristics, "What is there about Victor's deviant behavior in society that cannot be explained by his adaptive behavior in the forest?" Furthermore, if he had been autistic when his parents abandoned him at age five, could he even have begun to survive in the woods?[59]

Whatever the case, these children were so rare and such intense objects of fascination as to argue *against* the idea that autism was already common during their times. They recall Leo Kanner's identification of Thomas Robertson, the Native American with general paralysis of the insane, which he said highlighted the fact "such a case is so rare that it is really regarded as a curiosity." A recent survey of the wild child phenomenon points to an early mention by Charles Linnaeus of just nine "wild men" over a period of several centuries.[60]

Autism, then, appeared to be what Leo Kanner said it was—a new disorder that differed strongly from those already described, rather than one that Kanner's discerning clinical eye finally managed to spot. The implications are enormous, because if autism was a new disorder, that argues for a largely environmental, rather than a genetic, cause.

In sum, both common sense and a careful review of case histories suggest that Leo Kanner meant what he said, and that what he said was right—autism was different. Bernard Rimland, a researcher and autism parent whom we will introduce in the next chapter, noted that Kanner earned his M.D. in 1919 in Berlin, came to Hopkins in 1928, "and has been reported to have seen well over 20,000 children in the course of his psychiatric career. . . . It is remarkable, in retrospect, that none of the [autistic] children were seen in Kanner's first 12 years of practice, and all 11 were born after 1930."[61]

It is also remarkable that a similar cluster of children appeared on another continent at the same time.

Vienna Again

In 1943, the same year Leo Kanner's landmark paper was published, an Austrian pediatrician, Hans Asperger, finished a study that centered on a case series of four boys and submitted it to a medical journal. It was titled "Autistic Psychopathy in Childhood" and published in 1944 at the height of World War II.[62] There was no contact between Kanner and Asperger before its publication and, based on a thorough review of Kanner's archives, no evidence of communication afterward.

"The aim of this paper was to report on a personality disorder already manifest in childhood which to my knowledge has not yet been described," Asperger wrote, echoing Kanner's comment about a fundamentally different disorder. "In what follows I will describe a particularly interesting and highly recognizable type of child. The children I will present all have in common a fundamental disturbance which manifests itself in their physical appearance, expressive functions and, indeed, their whole behavior. This disturbance results in severe and characteristic difficulties of social integration." In other words, they displayed as their central feature autistic disturbances of affective contact—and although they were higher functioning than the majority of Kanner's cases because they had functional speech, in many ways they were clearly a mirror image from across the Atlantic of the same striking, "highly recognizable" childhood disorder.

Asperger's case series was smaller than Kanner's—a sufficient number for him to believe in a pattern, but he provided nowhere near the background information that Kanner did. Still, he started in a similar fashion with Fritz V., who was born in June 1933 (a mere three months before Donald Triplett) and first seen in autumn 1939, a year after Donald's arrival at Hopkins:

> We start with a highly unusual boy who shows a very severe impairment in social integration. . . . He was referred by his school as he was considered to be 'unteachable' by the end of the first day there.
>
> Fritz was the first child of his parents. . . . Motor milestones were rather delayed. He learnt to walk at fourteen months, and for a long time was extremely clumsy and unable to do things for himself. . . . In contrast, he learnt to talk very early and spoke his first words at 10 months, well before he could walk. He quickly learnt to express himself in sentences and soon talked 'like an adult.'
>
> From the earliest age Fritz never did what he was told. He did just what he wanted to, or the opposite of what he was told. . . . He was never able to become integrated into a group of playing children. He never got on with other children and, in fact, was not interested in them. . . . He had no real love for anybody but occasionally had fits of affection. . . . Another strange phenomenon in this boy was the occurrence of certain stereotypic movements and habits.

So it went through the next three cases—Harro L., Ernst K., and Hellmuth L. All were born in the 1930s except Harro, who was born in the mid-1920s and "had severe asphyxia at birth and was resuscitated at length. Soon after his birth he had convulsions." He, too, was delayed physically, starting to walk and talk only at the end of his second year. "However, he then learnt to speak relatively quickly, and even as a toddler he talked 'like a grown-up.'" He was also "grotesquely fat" and, unlike the other Asperger and Kanner cases, "His appearance was grotesque. On top of the massive body, over the big face with flabby cheeks, was a tiny skull. One could almost consider him microcephalic." In retrospect, Harro appears to be an outlier in this group, which would make Asperger's true case series really three.

The mothers and fathers were more of a mixed lot than Kanner's well-educated and mostly well-to-do parents. Fritz's mother came from the family of one of Austria's greatest poets, the father from an ordinary farming family; Harro's father was a painter and sculptor "but out of financial necessity he was making brooms and brushes"; he came from peasant stock but was "a typical intellectual." Ernst's father was a tailor's assistant and his mother "a very bright and extremely nice woman whose life was not easy," nervous and prone to headaches; Hellmuth's parents were described only as "without any peculiarities" in contrast to their grotesque-looking child.

In discussing "the clinical picture of autistic psychopathy," Asperger noted "the autistic personality is highly distinctive despite wide differences. . . . From the second year of life we find already the characteristic features which remain unmistakeable and constant throughout the whole life-span."

About Fritz, Asperger provides this haunting description: "His gaze was strikingly odd. It was generally directed into the void."[63]

Most discussions of the timing and similarities of Asperger's and Kanner's reports treat them as a remarkable coincidence. We find *that* remarkable. "Child psychiatry was emerging on both continents simultaneously," writes anthrolopologist Roy Richard Grinker in *Unstrange Minds*. And he proposes that "today, most mental health professionals think that Kanner and Asperger were treating different kinds of patients."[64]

The idea fits neatly with Grinker's belief that autism is a constant-prevalence genetic disorder that merely escaped the attention of everyone before it was observed by not one but two clinicians, on two continents, in papers submitted for publication the same year. But there is another possibility: Starting about 1930, the ethylmercury seed treatment Ceresan was jointly marketed by DuPont in the United States and Bayer in

Europe under a partnership called DuBay. The diphtheria toxoid was also introduced in Austria in the 1930s, but with an intriguing difference: It was generally administered *after* the age of two and primarily targeted at schoolchildren.[65] In the United States, the recommended age was much earlier: "Six months is the best age," the Baltimore City Health Department reported in 1932; it was routinely administered at nine months in Boston's Harvard School of Public Health well-baby clinic.

Could the later exposure to the diphtheria shot in Austria have allowed Asperger's children to acquire functional language, the main distinction between the two syndromes?

Gold Salts

Although Leo Kanner fought off the Freudians as he built his reputation as a child psychiatrist, even ridiculed their founder and his ideas, he was not immune to the possibility that parents were complicit in autism. His 1943 paper contains this penultimate paragraph:

> One other fact stands out prominently. In the whole group, there are very few really warmhearted fathers and mothers. . . . [They are] limited in genuine interest in people. Even some of the happiest marriages are rather formal affairs. Three of the marriages were dismal failures. The question arises whether or to what extent this fact has contributed to the condition of the children.[66]

In keeping with this vague concern, Kanner suggested that Beaman and Mary Triplett send Donald to live on a farm with a simple, "warmhearted" couple, as Kanner called them.

One of us went to Forest, Mississippi, in 2005 and met Donald's brother, O.B., who described an unknown aspect of this story: When Donald was nearly fourteen, he became quite ill, and the farm family that he had been sent to live with, the Lewises, brought him back to the Tripletts. By then he had a high fever, his joints were severely swollen and he'd stopped eating. As they had done when his behavioral problems surfaced a decade earlier, the Tripletts looked far and wide for help, even taking him to the famed Mayo Clinic in Minnesota. But no one could figure out the problem, and his health continued its sharp decline. As his father told a doctor and family friend he encountered in nearby Raleigh, Mississippi, "It looks like Don's getting ready to die." That doctor proved a lifesaver when he suggested the child might have a very rare condition called juvenile rheumatoid arthritis (JRA), also known as Still's disease—named after the London physician George Still we mentioned in chapter 4 who also first described ADHD. They immediately took Donald to the Campbell Clinic in Memphis, which specialized in orthopedic problems like arthritis, and he underwent a series of treatments with gold salts that lasted several months. Gold salts were then the standard remedy for JRA (they are still FDA-approved, but newer treatments with fewer side effects are now the standard of care).

In Donald's case the results were astonishing. His arthritis cleared up, leaving behind the minor reminder of one fused knuckle. But something even more remarkable happened. As the treatment came to its end, "the nervousness and extreme anxiety that had heretofore afflicted him all but disappeared," his brother recounted in courtly fashion. "He became more social"; the defining features of his disability lessened dramatically and permanently. "It was the most amazing thing I've ever seen. . . . He just had a miraculous response to the medicine."[67]

In the medical world, Donald's recovery in association with the gold salts treatment barely registered and was quickly forgotten. Leon Eisenberg, a Hopkins colleague of Kanner's, wrote in 1956: "Donald, at 14, developed an undiagnosed illness manifested by fever, chills, and joint pains. He became bedridden and developed joint contractures. On the basis of a tentative diagnosis of Still's disease, he was placed empirically on gold therapy with marked improvement. After 18 months he was once again ambulatory. He emerged with little residual deficit from a second episode of arthritis two years later. The clinical improvement in his behavior, first observed during his rural placement, was accelerated during and after his illness and convalescence at home."[68]

In a 1971 follow-up, Kanner mentioned the arthritis attacks but not the gold salts treatment, focusing instead on the "intuitive wisdom" of the farm couple that so clearly contrasted with the "very few really warm-hearted fathers and mothers" of the eleven children.[69] In fact, Eisenberg's reference seems to be the sole published mention of the treatment. Thus did the very first child with autism stage a recovery that his family attributed to a biomedical intervention. The leading experts in autism missed this entirely.

———

When Leo Kanner looked back on his discovery of autism, he linked it to his admittedly superstitious belief in serendipity. Noting in 1979 that there were 102 chapters of the National Society for Autistic Children in the United States and 66 more in thirty-one countries around the world, he marveled: "All this started 40 years ago with Donald T. . . . the first reported specimen of what many of my colleagues call 'the Kanner syndrome.' How is *that* for serendipity?"[70]

But the head of a prominent clinic and author of the standard diagnostic manual cannot claim to be "endowed with serendipity, or 'the gift of finding unsought treasures'" simply because "the first reported specimen" of a new childhood psychiatric disorder is referred to him. True serendipity would have required a greater degree of sagacity—deducing the *reason* these first cases suddenly appeared, the real treasure buried in the shared backgrounds of those eleven children's families.

For Leo Kanner, that was not to be—and not for the first time. Two decades earlier in South Dakota, he identified the rarity of general paralysis of the insane among Indians with syphilis. The observation was correct, but he missed the clue hidden in plain sight—Indians did not treat syphilis with mercury—and he fell into groundless speculation ("the relative absence of general paralysis among the Indians can be explained by the old age of syphilis in the race").[71] When autism arrived a decade later on his doorstep in Baltimore, he identified the disorder but overlooked the same clue—mercury exposure. And once more he wandered onto shaky ground. His suspicions about parents, which would grow from an afterthought into a malignant theory, was all the more unfortunate given his contempt for Freudian parent bashing.

In *The Travels and Adventures of Serendipity*, a marvelous book on the history of the word in the English language and its role in medical discovery, scientific sociologist Robert King Merton and Elinor G. Barber quote an essay by David Seegal titled "Chance and the Prepared Mind":

Many of the great advances in medical science have come by simple means and often by *chance* [emphasis in original]. It would seem as if Providence were exercising wit and playfulness in hiding the missing piece of the scientific puzzle behind a nearby elm tree, while the search went on in a distant and exotic forest. But the rewarding chance observation may be missed even when the investigator finds the elm tree unless he has a sound training in his chosen field. He may lack the receptors characteristic of the trained mind to take advantage of the chance observation.[72]

"Where observation is concerned, chance favors only the prepared mind," Pasteur said. Leo Kanner's mind was prepared only to identify cases rather than causes. The missing autism puzzle piece—strong evidence of a role for environmental exposure, including mercury—has remained hidden almost literally behind a nearby tree while the search wandered through ever more distant and exotic forests.

That is not serendipity. That is tragedy.

CHAPTER SEVEN

THE WRONG BRANCHES

The challenge for the 21st century is to place human behavior on a more solidly scientific foundation and to ensure that all children have the maximum opportunity to develop the potentials with which they have been born. Freudian theory would appear to have no role in this endeavor since it has no scientific base. It will slowly fade from view, therefore, just as the Cheshire cat once did, except that in this case the grin will fade first, and the genitals last of all.

—E. FULLER TORREY, *FREUDIAN FRAUD*[1]

The medical profession embraces the conceit that when errors occur in understanding a disease condition, devotion to the scientific method makes these errors transient and self-correcting. But in the latter half of the twentieth century historians and sociologists of science began calling attention to the idea that errors in science are often caused, and therefore perpetuated, by the beliefs and prejudices of practitioners. Out of the complex interaction between facts and evidence and deeply held beliefs, scientific errors can be pervasive and long lasting, while the truth remains hidden. And because of the economic incentives of drug manufacturers, practicing physicians and powerful specialists, the medical industry is especially vulnerable to long-lasting error, as we've seen in the cases of syphilis, hysteria, and acrodynia.

So it shouldn't be at all surprising that Leo Kanner's early failure to observe important patterns in his first cluster of cases didn't correct itself very quickly. Quite the contrary, Kanner's error metastasized. And unfortunately, Kanner himself played an active role in that process. Perhaps he was lured by the prospect of the immortality that might accrue to the discoverer of "Kanner's syndrome"; more likely, he was over-whelmed by the profound influence of the Freudians in America's post-war psychiatry community. Regardless of his motivations, for a man with such independent habits of mind early on, the latter part of Kanner's career was marked by far lesser contributions than the first.

Still, among the many errors of the medical industry as the Age of Autism spread like a cancer, Leo Kanner's contributions were far from the most harmful. Autism's leading Freudian theorist, Bruno Bettel-heim, turned an accusatory eye on the mothers of autistic children, ar-guing that women like Elizabeth Peabody Trevett, Miriam Partridge Speck, and Rachel Cary Muncie were at fault for their children's autism. While conventional wisdom has it that Bettelheim promoted the concept of "refrigerator" mothers, it was Kanner who first used the term. But Bettelheim's view was far darker than that.

Autism science pursued the wrong branches at almost every turn. Bettelheim's views were celebrated, while clear evidence of a role for oc-cupational chemical exposures in families was ignored. And as one par-ent's personal crusade to debunk Bettelheim succeeded, rising interest in "the biology of the autistic syndromes" turned the field not to environ-mental injury but instead to genetics, launching decades of research from which little has been gained.

Fortunately, there were a few bright spots in an otherwise dark period for families affected by autism, Bettelheim's fall from repute foremost among them. Since the clues about the role of environmental factors in autism have been ignored for so long, it is worthwhile to expose the erro-neous commitments made by former "experts" in autism so that we can trace their roots into the present day and correct the record. For as David Wootton observed in the case of penicillin, discovered two centuries after the requisite technology for its discovery was in place, the question is not so much what led to the truth in the end. It's what took so long.

Autism Grows

In 1956, thirteen years after Kanner published his original paper on autism, a Navy psychologist in San Diego named Bernard Rimland and his wife, Gloria, had their first child, a son they named Mark. Mark showed all the hallmarks of early infantile autism and was soon formally diagnosed. By then autism, while still rare, was well-known in the medical community: Since Kanner's 1943 paper, the syndrome had gained increasing attention for its remarkable combination of features. In 1952 Dutch psychiatrist Arn Van Krevelen said that he had started to doubt autism's existence because he hadn't yet seen a case, but when he finally did, the doubts disappeared: Each child "was as much like those described by Kanner as one raindrop is like another."[2] (And, of ten early cases he saw, interestingly enough, one was the child of a horticulturalist and another the child of a florist's salesman—both possible signs of fungicide exposure, as we saw in Kanner's original case series.)[3]

Like Beaman Triplett, Rimland sent Kanner a case file on his son Mark and corresponded with him. He also began a treatment for him, an approach that has since come to be described as biomedical, making use of supplements, dietary changes, and other interventions rather than prescription drugs to blunt unwanted behaviors. The practice is based in the belief that autism has its roots in a child's metabolic and immune processes, as well as his or her susceptibility to toxins. Rimland told Kanner he had been trying a product called Deaner, a substance some believed could elevate mood, intelligence, and memory.[4]

Like Donald Triplett, who unbeknownst to Rimland had improved dramatically after gold salts treatment seven years earlier, his son seemed better. "Many people have commented on Mark's improvement," Rimland wrote Kanner. "He is using a little speech now—not just fragments in a high piping voice. He is naming pictures in books for the first time, and there is progress in toilet training. . . . Where before, on returning from work it was common to hear him screaming in part of an hour-long tantrum, I now often find him opening the door for me with a smile."

Convinced that he and Gloria had done nothing to make Mark this severely disabled, and encouraged by his medical interventions, Rimland put every waking moment outside his day job into autism research. "I have spent many hundreds of hours studying the literature on infantile autism and related subjects. . . . I still have not finished, but I believe I have come close to reading all that has been written on the topic in English. I have been mainly concerned with trying to find biological factors which might eventually help beat the problem." Rimland fell asleep many nights on the floor of his study, but even getting his hands on the material was a challenge. He told Kanner he was waiting for the July issue of the *American Journal of Mental Deficiency* but "it is three weeks overdue at the college library, and I'm tired of stopping there almost daily to see if it would have arrived."

It would be another two decades before Rimland would help put together the first study to search for the biological factors he suspected—and stumble across systematic evidence of a "chemical connection" in the parents' backgrounds. And it would be even longer before these insights blossomed into a widespread movement by parents who, frustrated with the medical profession, tried the kinds of approaches that appeared to help Donald Triplett and Mark Rimland.

Meanwhile, reports of autism increased—first a trickle, then a torrent.

By the time "Autistic Disturbances" was published in 1943, two more cases of autism had been referred to Kanner.[5] He called the disorder "rare enough, yet it is probably more frequent than is indicated by the paucity of observed cases"—a comment that may have reflected what he knew but his readers had no way of telling, that many of those first eleven cases were close at hand, clustered in Maryland and among families with some sort of medical connection to Hopkins.

By 1946, just three years later, he already had "the occasion to observe 23 children whose extreme withdrawal and disability to form the usual relations to people were noticed from the beginning of life." In this first follow-up he focused on the language difficulties demonstrated by autistic children. Repeating the tale of "Donald T.," he added several new accounts. "Jay S., not quite four years old, referred to himself as 'Blum' whenever his veracity was questioned by his parents. The mystery of this 'irrelevance' was explained when Jay, who could read fluently, once pointed to the advertisement of a furniture firm in the newspapers, which said in large letters, 'Blum tells the truth.' Since Jay told the truth, he was Blum."[6]

Kanner took the occasion to defend his cases as a new disorder, showing how each additional child fit with the striking peculiarities observed in the first eleven. "I have designated this condition as 'early infantile autism,'" he wrote, having settled on the phrase in 1944. "Phenomenologically, excessive aloneness and an anxiously excessive desire for the preservation of sameness are the outstanding characteristics. Memory is often astounding. Cognitive endowment, masked frequently by limited responsiveness, is at least average." And he continued to observe what he thought was an important pattern. "Most patients stem from psychometrically superior, though literal-minded and obsessive, families."[7] By 1949 it seems likely that the shadow of Sigmund Freud was darkening his view. He wrote, "The parents' behavior toward the children must be seen to be fully appreciated. Maternal lack of genuine warmth is often conspicuous in the first visit to the clinic." He described Donald and his mother: Donald "sat down next to his mother on the sofa. She kept moving away from him as though she could not bear the physical proximity. When Donald moved along with her, she finally told him coldly to go and sit in a chair."[8]

Kanner seemed not to consider that the parent-child relationship was mutual, that the failure of the child to respond was difficult for the parents, and that many of the children had physical problems that added to the difficulty. Nonetheless, he had to acknowledge that the parents behaved responsibly. "Most of the patients were exposed from the beginning to parental coldness, obsessiveness and a mechanical type of attention to material needs only. . . . [Yet the mothers] were anxious to do a good job, and this meant mechanized service of the kind which is rendered by an overconscientious gasoline station attendant. . . . Pediatricians' instructions were carried out to the letter."[9]

In 1952 he wrote about two more cases and began introducing language that would turn the parents into an unfeeling appliance. He claimed that the children's "therapy has been sabotaged by emotionally refrigerated parents incapable of defrosting. . . . The vast majority of parents, though competent in their chosen profession, are cold, detached, humorless perfectionists, more at home in the realm of abstractions than in the world of people."[10] In Kanner's early writings, then, we can find the roots of the concept of the "refrigerator mother." In the journal article "Early Infantile Autism, 1943–55," he and Hopkins colleague Leon Eisenberg crossed explicitly into causation: "The emotional frigidity in the typical autistic family suggests a dynamic experiential factor in the genesis of the disorder in the child."[11] Emotional frigidity . . . in the genesis of the disorder. Here, Kanner first places autism squarely on the parents; a lack of affective contact *toward* their children led to a lack of affective contact *from* their children.

To convey just how coldly these parents treated their offspring, Kanner cited the case of Brian, "who was one of twins born despite contraceptive efforts, much to the distress of his parents; their plans centered about graduate study and had no room for children." The mother, a psychology student, decided to raise the twins "scientifically—that is, not to be picked up if crying except on schedule." At five months, the other twin died—this, Kanner said, resulted from their rigid approach that led them to ignore the child's health crisis—and "the mother withdrew from the remaining child even more completely, and spent her days locked in the study reading. . . . This case, an extreme instance chosen for emphasis, can serve as a paradigm of the 'emotional refrigeration' that has been the common lot of autistic children."

This extraordinary turn against the parents, less than a decade after Kanner's first description of the disorder, may have effectively blinded him. Perhaps if he had looked away from the parents' behavior, Kanner might have seen clues to environmental harm of a different kind. But as Kanner bore deeper into the parents' psyche, he grappled with the inconsistencies of his theory: Why didn't *all* of their children have autism, and why did many parents simply not fit the pattern of emotional refrigeration? "It is difficult to escape the conclusion that this emotional configuration in the home plays a dynamic role in the genesis of autism," he wrote. But he also began devising an escape plan, conceding that "it seems to us equally clear that this factor, while important in the development of the syndrome, is not sufficient in itself to result in its appearance."

With every new case, Kanner saw parents' backgrounds as signs of toxic parenting, not toxic exposures. When he reached one hundred cases, Kanner reported that the children "almost invariably came from intelligent and sophisticated stock." Seventy-four of the fathers were college graduates—almost twice today's percentage—and he meticulously compiled their professions: thirty-one businessmen, twelve engineers, eleven physicians, ten lawyers, eight tradesmen, five chemists, five military officers, three with a Ph.D. in science, two with a Ph.D. in the humanities. The clear subsets of chemical connection within this group—chemists, engineers, tradesmen, doctors, scientists—are flagrantly obvious, and this is without even considering the mothers' backgrounds, some of which pointed just as strongly to toxic exposures that could even more directly harm the fetus and infant.[12]

The cases kept coming: There were 120 by 1957,[13] 150 by 1958.[14] The syndrome was static—the children identical as raindrops, to use Van Krevelen's phrase—but something new began to emerge. Kanner noted in 1955: "The case material has expanded to include a number of children who reportedly developed normally through the first 18 to 20 months of life, only to undergo at this point a severe withdrawal of affect, manifested by the loss of language function, failure to progress socially, and the gradual giving up in normal activities. These latter cases have invariably been severe and unresponsive. When seen, they could not be differentiated from the children with the more classical account of detachment apparently present in the neonatal period. But even these cases are much earlier in onset and phenomenologically distinct from cases of childhood schizophrenia."[15]

Regressive cases were starting to appear, yet Kanner took pains to group these cases who regressed during infancy together with those in whom autism seemed inborn, separating them from children who exhibited some form of later-onset regression, i.e., during the childhood period after three years of age. And while the timing of autism's onset began to vary in these reports from what he gave in his original paper, Kanner remarked in 1958 that autism continued to be both rare and remarkable. "The fact that an average of not more than eight patients per year [over a span of twenty years] could be diagnosed with reasonable assurance as autistic in a center serving as a sort of diagnostic clearinghouse, speaks for the infrequency of the disease, especially if one considers that they recruit themselves from all over the North American continent."[16]

But if autism was rare, exactly how rare was it? What was the prevalence rate not just in the United States but in other countries that were starting to take note of this striking syndrome?

The First Surveys

The earliest studies of autism rates are interesting not only for what they found, but for where they were done. The locations of these early surveys align remarkably with the places we have already visited on our journey through the history of mercury poisoning and pollution.

Victor Lotter's 1966 survey in Middlesex County, England, was the first of its kind: the oldest survey ever published of autism prevalence rates in a defined population. His prevalence estimate of 4.1 per 10,000 (1 in 2,400) set the standard for the generally accepted disease frequency of autism, repeated for decades to follow.[17] (For many current parents whose children were born in the 1990s, Lotter's rate of 4–5 per 10,000 was still the rate of autism quoted when they wanted to know how unlucky they really were.)

The first attempt to scientifically establish the autism rate in the United States was in Wisconsin in 1970. Darold Treffert found a very low rate of "classic infantile autism" in 0.7 per 10,000 children born in the 1950s and 1960s; using a broader definition that included onset later in childhood, he reported an overall rate of 3.1 per 10,000.[18] Treffert was assigned to the children's unit of one of Wisconsin's mental health institutes, among the few such specialized child psychiatric units in the country. Out of eight hundred patients at the institute, thirty were children under of the age of eighteen, and most of these were autistic. Soon it was decided to separate them out.

Treffert was well aware that the idea of "refrigerator mothers" was then in vogue, and that Kanner's studies had shown a high level of education in the parents of autistic children. But he took issue with Kanner's interpretation. "The mothers of the autistic children on our unit looked to me like any other mothers," he told us. "They were caring, concerned, involved and not aloof. Certainly not 'refrigerator,' and adding guilt to an already heavy burden seemed so cruel. And I thought also that Kanner's observations regarding educational level, which fed into the refrigerator stereotype somewhat, was probably a reflection of the nature of his referral practice at Johns Hopkins."[19]

Treffert concluded that the study of a statewide sample might help refute the "refrigerator parent" theory. He was confident that his role in the children's clinic put him in touch with the full population of autistic children in Wisconsin at the time. Although autism was not a recognized diagnosis in *DSM* until 1980, Treffert knew children with autism were likely to have a diagnosis of childhood schizophrenia, and he collected records for all such children throughout the state. Given Frederick Wellman's roots in the plant pathology scientific community that was centered around the University of Wisconsin, Treffert's pioneering effort there doesn't surprise us; still, the low rate of autism—just one in ten thousand, excluding later-onset cases—provides validation for Kanner's belief that autism remained rare.

Studies began cropping up in other countries around the same time.

Japan, where we already observed a tragic history of environmental mercury contamination, had the most. Sweden, where alkyl mercury poisoning triggered the first so-called Silent Spring, was second. Of twenty-four studies published by 1991, nine were in Japan, four in Sweden, four in the United States, and three in the British Isles (including the first study to be published). This distribution raises a question: Does the creation of a diagnostic category stimulate a demand for corresponding surveys, or would a greater number of epidemiological surveys reflect those places where autism was first emerging?

Despite its discovery in the United States, surveys conducted here reported lower rates than in Japan and Scandanavia. But one American study conducted in 1975 provides perhaps the best marker against which to judge the trends that have since unfolded. E. Fuller Torrey and colleagues used data from the National Collaborative Perinatal Project to conduct a study. Instead of looking for cases in a set population at one point in time, this prospective study followed a population of newborn babies and observed their development. Torrey's study was specifically designed to investigate bleeding during pregnancy as a risk factor for autism and childhood psychosis. To do so, it examined the computerized records of thirty thousand children—a huge sample—born between 1959 and 1965 at fourteen university-affiliated medical centers. All the children received several neurological, psychological, speech and hearing exams by age eight.

"From this group 14 were selected as conforming to the syndrome of infantile autism," Torrey reported.[20] That translated to a rate of 4.7 autistic children per 10,000. The researchers wrote that although they "make no claim to having identified every autistic child among the 30,000 children, the rate of 4.7 per 10,000" was almost identical to that reported by Lotter's Middlesex County study in England, "leading us to believe that most such children were included." The researchers also reviewed the examination reports of "additional children who, although not having the classical syndrome of infantile autism, were apparently psychotic. Six such children were found, all labeled by at least one observer as severely disturbed, psychotic-like, autistic, or childhood schizophrenic." Adding in those children gave a combined rate of 6.7 per 10,000 children.

The power of this study, besides its large size, came from the fact that it was prospective and followed a large population closely to observe a whole range of developmental outcomes. These autism rates, of course,

Syphilis patients shown in a 1498 woodcut, the first medical depiction of the disease. Fairly quickly, syphilis spread through Europe and became widely portrayed in art and literature.

Emil Kraepelin, widely credited as the father of biological psychiatry, was fascinated by general paresis of the insane. He traveled the world looking for cases and wrote a lengthy treatise on the subject.

Thomas T. Robertson, a Sioux Indian who carried his Scottish great-grandfather's name, was admitted to the Hiawatha Asylum with a diagnosis of general paresis of the insane. He is pictured here in Western garb; a coat and tie. *American Journal of Psychiatry*

Gerard van Swieten, personal physician to Empress Maria Theresia and inventor of "van Swieten's liquor," the first syphilis treatment to introduce the internal administration of mercuric chloride.

Some of the subjects in the infamous Tuske-gee experiment, in which poor black men from rural Alabama were recruited to be subjects in a study that tracked the course of untreated syphilis. They were denied peni-cillin after it was clearly shown to completely cure syphilis. *Centers for Disease Control and Prevention*

Public Health Service officers involved in the Tuske-gee Study. Standing from left: Nurse Eugene Riv-ers, Lloyd Simpson, Dr. G. C. Branch, Dr. Stanley H. Schuman. Seated from left: Dr. Henry Eisen-berg, Dr. Trygve Gjestland (author of the Oslo Study of Untreated Syphilis). *Centers for Disease Control and Prevention*

Charcot's Tuesday lectures on hysteria became a sensation in Paris and attracted large audiences. Contemporary and later skeptics argued that Charcot's female patients were play-acting. *National Library of Medicine*

Freud in 1885, the year he went to study with the famous neurologist Jean-Martin Charcot at the Salpêtrière in Paris. *Library of Congress*

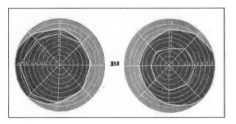

A figure from Charcot's *Clinical Lectures on Diseases of the Nervous System* showing one of the "hysterical stigmata"; in this case one of many diagrams showing visual-field constriction.

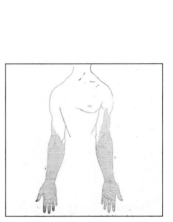

Another diagram from Charcot's Lectures illustrating a case with another one of the hysterical stigmata; in this case loss of sensation in the peripheral nerves.

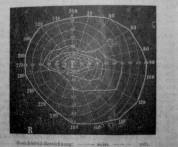

Freud's first diagnosed case of hysteria, August P., with an ophthalmological chart prepared by Dr. Königstein showing clear signs of visual-field constriction. *Freud Library in London*

Bertha Pappenheim, Josef Breuer's hysteria patient, inspired Freud to develop the basic principles of psychoanalytic theory. Called Anna O. by Breuer, Pappenheim exhibited clear symptoms of mercury poisoning, including visual-field constriction, contractures, and numbness in her extremities. *Library of Congress*

Sergei Pankejeff and his wife in 1910, the year he began his psychoanalysis with Sigmund Freud, who called him the Wolf-Man.

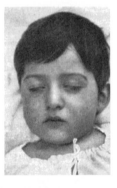

A child suffering from acrodynia. He died shortly after this picture was taken by Charles Rocaz.

Dr. William Alexander Hammond's opposition to the use of calomel during the Civil War provoked the Calomel Rebellion, when army doctors objected to the banning of mercury treatments. Hammond was court-martialed in 1864.

Josef Warkany discovered that acrodynia was caused by mercury poisoning from childhood mercury treatments such as teething powders. *Journal of Toxicological Sciences*

An advertisement for Steedman's Powder uses Mother Hubbard to market mercury-containing medications to large families.

Considered the father of organic chemistry, Morris Kharasch, at the University of Chicago, filed a series of patents in the 1920s and 1930s that paved the way for the commercialization of ethylmercury in agricultural and pharmaceutical products. *Michigan State University Department of Chemistry*

A pamphlet for Ceresan, the ethylmercury fungicide developed by Morris Kharasch for the joint venture between DuPont and Bayer known as DuBay. *Special Collections Research Center at North Carolina State University Libraries*

Bridget Muncie at age 4, one of the first girls ever diagnosed with autism, was Case 5, Barbara K., in Kanner's 1943 paper. *Courtesy of Peter Muncie*

The Muncie family: Rachel Cary Muncie, Bridget (age 6), and Peter (age 2). *Courtesy of Peter Muncie*

Dora Wellman holding her son, Frederick Creighton Wellman, III. "Frederick W." was the second case listed in Kanner's landmark 1943 article. *Special Collections Research Center at North Carolina State University Libraries*

Leo Kanner, who wrote the paper that introduced autism to the world in 1943. Considered the father of child psychiatry, he later said the syndrome of behaviors was "not known to me or anyone else theretofore." *Johns Hopkins Medical Archives*

The papers of the late Frederick L. Wellman include a study of organic mercury on plant fungi as well as brochures for commercial fungicides containing organic mercury.

Bruno Bettelheim *University of Chicago Library*

Bernard Rimland with his son, Mark. Mark was born in 1956 and diagnosed with autism. *Autism Research Institute*

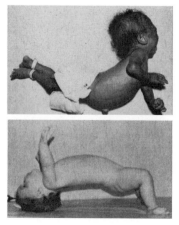

Infants with congenital rubella syndrome (CRS) born to mothers in Houston during the rubella epidemic of 1964–5. Although CRS was known to result in vision, hearing, and cardiac defects, the degree of neurological impairment in these American children was unprecedented. Could gamma globulin treatments, then the standard of care for women exposed to rubella in pregnancy, have combined with the rubella virus to create a "disease of the remedy"?

According to her parents, this nine-year-old Old Order Amish girl developed autism after she was removed from her home by health officials and vaccinated at a local clinic. *Dan Olmsted*

Dr. Andrew Wakefield

Sallie Bernard
Angela Magee

Hannah Poling and her parents, Jon and Teri Poling, at a news conference. *W.A. Harewood /AP*

are far below later prevalence studies; a comprehensive 2004 review put autism at around thirty or forty per ten thousand for full-syndrome or "Kanner autism," and about sixty-seven per ten thousand for the broader diagnostic category that includes Asperger's and pervasive developmental disorder—at least ten times higher than Torrey's prospective analysis.[21] The most recent estimate puts rates even higher than this.

When early researchers went looking for autism in the Third World, they found even lower rates. More than thirty years ago, Victor Lotter took a tour of Africa looking for autism cases. He didn't attempt a full prevalence study; instead he simply went to visit "collections" of mentally handicapped children in institutions in hopes that he would be able to find evidence of autism in these high concentrations of mentally impaired children. He visited nine cities in six African countries (Ghana, Nigeria, Kenya, Zimbabwe, Zambia, and South Africa) in search of as many cases of autism as he could find. Although not a full-scale population survey, Lotter personally screened more than thirteen hundred mentally handicapped children during a two-year period.

So what Lotter found in Africa surprised him, namely, that "the number of autistic children found was much smaller than expected." Within a population already diagnosed with a mental handicap, one would expect to find a higher rate of autism, since the population had been screened to exclude any typical children. Only 9 of the 1,312 mentally handicapped children he saw in nine cities were autistic, a rate of 1 in 145, *less than* the autism rate today in the entire U.S. childhood population. He had expected to see more than one in twenty in such a high concentration of mentally disabled children.[22] Around that time, clinicians in Nigeria[23] and later in Kenya[24] confirmed that autism indeed was present among African children but found it rare enough that it was worthwhile for them to give detailed profiles of just four and three cases, respectively.

Unfailingly, when autism was found by early researchers in Africa, it occurred in "elite" families. Lotter reported that "there was amongst all the children originally selected as possible cases an excess of the elite . . . this excess was even greater amongst the autistic children than amongst non-autistic children." Lotter defined as elite "any child who had been born abroad [Britain, Europe, or North America], or had lived for any period abroad, or whose parent(s) had lived for any period abroad, or whose father had a non-manual job." Lotter's finding was supported by other researchers as well: All four cases in the Nigerian report came from "elite" families, as did the three Kenyan children, the parents of whom included a medical doctor, an engineer, and the "chairman of a parastatal organization."

This interpretation of autism suited some academic observers, who were eager to blame, if not simply the parents, then society and social class for autism. "Infantile autism," wrote Victor Sanua in a 1984 paper that reviewed the evidence of autism in Africa, "appears to be an illness of Western Civilization, and appears in countries of high technology, where the nuclear family dominates." The idea that the risk of Western civilization might be real but boil down to something different, concrete, and quite specific seems never to have occurred to Dr. Sanua. And in this we hear the echo of Emil Kraepelin—and Leo Kanner—in their search for general paralysis of the insane in indigenous cultures.

The Mutant Spawn of Sigmund Freud

As we've seen, for a time Kanner hesitantly supported a Freudian-influenced view of autism even though he reported its presence from the beginning of life. Pure Freudians like J. Louise Despert had no such hesitation. But the clear leader of the pack was Bruno Bettelheim. He commented in 1981, "All my life, I have been working with children whose lives were destroyed because their mothers hated them."[25] Bettelheim was perhaps the most malignant force ever unleashed on families coping with autism.

Bruno Bettelheim was born in Vienna in 1903, three years after Freud's pivotal analysis of eighteen-year Dora Bauer. Like Dora's father, Bettelheim's had syphilis. And while we think Dora was affected by the mercury treatment Freud almost certainly prescribed her father, Bruno Bettelheim's circumstances do appear to reflect psychological dysfunction—gloom hung over the household, a biographer writes. "Decades later, Bruno would tell his own children that as a young boy he did not know what caused the oppressive climate in his home but a fear that he may have created it caused him great anxiety about his own sexuality."[26] As a teenager, Bettelheim read Freud, initially to impress a girl whose interest in both Freud and Bettelheim quickly waned, but Bettelheim remained captivated by the sage of Vienna. He hovered around the outer edges of the intellectual milieu, taking art and aesthetics at the University of Vienna, but he also had family obligations—his father owned a company, and so, aware of his father's precarious health, Bettelheim also studied business and bookkeeping. That ended in 1938 when the Anschluss handed Austria to its native son Adolf Hitler, now the Reichsführer of Germany. Soon thereafter, Bettelheim ended up in Dachau and then Buchenwald. Released before they became extermination camps, he made his way to the United States; settled in Chicago, where he established contacts with the University of Chicago; and remade himself as a student of Freud.

In 1943—the same year, coincidentally, that Leo Kanner published "Autistic Disturbances"—he recounted his concentration camp experiences in a journal article, "Individual and Mass Behavior in Extreme Situations."[27] Its early glimpse into the depravity of the camps, along with a detached and objective tone, made his name in the United States, where he became an overnight sensation.

Hired by the University of Chicago, he began to treat disturbed children and developed a theory of autism that compared the experience of an autistic child with that of a concentration camp inmate: emotional withdrawal in fear of their lives. In his book *The Empty Fortress* (1967) he wrote of a type of prisoner called "moslems" (interestingly, he had not mentioned them in his original 1943 paper on concentration camp life) who broke down after being terrorized by the guards:

> Thus what was startling about the experience in the camps was that though the overpowering conditions were the same for many prisoners, not all succumbed. Only those showed schizophrenic-like reactions who felt they were not only helpless to deal with the new situation, but that this was their inescapable fate. These deteriorated to near autistic behavior when the feeling of doom penetrated so deep that it brought the added conviction of imminent death. Such men were called "moslems" in the camps and other prisoners avoided them as if in fear of contagion.[28]

It is not an overstatement to call Bettelheim a fraud. He falsely claimed degrees in philosophy, psychology, and the history of art. Far worse, given what was to come, he maintained that he was an experienced professor, had "taught courses . . . in normal and abnormal psychology" and belonged in Vienna to "an association of professional psychologists and educators which studied the developmental problems of children and adolescents."[29]

But given the gripping backstory of his time in a concentration camp and his personal charisma (not to mention the fact that the Nazis had destroyed most of the documentation necessary to check such claims), Bettelheim gained a wide and admiring audience. His home base was The Orthogenic School at the University of Chicago, which became the home for several dozen children at any one time undergoing his intensive but supposedly benevolent treatment. (In fact, multiple witnesses came forward after his death to say he held the parents at bay, browbeat the staff, and physically beat the children.) He turned these children's stories into literary sensations, such as "Joey, the Mechanical Boy" in 1959 in *Scientific American*.[30] It was a portrait of a "schizophrenic child" and a masterpiece of Freudian mumbo jumbo. Placing the blame exclusively on the mothers, Bettelheim elaborated an extravagant theory that could even explain what to Kanner appeared an "inborn disturbance":

> The conditions of life that made Joey decide to be a mechanical contrivance instead of a person began before he was born. At birth, his mother "thought of him as a thing rather than a person." But even before that he made little impression. "I never knew I was pregnant," she said, meaning that consciously the pregnancy did not alter her life. His birth, too, "did not make any difference."[31]

Of course, to Bettelheim, all this had roots in the parents' own deep-seated problems. It was all about the parents, whom Bettelheim proceeded to "treat": "Psychotherapy helped the mother to realize how much she initially felt 'trapped' in her marriage; how for years she had only thought she loved her husband [poor misguided woman!] while all her deeper feelings had lain dormant. . . . The father needed much less therapy."[32] Of course he did—he was not the one whose pathology was so severe it made Joey autistic.

Bettelheim has been derided as inventing the term "refrigerator mothers." As we've seen, Kanner's use of "refrigerators" actually predated Bettelheim. But Bettelheim's critique went far deeper. They were *homicidal* mothers, and the infants knew this. They sensed their mothers' murderous intent and withdrew from the world. This sounds so implausibly extreme that it is worth letting Bettelheim spell it out himself:

> Despite the incredible variety of symptoms among the several hundred schizophrenic children we have worked with over the years, they all shared

one thing in common: an unremitting fear for their lives. . . . The more autistic the schizophrenic child, the more debilitating his symptoms, the greater is his mortal anxiety. Autistic children in particular not only fear constantly for their lives, they seem convinced death is imminent; that possibly it can be postponed just for moments through their not taking cognizance of life. . . .

I believe the initial cause of withdrawal is rather the child's *correct interpretation* [emphasis added] of the negative emotions with which the most significant figures in his environment approach him. This, in turn, evokes rage in the child till he begins—as even mature persons do—to interpret the world in the image of his anger. All of us do that occasionally, and all children do it more than occasionally. The tragedy of children fated to become autistic is that such a view of the world happens to be correct for their world.[33]

In this way, Leo Kanner, fixated on the aloof parenting of autistic children, and Bruno Bettelheim, focused on the mother's actively homicidal impulses, never noticed chemical exposure in the background of families with autistic children. But others did.

Chemical Exposures

In the spring of 1974 Bernard Rimland's group, the National Society for Autistic Children, held its annual conference, meeting that year in Washington, D.C. Since a number of autistic children would be gathered in one place, Rimland decided it might be an opportunity to research the biological basis of autism, and he reached out to the Children's Brain Research Clinic, which agreed to conduct a detailed study. The lead researcher was Dr. Mary Coleman of Georgetown University. A total of seventy-eight autistic children participated, and the local chapter also provided the necessary "controls," unaffected children matched by age and sex.

For the first time, Coleman and Rimland began to explore the question of subgroups and biological causation. They hypothesized there were three clusters of autistic children. One was made up of cases that seemed to run in families. Another was a group that had gastrointestinal issues and sensitivity to wheat; they called this group celiac autism. The third group showed signs of a metabolic disturbance; in particular, the purine pathway, which produces molecules like adenosine and uric acid, seemed abnormal.[34] Each of these three clusters reflected themes—genetic susceptibility, gastrointestinal difficulties, and disturbances of a particular biological pathway—that have endured to some degree.

In terms of causation, some interesting additional data emerged from the detailed questionnaire: There were "two areas of marked difference between the parents of the autistic children and parents of controls. One of these areas was exposure to chemicals. In twenty families of autistic patients, an unusual amount of exposure to chemicals had occurred during the preconception period. In four of these families, both mother and father had been exposed to chemicals, mostly with the parents working as chemists. Of the control parents, there was only one family (again both the father and the mother) who were working as chemists in a laboratory."[35]

· Was this an alarm bell, thirty years after Kanner's original signals were missed, to home in on toxins in the etiology of autism? Coleman said it should be: "Since the incidence of individuals exposed to chemicals in all related occupations in the United States is . . . 1.1 percent of the population . . . to find that 25 percent of any sample has had chemical exposure is quite startling."[36] (The other difference Coleman found in parents of autistic children was the increased rate in the mothers' preconception histories of hypothyroidism—an autoimmune disorder.)

These results were, indeed, quite startling. But they also reflected a self-selected sample of parents coming to Washington for a meeting of a national autism group. Coleman reasoned that perhaps only children whose families reflected a chemically induced illness would participate in this kind of study, thereby skewing the results. So the question remained: Would a chemical connection hold up if the possibility of selection bias were eliminated? One of Coleman's graduate students, Thomas Felicetti, put the theory to an additional test.

The experimental design compared the occupations of twenty parents of autistic children, twenty parents of mentally retarded children, and twenty parents of "normal" children who were friends and neighbors of those attending the Avalon School in Massachusetts, where he taught at the time. The results confirmed Coleman and Rimland's original finding. "Eight of the 37 known parents of the autistic children had sustained occupational exposure to chemicals prior to conception. Five were chemists and three worked in related fields. The exposed parents represent 21 percent of the autistic group. This compared to 2.7 percent of the retardation controls and 10 percent of the normal controls." Felicetti concluded, "The results of this study point in the direction of chemical exposure as an etiological factor in the birth of autistic children."[37]

Felicetti, now executive director of Beechwood Rehabilitation Services in Langhorne, Pennsylvania, is quick to acknowledge that such a small study was not definitive. "This particular study was occupations, and it was all different occupations," he told us. "But again that's as far as I went with it. It was a pretty good study but suggestive—because we couldn't find any particular chemical and because we only looked at occupations." Felicetti acknowledged that careers like plant pathologist and forestry professor—Cases 2 and 3 in Kanner's original paper—met the criteria for a "chemical connection." The study also went against the "class" observations of so many other reports. "It did try to have the control groups of equal occupation and social class," Felicetti said. Contrary to all the speculation that brainpower and education correlate with autistic offspring, job status seemed to have nothing to do with it.[38]

Nor was that the last sign of a chemical connection. Another research effort looked again at the same prospective study of children in which Torrey and colleagues found a 4.7 per rate of autism; it, too, found a higher incidence of occupations involving exposure to chemicals among the small set of parents of children with autism.[39]

Despite the power of these findings—at least to generate hypotheses about toxic exposures in the etiology of autism—they failed to produce further studies. The call from Coleman, a widely respected and thoroughly mainstream scientist, for more research was ignored. One of Felicetti's observations in the 1981 article is haunting: "It is especially ironic that many of the parents of the autistic youngsters in our study could not specify the nature of the chemical agents. One can only speculate that they had blind faith in the safety precautions of the plants and in the reassurances of their employers."

In a similar spirit, we do not argue that ethylmercury exposure would have been identifiable in every one of these cases, only that the original eleven Kanner cases showed a link to newly commercialized ethylmercury compounds. Moreover, the subsequent studies that found convincing evidence of chemical exposures by then could have included a wider array of toxins, both from industrial and household chemicals and from

more widely administered and more frequent vaccinations. It is important to note that the field of toxicology research has identified multiple
instances in which different chemicals converge on identical pathways.
We'll return to the implications of these findings for analyzing the association between chemical exposure and autism (or any other disease)
later. Meanwhile, as autism reached epidemic proportions, the "chemical connection" signal would become harder to detect because it was
more universally shared. Eventually, this first suggestion of chemical involvement faded away entirely and was overwhelmed by other biological
concepts, including the familiar territory of germ theory and ultimately
genetics.

Indeed, one germ in particular caught the attention of scientists
around this time. This was fueled in part by an epidemic that swept the
world in the 1960s and seemed to trigger, at least in a few places, an unusually high rate of autism.

The (Brief) Age of Rubella-related Autism

Scientists are uncertain about the origins of the rubella virus. We do
know that it has been around for a long time and is in large measure
harmless, lasting a few days with a course so innocuous that no one ever
really commented on it. Rubella was only identified as a distinct disease
by German physicians in the 1700s—hence one of its names, German
measles, to differentiate it from regular measles and chicken pox.

But if a young woman who has not gotten rubella in childhood becomes infected during pregnancy the risk can be quite serious for the
developing embryo. The disease known as congenital rubella syndrome
(CRS) can cause deafness and muteness; we have witnessed conditions
like these for eons, and it's likely that a significant number of them were
triggered by rubella in the mother. Congenital rubella can also be life
threatening, with a high rate of spontaneous abortion, infant mortality,
and infant heart defects.

For a long time, this severe manifestation of the disease went unnoticed,
in part because rubella was similar to measles (rubeola) and other diseases
that come with rashes, like chicken pox or even syphilis. As Australian

physician Charles Swan remarked: "In view of the universal occurrence of German measles, it seems curious that if congenital defects frequently followed a maternal attack during pregnancy, the connexion [sic] between the two conditions was not discovered earlier."[40] But frequently, the mothers didn't realize or remember they had been infected, given the generally mild course of the disease.

More to the point, the problem with identifying the effect on pregnant women and their fetuses was latency—the gap between the infection in the mother and the symptoms in the child. We now know the earlier the infection during pregnancy, the more severe the damage to the fetus; at the same time, that puts a longer distance between the timing of the exposure and the recognition of the damage.[41]

For all these reasons, it's easy to understand how congenital rubella syndrome was not recognized until relatively recently. In 1940 a particularly severe outbreak of German measles hit army training camps in Australia, and a large number of troops brought it home and infected their wives. The next year, Dr. Norman McAlister Gregg of Sydney, an ophthalmologist, noticed he was being referred an unusual number of infants with congenital cataracts. Some also had serious heart problems. Gregg checked with colleagues in New South Wales and Victoria, and soon had compiled seventy-eight such cases. In sixty-eight of them, he realized, the mothers reported having had German measles either right before or very early in pregnancy. Other such cases showed a high rate of deafness.

The *Medical Journal of Australia* broadcast the news in its bulletin for December 6, 1941, while Gregg's paper was awaiting publication in an ophthalmologic journal.[42] Meanwhile, Gregg had little doubt the finding would be confirmed—and it was. First in Australia, a series of retrospective studies went back and looked at "deaf-mutism" in earlier known rubella epidemics—and found that when a rubella epidemic hit Australia, the birth cohorts that followed shortly thereafter had an unusually high level of deaf-mute cases.[43] An island continent like Australia, where rubella epidemics came in identifiable bursts, made a particularly good laboratory for observing the impact of the rubella virus, but the finding was confirmed in the United States and Europe as well.[44]

From the beginning there were questions about the degree of brain damage that went along with the defects in vision, hearing, and heart function in these cases. Australian clinicians observed that the children had difficulties in intellectual development and learning capacity. Early on this was a subject of controversy and research, as a debate grew over whether the rubella virus was a primary cause of mental retardation or whether cognitive issues were secondary to the deaf-mute condition. Shortly after Gregg's discovery in 1941, a number of studies around the world took up the question of the mental capacity of congenital rubella victims. By and large these studies found evidence for some levels of mental retardation, but these rates were generally low, and most of the authors found that the deaf-mute condition explained most of the developmental difficulties. These early studies assigned a rate of mental retardation in congenital rubella anywhere from 2 to 20 percent.[45]

As physicians identified groups of congenital rubella victims, many of them in childhood, several groups were followed over the course of their lifetimes to assess the long-term course of the disease. For example, Dr. Gregg's collection of seventy-eight children was followed for sixty years with reports in 1967, 1992, and 2002.[46] These long-term studies showed that CRS took a serious toll, including heart problems, endocrine abnormalities, deafness, and vision loss. Similar long-term studies were conducted in London and New Zealand.[47]

By the mid-1950s it seemed clear what CRS involved—a seriously disabling condition of vision and hearing that included serious health complications, particularly heart disease. Beyond that, there were scattered cases of mental retardation and even a rare case of schizophrenia, but for many CRS victims, the long-term outlook was surprisingly good. As for the effects on the brain, it wasn't clear these were higher than in the general population, and they were difficult to separate from the learning disabilities that went along with deafness and cataracts.

Soon after Gregg made his discovery, scientists began to look for a rubella treatment, borrowing from the earlier diphtheria treatments that used antitoxins. To obtain rubella antitoxins, an infected person or animal was found and the blood extracted and processed to concentrate the antibodies that had developed to the disease; those were then injected in a person who had become infected or exposed to the virus. Early on there were two varieties of what was called gamma globulin—the first was made from generalized sets of antibodies pooled from large collections of human blood; the second was more targeted, taking blood from a convalescent group that had recently been infected with rubella and presumably had more active and specific antibodies.

For most, rubella infection was not a dangerous event, but there was an obvious question about how to prevent or moderate the infection in pregnant women during a rubella outbreak. A number of experiments, some in pregnant women, some in schoolchildren, set out to identify a method in the mid-1940s. The goal was to see whether, in the midst of an epidemic, gamma globulin could prevent an infection. Though relatively small and hard to control, the studies generally reported some benefit from treatment. In some cases the reported benefits were dramatic, in others more equivocal; but the medical profession was persuaded enough that a 1959 study reporting a limited benefit commented: "Gamma globulin is commonly used to prevent rubella in pregnant women exposed to the disease."[48]

By the early 1960s pooled gamma globulin products, much of them under the name poliomyelitis immune globulin, were produced on a large scale and considered effective. The preservative of choice was thimerosal (ethylmercury), so just as diphtheria toxoid and later the DPT vaccine had been first introduced to large populations, the commercial immune globulin preparations for rubella treatment were first launched into large populations of pregnant women.

Then, in 1962, scientists isolated the rubella virus, which allowed work on the vaccine to begin. But before long, there was a more urgent need to swing into action.

With a worldwide rubella epidemic at the start of 1964 a whole new picture began to emerge. Instead of the infection that caused deaf-mute syndrome and occasional cases of mental retardation, the disease as it swept across the United States seemed to have become far more dangerous, with dramatic rates of infant mortality and mental defect. Studies in Baltimore, Houston, and New York showed a far higher incidence of mental retardation and a general picture of devastation in the affected infants that exceeded anything previously reported. A study at Johns Hopkins noted the discrepancy and said that reports from past epidemics "would suggest, at most, a small increase in severe intellectual defects in children suffering from congenital rubella." By contrast, "The experience of several groups, following patients affected by the 1964 epidemic in the United States, suggests that the frequency of severe mental defect is quite high." The Johns Hopkins survey of Baltimore victims of CRS showed at least 29 percent were severely mentally retarded and roughly half were severely subnormal.[49]

If the Hopkins data were concerning, the implications of a study by Baylor University scientists were even more vivid and disturbing. The Houston group followed one hundred patients from birth through the first eighteen months of life. In their 1967 report titled "Congenital Rubella Encephalitis" they painted a picture of devastation unlike anything seen before. Out of the one hundred cases, twenty died in infancy; of the remainder, sixty-four were followed. Thirty of those had severe neuromotor impairment at eighteen months; only twenty of the original one hundred seemed unimpaired. Many of the infants had seizures and there were frequent reports of abnormal postures and movements—spastic rotations of the legs and feet, dramatic arching of the back, and retracting of the head.[50]

For the first time in any CRS study, the Houston group also reported signs of autism. This mention of autism caught the attention of a third research collective in New York City, the Rubella Birth Defect Evaluation Project in the Department of Pediatrics at New York University. "In the Baylor series, of the 64 children surviving at 18 months," the New York group observed, "8 appeared autistic, isolated and out of communication with the environment. Two actively rejected (by screaming, crying, back-arching) any attempt at communication or contact." This NYU group pursued the most organized and careful plan of diagnosis and follow-up, one that continued for several decades thereafter.

They recruited a group of CRS cases, carefully characterized them, and stayed in touch for many years. In their first report, they investigated 271 cases of CRS and found a high rate of "psychomotor retardation"; 65 of the 271 were severe or moderately severe, and 44 additional cases were affected, a rate of 40 percent of the group.[51] The researchers decided to look more intensively at the rate of autism in the New York CRS cases, and found a rate of 7.4 percent—18 out of 243 children evaluated were diagnosed with autistic spectrum disorder. They wrote that this revealed "a much higher prevalence of behavioral disorders than one would normally expect. This was particularly striking in regard to autism." They went on to describe the rates found by Victor Lotter in England (4.1 per 10,000) and Darold Treffert in Wisconsin (0.7

per 10,000) and remarked, "In striking contrast, the prevalence rate in our rubella children would correspond to 412 per 10,000 for the core syndrome of autism, and 329 for the partial syndrome, yielding a combined figure of 741 per 10,000."

This was no casual estimate. The authors took pains to emphasize the validity of their assessments. "We recognize that the diagnosis of autism requires rigorous justification. The condition is often loosely defined and overdiagnosed." They described their diagnostic criteria in detail. Over the next several years, they followed up on their sample. In a 1978 follow-up, two of the original eighteen children had improved and three new cases had emerged.

So what happened to these children? What caused this dramatic shift in the neurological outcomes of this preexisting disease? Was the strain of rubella that hit the United States in the 1960s more neurovirulent? That's certainly a possibility, although few observers seem to have made that argument, intimating that their observations were simply more accurate than those of their predecessors.

One possible explanation for this outbreak of severe outcomes is changes in the virus itself. But, as we have argued for the effects of mercury, treatment on individuals infected with syphilis, it is also important to consider the possibility that there are unexpected complications of the treatment when it is combined with the underlying pathology of the disease itself. As with the rise of a more toxic presentation of neurosyphilis three hundred years after syphilis came to Europe, we're left to consider a "treatment effect" as a possible factor. As we've seen, the standard of care for women exposed to rubella during pregnancy changed dramatically by the early 1960s, just before the first observations of autism in CRS children, the sharp spike in mental retardation, and the generally worsened outcome.

Did gamma globulin treatment and thimerosal that was used to preserve the commercial preparations have something to do with these surprising outcomes? Only one study sheds any light, and that is the New York City group's. Cooper and Krugman in their discussion of the NYU group, note, "The use of gamma globulin for the prevention of rubella has been a controversial topic for many years." They go on to say, "During the course of the present study, we have identified 31 infants with proved congenital rubella associated with one or more defects in spite of attempted prophylaxis with gamma globulin following exposure."[52]

Soon thereafter, in 1969, the rubella vaccine was introduced based on the identification of the virus itself seven years earlier. The vaccine proved to be a more effective weapon against congential rubella than thimerosal-containing gamma globulin, a treatment strategy Cooper and Krugman called "unpredictable and unreliable." The successful subsequent introduction of the rubella vaccine counts among the most successful vaccine programs ever instituted, as congenital rubella has disappeared from the United States (although it persists around the world).

Looking back, the verdict on gamma globulin treatment becomes substantially more negative and it seems likely—as in the case of syphilis—that using no treatment would have been better than injecting pregnant women with a mercury-containing product. In fact, the combination of the treatment and the rubella exposure seemed to be the most dangerous outcome of all. A 1961 study in North Carolina (admittedly a small sample) showed a rate of 16 percent abnormal outcomes in congenital rubella exposure alone; 6 percent of these were mentally retarded. Gamma globulin treatment by itself also showed a high rate of abnormal outcomes—with no rubella exposure, 6 percent of these pregnancies had an abnormal outcome. But the highest rate of abnormal outcomes came in children exposed to both gamma globulin and rubella. Out of eight children exposed to both gamma globulin and rubella, two were abnormal and one was mentally retarded.[53]

Was autism as an outcome of congenital rubella another example of a "disease of the remedy"? It certainly appears possible that infection of the rubella virus combined with an ineffective and toxic treatment could have contributed to the number of cases of autism observed in the United States in the mid-1960s. As gamma globulin therapies fell out of favor in the 1970s, the connection between autism and congenital rubella has faded, both from memory and the current clinical case record.

Yet although congenital rubella syndrome has disappeared from most developed countries because of the herd immunity gained from widespread use of the rubella vaccine, it persists in many less developed parts of the world. Surprisingly, in more recent reports from developing countries, the familiar profile of deaf-mute syndrome, cataracts, and heart disease is reported, but with a far more benign neurological picture than the horrific one that emerged in the Houston area after 1965. In the meantime, the World Health Organization estimates one hundred thousand new cases of CRS still occur every year and cites the numerous birth defects that go along with these cases, including deafness, blindness, heart disease, and mental retardation—but it does not mention autism.[54] In one example, a 2005 study in Oman of forty-three children found eye, ear, and heart problems as well as neurological manifestations including microcephaly, cerebral palsy, and seizure disorder—but no autism.[55] In a second report following a large outbreak in Brazil, investigators identified several dozen cases of CRS and similar outcomes—but no autism.[56]

Congenital rubella has long been a puzzle. Josef Warkany, the doctor who first identified acrodynia, commented on difficulties of connecting maternal rubella infections and subsequent deaf-mute syndrome in their children, offering "an apologia for pediatricians who for many years missed the correlation between the maternal disease and the anomalies in the offspring."[57] In that light, it would not be surprising if the "disease of a short-lived remedy" would also go unnoticed.

Bernie's First Revolution

The same year the rubella epidemic hit the United States, 1964, Bernard Rimland drew together his long search for a theory of autism into a book, *Infantile Autism: The Syndrome and Its Implications for a Neural Theory of Behavior.*[58] Although its full impact would take years to unfold, it powerfully countered the idea that parental behavior had anything to do with autism.

Rimland's voluminous reading had continued since his first communication with Leo Kanner in 1959 about his son, Mark. As a Navy psychologist, Rimland was occasionally sent to other cities that had medical school libraries. (San Diego did not.) "Between sessions and at the end of each day's work, Rimland would race to the nearest university library," according to one account. "In New Orleans, for example, he skipped the French Quarter and headed off to Tulane, where he talked a guard at the library into letting him into the locked building after hours."[59] He also persuaded friends fluent in other languages to translate medical journal articles.

All this played out against the background of Mark's severe autism. Mark's screaming and headbanging were extreme even by autistic standards. "When he got to be about a year old," Rimland's wife, Gloria, said, "he only cried twelve hours by the clock in a 24-hour period, and we thought we were really living—that was so wonderful, only twelve hours."[60]

Rimland's book never mentions Mark or a personal connection, instead unraveling the case against parents of autistic children in a methodical fashion. Rimland did believe that such parents were unusually intelligent and accomplished, but he didn't think that meant they had personality traits that made their children autistic. He summarizes the arguments for "psychogenesis"—the idea that the child's emotional environment (i.e., parental coldness) triggers autism—and exposed them one by one. Against this list, Rimland lines up nine reasons to support "the case for biological causation." These include the fact that not all parents of autistic children fit the cold and detached profile, that "pathogenic" parents have normal children, that the siblings of autistic children are generally typical but that when one identical twin has autism the other one almost always does, too, that autism is usually present "from the moment of birth," and that autism is often seen with manifestations of other organic brain damage, suggesting a biological trigger in at least some cases.

Finally, he notes an "absence of gradations and blends" among children with autism—the disorder was always well defined and severe; it fell within narrow parameters. "If autism were a reaction to environmental factors we would expect it to exhibit not only the diversity of manifestations from case to case as a consequence of situational differences," Rimland writes, referring here to family dynamics with his use of the term "environmental factors," "but in addition, the usual gradations in intensity, depending on the adverseness of the environment. . . . While there is variation in severity and in prognosis, the degree of variation does not account for the large void between autism and normal behavior. There have been few serious attempts to deny the existence of this void."[61]

Rimland appealed to the heart as well as the head, arguing from a moral basis: "Whatever may be the merit in being patient with psychogenesis as a hypothesis, there is much less in being patient with it as an assumed force-in-fact. The all too common practice of blatantly assuming that psychogenic etiology *can* exist or *does* exist in any individual case or in any given class of disorders is not only unwarranted but actively pernicious."[62]

In 1964, at a time when fissures were starting to appear in the Freudian foundations of psychiatry, these were winning arguments, buttressed by the fact that Leo Kanner himself wrote Rimland's introduction.

From that point on, Kanner moonwalked smoothly backward from his long litany of harsh comments. "We have in this country the National Association for Autistic Children," Kanner said, referring to Rimland's organization in a speech in Saint Louis. "The parents [are] finally rebelling against this assumption of guilt [and] being made to feel the culprits and [they] have encouraged further research and got together to help themselves as well as those who were interested in the topic."[63]

And against *whom* were these parents rebelling? Why, certainly not Leo Kanner—he made it clear he was talking about Bruno Bettelheim. "In the first publication of the eleven children," Kanner said, "I said all the other things I reported were facts and this was an opinion, at that time, that I felt very definitely that these children have some inherent, innate difficulty of relationship with people. . . . But there were others who felt, even so, that this is caused entirely and exclusively by some emotional conflict of the parents, especially the mother. In fact, a book appeared, a best seller, by a well known psychologist, describing the behavior of these children beautifully, but then decided that it's the parent's wish to see the child dead that causes the child to play possum more and more definitely. That book many of you know called *The Empty Fortress*, I found it an empty book."[64]

Kanner's turnabout reflects the revolution wrought by Rimland, creating a new disease model atop the ashes of the old Freudian theory. In its place is the alternative that Rimland pointed to as early as his 1959 letter to Kanner: "I have been mainly concerned with trying to find biological factors which might eventually help beat the problem." Autism in this model belongs to biology, not psychiatry; it is a specific disease entity, a complex response to genetic and/or biological events. Mothers have nothing to do with causing autism. Autism is a lifelong disorder.

But it took time for this paradigm shift launched by Rimland to take hold. Bettelheim's *The Empty Fortress* actually came three years *after*

Rimland's book, in 1967, and if there were any doubt who was the mainstream's approved autism specialist, one need look no further than the pages of *The New York Times* in 1967. In a lengthy bylined piece in *The Times Magazine*, Bettelheim was given ample room to elaborate his theories under the title "Where Self Begins."[65] The *Times* put its full editorial seal of approval behind Bettelheim two weeks later. "Foremost among the handful of psychiatrists and psychologists who have dedicated themselves to unraveling the puzzle of autistic behavior is Bruno Bettelheim," wrote the paper on February 26. "No brief review can do justice to his wisdom or his compassion."[66] A full-scale review followed in March.[67] And two months after that, the book was on the recommended summer reading list.[68] (The *Times* did run a brief letter from Rimland blasting Bettelheim: "To heap guilt, based on disproven, circumstantial evidence, on these parents, is an act of irresponsible cruelty.")[69]

But time and truth were on Rimland's side, and a moment of triumph came at the 1969 meeting of the National Society for Autistic Children, which he founded. According to a transcript of a tape recording, Kanner again blasted Bettelheim's "empty book" and said, "And *herewith* I especially acquit you people as parents. I have been misquoted many times. From the very first publication until the last I spoke of this condition in no uncertain terms as 'innate.' But because I described some of the characteristics of some of the parents as persons, I was misquoted often as having said 'it is all the parents' fault.' Those of you parents who have come to see me with your children know that this isn't what I said. As a matter of fact, I have tried to relieve parental anxiety when they had been made anxious because of such speculation."[70]

So if autism was innate, and it wasn't the parents' fault, what caused it?

Twin Studies and Genetics

"One of the strongest lines of evidence against psychogenic etiology of autism has come to light only in recent years," Bernard Rimland wrote in *Infantile Autism*.[71] He was referring to increasing reports in the 1950s of identical twins with autism. Compiling his own list of previous reports—in effect, the first survey of twins and autism—he found eleven cases in which both twins were autistic. All of them were monozygotic, or identical, twins, a remarkable finding given that only 1 birth in 285 is an identical twin.

By then, Leo Kanner had reported a total of fewer than 150 cases of autism in total. With so few cases reported, to find that eleven were cases in which both identical twins were affected was highly unusual. Rimland concluded that this high rate of autism in twins "seems highly significant in terms of the biological etiology of the disease."

When he and Mary Coleman had studied autistic children at the Washington gathering, one of their observations was that there seemed to be familial clustering. They noted the then-current estimate of between three and four autistic children per ten thousand, meaning that "one would expect to find family groupings only in extremely rare instances." Yet in their study of seventy-eight autistic children, they found six families in which there was more than one child afflicted, a total of more than 8 percent of the families in the sample. They also found "a rather high incidence of twins" and suggested the reason might not have to be genetic: "Of course, twins share the same intrauterine environment so evidence from twin studies can apply to gestational insults as well as patterns of genetic inheritance."[72] Twins provide a unique opportunity to compare the effects of genetics and environment. Identical twins have identical DNA, while fraternal twins have no more shared DNA makeup than regular siblings. As a result, numerous studies compare disease rates in identical and fraternal twins.

Three years later came the first formal autism twin study; it was authored by Susan Folstein and Michael Rutter, the man who developed the modern classification system for autism, the first post-Kanner update. They reported twenty-one twin pairs, eleven identical and ten fraternal, in which at least one of the twins was autistic. They found a relatively modest rate of both twins having autism (the "concordance rate"): four out of the eleven identical twins, or 36 percent, were both autistic (they said the remaining twin in five more pairs had a cognitive disorder like language delay); among fraternal twins, the concordance rate was zero.[73]

While the higher concordance rate among the identical twins pointed to a potential biological role, the fact that the majority were discordant is a point that quickly became lost: Subsequent investigators, bent on establishing the solely genetic basis of the disorder, blurred or glossed over the differences in the remaining cases.

Take Case 8, in which Folstein and Rutter described the identical twins, ten-year-old boys, as "discordant for autism, concordant for cognitive and social/emotional disorder." The firstborn was classically autistic. His twin, by contrast, was described in detail in the study as a "cuddly, responsive baby. Single words 23 months, phrases after 3 yr. Vocab. adeq. But limited social speech. Normal relationship parents. Only recently started to play peers; does not initiate interaction. Anxious. No resistance to change. Series of circumscribed solitary interests (currently marbles) . . . Shy but friendly boy."[74]

There is a world of difference between these two children, obviously. A shy but friendly boy with a normal relationship to his parents, going through a phase of fascination with marbles, does not belong in the same diagnostic category as a child with no functional language, who rocks and flaps and has repetitive behaviors and no affective contact—the hallmarks of autism. This suggests that "concordance for cognitive, social and emotional disorder" vastly overstates the genetic case for autism.

The contrast in other cases was even starker. In twin girls age five, one of whom was "severely autistic," the other was diagnosed as "concordant for cognitive disorder" but developed speech normally and had "normal relationship with parents but slightly less sympathetic and affectionate than sibs. Plays well with sibs but less with peers at school. . . . Drawing immature . . . At interview appears friendly, responsive, inquisitive girl." From this description, it is frankly difficult to see how the second twin can even be classified as having a "cognitive disorder." In addition, being raised with a profoundly disabled twin might have had subtle adverse effects on the typical one.

For almost a decade, there was nothing more published on autism and twins. Then, in 1985, Edward Ritvo and colleagues at the University of California, Los Angeles, came up with a strikingly different result. In a larger sample of forty twin pairs (twenty-three identical and seventeen fraternal), they found that 96 percent of the identical twins were concordant for autism, and 23.5 percent of the fraternal twins were concordant. Both numbers, obviously, were far higher than those in Folstein and Rutter's study. Ritvo made the suggestion that based on the arithmetic—nearly 100 percent concordance in identical twins, close to 25 percent in fraternal twins—autism could be the result of a simple recessive gene. While that theory was not borne out, the higher rate of fraternal concordance was striking. Researchers who expected to confirm a genetic basis for autism would anticipate low concordance for fraternal twin pairs because their genetic material is not identical, and while there is some suggestion of a high shared rate of autism among siblings, it is nothing close to 25 percent. Ritvo's findings, contrary to his own interpretation, suggested that fraternal twins shared some kind of environmental risk factor in the womb—a risk that might explain the higher rate in identical twins as well.[75]

In a sharp critique of the autism twin studies, Jay Joseph, a vocal critic of the way such studies are used to support genetic theories and diminish the role of the environment in disease, noted the incoherent interpretations of Ritvo's evidence, which clearly argued for environmental risks in the womb. "Rather than explain how Ritvo's 23.5% concordance rate is explainable on genetic grounds," wrote Joseph, "Folstein, Rutter, and the authors of the two subsequent twin studies attempted to discredit, dismiss or ignore this finding."[76] He notes that a 1991 review by Folstein criticized a "number of methodological problems" in the Ritvo study.[77] A Scandinavian group demeaned the Ritvo investigation as unacceptable because "cases were recruited largely from a pool of replies to a newsletter announcement of the National Society for Autistic Children," which could "lead to an over-inclusion of concordant and monozygotic cases."[78] Finally, in a 1995 twin study the authors wrote Ritvo et al. out of the history of autism research, citing only the Folstein and Rutter and Swedish studies as the "two previous epidemiological studies of autistic twins."[79] Indeed, Ritvo's study was not mentioned or cited at all by the 1995 authors.

After Folstein and Rutter and Ritvo came up with two wildly different findings, two subsequent studies followed that would soon come to dominate the discussion. The small Scandinavian study mentioned above found that ten out of eleven identical twin pairs were concordant for autism, and zero out of ten fraternal twin pairs.[80] Joseph is highly critical of their methods as well and points to their self-serving analysis of the Ritvo study: "Given the methodological problems, biases, and dubious assumptions in twin research in general, however, this study *does not* stand out as a noteworthy example of biased research. I mention these issues only to point out that [the Scandinavian] study—like Ritvo and colleagues' and most other twin studies—is subject to several potentially invalidating methodological problems and biases. Thus, it was improper for [the Scandinavians] and others to single out Ritvo's study as being qualitatively more biased than other twin studies of autism."[81]

In 1995, nearly twenty years after Folstein and Rutter's first study, a fourth study by British researchers including Rutter added a new group of seventeen identical and eleven fraternal twins. Their desire to settle on a conclusion seemed evident in their title, "Autism as a Strongly Genetic Disorder: Evidence from a British Twin Study."[82] These British researchers pooled their new twin sample with the twenty-year-old sample from Folstein and Rutter's original study and argued that they had found a 69 percent concordance rate in identicals and zero concordance in fraternals. This had the effect of diminishing the findings of the older identical twin set in Folstein and Rutter, which was discordant in 64 percent of cases. In the British study, like the previous Scandinavian study, none of the eleven fraternal twin pairs included in the sample were concordant for autism. In our view, this finding supported the bias of the investigators, which was to create the widest possible gap between the genetically identical group and the fraternal twins.

The British group went on to perform a calculation of heritability, the percentage of autism's causality that could be assigned to purely genetic factors. They estimated the heritability of autism at 92 percent. Jay Joseph points out an important inconsistency in their methods; the heritability calculations would have been thrown off by the zero rate of concordance in fraternal twins, a rate that was too low for the formula they were using. The investigators came up with a solution to this: As they continued to collect cases after the study period was closed, they reported that "*the next DZ pair seen* [emphasis added] was concordant for autism." Joseph noted that although the British researchers used this concordant set of fraternal twins in their calculation for heritability they did not include it in their published results, which listed a 0 percent rate. In reality, the British concordance rate for fraternal twins was 9 percent, a result that fell awkwardly between Folstein and Rutter's 0 percent and Ritvo's 23.5 percent in fraternal twins. Most important, the rate of fraternal concordance they used for their heritability calculation was only 3 percent.

The pooled concordance rates for all four studies were 77 percent for identical twins and 10 percent for fraternal twins, if Ritvo and the late addition to the British study are included. This is still a big difference, but the British study and the 92 percent heritability rate have become articles of faith rather than analysis and are frequently repeated in more than a decade's worth of autism and genetics papers. Subsequent twin studies would suggest that the gap between identical and fraternal concordance rates has grown even narrower in recent years, arguing that environmental factors in the womb have more to do with the finding than the genetic profile of the twins themselves; a recently published concordance study from Japan is closer to Ritvo's results than anything else.[83] In the meantime, a host of other technical arguments (such as that identical twins are more likely to share an intrauterine environment, specifically a single chorion—the same fetal membrance and placenta) point out the dangers of overinterpreting these and other concordance findings. But none of that has mattered as the rush to genetics has taken autism research by storm.

The Path Not Taken

Autism is remarkable for having been the subject of two fully developed— but fundamentally faulty—theories of causation within the first few decades of its discovery. In retrospect, the parental-behavior model was just waiting to be demolished—it could not withstand the rigors of Bernie Rimland's penetrating critique nor the rising observations of genetic susceptibility contained in the twin observations. Its roots in Leo Kanner's misunderstanding of the parents' backgrounds and behavior were taken to such a bizarre extreme by Bruno Bettelheim that even Kanner distanced himself from the implications.

The genetic model that rose in its place seemed better grounded in science and, at the same time, more humane—the parents had done nothing wrong, and there was no disputing some biological factor was at work based on the twin concordance data. But once again the possibility that this factor reflected a shared environmental risk in children with genetic vulnerabilities, rather than simple heritability, was overlooked. Rutter himself in 2008 acknowledged that "the truth may be that there is much more gene-environment interdependence than has been appreciate[d] until now,"[84] effectively returning the argument to the same point Rimland and Coleman made in 1974: the likelihood that evidence from twin studies could just as easily apply to gestational insults as patterns of genetic inheritance.

With Freud's influence on the wane and funding for biological and genetic research on the rise, genes became the new target of opportunity. Refrigerator mothers were exorcised. But chemical exposures were ignored. The triumph of Bernard Rimland and Mary Coleman was to turn autism into a biological disorder, but science promptly forgot environmental biology as it veered single-mindedly to genetics.

In the meantime the diagnostic tools for autism were being honed. Rutter himself systematized Kanner's diagnostic markers in 1978; after two subsequent updates, the 1994 edition of the *Diagnostic and Statistical Manual of Mental Disorders* included Asperger's syndrome. The medicalization of autism had begun.

In reading the different generations of diagnostic criteria from Rutter to the 1994 update, it's clear that none of the revisions marked a point of departure from Kanner's original vision; each revision was simply an attempt to make diagnosis easier for the practicing clinician. Indeed, the latest update in 1994 was defined as "a corrective narrowing." It's impossible to read the post-Kanner discussions of autism without coming across complaints that autism was overdiagnosed. And nowhere is it suggested that vast hordes of autistic cases were going overlooked.

Despite all this new interest in biological issues, not much progress was made in finding causes; genes in particular stubbornly refused to submit to discovery. And then something important happened. The early autism prevalence estimates of one in twenty-four hundred to one in ten thousand, which had held constant for three decades, suddenly began to look obsolete. Autism rates started to rise.

—

CHAPTER EIGHT

GROWING LIKE A WEED

It's time to start looking for the environmental culprits responsible for the remarkable increase in the rate of autism in California. There's genetics and there's environment. And genetics don't change in such short periods of time.

—IRVA HERTZ-PICCIOTTO,
A PROFESSOR AT UC DAVIS'S M.I.N.D. INSTITUTE[1]

The prevailing model of autism that has developed over the last few decades depends on epidemiological data for crucial support. Autism has been viewed as a rare, if tragic, disorder, with prevalence rates in most populations around five per ten thousand. This prevalence rate has been considered constant, with any variations in rates across studies a result of variations in study methodologies and criteria rather than differences in incidence. Consistent with this epidemiological view, and alongside a number of twin studies, autism has been characterized as an inherited disorder, with clear, if complex, genetic causes. Despite the fact that few, if any, polygenic diseases have ever been described, the research into autism has proceeded diligently in search of the multiple genes that supposedly "cause" autism. Autism is therefore grouped together with a host of other inherited diseases, many of which have had well-characterized, single-gene loci.

Autism thus entered the 1990s as a disease of neurologists and geneticists. The approved therapies, almost exclusively psychotropic drugs and behavioral programs, presumed that the genetic condition was unchangeable, if manageable. To the extent that parents reported puzzlement with a history of apparently normal development followed by unexplained regression and loss of function, these events were explained away as the progressive consequence of developmental defects. But then a phenomenon occurred that challenged this perspective on autism.

In 2004 Marshalyn Yeargin-Allsopp, the CDC's lead autism epidemiologist, gave a presentation on autism outside of Boston that one of us attended. In the course of her lengthy talk, she said something that surprised us. "About ten years ago, we began to hear concerns from around the country that people were seeing more cases of autism," she said.[2] Certainly, the CDC, as the agency on the front line of all emerging public health problems from HIV to swine flu, would have had some idea that there was an autism problem far before any of the rest of us did.

What did the CDC know about the autism epidemic and when did they know it? A case study in a small New Jersey township offers a revealing glimpse.

Stonewalling in Brick Township

The Centers for Disease Control was once a prestigious agency, staffed by an elite corps of disease fighters manning the front lines of the most threatening health problems of our time. In recent years, riven by dissension, it has failed in many areas to get to the roots of the most critical public health challenges of the day, including, but not limited to, autism. Morale has deteriorated and Congress has been investigating the agency.

The CDC has the dual responsibility for monitoring vaccine safety and promoting the vaccine schedule; at the same time it's also responsible for surveillance on diseases like autism. In light of widespread concern within the autism parent community over the link between autism and vaccines, when the CDC announces that it's launching a new effort to find the cause of autism, parents have been skeptical.

Was there a point in the history of autism when CDC leaders had the chance to honor its history and raise the alarm over the autism crisis? From Yeargin-Allsopp's intriguing comment, it's clear that CDC was at least beginning to hear reports of rising autism rates in 1995. There were few signs of a broader recognition of an autism problem that one can find before that. But then, in a small town in eastern New Jersey, the CDC's first chance to raise the alarm appeared. In the fall of 1997, at a parent support group meeting, a few people started commenting about how many new autism cases seemed to be cropping up in Brick Township, New Jersey, and how there seemed to be an unusual number of three- to four-year-old children with a new autism diagnosis. One of the attendees at the support group, a mother named Bobbi Gallagher who had two young children with autism, was struck by this coincidence. She wondered if there might not be a cluster of autism cases in Brick. Perhaps, she thought, there was something in the water. So she resolved to do something about it. She decided to send around a survey to see if she could count the autism cases in all of Brick, a town of some seventy thousand people.[3]

So as the new 1997 school year began, Bobbi Gallagher distributed her survey form everywhere she could think of in town. And in a few short weeks, she got a surprising result. Based on the responses to her impromptu survey, she counted more than forty autistic children in Brick Township alone and more than thirty who were just three or four years old. Armed with these results, Gallagher formed a group called the Brick POSSE (Parents of Special Services and Education) and organized a meeting at the local library a couple of months later. They contacted the National Alliance for Autism Research (NAAR), who in turn invited a number of academic epidemiologists. To a full house at the library meeting, Bobbi Gallagher shared her findings. One of the epidemiologists present decided the numbers were disturbing enough to contact the New Jersey Department of Health and Senior Services, who in turn contacted the CDC. In the meantime, the Brick POSSE arranged a meeting with their congressman, Representative Chris Smith, who invited them to his office in Washington.

Within weeks, a more organized response took shape. Bobbie Gallagher received an invitation to another meeting in Washington, this time in then New Jersey senator Robert Toricelli's office. Gallagher remembers the meeting vividly and she was astonished at how quickly plans had emerged. She had expected to play the role of supplicant, pleading with the government officials to take action. Instead, she found a prompt and aggressive action plan being put on the table. In the room that day were representatives from multiple departments within the CDC who had come to the senator's office equipped with a multipart plan, the first part of which was a prevalence study for Brick Township, an in-depth survey of the town's autistic population that would pick up where Gallagher's survey left off. The CDC had identified a core team of staffers to lead the effort, including Jacquelyn Bertrand and Marshalyn Yeargin-Allsopp from the National Center on Birth Defects and Developmental Disabilities (NCBDDD) and Frank

Bove from the Agency for Toxic Substances and Disease Registry (ATSDR). Their proposal: to diagnose every child with autism in Brick Township between the ages of three and ten years old. They would start canvassing for cases and conducting interviews beginning with the start of the 1998 school year in September. And they planned to move quickly (at lightning speed really), to have their initial results ready by the end of the year.

They were true to their word. Two diagnosticians spent several days a week diagnosing children in the fall of 1998. And by January 12, 1999, the CDC had confirmed the findings of Gallagher's initial survey. Out of an initial estimated Brick population of six thousand children from three to ten years old, they had found more than forty cases of autism, giving a preliminary rate that was twelve times the estimated prevalence in the rest of the country. "I think there is a cluster here. I don't know why," the lead investigator said in an article by the Associated Press the next week. "If [we find] it's something that can be taken out of the community, that will be done," she said.[4] According to the AP she also added another intriguing tidbit: that "the researchers are eager to solve the puzzle here because of escalating calls the last few years about possible, but less credible, clusters elsewhere in the nation."

It all seemed to Gallagher like a dream: The cavalry had arrived and somehow they were going to get to the bottom of the issue. But then something strange happened. Suddenly, the lines of communication with the CDC team went dark. After several months of intensive planning, intensive collaboration, and rapid response, the CDC team told Gallagher that they were not at liberty to discuss the results with the parents any longer. According to Gallagher, one of the CDC staffers informed her that the mere mention of the word "cluster" had provoked a reaction from the higher-ups within the CDC. Apparently, there was now even a debate as to whether they could use the word "elevated" when describing the prevalence rates. So from January 1999 until the release of the final study in April 2000, there was no more interaction with the CDC. Not a single word.

Perhaps this was due to concern about the legal questions it raised if there was indeed something in the water (class-action attorneys had begun recruiting local families). Perhaps the Brick results weren't a cluster after all but part of a larger pattern that caused a more generalized concern within the CDC (maybe it wasn't the water after all, since in February 1998 *The Lancet* had published a controversial study implicating vaccines in autism). But there was no doubt about the silence coming from Atlanta. Something had changed the behavior of the CDC team.

Vague political rumors circulated as an explanation for the new sensitivity from the feds. But whatever the cause, it wasn't until well over a year later, April 2000, that the CDC's Brick study team would resurface. And when they did, all talk of a cluster was gone. All concern expressed in mid-1997 for the surge in three- to four-year-old kids (who were four to six years old in 1998) was gone as well. Politics and public relations priorities, it seems, had taken precedence.

There was, to be sure, more work to be done after January 1999. The team added more autism cases to its count of "over 40" reported in their first press conference. By the time of their final report in April 2000, the CDC had identified sixty cases of autism spectrum disorder (ASD) in a population of just 8,900 children between the ages of three and ten. This rate, 1 in 150 children, was the highest autism rate ever reported anywhere in the world up to that time. And Bobbie Gallagher believed the CDC's count left out quite a few families that had left Brick and that an approach that accounted for migration would have yielded more than seventy cases.

But by early 1999, the CDC team had virtually all the information it would ever get on autism rates in Brick. What did they do with that information?

They had two questions they really needed to address in any final report. The first was the issue of locally elevated environmental toxins: the kind of industrial contamination that might have provoked a Brick autism cluster. The Brick POSSE certainly believed that they had discovered a cluster, and so there was great concern over specific chemicals that might be harming Brick's unborn children. Gallagher expressed skepticism that vaccines had anything to do with her own children's autism. "It's possible that vaccines are a factor in some families, but I don't think that's what happened with my two children," she told one of us. "I brought two autistic babies back from the hospital."

So with the support of local parents, the CDC team focused on water quality. And they had a specific hypothesis about the nature of the contamination. Frank Bove, the CDC team member from the ATSDR, had written a paper just a few years before that linked trihalomethanes (THMs) to a variety of birth defects, including neural tube defects. Bove believed that these neural tube defects could be the missing piece in the puzzle. Bove consulted with Patricia Rodier, a researcher from Rochester who had worked on toxins that she believed could cause neural tube defects in autism. The ATSDR report on Brick went on at some length about their concerns over THMs and neural tube defects.[5] But in Bove's particular approach to the analysis of Brick's autism cases and THM exposure, there was no smoking gun. In fact, any way they cut the data, they could find no link between the elevated THM rates in the local water supply and the local autism cases.

In short, the ATSDR's quest for a singular environmental toxin that might provide an easy explanation for Brick's autism problem came up empty. So despite autism rates in Brick that were far higher than anything ever seen before, the CDC and the ATSDR were unwilling to declare the Brick community an autism cluster. To this day, autism rates in New Jersey are among the highest in the nation and among the highest reported anywhere in the world (one recent survey reported a rate in New Jersey of one in ninety-four children). But partly because no obvious and easy toxin presented itself for blame and removal, the CDC took no position on Brick's high autism rates, and they pursued the issue no further.

The second question on the CDC's plate was the rising trend in autism rates. In Gallagher's support group meeting in 1997, everyone had remarked on the unusually large numbers of three- to four-year-old cases of autism. And by January 1999, the CDC had a great deal of data on ages and birth years of their affected population. Despite much evidence to the contrary, they declared that there was no statistical support for higher autism rates in younger children. "Age-specific rates were calculated for preschool (3- to 5-year-old) and school-aged (6- to 10-year-old) children. . . . CIs [confidence intervals] for the 2 age groups overlapped, indicating that the prevalence rates for the 2 age-groups were not different."[6]

How could this be true? It seemed to fly in the face of everything observed by the parents and professionals on the ground, not to mention the hints that the CDC had been hearing for years about rising autism rates all over the country. Unlike the search for environmental toxins in the water, there was nothing complicated about the trend. Either there were more cases or there weren't. And if the rates were rising, however hard it might be to pin down the cause, it was important to keep looking, because too many children were sick.

In mid-2002, it occurred to another New Jersey mother, Sallie Bernard, that the CDC's conclusion in their Brick Township report was likely to be flawed. Not only was the rising trend apparent in the CDC's data, there were also a number of odd elements in the report's design and write-up. For one thing, the age groupings were strange—the sample was separated into two groups of unequal size, three- to five- and six- to ten-year-olds. Why would they not divide the population into equal sizes, putting three- to six-year-olds and seven- to ten-year-olds together? For another, autism time trends can be easily misinterpreted if the analysts don't factor in the lag time that the youngest children face in getting recognized (the technical term is "ascertainment bias"). What if the Brick team, as most survey teams had done before them, had simply undercounted three-year-olds?

So Sallie Bernard sent an e-mail to Frank DeStefano of the CDC, whom she had met at a recent meeting. She asked him what would happen to the Brick rates with three-year-old cases removed. And he responded in a May 10, 2002, e-mail, "For overall ASD, the prevaleces [*sic*] were: 10.2 per 1,000 among children 4–6 years old, 4.4 per 1,000 among those 7–10 years old." Sallie promptly thanked him and, noticing that this rate differential seemed larger than the published study, asked him if these were statistically significant. DeStefano responded in detail that they were: "The results are based on 35 cases out of an estimated 3442 children 4–6 years of age, and 19 cases out of an estimated 4272 children 7–10 years of age. The difference in prevalences noted below is statistically significant." In other words, the published conclusion changed completely if you simply removed a single age group, the three-year-olds.

Despite providing a stunning admission, DeStefano had still not given Sallie what she really wanted, which was the breakdown by age category. So Sallie asked him again. And a few months later, she received this response from Marshalyn Yeargin-Allsopp:

Hi Sallie, Happy New Year! Frank DeStefano has asked me to respond to your question about rates of autistic disorder for Brick Township.

They are: (per 1,000), rounded

3 yo	2.5
4 yo	6.1
5 yo	7.8
6 yo	7.0
7 yo	6.4
8 yo	2.0
9 yo	—
10 yo	—
TOTAL	4.0

This was even more of a shock. What Yeargin-Allsopp had revealed was that there was not a single case of full-syndrome autism in the entire Brick Township population of nine- and ten-year-olds. While this was a different case definition than the one DeStefano had given, which included PDD-NOS* and Asperger's cases, it provided clear statistical support for the concern over the unusual number of cases in the younger children. And here it was in black and white—the CDC had had this data all along.

So on the second crucial part of their charge, the evidence was clear. The CDC knew there was an autism epidemic in Brick Township in 1998. And they neither said nor did anything about it. In fact, they did exactly the opposite: They used a clever bit of statistical trickery to cover it up.

In fact, once you have the real trend data, you can figure out how hard the CDC had to work in order to report a result that said there was no trend. In the months between their January 1999 press conference and their April 2000 report, the CDC had figured out the only possible way to claim that autism rates weren't rising. They took the six- to ten-year-old group—in which autism rates went from 0 in the group born in 1988, the ten-year-olds, to 1 in 143 for the group born in 1992, the six-year-olds—and put them in one bucket. They took the three- to five-year-old group, which due to ascertainment bias had a declining rate (from 1 in 128 for children born in 1993 to 1 in 394 for the youngest children, born in 1995), and put them into another bucket. And they compared these two ratios and reported that there was no significance to the rising trend. And if you run the statistics on just this arrangement of the data, they are correct. But virtually every other reasonable grouping shows a significant increase:

- DeStefano's analysis comparing ASD rates in four- to six-year-olds with seven- to ten-year-olds gave a significant increase with 99 percent confidence (statistical "significance" kicks in at 95 percent confidence).

- If you take the full-syndrome autism group and divide it into two equally sized buckets, comparing three- to six-year olds and

*"Pervasive developmental disorders" is the diagnostic category often referred to as autism spectrum disorders. The three main categories of pervasive developmental disorder (PDD) include autistic disorder, PDD-NOS (not otherwise specified), and Asperger's syndrome. A diagnosis of PDD-NOS is similar to but less severe than autistic disorder and includes language and communication delays, unlike Asperger's.

seven- to ten-year-olds, you also get a significant result with 99 percent confidence.

- If you take the five- to six-year-old group of full-syndrome kids and compare it to the nine- to ten-year-old kids, you get an even more significant finding, more than 99.9 percent confidence.

If this wasn't a cover-up, it's hard to think of a polite synonym.

Assuming the problem in Brick was more than a cluster, if there was a broader national trend toward rising autism rates, then what matters is not just the age of the Brick children but their birth years. A more consistent national trend would be revealed if we could find similar changes in autism rates in the same birth years. And a clear picture of the increasing trend would help us identify the potential environmental causes aside from elevated local toxins in the Brick water supply.

The age groupings in the Brick team's study were based on the "attained age in 1998." So the ages are easily converted to birth years. The chart below shows the data Yeargin-Allsopp sent to Sallie Bernard and compares it to the data the CDC published. As you can see, the rates exploded in the 1990–94 birth years and then dropped off a bit in the three-year-olds, due to the ascertainment effect. Looking at the numbers year by year (the dotted line), and comparing them to the published rates (the flat solid line), it's easy to see just how deceptive the CDC's reported findings truly were.

After such a diligent and responsive start, what moved the CDC team to do something like this? In March 1999, just two months after the CDC's first press conference on Brick Township, the California Department of Developmental Services issued a report showing a sharp increase in the number of autism cases in California. A few months after that, in July 1999, the Public Health Service announced its plans to remove thimerosal from childhood vaccines. So as the team completed their work, it's almost certain that the public posture the CDC was deciding to take in the Brick report took on added importance.

After all, as the chart shows, the real surge in Brick was in line with the expansion in the required immunization program, and certainly correlated with thimerosal exposure. So there's little doubt that the CDC was worried about its own role in provoking an autism epidemic. At the same time, as the durable evidence of elevated rates in New Jersey has shown, the local trend may also have been part of something more specific to the Brick environment. This was a moment of choice for

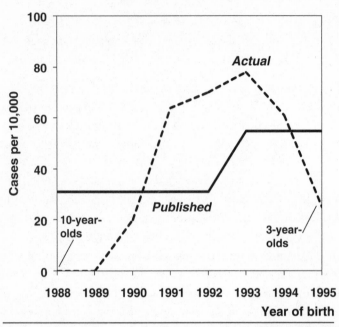

Figure 6—Comparing Reported and Actual Time Trends for Autistic Disorder in Brick Township

Source: Adapted from data reported in J. Bertrand et al., "Prevalence of Autism in a United States Population: The Brick Township, New Jersey, Investigation," *Pediatrics* (2001)108: 1155-61; and from data provided by the authors to Sallie Bernard of SafeMinds.

CDC. And in a moment that required continued professionalism, openness, and candor, something else happened.

In April 2000, after many months of silence, Bobbie Gallagher got a call from the CDC. They were coming to town to release their study, both the CDC prevalence report and the ATSDR analysis of local toxins. They came to her house, gave her two lengthy documents, asked her to respond in the moment if she had any questions. They confessed that the autism rates in Brick were three times higher than rates they were seeing elsewhere. But they had no plans to do anything more about it. Then they left the Gallaghers' house to go to the public meeting, where they took the same basic approach. They made no presentations, simply put the two reports on the table and made themselves available for questions. They had two sessions, one for the press and one for the residents.

And at the front of the room, Gallagher reports, there were two groups of people. One was the familiar team, who had done the work and been part of the initial outreach. Next to them was another group "we had never seen before." Their job, according to Gallagher, was to watch the original group and "make sure nobody said the wrong thing." At 8:00 P.M., the session ended and "you've never seen a group leave a room so fast.

"And we never heard from any of them ever again."

In the midst of the AIDS epidemic, it was CDC researchers that took the lead—often against the intransigence and conservativism of National Institutes of Health (NIH) researchers—in tracking down the causes and taking steps to reduce its toll on society. For many years, the CDC was held up to the world as a model government agency. Yet in autism, there seems to have been a downward spiral; and many feel that the agency has been defensive, secretive, and nonresponsive to a health crisis. There are undoubtedly larger forces affecting the agency and its leadership. But if there are turning points in the lives of large institutions, crossroads at which difficult choices are made, then the CDC's handling of the autism epidemic is certainly one such turning point.

Fombonne's Follies

While the federal government managed to avoid coming to grips with the alarming increase in autism in Brick Township, even more startling evidence from figures compiled at the state level was already overtaking it. Data from California released in March 1999 showed a 273 percent increase in the number of new cases of autism entering California's developmental services system from 1987 through 1998. The actual cases jumped from 3,902 to 12,780, a rate of increase more than four times greater than those seen in other diagnostic categories like cerebral palsy, epilepsy, and mental retardation.[7]

But these California numbers came under sharp attack from a London psychiatrist, Eric Fombonne. "There is no need to raise false alarms on putative epidemics," he wrote, "nor to practice poor science to draw the attention to the unmet needs of large numbers of seriously impaired children and adults."[8] The assault on the California numbers had extra weight coming from Fombonne, who had become one of the most prolific authors in the field of autism epidemiology. Fombonne himself was not a trained epidemiologist but a psychiatrist who had gotten into the field of autism by designing diagnostic tools and using those for prevalence surveys of autism. At the time the California report was released, no single author had published more surveys than Fombonne.

More to the point, he was also a prolific reviewer of the epidemiological literature. Starting in 1998 he wrote a series of review articles on autism, in which he collected and summarized findings from the past several decades of research in autism epidemiology. These were careful, meticulous comparisons of the differences and similarities in published autism surveys. Inevitably, in a review of the body of literature, the question of trend would arise, and Fombonne took a position—there was no trend.

In the early reviews it was possible to justify this conclusion because in most of the studies before 1995 the rates were consistent and low, along the lines of Lotter's original survey of 4.1 per 10,000 in England—with the exception of a few higher reported rates in some Japanese surveys. But as time went on and the numbers began growing like a weed, Fombonne appears to have dug in his heels to defend the orthodoxy: that autism was a genetic disorder with constant prevalence. This required an attack on the California study, and he delivered. He said the diagnostic practices failed to account for increasing population, their case definitions were inconsistent, autistic children were being diagnosed earlier, and that a chart showing the rising number of cases was distorted. "This graphical display deliberately transforms what is an age effect into what seems a cohort effect," Fombonne argued. "By analogy, any sample with a marked skewed age-distribution (for example, take a survey of Army personnel) could be misleadingly portrayed by replacing age by year of birth and giving the same impression of an upward trend over time . . . (but nobody would interpret the transformed personnel Army data as indicative of rising numbers of militaries!)."[9]

At the most basic level Fombonne's aggressive attack was flawed and assumed that age effects could be separated from cohort effects. He failed to consider the notion that the army has a thing called discharge; there may be a parallel in autism—the kind of recovery we saw when Donald Triplett was treated with gold salts—but by no means more than 10 percent. In the vast majority of autism cases, after they are "enlisted" there is no discharge.

In 2002 a follow-up study by the M.I.N.D. Institute at the University of California, Davis, showed that Fombonne's objections were baseless— that the increase was stark and real. The study concluded: "The observed increase in autism cases cannot be explained by a loosening in the criteria used to make the diagnosis; some children reported by the Regional Centers with mental retardation and not autism did meet criteria for autism, but this misclassification does not appear to have changed over time; children served by the State's Regional Centers are largely native born and there has been no major migration of children into California that would explain the increase in autism."[10]

The next year, a study that adjusted for population also found rising rates—of full-syndrome autism, not including the broad spectrum of other varieties—of more than thirty per ten thousand, close to the Brick Township rates.[11] Still, there were many attempts to nullify the California numbers and other signs of a huge increase, most of them based on the idea of "diagnostic substitution"—that autism rates were rising because more cases were being recognized that had once been classified under other diagnostic categories such as mental retardation.

One study led by Lisa Croen[12] appeared to show exactly that, and drew praise from Fombonne in the *Journal of Autism and Developmental Disorders.* "Croen et al. carefully analyzed the California dataset from the Department of Developmental Services," Fombonne wrote, "looking at factors that might explain the increase of prevalence reported during the 1987–1994 period." He summarized the basic case for diagnostic substitution: "The findings indicate that the administrative prevalence of autism increased during the study period but that the increase in the rate of autism was paralleled by an almost identical decrease in the rate of mental retardation not associated with autism."[13]

Fombonne's conclusions about Croen's analysis were flatly wrong. One of us reviewed the study and identified basic errors in Croen's analysis, particularly the tendency we've seen in the Brick Township numbers for the ascertainment levels to fall off sharply in children under five years of age (two- and three-year-old children with autism are far more frequently overlooked during screening efforts).[14] This is true for

both autism and mental retardation. Correcting for this bias dramatically changed the results that Croen reported. When challenged with
this criticism, Croen and colleagues looked at the data again, were
forced to acknowledge that the criticism was correct, and retracted their
original analysis.[15]

The diagnostic substitution argument has since been tried out on many
occasions, but two studies using special education data, one in Minnesota
and another using data for the entire United States, found no evidence
supporting this speculation. The Minnesota analysts found that prevalence rates were not falling in other special education categories, while at
the same time they observed sharp increases in autism rates.[16] In the
nationwide analysis, a different analyst group found no evidence of substitution at the national level when comparing autism to its closest diagnostic
neighbors: mental retardation and speech/language impairment.[17]

In 2003 another group of investigators examined trends in autism
rates in the United Kingdom, observing an increase in autism rates while
comparing this trend to what they suggested was a declining trend in
rates of "certain developmental disorders"; in our view, the authors of the
study offered the clear inference that the increased rates of autism were a
result of diagnostic substitution.[18] But the analysis also suffered from serious errors, some of which the authors subsequently acknowledged, even
as they disavowed having raised the idea of diagnostic substitution at all.[19]
Then, in 2005, a group from the Mayo Clinic examined the possibility of
diagnostic substitution in a population in Olmsted County, Minnesota.
They found no evidence of substitution between diagnostic categories,
since both autism rates and rates of possible substitute disorders increased
during the study period. In light of this, the group was forced to concede,
"We cannot exclude the possibility that environmental factors caused this
increase; additional studies are needed to address this possibility."[20] This
was a crucial point, yet these observations were buried in the detail of the
report and the authors downplayed this concession in the short abstract
that summarized the results of their analysis.

Besides diagnostic substitution, two additional arguments have been
proposed to explain the rising numbers. The first was diagnostic expansion: in other words, the suggestion that the criteria themselves changed
and other kinds of disorders that had not been included in the autism
spectrum before were now being included in the numbers. This conten-
tion is true in a sense, but only in the narrowest of ways. In 1994 Asperger's syndrome was specifically included in the fourth edition of the *DSM*

as part of the pervasive developmental disorders (PDDs). Most careful surveys of autism prevalence rates take care to distinguish between the three main categories of PDDs: PDD/autistic disorder, PDD-not otherwise specified (PDD-NOS), and PDD/Asperger's syndrome. In fact, Asperger's syndrome was rarely included in autism surveys published until very recently; in most such surveys the researchers provided a clear distinction between the Asperger's cases and the other PDDs. In those cases in which Asperger's syndrome data were reported, the numbers represented less than 20 percent of the total. And in all the surveys in which "apples to apples" comparisons can be made, the upward trend in autism is clear.[21]

It's only been the studies designed by the CDC itself in which enough confusion has come into play to make the claim of diagnostic expansion remotely credible. The CDC's formal autism surveillance program is called the Autism and Developmental Disabilities Monitoring Network, or ADDM. The program began measuring birth cohorts from 1992, therefore *excluding by design* the birth years with lower rates; and ADDM's reported statistics include all PDDs under "autism" (including Asperger's syndrome) with no segmentation between subcategories. Regardless of this confusion, there's plenty of evidence from the broader autism survey literature that full-syndrome autism rates (PDD/autistic disorder) have risen by a factor of ten or more, with no contribution at all from Asperger's cases.

Two other perspectives provide evidence refuting the hypothesis of diagnostic expansion. First, by simply looking back at their stated goals, the clear intention of the group that designed the latest set of diagnostic criteria for the PDDs is clear. "The change from DSM-III [1980] to DSM-III-R [1987] is an example of the broadening of the concept of autism," states Fred Volkmar, a leader of the design team for the most recent criteria. By contrast, "From DSM-III-R to DSM IV [1994], a *corrective narrowing* occurred [emphasis added]."[22] Despite the efforts of the designers to tighten the standard, the numbers exploded anyway. Second, by looking back at actual diagnostic practices, the only group to perform an audit of diagnosis quality over time found an equally clear result: In comparing two birth cohorts with diagnoses separated by a decade in California, they concluded there was "no evidence that loosening in diagnostic criteria contributed to an increase in the number of children with autism."[23]

The final epidemic-denial argument, in addition to diagnostic substitution and diagnostic expansion, is one that instead posits a widespread and systematic pattern of diagnostic oversight. One of us previously labeled

this theory the "hidden horde hypothesis"[24]—the suggestion that somewhere out there are hundreds of thousands of adults and older children
with a diagnosis of autism whose condition previously eluded detection
and have gone through life underserved and undiagnosed. Besides the
logical impossibility of this hypothesis, a number of investigators have
searched for this "hidden horde" and failed to locate one:

- In two instances, research groups went back to populations in
  which low autism prevalence rates had been measured previously
  and looked for new cases. In one of these, a North Dakota group
  found that 98 percent of cases had been found in their first survey,[25] while in the other, no new cases were found in a 1975–77
  Swedish birth cohort after adjustments for immigration.[26]

- Using a different approach, two studies have sought to find undiagnosed autistic individuals in adult psychiatric outpatient settings. In each investigation, one in Taiwan,[27] another in Sweden,[28]
  the rate of undiagnosed autistic cases was low (less than three per
  ten thousand in the population) and only a small percentage of the
  outpatient groups that were examined (less than 1 percent).

- Most recently, a group of researchers at the Mayo Clinic developed an aggressive method to reclassify as autistic older individuals never diagnosed with autistic disorder. They described these as
  "research-identified autism" cases. In their earliest cohort, their
  method routinely designated teenagers as autistic without regard
  to age at onset of symptoms (one of four essential criteria for autistic disorder). Despite this search for overlooked cases, the authors
  found that autism rates increased by more than eight times in a
  fifteen-year period.[29]

But consider for a moment a commonsense test of the hidden horde hypothesis. By one estimate, in the history of mankind, well over 100 billion people have been born on Earth, 99 billion of them before 1930.[30] If
autism rates were truly 1 in 150 throughout that period, then we would
expect to have seen close to 700 million autistic people born before Leo
Kanner's first case in 1931. Yet, try as we might, we find no mention of
these people in the history books, in literature, in folklore, or in family
records of any kind. How could this many cases go unnoticed and unrecognized for so long? How could this many severely ill people have re-

mained hidden, much less functioned adequately without help for so many years? How could Leo Kanner have described with a straight face a condition that differed "markedly and uniquely from anything reported so far" if they had been present in the hundreds of millions before?

It is true some modest forces are helping to fill out the case numbers in some reports. There's probably some shift toward an earlier age of diagnosis due to more active screening, and this earlier diagnosis can limit the ascertainment effect we've described before and speed up the rate at which true cases of autism can enter a services system. There are certainly more administrative databases to register formal autism diagnoses as part of an official record, and this expansion of registration practices provides more systematic reporting of prevalence rates without the need for special survey projects. But none of these forces come even remotely close to explaining the dramatic increases we've seen in reported autism rates.

The reason reported rates are higher is because the real rate is higher. Some may find it hard to accept, but the truth is inescapable; something new and terrible is happening to a generation of children.

Meanwhile, more anomalies have offered clues not only to the rising rate but to the reasons behind it.

Out of Africa—and the Amish

As if on cue, the latest autism tragedy emerged: In the Somali community of Minnesota. Escaping the horrors of a civil war that has lasted nearly two decades, these families immigrated to the United States in large numbers looking to replace their nightmare with the American dream. The rapidly evolving Somali experience is unfolding in familiar form: first with their own rising awareness of the autism anomaly as inexplicably high numbers of autism diagnoses show up in their children, followed closely with organized denial by public health authorities of both the rising numbers and the potential causes.

As we noted earlier, autism has always been rare in Africa, with low rates that have surprised researchers. Most autism there occurred in what was termed "elite" families with access to Western health services.

Now, among Africans who migrate to Western countries, autism rates are remarkably high. This raises an interesting set of questions.

The obvious risk that immigrants to any Western country face is over-vaccination. As vaccination programs have spread around the world in recent years, future immigrants are increasingly likely to be vaccinated in their home countries. When they travel, they are forced to receive another round of vaccinations in their home countries before they leave. When they reach their new countries, their previous vaccination records are generally not recognized as valid and they often must be vaccinated again. This unique migration risk is especially relevant for population groups that can influence autism risk: women of child-bearing age, pregnant women, and infants. It's hard to know what kind of havoc these redundant treatments wreak on the immune system of such targets when they receive excessive vaccine doses. All we know is that children of modern immigrants are at high risk of both overvaccination and of autism. But no one has ever bothered to investigate overvaccination as a specific risk factor of obtaining the medical entry visa to Western civilization.

Well before the Somali anomaly in Minnesota, autism surveys noted an increased risk of autism among African immigrants. The first hint came not from Minnesota but from Sweden. In 1991 Christopher Gillberg, one of the more prolific autism survey authors, published a study titled "Is Autism More Common Now Than Ten Years Ago?," in which he made the following observation about the city of Göteborg: "Almost 60% of all new children with autism in the urban region detected between 1984 and 1988 were born to immigrant parents. Almost all of these parents had been born in non-neighboring countries and more than half came from southern Europe, Asia, Africa, and South America. So far, this represents an unusual distribution of immigrants as compared with the Göteborg population in general."[31]

In subsequent studies Gillberg went on to investigate the idea that children born to parents of immigrants in Sweden (including but not limited to African immigrants) had higher autism risk, but Gillberg didn't consider the vaccination risk in any of these papers. Instead, he raised for the first time the notion that "men with Asperger syndrome (whose children would be more likely than others to develop autism) might marry women from other cultures, who, in turn, might not initially be as aware of the social and communication deficits shown by these men as native women would be."[32] But in a detailed study of these specific cases, Gillberg rejected the parental mating theory. He did consider the idea that the Ugandan mothers were exposed to a novel virus while pregnant and that this exposure provoked autism in their children. The suggestion that the virus might come from a vaccine rather than a wild type of virus never came up.[33]

Only recently has Gillberg even raised the specter of the vaccination hypothesis: this time indirectly in a 2008 analysis of Somali immigrants in Stockholm.[34] Most important, this new study found a rate of autism among Somali immigrant families (1 in 142) that was three to four times higher than the rate in the non-Somali group from Stockholm (1 in 526). In their paper, the authors noted that the Stockholm Somali community was suspicious of the MMR vaccine and had a reduced vaccination compliance rate (70 percent vs. 95 percent in most other areas of Stockholm). They also noted that they had collected extensive medical records for all the Somali immigrants. But despite collecting all the information on Somali vaccine records, they did not disclose any vaccination risk analysis of any kind in the paper.

By now, the official response that the Somali community in Minnesota experienced is predictable: Autism rates can't be low in Africa, "we simply don't know what the prevalence is." When higher rates of autism showed up in the children of African women who immigrated, certainly it wasn't the experience these women had while immigrating that could shed light on their infants' risks; it must have been due to the innate autistic features of their husbands. And, of course, when the Somali community in Minnesota began to mobilize around the possibility that the excessive rate of vaccination to which they'd been subjected during their immigration process might have increased their children's risk of autism, they were dismissed with the same contempt with which native-born parents have been treated.

But the findings speak for themselves: Lotter found 1 in 145 cases of autism in a population of mentally handicapped children in Africa. By contrast, in Somalian immigrants in Minnesota, we are finding one in twenty-eight in the entire population of children.[35] The Somali anomaly is no anomaly at all. Instead, it is a bright beacon that shines an uncomfortable light on the root causes of autism.

As interesting as clusters with high autism rates might be, groups that appear to have a low prevalence of autism are also highly significant. Starting in 2005, one of us began looking for autism in major Amish population centers.[36] There are just a few of them in the United States, with an overall population of close to two hundred thousand Amish (over two-thirds of whom reside in three states). If we had applied a recent estimate for autism prevalence of 1 in 150, we would have expected to find quite a large autistic population among the Amish, well over a thousand, but so far have identified only a small handful of cases, a minute fraction of the autism population size one would expect to find. The most aggressive possible count of autistic Amish comes to fewer than twenty cases, which would give us a rate of no more than one in ten thousand, nearly one hundred times less than the best current estimates.

Dr. Heng Wang, director of the Clinic for Special Needs Children in Ohio, told us the rate of autism in the Amish there was one in fifteen thousand—literally. Of fifteen thousand Amish who live near Middlefield, Ohio, Wang is aware of just one who has autism.[37] The consensus over low autism rates in the Amish population is as true in Lancaster County, Pennsylvania, as it is in Middlefield. A Lancaster County doctor named Frank Noonan who has cared for thousands of Amish patients over nearly twenty-five years confirmed the same assessment. "We're right in the heart of Amish country and seeing none," said Dr. Noonan, "and that's just the way it is."[38]

One medical center, the Clinic for Special Children in Lancaster County, says it does see Amish autistic children, but only in connection with genetic disorders. A pediatrician there, Kevin Strauss, described the cases as "syndromic"—occurring along with genetic defects as opposed to "idiopathic autism" with no evident organic or genetic anomalies. He told a blog writer, "We see autistic behaviors along with seizure disorders or mental retardation or a genetic disorder, where the autism is part of a more complicated clinical spectrum" such as mental retardation, chromosomal abnormalities, unusual facial features, and short stature, as well as fragile X syndrome. "We see quite a few Amish children with fragile X," he said.

Strauss says he doesn't see cases of "idiopathic autism"—children with average or above average IQs who display autistic behavior—at the clinic. "My personal experience is we don't see a lot of Amish children with idiopathic autism. It doesn't mean they don't exist, only that we aren't seeing them at the clinic."[39]

All of this suggests that autism as it presents in mainstream American society is markedly absent among the Amish. In interviews with dozens of Amish residents and those who serve them, we came across a single Amish child who met the description of "idiopathic" autism: the exception that could prove the rule. A decade ago, as an infant, she was taken from her family by public health authorities who did not approve of alternative treatments she was given to treat an ear infection; while in their care, she was vaccinated at the Clinic for Special Children before being returned to her family a year later. At that point, the family said, they first noticed autistic behaviors; she now has a diagnosis of full-syndrome autism.[40]

Like Native Americans without general paresis, the Amish are living a different lifestyle—they grow much of their own food, often give birth to their children at home, work in Amish-owned enterprises like furniture building, and make far less use of mainstream medicine. Although there is no prohibition against medical interventions, their vaccination rate tends to be lower and slower and many Amish have never been vaccinated; after a 1991 rubella outbreak led to cases of congenital rubella syndrome, the CDC studied eighty-nine mothers and found that only one had received a rubella vaccination.[41] The rate of immunization has been rising as public health workers go door to door offering free vaccines, but the overall coverage remains substantially lower.

Some have suggested that because the Amish intermarry they may be genetically protected from autism susceptibility genes, but it is far more likely that some environmental factor is at work. Former CDC director Dr. Julie Gerberding has said that studies of the autism rate in never-vaccinated American children "could be done and should be done," but to date that has not happened.[42] U.S. Representative Carolyn Maloney (D-N.Y.) has introduced (and reintroduced) a bill requiring the federal government to conduct such a study, informally referred to as the Amish Bill.[43]

Autism appears rare in two other settings with different lifestyles and lower vaccination rates—homeschooled children, many of whom are not vaccinated; and patients who choose health care practices such as Homefirst Health Services in Chicago, which does not push vaccines for families that don't want them. Dr. Jeff Bradstreet, who treats several thousand autistic children from around the country at his practice in Florida, said there is virtually no autism in homeschooling families who decline to vaccinate for religious reasons. "It's largely nonexistent," Bradstreet told us. "It's an extremely rare event." Bradstreet, who describes himself as a "Christian family physician," has a son whose autism he attributes to a vaccine reaction at fifteen months. His daughter has been homeschooled, and he knows many of the leaders in the homeschooling movement.

"There was this whole subculture of folks who went into homeschooling so they would never have to vaccinate their kids," he said. "There's this whole cadre who were never vaccinated for religious reasons." In that subset, "Unless they were massively exposed to mercury through lots of amalgams (mercury dental fillings in the mother) and/or big-time fish eating, I've not had a single case."[44]

Homefirst Health Services in Chicago also says it has a virtual absence of autism among several thousand patients who were delivered at home by the practice. In a group that size, there should be several dozen. "[Our practice] has virtually no autism," the director, Dr. Mayer Eisenstein, reports. "I got all my partners together; we scoured the records. We looked at ICD codes for neurological disorders, and first of all, we didn't see it.

"But it's more than just no autism," he said. He and his three partners, in practice for twenty-five years, decided at the beginning not to treat children with asthma and insulin-dependent diabetes—they would instead refer them to specialized practices. Asthma now afflicts one in ten American children, and a growing number are diabetic, but neither diagnosis has occurred in the thousands of never-vaccinated children in the practice who were delivered at home.

"And I can tell you this would be a nightmare when you have to start referring one person a week, two people a week, three people a week, in a large practice, only because, you know, they would say, 'But Dr. Eisenstein, I want you to take care of me,' [and I would have to say,] 'No, there are people who are much better at taking care of asthma than me, there's people who are much better at diabetes than me.'" But according to Eisenstein, "It never came up."[45]

Separated at Birth

As evidence for environmental factors increases, the twin studies that form the basis for the genetic argument have continued to look shakier.

In the ten years since the last twins study, in Britain, there has been remarkably little published in terms of concordance studies. But more data
about twins and autism have continued to come in, and they tend not to
support the orthodox view of a genetic basis for autism.

There are several ways in which the evidence refuses to cooperate
with the theory. First, as we've noted above, some authors have emphasized the high concordance rates in identical twins—rates that were 90
percent or above. But more accurate analyses of identical twin concordance rates come in at 70 percent and often lower. For example, a 2004
study found an identical twin concordance rate of only 44 percent[46]
and a study in California produced a rate that could be as low as 59 percent.[47]

Second, there's a fair amount of evidence suggesting that even when
the identical twin concordance rate is high, that's simply because twins
themselves are at a higher risk for autism, including fraternal twins. The
reasons for this aren't known but might have something to do with the
unusual gestational environment facing twins. This is an obvious conclusion to draw from the Ritvo study, which had an astonishingly high
rate of fraternal concordance.

The only concordance study done in the last fifteen years came out of
Japan and reports results that echo Ritvo, close to 100 percent concordance in identical twins but close to 30 percent in fraternal twins.[48] This
may reflect an increased genetic susceptibility in the identical twins, but
it may also point to their more often sharing an environment than do
fraternal twins. Three other studies have suggested that high rates of
autism in twins may simply result from the extra demands the twins put
on mothers and babies in pregnancy—implying that being a twin is a
risk factor for autism all by itself.[49]

Third, the idea that autism is inherited relies on the difference between the identical twin and the fraternal twin concordance rates, based
on the idea that identical twins have identical DNA, and the higher the
ratio between the two concordance rates, the more inheritance plays a
role; the lower the ratio, the less convincing the case. The Japanese
study, for example, with a high rate of concordance in identical twins, still
has a ratio of identical to fraternal of only three to one. Another study
reported an identical-to-fraternal rate of less than two to one, although
they did so as a parenthetical aside.[50]

In short, the quest to confirm the heritability theory with the twin
data is a numbers game and requires good behavior from the twin study

data. Overwhelmingly the data suggest that there are much more subtle interpretations of the twin evidence, none of which rely exclusively on genetics.

In contrast to the numbers game of the orthodox geneticists, the case for the environmental perspective requires a different approach to evaluating the twin experience. From an environmental perspective, a high rate of fraternal twin concordance—much higher than any reasonable sibling rate—would be an occasion to inquire about the exposure history of the mothers and the affected twin pair because of their shared prenatal environment. Similarly, a low concordance rate in an identical twin provides an opportunity to learn what differed for the two children, who, despite sharing genetic material, have dramatically different outcomes.

In our research we've come across at least eight such identical twin pairs with dramatically different outcomes. It is worth listening to three of the mothers tell their own stories.

Jeana and Darryl Smith of Baton Rouge had identical twins, Jesse and Jacob, in 1995. The only difference in their health history was that a month after the births, "we found dark blood mixed in Jacob's diarrhea," Jeana told a congressional hearing in 2000. "Jacob had never had diarrhea before. We immediately took him to the doctor, who assured us the blood was from a rectal tear. He mentioned that in the chaos that generally follows the birth of a baby, much less twins, we had been released from the hospital without vaccinating the twins with Hepatitis B. He wanted to vaccinate Jacob right then. We questioned him because it did not seem right to give a potentially ill child a vaccine, but he convinced us that it was routine and safe. Not to worry."

Jeana Smith believes that was the decisive difference. "Two months later, Jacob received his second Hepatitis B vaccine and Jesse his first. On this same day Jacob and Jesse both received their first DPT, Polio and Hib vaccination. From that day, Jacob was constantly coming down with one ear, respiratory or sinus infection after another. Jacob was constantly on antibiotics.

"At only 16 months of age Jacob and Jesse received their first MMR vaccine, along with their fourth DPT, fourth Hib, and their third Hepatitis B. The following 24 hours both twins slept most of the time with 100 degree temperatures, in spite of receiving the recommended dosage of Tylenol every six hours. Just days later, Jacob began exhibiting strange behaviors. He was no longer excited or responsive when Daddy came home from work. He became preoccupied with certain toys. He would spend long periods of time studying the way their wheels would spin or whether or not they were lined up just right. Any attempt to interrupt or distract him was met with great resistance and an eventual fit. During this time, Jesse went along with business as usual.

"Back to the doctor we went again, this time with very serious concerns about the growing developmental difference between Jesse and Jacob. And once again, we were met with the dominant twin theory. Jacob would probably be more quiet. Jacob would probably want to play by himself more often. 'Jacob is fine, stop worrying.'

"Finally we could not stand the undeniable difference in their language and communication skills. Something was most definitely wrong with Jacob. He could not express even his most simple needs or wants. He couldn't ask for juice or something to eat. Jesse was chattering constantly. And at times, Jacob was so withdrawn that we absolutely could not reach him.

"In a waiting room, in front of several other parents, we received Jacob's first official diagnosis. The Director of LSU's Speech and Hearing clinic callously and simply stated, 'Mrs. Smith, Jacob is autistic.'"[51]

Diane Powell of Harrisburg gave birth on November 25, 2000, fourteen weeks prematurely. Casey was 13.8 ounces, one of the smallest premature infants ever to survive; identical twin, Sean, was 1 pound, 7 ounces.

"Casey was diagnosed at two and a half with classic autism; he had been developmentally delayed since birth but did have regression—loss of speech and eye contact," Diane Powell says. "He remains nonverbal (makes sounds and some word approximations)—still hand-flaps, stims, etc." He's affectionate, but still has a diagnosis of classic autism.

"Sean was tracked for developmental delay due to prematurity early on and received speech and OT. At eight, he is now in a regular school class with no special support or services.

"Certainly I think genetics plays a role, but not the only role, since we disprove this," their mother says. "Casey was, and is, still the most immune compromised of the two. He has also been diagnosed with PANDAS—so his immune system is all out of whack, and has been since birth." In the neonatal intensive care unit, he had a staph infection and pneumonia among other problems, and later "tons of ear infections."[52]

———

One of the strongest tests of heredity versus environment is the "separated at birth" phenomenon. That is what happened to the identical twin boys of Kim Stewart.

"When I was nineteen and in college in Massachusetts, I got pregnant. My first ultrasound revealed I was carrying twins. After weighing my options (along with the babies' father, my boyfriend at the time), we decided on adoption. I gave birth to two healthy identical twin boys. I had hoped that the boys could be kept together, but in the end they were adopted by two different families, one in Nashua, New Hampshire (Kevin) and one in Portland, Maine (Brian). The families kept in touch with each other, and also sent me periodic updates.

"Both boys were developing normally and were healthy, happy little boys. At fifteen months, Kevin began regressing and losing skills and was diagnosed with severe autism at age two. Brian continued to develop normally. At the time, the vaccine question never came up, and I wasn't aware of the vaccine status of the boys. I just assumed they were both vaccinated, because that's what everyone did.

"When the boys were six, a friend had a severe reaction to a flu shot while pregnant, and subsequently gave birth to a baby girl (who was also vaccinated with hep B at birth, against my friend's wishes) who never developed normally and was diagnosed with early infantile autism. This caused me to wonder about what might have happened to Kevin, and I discovered that his initial regression coincided with his fifteen-month shots. Brian's family are Christian Scientists and did not vaccinate him. Obviously, there can be other factors involved, since they live in different places and are exposed to different things, but after what happened to my friend's daughter, I became convinced that Kevin's vaccinations played a significant role in his regression. Additionally, Kevin has gut problems and food and environmental allergies, while Brian does not. The boys will be fifteen next week.

"I am now married with three daughters. Interestingly, I had another set of identical twins, who are now five, and I also have a two-year-old. None of them are vaccinated and they are all incredibly healthy and vibrant kids."[53]

Scientific Revolution

The incidence of autism is increasing at disturbing rates. Yet this simple observation, affirmed by clinicians, parents, educational providers, and a wide range of "front line" professionals, has been surprisingly controversial. Leading news journals hesitate to report it. Leading scientists carry on in their research without considering the implications of the increase. And most of the epidemiologists who have taken on the special challenges of analyzing and interpreting what little data exist on the incidence of autism have sidestepped this crucial issue.

Why is there such resistance to such a simple finding of fact? Because, in the language of historians of science, rising autism incidence is an anomaly, a novelty that the prevailing model of the disease cannot explain. Anomalies are often unwelcome events in the regular course of scientific progress. But when such events occur in the context of a community struggle, they can be even more unwelcome. And indeed, over the last few decades there has been a meaningful struggle to establish a medical model for autism, a disease that was once thought to result from the pathological neglect of so-called refrigerator mothers.

In the context of such a recent struggle, the emergence of an anomalous finding has met with more than its usual share of scientific skepticism. Yet the alarming rates of autism have continued to attract widespread publicity and attention. In the meantime, the prevailing disease model continues its collapse in the face of novel information it cannot explain—specifically, the soaring autism rates in the United States and Britain starting around 1990 that many parents associate with the rise in vaccinations. And it is the parents—and a vanguard of courageous scientists—who are putting together the puzzle pieces and building a new environmental paradigm for the disorder.

CHAPTER NINE

FRUIT OF THE POISONED TREE

The act of judgment that leads scientists to reject a previously accepted theory is always based upon more than a comparison of that theory with the world. The decision to reject one paradigm is always simultaneously the decision to accept another, and the judgment leading to that decision involves the comparison of both paradigms with nature and with each other.

—THOMAS KUHN, *THE STRUCTURE OF SCIENTIFIC REVOLUTIONS*[1]

As we've seen, Leo Kanner liked to invoke the concept of serendipity, the notion that scientific discoveries result from the happy combination of "accidents and sagacity."[2] More to the point, he liked to say he was personally endowed with serendipity (what he called "the gift of finding unsought treasures"), citing his observation of the early cases of autism as a case in point.[3] But Kanner's discovery was remarkable as much for what he failed to observe as for what he did. His mind was well prepared to draw a clear distinction between the children he examined and those described before him, and that part of his discovery has stood the test of time, but he did not possess the sagacity to ask obvious questions: Why had no one ever observed the pattern before him? What attributes did those early families really share that could explain the sudden arrival of this new condition? The combination of autism's rarity and Kanner's vanity made it possible for both him and others to credit his acute observational skills for the discovery. But as rising autism rates brought the tragedy home to increasing numbers of families, true serendipity would soon have to benefit from the greater sagacity of fresh observers.

Within a short period during the 1990s, three different observers launched the search for a new environmental paradigm based on two separate causation theories. Both theories involved infant vaccines, a hot-button area that would soon mire the autism community in new controversies. But none of these three began their autism journey with a particular bias against vaccination; instead, they all had prior experiences that simply prepared them to offer a risky theory. The father of germ theory, Louis Pasteur, famously remarked that "where observation is concerned, chance favors only the prepared mind".[4] So far, we've focused on the roots of only the autism-mercury theory. For the other theory, however, the causal roots came from a surprising direction. Real insight into the causes of autism would require observing not just the brain, but also the bowel.

Frankenstein's Monster Evolves

Rosemary Kessick, or Rose, was prepared for autism in ways few parents are. Her parents, Glover and Dorothy Lunn, were both medical professionals. Her father, first a scientist and then a medical doctor in England's National Health Service, did early research on nutrition. Her mother, a nurse who worked alongside her father in their general medical practice, raised three children while juggling a career translating medical jargon into practical patient advice.

One of those children posed a special challenge to the family. Rose's older brother David was schizophrenic, struck with the disease in adolescence when Rose was just six years old. Like many family members affected by mental illness, Rose was forced to "survive schizophrenia" along with her parents and brothers. Her parents didn't survive very long: Glover Lunn died at fifty-two when Rose was just eleven; Dorothy died ten years later at the age of fifty-three.

Rose notes with pride that her parents' former patients still come up to her on the street to tell her how much they appreciated the care her parents provided. Rose sees this as a product of her parents' strong values: They always treated their patients with respect, had a healthy skepticism of commercial medicine, and worked incredibly hard. Rose's pride comes with battle scars. Back when she was growing up, parents of schizophrenics—like autism parents—had a tough time; Freudian theorists also blamed schizophrenia on bad parenting. Although her parents never bought the Freudian line—Rose remembers her father telling her schizophrenia was clearly biological—there was little they could do about the prejudices of others.

When her own children were born—her oldest son James in 1981 and her second son William in 1988—Rose followed in her mother's footsteps. She juggled raising children with a career, starting as a college lecturer in communications and drama, and then going into business. Making the transition back to work had gone smoothly with James and so she was optimistic for a similar transition with William.

Always lurking in the back of Rose's mind, however, was a fear for her own family's survival. "I always had a real terror that my children would be schizophrenic," she recalls. So she had a vivid memory, when she was pregnant with William, of hearing a radio report claiming that English scientists had discovered the cause of schizophrenia. It was a gene, of course. Rose approached her doctors to see if she could test for the gene. They told her that, well, the claim reported on the radio was a bit premature, the gene didn't really explain much after all, and there were no tests. Nonetheless, Rose and her doctors did scrutinize William's early development closely. Everyone assured her, "There's absolutely nothing wrong with this baby," and everything Rose saw with her own eyes led her to believe them.

In fact, William seemed to be ahead of typical infants in many ways. Rose remembers him as clear and focused within hours of birth; after leaving the hospital, he hit all his early developmental milestones on or ahead of schedule. Even beyond those things pediatricians measure formally, William was the sort of baby that gives parents great joy: He was physically affectionate and cuddly; he gleefully played peekaboo games, extending the interactions with delight; he pointed and made eye contact; he understood language clearly; and he had developing vocabulary of his own, words like "drink," "book," "call," "James," and "cat" (a special favorite).

All that changed at fifteen months. Within days of receiving his MMR vaccine, William became a different child. Almost immediately, he began having digestive problems: More bowel movements each day and these with unusual colors and smells. Also immediately, his sleep patterns changed. A child who used to wake up just once a night became a fitful sleeper. The slightest noise awoke him and he almost never settled for a period of extended sleep. Most of all, Rose remembers that he just never looked right, as though he was simply sick all the time. Before long, William began banging his head and presenting with symptoms of autism, losing all his language and social connection.

Rose found it nearly impossible to get help for William's mysterious set of symptoms. Most medical doctors had never heard of autism, and those who had some dim awareness insisted that William was not autistic. "I can tell you absolutely, he's not autistic," one said. "William needs speech therapy." They were even more flummoxed by the link between his brain and gut problems. "Not one doctor could look at William and say, 'I've seen this pattern before,'" said Rose, "not a one." When Rose mentioned her suspicion over the connection between the MMR vaccine and William's downward spiral, the conversation closed down almost immediately. "Don't worry your pretty head about MMR," one specialist told her. The possibility of an adverse vaccine reaction wasn't even worth considering. "I've seen vaccine damage before," said another, "this is not a vaccine reaction."

About this time, Rose's local pediatrician commented to her, "You know, this is funny. I'm seeing quite a few local children that are presenting a bit like William. You should all get together." As Rose met these families, it became obvious to her that many of these children were similar to William in having both developmental and digestive issues. None of the other children were quite as severe as William, but the same symptom pattern jumped out at her, even when the parents were in denial.

Out of necessity, Rose began to put the pieces of the puzzle together on her own. She started wondering about William's diet. Perhaps something he was eating was causing the diarrhea. So she went through an exercise of rotating individual foods out of his diet, one by one. This process of elimination yielded two clear culprits, milk and wheat. When she removed just these foods from William's diet, his sleep and behavior improved noticeably (although not his diarrhea). So when William was three, she put him on a diet free of wheat and dairy products and it worked, not as a cure but rather as a clear continuation of the results she had seen in her little experiment. It was the first intervention Rose had ever found for William that made a difference, and the experience marked an emotional turning point. She realized that no doctor was going to give her the answers about William; she was going to have to figure things out for herself.

William's initial diagnosis was not autism (he wouldn't get a formal autism diagnosis until later), but rather "receptive dysphasia," a speech disorder. So Rose began looking for the best speech program she could find and soon pinpointed the best in the country. An initial three-day assessment went well and a few months later, William went back to start the program. Then her phone rang. "This is not the same child we assessed," the school told her. No longer simply nonverbal and not sleeping, William was now throwing tantrums and screaming nonstop. "You'll probably need to institutionalize him for life," the speech teachers told her. "This child is seriously damaged."

After months of progress, William had crashed again, this time more violently than after his MMR vaccination and for no discernible reason. Rose felt she had little choice but to redouble her efforts on the biological-treatment front. Intrigued by William's progress from a simple elimination diet, she wondered if his recent crash might have to do with something that was now *missing* from his diet. Perhaps he had some kind of vitamin deficiency. Not knowing how to connect specific vitamins and symptoms, Rose set out to find a reference book that could help her diagnose a vitamin problem. She called every vitamin and pharmaceutical company she could track down and before long, she found something. Stored back in the shelves of a veterinary medicine department was a little red book titled *Vitamin Compendium: The Properties of the Vitamins and Their Importance in Human and Animal Nutrition.*

Published in 1976 by the Vitamins and Chemicals Department of Hoffmann-La Roche, the chapters of the book went through the symptoms of individual vitamin deficiency, often using animal models to spell out the symptoms of each. When she saw a picture of an unhappy little pig that was deficient in vitamin B_{12}, Rose felt as though she was looking at an animal model of William.

So she began a new search for vitamin B_{12} treatment. Before long, she had begun B_{12} injections and found a specialized vitamin B_{12} unit where she entered William into an intensive program of daily injections for two weeks. Sure enough, Rose's intuition appeared right again. After the injections, William's behavior improved; the crisis that had come on so suddenly was gone just as fast. Still, the diarrhea remained.

Encouraged by her second success, Rose next turned her attention to the underlying condition of William's gut. She had long been interested in the gut flora, the natural bacteria that line all of our intestinal walls. So her ears perked up when she heard of a nearby clinical trial that targeted the gut flora: Some local doctors were giving probiotics to patients with Crohn's disease, a form of inflammatory bowel disease. Rose knew almost nothing about Crohn's disease, but she contacted the investigators who were conducting the trial anyway. Displaying her formidable powers of persuasion, Rose obtained a course of the experimental treatment and was delighted to see yet another puzzle piece fall into place: no more diarrhea. After taking the special formulation, William had consistent, solid stools for the first time in his life.

Following this string of discoveries—wheat and milk reaction, vitamin B_{12} deficiency, gut flora problems—Rose felt encouraged and frustrated at the same time. It seemed she was collecting pieces of the puzzle without connecting any of them to the triggering event. Try as she might, Rose couldn't come up with a theory for a mechanism that could connect William's MMR vaccination with his bowel disease and autism symptoms.

In May 1995, she picked up the phone and called Jackie Fletcher at Justice Awareness & Basic Support (JABS), England's leading vaccine safety group. Rose's interest in bowel disease diverged from most of Fletcher's work at JABS, which focused on brain injury from vaccines. But it sparked a thought. Fletcher, who closely followed the scientific literature on vaccine viruses, told her there was a doctor at the Royal Free Hospital who had just published some interesting work on the measles virus and Crohn's disease in Scandinavia. He might be open to your ideas on this, Fletcher told Rose.

The conversation with Fletcher inspired Rose. For the first time, she could trace a direct line between bowel disease (and the Crohn's disease trial) and measles virus (from the MMR vaccine). Was this the missing piece in the puzzle that could explain William's reaction to the MMR? She hung up the phone with Jackie and called "directory inquiries" for the number of the Royal Free Hospital. Reaching the switchboard, she asked for the researcher's direct line and they put her through.

The researcher picked up his own phone. "Hello, my name is Rosemary Kessick," she began, "and I'm not mad."

The Scandinavian study that Jackie Fletcher described to Rose Kessick— one that was soon to launch the biggest medical controversy in autism since Bettelheim—actually had nothing to do with either vaccines or

autism. Rather, it was an investigation of the possible role of measles infection in a particular form of inflammatory bowel disease. The connections would prove to run deeper than even Rose expected in her moment
of discovery.

Crohn's disease is yet another of the new diseases of the industrialized
world, although in the case of Crohn's, its novelty, late emergence, and
rapid rise are more generally accepted. Like other diseases we've described, some of the earliest signs of Crohn's disease emerged in Great
Britain (a Glasgow surgeon named Thomas Dalziel was among the first
to describe a case series in 1913),[5] but by now the disease has spread all
over the world.

Scattered cases were characterized in the nineteenth century, but the
first comprehensive description came from a New York doctor named
Burrill Crohn and two colleagues in 1932, who first described "a disease
of the terminal ileum, affecting mainly young adults. The disease is clinically featured by symptoms that resemble those of ulcerative colitis,
namely fever, diarrhea, and emaciation, leading eventually to the obstruction of the small intestine."[6] They called their disease regional ileitis, but due to Burrill Crohn's subsequent efforts to promote awareness
of the disease, the condition eventually bore his name.

Crohn's observations were centered on some striking and visible
symptoms in the "terminal ileum," the last segment of the small intestine
before it feeds into the large intestine and colon. Later, the inflammatory
profile of Crohn's disease would be found beyond the terminal ileum,
but this was at least in part because of the evolution of the disease, not an
error in Crohn's observations. For these first patients described in 1932,
the florid and painful inflammation in the tail end of the small intestine
was no mere inconvenience: Crohn's disease was always an agonizing
experience for its sufferers and sometimes fatal.

Unlike autism and schizophrenia, there was little disagreement among
specialists that Crohn's was new, nor was there much difficulty in concluding that its growth rate was explosive. Over two decades later, Crohn
looked back on his 1932 article and wrote, "From this small beginning,
we have witnessed the evolution of a Frankenstein monster that, if not
threatening to life, frequently results in serious illness, often prolonged
and debilitating."[7] And in the half century since Crohn first invoked the
classic specter of cinematic horror, this monster has continued to grow,
evolve, and raise difficult new questions. Forty years after Crohn's own
retrospective, leading authorities on Crohn's disease continue to empha-

size the obvious: Some change in the environment must be involved in the rise of this intestinal scourge.[8]

Even more disturbing to some observers has been the rise of Crohn's disease in children, a rise that was noted with special urgency in Great Britain. One study found a threefold rise in Scottish children in a fifteen-year period. The study authors treated these increases seriously and took pains to emphasize that this increase was a real one and couldn't be explained by changes in diagnostic criteria or other changes in diagnostic patterns.[9] Inevitably, the rising pediatric caseload called forth a new supply of specialists to treat the affected children. Pediatric gastroenterology had been practically unheard of as a practice, yet this rise in pediatric Crohn's cases helped to recruit a new cadre of both clinical and research talent to the field.

An Australian gastroenterologist named John Walker-Smith became one of the main referring physicians in the United Kingdom. Starting in the 1970s, children with Crohn's disease throughout England, Scotland, and Wales were referred to his clinic at St. Bartholomew's Hospital in London, where he became the world's leading expert on pediatric Crohn's. He wrote the seminal textbook *Diseases of the Small Intestine in Childhood* in 1974. By 1999, as the textbook went into its fourth edition (and joined this time by a younger coauthor named Simon Murch), he commented at some length on the continued rise of childhood Crohn's disease and the likely role of new environmental factors. We can hear the echoes of Kraepelin's global surveys of GPI in his sobering analysis.

> The geographical distribution of Crohn's disease is of interest as it appears to be more prevalent in North West Europe and America, suggesting a factor related to Western societies and more specifically urbanized areas. It is found in African American but rarely in African children. In the authors' UK practice, the incidence of Crohn's disease in Afro-Caribbean children increased in a decade from a notable rarity to commonplace. More remarkable increases in children of Indian subcontinent origin are also now being seen with Crohn's disease, whereas the disease remains very uncommon in children in the subcontinent itself.

He concluded, "The appearance of the disease in children of immigrants, together with the increases in incidence of Crohn's disease in general in Western societies, suggest that an environmental agent or agents may be important in the pathogenesis of Crohn's disease."[10]

Not surprisingly, getting to the bottom of the Crohn's disease epidemic in both adults and children was a hot topic for research gastroenterologists. By the mid-1990s, when Jackie Fletcher spoke to Rose, there were a number of theories in circulation, with quite a lot of interest centering on infection as the unknown environmental factor. The specific pattern of the Crohn's disease inflammation led many to suspect that a microbe was involved, either a viral or bacterial infection.[11]

Starting around 1990, two research groups began to focus on the connection between Crohn's disease and measles. One of them, the Inflammatory Bowel Disease (IBD) Study Group based at the Royal Free Hospital in London, started out by taking a fresh look at the bowel tissue itself, and especially the terminal ileum, employing a host of innovative new methods and technologies.[12] In 1993 the IBD Study Group set out to look specifically for measles DNA and made a surprising discovery. In almost every case of Crohn's tissues they examined, genetic testing showed the presence of measles virus; the same testing showed the virus in only a minority of the controls.[13] They became intrigued by the idea that Crohn's disease might be caused, or at least promoted, by a persistent measles infection.

Meanwhile, another group from Sweden, the Cancer Epidemiology Unit of University Hospital in Uppsala, came at the measles issue from a different perspective, by looking for evidence at the population level. Data from a comprehensive sample of Swedish Crohn's cases, ninety-three in all, showed a high rate of early-life infection, either prenatal in the mother or postnatal in the child.[14] Out of eighteen identifiable infections, measles was part of the picture in two of the patients' mothers, both of whom, the Swedish investigators learned, were infected in the last weeks of their pregnancy.

So in 1993, representatives from these two groups, including the head of the IBD Study Group and the head of the Swedish team, got together to perform a series of studies focusing on measles infections in the population that included the Swedish Crohn's cases. They first found an elevated risk of Crohn's due to measles exposure, but only when the measles infection came within weeks of the birth date.[15] (This, interestingly enough, was the "Scandinavian study" from the Royal Free that Jackie Fletcher mentioned to Rose Kessick.) Next, they decided to seek out and investigate each individual case of maternal measles infection they could find in a large population where the infection took place during pregnancy.

What they found amazed them. Out of twenty-five thousand babies delivered in Uppsala's University Hospital between 1940 and 1949, there were only four known cases where the mother had measles during pregnancy, two of whom had surfaced in the earlier study of known Crohn's cases. Following up on each of these cases, researchers found that three out of the four children went on to develop Crohn's disease. "Although this study is biased by the selection of a period when it was known that two cases of measles in the mother were followed by Crohn's disease in the offspring," the authors commented, "the detection of a third such case in the only four mothers to have had measles during pregnancy is extraordinary."[16]

This observation didn't appear to be universal, since population surveys of measles epidemics in the United Kingdom didn't show the same result. Still, both the Swedish and the British teams kept at it and produced a continuing series of papers. One of these was titled "Is Measles Vaccination a Risk Factor for Inflammatory Bowel Disease?" and followed up one of the original clinical trial groups for the measles vaccine administered in 1964 in the United Kingdom. They found that the vaccinated group had three times the risk of developing Crohn's than unvaccinated controls.[17]

The lead Swedish researcher was well rewarded for his work; in 1999 Anders Ekbom was appointed full professor of epidemiology at Sweden's prestigious Karolinska Institutet. The leader of the Royal Free's IBD Study Group, a young British researcher named Andrew Wakefield, had a different path ahead of him.

Paradigms Wars

Despite the inescapable rise in autism rates, most medical scientists have tried their best to escape its implications. It may not sound very scientific, but even for scientists, abandoning comfortable beliefs for an inconvenient truth is often painful business. Still, their resulting resistance has created extra hurdles for those who make the obvious case for the role of the environment in autism. It's not enough merely to demonstrate that what we thought we knew about autism was wrong. The scientific community has insisted on something nearly impossible to provide: a more satisfying *and* appealing explanation of what kind of disease model is at work. In other words, both a superior and more comfortable replacement theory. Unfortunately, the search for that explanation has put not just theory and evidence but also politics into play.

In part 1, we described quite a number of different archetypes for environmental diseases, each one of which has the potential to inform new theories of autism, none of them convenient or comfortable. Could autism be a simple case of undiagnosed mercury poisoning, like hysteria? Does it have its origins in well-meaning but dangerous medical treatments that produce a unique model of developmental mercury poisoning, like acrodynia? Is it instead a new and specific (if easy to miss) interaction between toxic metals and a single microbe, like GPI? Or is the situation worse than that, with autism an elusive disease of industrial civilization, like schizophrenia, one that risks being passed over indefinitely as just a basic part of the human condition?

Resolving these questions is more urgent than ever, because a full-fledged paradigm war has broken out and with it a race for the intellectual high ground on causation. Regardless of whether one accepts that autism rates have increased or not, its new prominence has raised indisputable interest in tracing its causes. There's no shortage of causal theories, either; just about everyone agrees that there is a seed that grows into a poisoned tree. And each theory brings with it a medical model for how best to avoid bearing more fruit from the poisoned tree.

Beyond that, any semblance of common ground vanishes. In numerous ways it's hard to imagine a more deeply antagonistic battle, between the medical industry on one hand and health consumers on the other, with the disciplines of science and the individual career prospects of scientists caught in the middle.

At their core, the paradigms most readily embraced by the medical industry have placed a defective seed somewhere in the heart of the family. Channeling Freud, Bettelheim blamed homicidal mothers. Rejecting Freud, biological determinists then turned to inherited genes, and the heritability theory swept the scientific community. This new turn managed to shift the blame, albeit not very far: from bad parenting to genetically unfit parents, from homicidal mothers to defective children. But at their core, these prevailing paradigms have offered little in the way of hope for the families of affected children, especially the heritability theory.[18] The target of much recent research has been finding the "autism genes," but that research begs a crucial question: What happens if and when you find the genes? The most obvious opportunities would then come before conception and birth; discovering genetic problems in "high risk" pairings and their progeny. In this guise, the therapy for autism prevention is unspoken but clear: abortion.

To be sure, the research program of the genetics camp is targeted at a model of action in the longer run. By specifying clusters of genes, these scientists point out, new insights might emerge on metabolic pathways that have gone awry. Understanding these faulty pathways may eventually lead to new therapies: new psychotropic drugs for autistic people and perhaps more sophisticated preventive measures for pregnant and susceptible autism moms.

Realistically, however, any such treatments are decades away at best. Unlike the impact of penicillin on syphilis, the genetic discovery model as a path to effective therapy may be an appealing prospect, but it has more to offer as a marketing tool than in achieving realistic results in the here and now. In terms of getting down to the core of the problem quickly, it's largely an evasion tactic.

By contrast, the model that Rose Kessick set in motion in both form and substance places the toxic seed squarely outside the family. Instead of defective children, the new model argues that the affected children would otherwise have been normal but instead became chronically ill. Not only that, but, largely ill served by a medical industry increasingly constrained by the cookbooks of reimbursement-based care, the new model has found its most powerful resources in an unorthodox place: with professional parents taking on a new prominence as both clinicians and citizen scientists. Like the genetic model, this revolutionary theory is biological in focus. But by placing the prospect of medical and manufacturing malpractice squarely on the table, this new model has made some powerful enemies.

Unlikely Revolutionaries

On May 17, 1995, Andrew Wakefield picked up the phone in his small, windowless office at the Royal Free Hospital. Rosemary Kessick was on the line, calling him about her seven-year-old autistic son, William.

Wakefield was impressed by Rose. "She was intelligent, articulate, and unemotional" as she described William's case history in painstaking detail. She had clearly done her homework. Her ideas on elimination diets and especially on vitamin B_{12} deficiency sounded reasonable to him. If William had some early onset form of Crohn's disease, it would make sense that he wasn't getting enough B_{12}; the terminal ileum was the place in the bowel where B_{12} was mostly absorbed.

Like others along Rose's journey, Wakefield was impressed not just by her logic but by her determination. Rose was not the sort of person to let you off the hook easily. She asked him for his advice, which was easy enough. But more to the point, she asked him for his help. As a medical doctor, he remembers his first reaction: Why hadn't anyone investigated William's obvious gastrointestinal distress? As a research gastroenterologist faced with a condition he had never heard of before, a rare bowel condition, possibly an early-onset form of Crohn's disease, coupled with autistic symptoms, he was also intrigued. He knew from experience that unusual cases like William's often provided the greatest opportunity for original insight. So he agreed to help.

Before that fateful telephone call with Rose, Wakefield's medical research career had been marked by a steady stream of success and accomplishment. Following his medical education, he received a prestigious research scholarship as a Wellcome Research Fellow. He spent the first year of his grant working with leading experts in small bowel transplantation at the University of Toronto and then moved back to England to continue his fellowship, joining the inflammatory bowel disease group at the Royal Free Hospital. Wakefield fast became a rising star within the Royal Free. He was named senior lecturer in 1993, skipping a step in the academic hierarchy, promoted to reader in 1997, and soon launched a dynamic new group within the Royal Free, the Inflammatory Bowel Disease Study Group.

The IBD Study Group represented the spirit of what is called, in modern medical jargon, translational medicine. The basic idea of translational medicine is to promote close collaboration between research and clinical practice so that insights from the "bedside" are reflected in research projects, therefore making the "bench" (or the lab) more relevant to real medical problems. Comprised of a cross-disciplinary group of clinical researchers and skilled clinicians, the IBD Study Group met weekly to discuss interesting patients, new research ideas, treatment outcomes, surgical procedures, and the medical writing they could do to disseminate their insights. Papers from the IBD Study Group were published in some of the leading journals in medicine. Collegial and collaborative, innovative and ambitious, it was a high-performance team that was just the sort to take on challenges of the type William Kessick posed. But before long, Wakefield (and also his colleagues in the IBD Study Group, John Walker-Smith and Simon Murch) confronted a series of choices that would forever change the course of autism research and their careers.

Rose Kessick's telephone call presented the first fateful choice, one that seemed quite obvious at the time. Wakefield had little difficulty in deciding to help William Kessick. Better yet, he knew just the doctor to refer her to, John Walker-Smith. Not only was Walker-Smith the author of the standard textbook on childhood bowel disease, he was at that moment bringing his pediatric gastroenterology practice over to the Royal Free and joining the IBD Study Group.

On Wakefield's suggestion, Walker-Smith saw Rose and William, just a couple of months after her initial contact with Wakefield.[19] Before long, in part through Rose's network, several other parents had called Wakefield looking for help with their children. Walker-Smith began meeting with these families as well, and the emergence of an apparent cluster of highly similar children reinforced Wakefield's original intuition that William might be an important case.

As the number of referrals started to expand (there were fewer than ten at the outset, but over several months, the number rose to a dozen), Wakefield and Walker-Smith found themselves faced with a second choice. Should they investigate the group of children to confirm a pattern? All of the children presented essentially the same profile: autism (ten of twelve, two with encephalitis) with clear regression within days after vaccination with MMR (ten of twelve, one after measles infection, another after an ear infection), alongside bowel symptoms (all twelve). For Wakefield and Walker-Smith, both committed to the model of translational medicine, this seemed to be another easy choice. Not only was it ethical to investigate whether these children shared a novel disease process, it was their obligation.

So as Walker-Smith continued his initial consultations with the families, the IBD Study Group began pursuing two related but distinct investigative tracks. They began scoping out a proposal for a full-scale research project, one involving a careful study of cases and controls, though they knew that "gold standard" research proposals like this took a long time to design correctly and required rigorous ethical approvals. The time required to obtain funding and approval would delay clinical work with the children and the consistency of any subsequent treatments, so they felt the need to investigate the basic patterns in this group faster than the basic research plan would allow. For clinical and treatment purposes, therefore, they moved ahead on a second, more expeditious, track. They laid out a testing schedule over the subsequent six months for all twelve children, including simple colonoscopies and urine collections to test for a marker of vitamin B_{12} deficiency.

Scheduling colonoscopies quickly had a side benefit; it created the opportunity to do some rudimentary research. As part of his agreement to bring his practice to the Royal Free, Walker-Smith had a standing approval from the Ethical Practices Committee to use biopsy and other tissue samples collected during his clinical work for research purposes. Case series of this size, although not adequate for a "gold standard" research design, frequently serve as the earliest evidence of a new form of disease, and the initial report of the pattern can often represent a lasting contribution to medicine. After all, Leo Kanner's first report on autism in 1943 had eleven cases and Burrill Crohn's landmark 1932 paper on Crohn's disease had fourteen.

As the schedule turned out, although William was supposed to go first in July 1996, his procedure was delayed until after the August holiday while another child went first (like David Speck in Kanner's referral sequence, this first case in July provided interesting results while also deferring the investigators' moment of true discovery). The first child showed definite evidence of bowel inflammation (technically, "chronic non-specific colitis" and "acute caecal cryptitis") but no clear sign of Crohn's disease symptoms, largely because the first colonoscopy procedure was the least successful of the twelve: Simon Murch (Walker-Smith's younger colleague who performed the colonoscopies) wasn't able to reach and observe the terminal ileum. William went second, in September 1996, and in his case Murch was able to obtain more definitive results. William had the same colitis as the first child, but upon entering the terminal ileum, Murch saw evidence of a far more dramatic kind: a striking pattern of swollen and inflamed lymph nodes, or "lymphoid nodular hyperplasia" (LNH) in medical jargon.

Wakefield calls William the "sentinel child"[20] and as the remaining ten children completed their procedures over the next four months, the LNH pattern observed in William held up repeatedly. Not just that, but the vitamin B_{12} markers came back confirming signs of abnormalities in all of the children. There was a real sense of excitement in the IBD Study Group. First of all, their preliminary investigation showed clearly that the parents were right. Despite widespread resistance to their concerns, their children did indeed have bowel disease just as they claimed. Second, and more important, Walker-Smith could help these children immediately by treating them for bowel inflammation. The standard treatment, a bowel medication called mesalazine, met with quick positive results in all of the children, especially for William.

But the benefits of the case series approach made the findings even better than that: Not only could the IBD Study Group help these twelve children, the consistency in the findings suggested they might help many more. The team agreed quickly to write up the results as an "early report" and submit it to *The Lancet*, where it was accepted promptly and published a year later, in February 1998.[21]

In the meantime, the IBD Study Group also agreed that the more comprehensive project proposal deserved the highest priority. But since this project was considerably larger than a simple clinical case series, it would require resources, patients, and more extensive sampling. The larger size and scope of the second project presented a third choice for the group, one with both financial and (for Wakefield) legal ramifications.

As Rose and the other parents were organizing to get their children bowel examinations and treatments, they also started to organize to get compensated through the established British government program for vaccine injury. They all believed the MMR triggered their children's autism, and since the future financial burden on these families in caring for their autistic children would be enormous, it was only natural that they take their case to the Legal Aid Board (LAB), the approved channel for taking vaccine injury claims to the government.[22] So as the research agenda took shape during 1996 and 1997, the economic distress and financial interests of the parents became intertwined with the IBD Study Group's research.

For Wakefield and his colleagues, this series of developments clarified their third choice. Should they take money from the parents' lawyers to sponsor the work they had planned, and permit their research to be connected to a legal process? The question here came down not to a funding question for the IBD Study Group, which had little to gain financially, but to a simple moral choice. Wakefield recalls that his moment of decision came when the mother of one of the twelve children verbalized a thought that many autism parents have shared (and an unfortunate few parents have acted on).

"Please don't judge me too harshly," she stated in an apologetic tone, "but when I go I will be taking my son with me."

Realizing the scale of the human problem facing these families, Wakefield didn't hesitate, and as head of the IBD Study Group made a decision to accept funding from the Legal Aid Board. This came in two forms. The Royal Free Hospital accepted £55,000 (just under $100,000) for the second study (but not the case series published in *The Lancet*). As research grants go, it was a modest amount. And although much of the research work was eventually done, it was never published due to all the subsequent controversy. Of greater potential concern due to the remuneration involved, Wakefield also agreed to serve as an expert witness for the parents. Working for the standard hourly rate for experts of £150 (about $270), over a period of eight years (most of it subsequent to *The Lancet* publication), he received about £300,000 (over half a million dollars) in fees, or £180,000 after taxes.[23] Although modest on an annual basis, that's a material amount of financial support, and it's appropriate to ask the question: What did Wakefield do with the money?

For all practical purposes, he donated it back to the hospital. More precisely, Wakefield used the LAB proceeds in an attempt to build intellectual capital for the practice of gastroenterology at the Royal Free. In June 1997 Wakefield filed a patent application on a treatment for persistent measles infections. (Most academic research institutions encourage their researchers to file patents on their medical innovations. No exception to this pattern, the Royal Free has filed close to twenty patent applications since 1986.) He had developed an idea about a treatment, and hoped the patent would help commercialize the invention while also generating funds for a new gastroenterology center for the Royal Free. Over half of the net proceeds from his expert services went into patent-filing fees; the rest funded administrative support for the autism project.

Looking back, any objective observer would conclude that the project was a clear financial failure: The treatment patent was never granted, no clinical trials were attempted, the investment capital was lost, and the hospital (and for that matter Wakefield himself) spent every penny it received with little subsequent benefit. But from a public relations standpoint, his donation to the hospital was a catastrophe. These LAB payments spelled career disaster for the young researcher, and soon became a media snowball: In the hands of a British journalist named Brian Deer, these payments were eventually skewed to make Wakefield look financially motivated and ethically compromised.

How this happened requires a framework, which takes us back to the concept of paradigm wars that inevitably occur during periods of revolutionary science. Scientific revolutions require revolutionaries. It's not a fun job, as scientists from Galileo Galilei to Ignaz Semmelweis have demonstrated. And for better or worse, Andrew Wakefield has taken on the mantle of revolutionary scientist in autism. This occurred not because he sought out the role, but simply because he had the courage to do the right thing when faced with a series of moral choices.

And unlike any other research scientist in recent memory, Andrew Wakefield has been singled out by the medical industry, not just for sanctions but for public excoriation. In part based on a letter filed by Brian Deer with the General Medical Council (GMC), Wakefield, Walker-Smith, and Murch were placed on trial before the GMC. The GMC hearings, which went on for more than 150 days over a period of more than two years, attempted the remarkable feat of turning the clinical and research choices of these men into a sinister narrative of conspiracy and bad medicine. The doctors' straightforward choices surrounding clinical care, research design, funding, and expert witness support were all woven into this narrative, and the length of the proceeding provided evidence, if nothing else, of the difficulty of making the alternative narrative plausible.

The prosecution's case started out with these experts' choices regarding clinical care and argued that if these twelve *Lancet* children had "autism," then by definition there was no other medical condition of any relevance whatsoever. Thus, according to the GMC, administering a procedure such as a colonoscopy, by definition, was unethical. Never mind whether a leading specialist like John Walker-Smith investigated the clinical symptoms of children with bowel disease all the time. These children were "just autistic" and therefore couldn't have it. It didn't matter if they had clear symptoms of bowel disease, diarrhea, or constipation (or both); the prosecution argued there was no ethical justification for performing a colonoscopy on autistic children, even if Walker-Smith had all the necessary clinical authority and even if the parents gave informed consent.

The second prong of the prosecution's case effectively rejected the innovative premise of translational medicine and argued instead that clinical medicine must be performed according to standard practice, and all research must be performed at the greatest possible distance from active clinical practice. It matters not that the published research at issue in *The Lancet* study was secondary to clinical care; the fact that a case series was written up and published in a research journal demonstrates that the three doctors were performing unethical experiments on children. This argument rests on outdated suppositions: that research can only be conducted at a complete remove from the patients; that autism is fully understood as a brain disorder; that there is no urgency for treatment; and that the IBD Study Group should never have pursued the research question to begin with.

Finally, the prosecution's case cut to the heart of the question—the money—and turned the tables on the question of financial motivation. They claimed it wasn't the companies and the health care providers who had the profit interest here, it was the patients. Since the MMR vaccine was the hypothesized exposure based on parental observation, it was not acceptable to investigate the legitimate question posed by the parents. More to the point, to permit a rigorous scientific investigation funded by legal counsel to financially interested parties to proceed was, according to the prosecution, malpractice by definition. And it wasn't just the parents' greed that was suspect, it was Wakefield's patent application that was the driving motivation; according to the narrative of the media, he wanted to invent a commercial product to replace the MMR. "He did it for the money," went the accusation. "He was just trying to get rich from his patent."

But all twelve children got excellent care from one of the best specialists in the world. Their parents were delighted with the services they received and never complained; indeed, parents of eight of the twelve protested actively and publicly against the GMC proceeding. The finding of a novel bowel condition has been consistently replicated,[24] although the subsequent finding of the persistence of the measles virus itself has been questioned. As for the legal process, the LAB work for the parents on MMR was simply shut down by the British government, which has full power over the resources available to plaintiff's counsel, a short four months before the case was to go to trial. In the meantime, a single journalist, the only man in the world ever known to have complained to the GMC about Wakefield, managed to generate the longest trial proceeding in GMC history. Along the way, Wakefield lost his position at the Royal Free, his sure path to a professorship, and all hope for a mainstream career. (In February 2010, the GMC ruled against Wakefield and his colleagues—an unsurprising though deeply unjustified finding—and in May 2010, as this book was in press, revoked his and Walker-Smith's licenses to practice medicine. *The Lancet* fully retracted the 1998 study; another journal, *NeuroToxicology*, owned by the same publisher, withdrew a separate crucial study on the impact of the U.S. infant vaccination schedule on primates—a study that had been peer reviewed, accepted by its editor, and published online—citing Wakefield's involvement; and Wakefield resigned from his position at Thoughtful House, the Texas treatment and research center he founded after leaving London. His powerful opponents may believe they have scrubbed the record clean of the work of an inconvenient scientist, but they have managed to galvanize a number of powerful autism groups behind him in an effort to enable his work to continue.)

Revolutionaries are always vulnerable to attack. But in the modern world, where religion has largely separated from science, taking a heretical position on a controversial scientific theory is not usually grounds for excommunication. But Wakefield's actions touched two deep chords. For one, he put vaccine-adverse events front and center as a possible cause of autism, a large and growing problem. Second, he confronted the anomaly of the autism epidemic and the obvious role of environmental factors. In the process, he turned the theory of autism, quite literally, upside down: from the brain to the bowels.

Sallie Bernard's first revolutionary impulse came from a simpler source. In her case it was little more than a natural parent's reflex. In early 1993 she heard about a new paper that Ivar Lovaas, a prominent autism theorist, had published that followed up on a group he first treated in 1987.[25] In his latest paper, Lovaas made some startling claims. His treatment had not merely helped the original study group; he argued that eight of nine of them had made dramatic gains after undergoing a rigorous program of behavioral modification. According to Lovaas, the children he had treated "were indistinguishable from average children on tests of intelligence and adaptive behavior."[26] In others words, they had *recovered* from autism.

The idea of recovery focused Bernard's attention. Up to that moment, she had heard little from her doctors that wasn't depressing. Recovery was serious business and if this was real, Bernard would have to change everything she was doing. She needed to know how credible this study was, to filter out the spin. There was only one way to do this; she simply had to read the full text of the article herself.

There were not many parents in 1993 that would seek out and read the full text of a scientific paper themselves. This was before technology made medical information widely available to anyone with an Internet connection and a credit card. "The lay public" were almost always forced to get scientific information through filters, and virtually never read the full text of a paper. This created numerous practical obstacles when it came to learning about medical science. In order to interpret scientific texts, the reader had to possess access to medical libraries and to go through a structured degree program (M.D. or Ph.D., for example). Without access to either of these privileges, health consumers were widely considered to be incapable of making independent judgments on scientific issues.

But Sallie Bernard was not your typical member of the lay public. A graduate of Harvard, where she majored in history and graduated with honors, she had gone into the field of market research. Like Rose Kessick, Sallie Bernard entered the world of autism well into a career that had given her considerable training in assimilating and mastering technical concepts and jargon.

Also like Rose Kessick, Bernard chose to juggle children and motherhood alongside a demanding career, and gave birth to triplets in 1987. The first two of the three developed normally, but her third son, Bill, had troubles from the beginning. He was the smallest of the three at birth, weighing in at barely three pounds, and frequently sick. At every stage, he developed more slowly than both of his brothers; by the time he was two years old, it was clear that something was wrong.

Bernard began searching around for help, but had trouble figuring out what to do because she didn't have a road map for understanding what Bill's issues were. Like William Kessick, Bill Bernard was diagnosed with language disorder before his autism diagnosis. In the meantime, it was clear to his mother that Bill had more problems than just language delay: he also experienced fine motor delays, appetite problems, vision and other sensory disturbances, and an increasing loss of social connection and eye contact.

It wasn't until January 1992 that Bernard first heard the word "autism."

She took Bill to the Cornell Medical Center in New York City, where a pediatric neurologist told her Bill's problem was largely his language disorder and "a little mild autism." Looking back, this was her first indication that Bill had autism, but it wasn't until February 1993, when she took him to a psychologist who specialized in Lovaas therapy, that a doctor told her without any qualification that Bill was autistic. By then, Bill was already five and a half years old. For some parents, hearing an autism spectrum diagnosis applied to their child is a devastating moment, but Bernard already knew something was seriously wrong with Bill. In fact, reading the Lovaas article was what had led her to the therapist in the first place, and for her, the diagnosis was liberating. An action-oriented, results-driven professional, she felt for the first time that having a concrete diagnosis, even if it was autism, could help to give her a plan and a focus.

More to the point, reading the Lovaas paper made her angry. Lovaas argued that there was a narrow window within which to address the symptoms of autism and that the window started closing after the child reached five years of age. By the time Bernard read the article, Bill was already five and a half. If there was indeed a window for effective intervention, all the delays and misguided focus on language had left her very little time before that window would be closed for good. But anger wasn't a productive emotion, so reading the paper simply steeled her resolve to get serious. She had a lot to do very quickly.

Her first step was getting more information, so she joined every mailing list she could find, including Bernie Rimland's original organization, now the Autism Society of America; a local New Jersey group called COSAC (Center for Outreach & Services for the Autism Community); and the Greater Philadelphia Autism Society. She also signed up for the newsletter from Rimland's current organization, the Autism Research Institute, which she liked most of all because Rimland reported on science directly, and had a good eye for relevant science beyond autism.

Still, there was something about all these activities that frustrated her. They seemed small and grassroots oriented, more focused on services and coping than on transformative science. Then she came across something that inspired her. At the end of 1996, she read the story of David Ho, when he was named Man of the Year by *Time* magazine. Ho was the scientist who had developed the cocktail of anti-HIV drugs that proved to be the first effective therapy for AIDS. If medical research can halt the AIDS epidemic in its tracks, thought Bernard, why not autism?

So when some new groups with more ambition and new energy started organizing to push for more groundbreaking research, Bernard was ready for their message. One group with such larger ambitions, the National Alliance for Autism Research (NAAR), was formed in nearby Princeton. In 1995 they issued a first appeal for biomedical research in autism. That same year, on the West Coast, another group with similar aims was formed called Cure Autism Now (CAN). Soon afterward, a group of parents formed a New Jersey branch of CAN, and Bernard attended some early meetings. She liked their sense of urgency and the focus on results and signed on as a member of the local CAN chapter.

Fairly quickly, the New Jersey CAN group became close. In addition to Bernard, the group included Albert Enayati, a passionate Iranian chemist who was the chapter's founder and first president. Albert got the group involved in several meetings down in Washington, at different agencies within the National Institutes of Health. This gave Bernard an early taste of the political landscape surrounding autism. These interactions did little to tamp down her frustration, as she wasn't at all impressed by the federal government's lack of urgency. They were about as far away from a breakthrough as she could imagine. She began to wonder how she could make a difference more directly.

Then, as their policy activism was increasing, the New Jersey CAN group encountered the controversy that would galvanize them. In 1997 Congress had passed the Food and Drug Modernization Act, a piece of legislation in which the FDA was directed to review the mercury content of vaccines and biologic products. Over the following months, it totaled up the mercury in three thimerosal-containing vaccines—DPT, haemophilus influenza type B (Hib), and hepatitis B—and realized that their cumulative ethylmercury content exceeded limits set forth by the Environmental Protection Agency (EPA) for mercury exposure. Within the first two months of life, infants could receive 75 micrograms of mercury from vaccinations; by the time they were two years of age, the total exposure could come to as much as 250 micrograms. On an average basis, this cumulative mercury exposure exceeded the EPA threshold, 0.1 micrograms per kilogram per day (mcg/kg/day) for the entire first year of life. On any given day, however, the one-time, or "bolus," exposure to mercury was nearly 90 times higher than the EPA threshold.[27]

Realizing it had a problem, on July 8, 1999, after months of internal deliberation and debate, the Public Health Service (PHS) announced a partial step.[28] It declared its intention to "phase out" thimerosal from the three infant vaccines, in a process that would delay (but ultimately never complete) the transition to zero exposure. Thimerosal-free vaccines were to be gradually phased into new production, though none of the details of the production transition were ever made public. None of the existing inventory would be recalled (vaccines have shelf lives of three years or more), and there was a crucial loophole. Vaccines targeted for pregnant women weren't included in the thimerosal withdrawal, nor were vaccines intended for adults as well as children. And so influenza vaccines were never affected. As public health authorities began ramping up their efforts to mandate the flu vaccine over this same period, an entirely new source of even earlier thimerosal exposure was introduced and remains to this day.

The 1999 PHS announcement marked the first public notification that the childhood vaccine schedule had exceeded the limits of mercury exposure. For a while the vaccine safety movement was slow to pick up on the issue. The autism parent community was the first to wake up. The announcement caught the attention of two parents immediately: One, a former nurse named Lyn Redwood, who was accustomed to performing weight-adjustment calculations to determine the proper dose of medications, was shocked by the degree to which the recommended schedule exceeded the EPA's 0.1 mcg/kg/day guideline. The other was Albert Enayati, whose training as a chemist and Iranian upbringing had given him a greater awareness of the Iraqi grain poisoning episodes, most recently in the 1970s. Albert approached Bernard and his other friends in the NJ CAN chapter about the announcement.

As a group, the NJ CAN team agreed to get to work on the issue. At first Albert led the way, starting by collecting articles that he then circulated within the group. Bernard remembers one in particular that struck them, a case report by a medical team from Saint Louis about a transplant patient. In 1996 a forty-four-year-old Hispanic man received a liver transplant after liver failure due to hepatitis. In the days following the operation, he received massive intravenous doses of a hepatitis B immune globulin product called HyperHep. Like the gamma globulin treatments for congenital rubella, HyperHep was preserved with thimerosal. During the course of the IV treatment, the transplant patient received more than 20,000 micrograms of ethylmercury.

The effects were immediate. Within three days, he began to have paranoid thoughts, lost muscle strength and his ability to walk. But most notable to the NJ CAN group was the effect on his speech: "On posttransplant day 4 he developed difficulty in verbalizing, although he was able to write his thoughts appropriately. . . . Nine days posttransplant . . . he continued to make no attempts to verbalize or phonate, although he remained fully alert."[29]

This selective loss of speech struck the NJ CAN group like a thunderbolt. After all, if large doses of thimerosal could selectively target speech in a grown man, what might happen if smaller doses were introduced to the brain of a developing infant? Autism parents understand regressive (and selective) speech problems. If thimerosal could selectively harm this man's speech, then perhaps it could help explain autism. They redoubled their research efforts.

The more they learned, the more they were intrigued about the possible connection between mercury and autism. Autism obviously affected the brain. But by 1999 it was clear that autism affected other body tissues as well. Wakefield's paper had been published the year before and it struck a chord among autism parents, many of whom had observed gastrointestinal distress in their children but never thought to connect the dots to autism. For a number of years Bernie Rimland's research group had been exploring the gluten-free/casein-free diet. The California report providing evidence of an exploding number of autism cases had just come out. And the Internet was growing rapidly. More and more parents were sharing medical experiences and realizing that their children had a host of immunological, gastrointestinal, and endocrine problems: diffuse and nonspecific but pervasive.

Albert wrote up a summary of what he had learned about the many symptoms of mercury poisoning and how they mirrored the symptoms being reported in autism. Bernard was impressed. By then, she saw clearly what needed to be done: They would need to reach out directly to the scientific community. For a trained marketing professional like Bernard, that meant speaking in the language of the target audience. And that wasn't just a bunch of parents in a support group talking about papers. They needed to write their own paper and have it published. And in order to make it convincing, it had to be good. After all, if they had any hope of achieving the kind of breakthrough that David Ho had made in AIDS, they would have to recruit a whole new cadre of scientists to work on the problem.

Resolving to get serious about publishing a paper on mercury and autism, Bernard took over Albert's working paper and began crafting a more ambitious article, one with convincing detail on the similarity in symptoms between mercury poisoning and autism. And not simply Leo Kanner's autism, but the real-world autism of the parents who lived it day-to-day, one that embraced Wakefield's full-body model of autism, with an autism physiology turned upside down.

As she spearheaded the writing process (writing with three other parents, including Enayati and Redwood, and a researcher), Bernard also investigated the journals to which they might submit the finished draft. She realized that the NJ CAN team would face difficulty in finding a receptive publication. The conventional process of peer review was generally hostile to ambitious conjectures, especially those that challenged medical industry dogma. She also knew that in order to reach their intended target audience, they would need to find a journal that was both respectable (this was easy to define: The journal needed to be indexed on PubMed) and willing to take risks with new and controversial ideas.

Bernard soon came across the journal *Medical Hypotheses* and quickly realized it was the perfect choice. She sent the editor, David Horobin, a hundred-page manuscript. He responded quickly and requested "a condensed version of around 25 pages." It was April 17, 2000, just nine months since the PHS announcement on thimerosal; only three years after the Wakefield article appeared, another front in the scientific revolution around autism was opened.[30] Like Wakefield's paper, the article from Bernard et al. produced strong medical industry resistance, and not just because of the content of the paper, but also because of the source. A parent had written a scientific paper. She didn't have a medical or scientific degree. She was self-motivated and self-taught, and her approach was something entirely new, translational medicine taken to a new level of engagement: the citizen scientist.

In a perfect world, one would hope that the rational process of scientific discovery would welcome and embrace the active involvement of motivated and critical consumers. A number of scientists have. Unfortunately, however, many in the medical industry would prefer that the "public" be left out of the messy process of setting scientific priorities, particularly when sensitive matters such as vaccination are involved. Especially in the culture of the public health profession, vaccine recipients are more generally seen as objects of instruction than informed consumers capable of making their own choices. Bernard's revolutionary act was especially unsettling for this segment.

But the issue Bernard and her friends at NJ CAN took up was not originally discovered by the PHS in 1999. In fact, some in the medical industry (specifically, a vaccine manufacturer) had discovered the problem years before. In 1991 Maurice Hilleman, a Merck scientist, had made the same calculation the FDA had performed in 1999 and reported his findings to his superiors. In a memo to the president of Merck's vaccine division, Hilleman wrote, "If 8 doses of thimerosal containing vaccine were given in the first 6 months of life (3 DPT, 2 HIB and 3 Hepatitis B) the 200 mcg of mercury given, say to an average of 12 lbs., would be about 87X the Swedish daily allowance of 2.3 mcg of mercury for a baby of that size. When viewed in this way, the mercury load appears rather large."[31]

But beyond this simple arithmetic, Hilleman's memo downplayed any concern. Instead, he discussed tactics to forestall any perception problems. Following Hilleman's lead, Merck chose never to bring the issue to light, obviously not eager to remove a preservative they deemed essential for their low-cost multidose vials.

So nearly ten years later, a parent and health consumer named Sallie Bernard became the lead author on the paper that confirmed Merck's worst nightmares about public perception. The product of the NJ CAN team's labors was formally titled "Autism: A Novel Form of Mercury Poisoning," and is commonly referred to now as "Bernard et al." As published in shortened form by *Medical Hypotheses,* the paper provided an extensive litany of symptoms of mercury poisoning (many of which we've explored earlier) paired with an equally extensive and parallel list of the symptoms of autism. And the paper concluded by using the disease archetype of acrodynia to illustrate the potential damage of low doses of mercury.

"Bernard et al." sparked a flurry of scientific and media attention. Early on, Morris Kharasch's development partner, Eli Lilly, quietly attempted to pass legislation protecting themselves from liability for the inclusion of thimerosal in vaccines. In short order, public health authorities rushed to publish epidemiological studies exonerating thimerosal from harm. The single study from the United States was prepared by a team of CDC epidemiologists close to the vaccine program. Their initial findings, connecting thimerosal exposure to autism and other neurodevelopmental disorders (NDDs), were unpublished. After numerous modifications to the study design, these findings were reduced to insignificance, and published in *Pediatrics* in 2003.[32] Other epidemiological studies, which were supported by parents working in the U.S. vaccine court (the U.S. legal equivalent of the LAB in the United Kingdom), found evidence implicating thimerosal in autism. The Institute of Medicine convened not one but two special panels to consider the thimerosal controversy. The first found reason for concern; the second effectively reversed the findings of the first.

Lab work and animal models competed in similar fashion. Most notable, perhaps, were two studies that mimicked the effects of thimerosal exposure on developing infants: One, a mouse model developed by researchers at Columbia University, showed that thimerosal caused developmental delay in genetically susceptible mice;[33] another, a primate model by researchers at the University of Washington, showed that ethylmercury remained trapped in the brain at significantly higher concentrations than other forms of mercury, including methylmercury.[34]

Before too long the media picked up the story. Investigative journalist and freelancer for *The New York Times* David Kirby wrote a bestselling book about the emerging thimerosal controversy, *Evidence of Harm*, in which he told the stories of Bernard, Lyn Redwood, Albert Enayati, and the other "Mercury Moms" (including work from one of us); Kirby became a frequent guest of the Don Imus radio show and appeared on *Meet the Press* in a debate with Institute of Medicine President Harvey Fineburg.[35] Environmental activist Robert F. Kennedy, Jr., lent his prestigious name to a blistering critique of the medical industry, *Deadly Immunity*, in *Rolling Stone* and *Salon*.[36]

Although Bernard succeeded beyond her expectations in raising awareness of the mercury issue by speaking directly to the scientific audience with "Bernard et al.," the backlash was far more intense than anything she had anticipated. To be sure, "Bernard et al." escaped the kind of direct personal assaults that had been directed at Wakefield. Nevertheless, the same kind of character assassination went on in indirect fashion, this time as intellectual class warfare disguised as news commentary. Bernard was derided as a "marketing executive," while other active parents were dismissed as desperate, emotional, and litigation-happy. Most audacious were the attempts to paint the most scientifically literate consumer activist movement in medical history as simply ignorant. *The New York Times* led the way in a June 25, 2005, front-page story titled "On Autism's Cause, It's Parents vs. Research," reducing the parent concerns to a caricature.[37] The medical industry was fighting back and working hard to declare the realm of science out-of-bounds for health consumers. The clear intention of this kind of coverage was an attempt, in David Kirby's words, to characterize parents like Bernard et al. as "bible-thumping conspiracy enthusiasts from red-state redoubts, who wouldn't know scientific proof if it plopped down next to them at the tractor pull."[38]

If Bernard's ultimate goal in writing the autism-mercury paper was to recruit scientists like David Ho to discover breakthrough autism treatments, she clearly had an uphill battle ahead of her.

Paradigms Lost?

Like Bernie Rimland several decades earlier, both Wakefield and Bernard provided critical challenges to orthodox autism science. For his part, Wakefield suggested that autism was not simply a genetic defect of brain tissue, but something more systemic, an insight Harvard neurologist Martha Herbert aptly summarized in a paper entitled "Autism: A Brain Disorder or a Disorder That Affects the Brain?"[39] He also focused attention on the regression following vaccination. For her part, Bernard provided a different theory about vaccine exposure, one centered on the most direct way ever invented to deliver mercury to the developing brain. She was the first to advance the theory we have been developing here: Mercury exposure through medical treatment can cause widespread harm that can go undetected, and ethylmercury exposures are implicated in the rise of autism.

The Bernard and Wakefield theories are not mutually exclusive, however; in fact, as time has passed, it has become increasingly clear how, in a slightly broader theory of microbes and metals, they might be complementary.

The two theories were also parsimonious. Neither offered themselves as the universal answer to all cases of autism. Wakefield simply observed a case series and suggested that "the consequences of an inflamed or dysfunctional intestine may play a part in behavioural changes in some children."[40] Bernard hypothesized a connection between mercury exposure from infant vaccines and regressive autism, a highly testable proposition. Crucially, neither theory pointed a finger at the more general expansion of the children's vaccine programs in both the United States and the United Kingdom.

Faced with the dual anomalies of rising numbers and systemic disease,

Wakefield's and Bernard's hypotheses were, and remain, far more plausible than the heritability model on a stand-alone basis. If, as Kuhn suggests, "the decision to reject one paradigm is always simultaneously the decision to accept another, and the judgment leading to that decision involves the comparison of both paradigms with nature," then health consumers, in this case the autism parent community, embraced these conjectures of the new environmental paradigm in such large numbers because the conjectures matched what they were observing more closely than the orthodox model did.

On the other hand, the comparison looked quite different to the medical industry. With both environmental theories placing blame in a targeted way on childhood vaccines, it was hard to imagine a challenge that was more threatening to mainstream medical science. For the medical industry, it became a choice between accepting the epidemic and defending the vaccine program, and this produced a reflexive response.

And so the paradigm of genetic determinism was defended with renewed fervor. Extravagant theories arose to explain the increasing autism rates with genetic causation. Autistic men were newly fit in the Darwinian process of sexual selection because of the rise of the computer industry that gave them employment, while global mobility brought autistic couples together in a process of "assortative mating" that produced an epidemic of more autistic offspring. The failures of early waves of genetic studies—the Hox genes,[41] the serotonin transporter gene[42]—were drowned out by announcements of new waves of success in full genome scans: the "hot spot" on chromosome 16,[43] the "suggestive linkage" on chromosome 11,[44] the "common genetic variant" on chromosome 5.[45] These were later (albeit quietly) negated when they, too, proved premature.[46] Meanwhile, in echoes of Torrey's account of the invisible plague, talking points of "better diagnosing" were advanced so consistently that they became widely accepted, despite no evidence at all to back the claims.

The single most prominent spokesman for the orthodox position, at least the one who has most actively sought attention, has been Paul Offit, the author of *Autism's False Prophets*.[47] Coming late to his autism activism, Offit spent most of his career as an infectious disease specialist and vaccine developer, and thus probably had reason to be troubled by the intellectual challenge posed to the vaccine industry by the new environmental paradigm. He soon turned his attention to the autism problem. With little background in autism, he reached out and adopted the views of an odd segment of the autism community, the "neurodiversity movement," a movement that claims that autism is ancient, that any role for the environment is impossible, that misguided attempts to treat or cure autism demonstrate intolerance toward autistic people, and that the suggestion that anyone anywhere might (however unintentionally) have done something wrong to cause autism is simply ridiculous.

Offit's message has been welcomed with enthusiasm by many in the medical industry, and his personal history provides an interesting contrast. Unlike Wakefield, Offit made a large personal fortune from a group of patents he filed on a rotavirus vaccine. While he was openly working in an active commercial partnership with Merck's vaccine division, Offit sat on the government Advisory Committee on Immunization Practices (ACIP) that mandated which vaccines—both categories and specific products—to include in the mandatory childhood program. Just months after his term ended, and supported by his votes establishing the rotavirus vaccine category, Merck's rotavirus vaccine product, RotaTeq, was approved for use by the FDA and ACIP and quickly reached over half a billion dollars in sales.

Offit's newfound interest in autism, in part funded by his share of Merck's vaccine profits and actively supported by media, raised the autism paradigm wars to a new level of acrimony. The debate wasn't about "Parents vs. Science," as *The New York Times* reported it, but rather between parents as health consumers on one side and the medical industry on the other. Both sides have been competing for the attention and resources of science: the parents armed with research and theories, but the medical industry with greater power and the clear resolve to deploy it.

___

And yet the initial conjectures of Wakefield and "Bernard et al." are not without problems. The biggest weakness with this first round of environmental hypotheses has been that they fail to pass some crucial tests. Any paradigm worth its salt must pass a rigorous gauntlet of challenges in order to gain scientific acceptance. Unfortunately, the strongest forms of both the MMR and thimerosal theories—the suggestion that each exposure might be both *necessary* and *sufficient* to provoke the autism epidemic—fail on a number of counts.

The limits of the MMR argument have been obvious from the start. In the United Kingdom, SmithKline Beecham's MMR formulation was introduced in 1989 just at the point when autism rates there began their sharp rise. But in the United States, pointing the finger at MMR was always far less satisfying. Merck's M-M-R II was introduced in the United States in 1979, well before American autism rates began to rise, and so it was hard to argue that MMR exposures could have triggered an autism epidemic in this country.

By comparison, in the United Kingdom, the limits of the thimerosal theory were similarly obvious. In the United States, the addition of two thimerosal-containing vaccines in 1990 and 1991 sharply increased mercury exposure around the time autism rates turned up. But in the United Kingdom, pointing the finger at thimerosal was also unsatisfying: The UK vaccination schedule never delivered more than 75 mcg of ethyl mercury to infants (although the timing of that 75 mcg dose changed in 1991), and so it was hard to argue that thimerosal exposures alone could have triggered an autism epidemic in that country.

These limitations have been apparent to everyone on either side of the debate. The real contest has always been about the complications surrounding the natural experiments under way in both countries. And although some may have hoped that a few natural experiments would provide satisfying tests of the Wakefield and Bernard theories, nature has proven more complicated than that. These complications bring to mind a comment from the famed philosopher of science, Karl Popper, who defended the need for bold conjectures like these. Popper wrote, "He who gives up his theory too easily in the face of apparent refutations will never discover the possibilities inherent in his theory. There is room in science for debate: for attack and therefore also for defense. . . . But do not give up your theories too easily—not, at any rate before you have critically examined your criticism."[48] And there are numerous limitations to the natural experiments in both the United States and United Kingdom that make it unwise to give up the theories too easily:

- The schedule for the DPT shot was changed in the United Kingdom in 1990. The changes tripled the ethylmercury received by a four-month-old baby around the same time the U.S. thimerosal exposures went up and the time UK autism rates rose as well.

- Meanwhile, in the United States, thimerosal-containing influenza vaccines were recommended and targeted at both pregnant women and six-month-olds just as the PHS phaseout of the other three vaccines was under way. On a weight-adjusted basis, the net recommended mercury exposure for infants remained essentially unchanged; as one exposure fell, an equivalent exposure rose in its place.[49]

- In many countries around the world, but especially in the United States, the overall vaccine program continued to expand even as thimerosal was phased out of three vaccines that remained on the schedule in reformulated fashion. In addition to influenza, new vaccines were added for rotavirus, pneumococcus, chicken pox, and hepatitis A, bringing the total U.S. childhood vaccine count to thirty-six doses of fourteen different vaccines in ten different products.[50]

- Thimerosal was an active ingredient in the three vaccines that first used it, and probably did more than act solely as a preservative; in markets where thimerosal-free formulations of these products were introduced, new preservatives as well as immune stimulants were added. In particular, aluminum content increased in several vaccines.

- Background mercury exposures have risen sharply due to rising coal consumption around the world. So as mercury exposures from medicinal sources have changed, mercury exposure from manufacturing has risen sharply.

For the purposes of Bernard's theory, however, one very important test was whether autism rates declined in California as the three thimerosal-containing vaccines were phased out. Unlike some CDC surveillance programs, the California autism data captured only "full syndrome" cases, children diagnosed with PDD/autistic disorder and not PDD-NOS or Asperger's. As reported in a 2008 study, these full-syndrome rates in California continued to increase without any apparent decline due to re-duced thimerosal exposure.[51] Unfortunately for those who hoped autism might be most comparable to acrodynia, reducing harmful infant expo-sures has appeared more difficult than banning teething powders, and rising numbers of children continue to be affected by autism.

One puzzling aspect of the CDC autism-tracking approach has been its inattention to critical details of autism measurement. Resolving con-troversies like these will require increased reporting of autism trends and greater precision in surveillance methods. To some degree, more reporting has been carried out, but unfortunately, government health authorities have made little progress in assessing the trends in the autism rate over time. In addition, they have done little to specify trends in the specific categories of varying autism severity. CDC surveillance programs have carefully excluded birth dates prior to 1990. Case counts that neglected to track case severity maximize confusion of diagnostic categorization, as Asperger's syndrome cases have been lumped into the autism totals. In both the United States and the United Kingdom, new surveillance programs that could provide crucial data on trends have been delayed for years before publication: One UK study reporting rates of one in sixty-four was first reported as an abstract in 2004[52] and not published until 2009;[53] CDC surveillance sites took until 2007 to report on autism rates that were measured in 2000 and 2002.[54]

Practical surveillance issues aside, what has become increasingly clear is that epidemiology has proven a blunt instrument for resolving the debates over autism's cause. What remains logically indisputable is that any satisfying resolution requires an explanation that can account for several phenomena at once:

- a sharp change in disease frequency over a short period of time; clear differences in rates across local environments (say, between Oregon and Alabama) while rate increases are pervasive across national environments;

- a convergence of rates within national borders alongside apparent discontinuity between different countries and regions;

- unusually high rates among immigrants (such as the Minnesota Somali community) while their countrymen back home are unaffected.

We've clearly observed such patterns before; these phenomena resemble the disease patterns that Emil Kraepelin saw in GPI, that Fuller Torrey described in schizophrenia, and that John Walker-Smith summarized in Crohn's disease.

One thing is certain: Victory in the paradigm wars won't be won at the level of epidemiology, especially when some vaccine safety studies have been conducted so carelessly by partisans on either side of the battle. One thing on which there is agreement among the warring camps is the centrality of biology, whether it's genetics or toxicology, in getting to the real roots of the autism problem. In the realm of biology, any truly satisfying resolution requires an explanation of the neurological processes that define the disorder. And in order to get down to the neurological roots, eventually all roads lead back to the infant brain.

▬▬▬

CHAPTER TEN

DIGGING UP THE ROOTS

Where do human minds come from? . . . Biologically, we are just another ape. Mentally, we are a new phylum of organisms. In these two seemingly incommensurate facts lies a conundrum that must be resolved before we have an adequate explanation of what it means to be human.

—TERENCE DEACON, *THE SYMBOLIC SPECIES*[1]

Wendell Muncie, the father of Bridget, "Barbara K." in Leo Kanner's 1943 paper, believed in the use of biology to study the mind. Muncie and Kanner were both students of Adolf Meyer, the man who inspired Kanner to write *Child Psychiatry* in 1935 and Muncie to write *Psychobiology and Psychiatry* in 1948. Muncie's own book defined his sense of mission in eerily poignant terms. Psychobiology, Muncie wrote, "is the study of those functions distinctively human, the things man is best known for, the mentally integrated performances."[2]

Bridget Muncie, the third girl formally diagnosed with autism, was close to fifteen as her father wrote those words. As one of the first parents to observe an autistic child, Muncie learned well how autism selectively targets "those functions distinctively human." Actually, the correspondence is uncanny.

As a species, *Homo sapiens* is unique in the capacity for language; and as we've seen, language and communication are selectively targeted in autism. Humans are particularly social, yet autism selectively disables the capacity for "affective contact." We are novelty seekers, we make tools, explore the globe, and invent new technologies; but autism brutally restricts the interests of the affected. In a sense, as we search for the roots of autism we are seeking out the distinctive biology of the human experience.

Beyond the three core domains of disordered language, impaired affective contact, and restricted interests, the final defining characteristic of autism is its onset early in life. Kanner emphasized the timing, using the redundant moniker "early infantile autism" to distinguish autism from childhood schizophrenia. As we've shown, he first argued that autism was inborn; later he acknowledged that regressive cases were possible if they came during infancy. Setting aside the question of the biological "point of no return," autism was defined by a symptom onset no later than thirty-six months of age and usually earlier. There's a clue in here, one that points to the uniquely human process of brain development that plays out in the earliest months of life.

Autism's Double Growth Surge and Infant Brain Energetics

In an evolutionary sense, a large brain is the organ that has made humans exceptional animals. A long journey of natural selection separated primates from the rest of the placental mammals, then separated the genus *Homo* from apes and ultimately left *Homo sapiens* the sole survivor among the genus: the world's only upright-walking, symbolic-thinking, language-speaking species. Most of that journey was marked by the increasing size of our most exceptional organ, our brains. Just as the large relative size of the primate brain is the key trait that distinguishes primates from other mammals, similarly, the large relative size of the human brain is the key trait that distinguishes humans from other primates. In adult humans (based on typical primate development models), the brain is bigger by about four times than it should be given our size.[3]

This difference in brain size between species develops unevenly, with most of the divergence between human and primate development occurring after birth. For example, a typical newborn chimp has a hefty brain that adds up to about 10 percent of its body weight,[4] while a human newborn's brain is only slightly bigger on a relative basis, averaging a bit less than 13 percent of body weight:[5] That's a difference of only 1.3 times at that stage.[6] But by the time each animal reaches adulthood, the brain size gap has widened dramatically. An adult human brain comprises more than 2 percent of typical body weight;[7] by comparison, an adult chim-

Figure 7—The Infant Brain's Postnatal Growth Surge

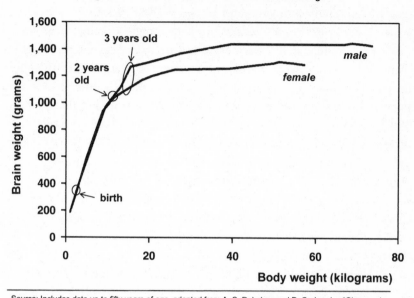

Source: Includes data up to fifty years of age, adapted from A. S. Dekaban and D. Sadowsky, "Changes in Brain Weights During the Span of Human Life: Relation of Brain Weights to Body Heights and Body Weights." *Ann Neurol (*1978); 4(4):345-56.

panzee brain is eight-tenths of a percent of its total weight, giving adult humans a brain proportion nearly triple their chimpanzee counterparts.[8]

Most of that difference occurs in a very short time. Whereas an infant's overall body grows to less than 20 percent of its adult size at two years of age,[9] its brain grows far faster. By two years of age, the human infant brain has grown to nearly 80 percent of its adult size. By three years of age the infant brain has more than tripled in size and reaches nearly 90 percent of its adult weight, thereby achieving almost two-thirds of its entire lifetime growth in just thirty-six months.

This incredible growth surge, completely unmatched by any other species and any other period of human development, is the single most significant event differentiating human and primate brain sizes. Surprisingly, variations in this same growth surge appear to mark some of the most crucial differences in human intelligence as well. British researchers have found that even if a newborn's brain is a bit on the small side, it's the growth after birth that makes all the difference. They observed that "*maximizing growth* [emphasis added] during infancy and childhood is critical for attaining peak cognitive capacity later in life."[10] Furthermore, they showed that the earliest months of life matter most, arguing that "infancy [as opposed to childhood] is the most important period of postnatal brain growth for determining later intelligence."[11]

In striking fashion, the very same tendency to develop large brains that drives human intelligence also appears to go into overdrive in autism. Harvard pediatric neurologist Martha Herbert, one of the leading investigators of autism neuroanatomy, has studied brain size in autism for many years. According to Herbert, "The most replicated finding in autism, and one that has been found in multiple reliably characterized cohorts and artifact-free samples, has been that the brains are on average unusually large."[12]

And just as in the typical development of human brains, it's less the size than the timing of brain growth that matters in autism. The normal surge in human brain growth occurs from birth through infancy, the first two or three years of life. In autistic children, this surge seems to run farther and faster, going into overdrive in ways that push the limits of a system already operating on a tight energy budget. "Brain overgrowth" in autism begins shortly after birth, when the autistic infant's brain is typically average or slightly below average in size, but then surges so rapidly that by five years of age, the autistic brain is almost indistinguishable in size from an adult brain.[13] This dramatic growth appears to begin in the first two months of life but continues for several years,[14] leaving the average autistic infant with a brain about 10 percent larger than a typically developing infant.

"This finding has had a paradoxical impact," Herbert continues. "On one hand, the consistency of an anatomical measure was an encouraging sign of convergence upon unraveling the neurobiology of this disorder. On the other hand, large brains did not make sense in terms of neural systems models of autism or brain-behavior correlations."[15] Despite producing highly specific autistic behaviors, the brain growth in autism was a generalized phenomenon, *pervasive* rather than specific.

This doubling down on brain growth (a surge within the surge of this developmental event), holds crucial clues to the resolution of the controversies in autism. How can the same event that makes humans smarter also turn against them? What is going on during this double surge that makes the autistic brain go haywire? This leads us into new terrain, and the overlap between evolutionary biology and what neurologists have labeled "brain energetics."

Growing a brain so large so quickly is a human infant's biggest job. In an evolutionary sense, it's dangerous because it prolongs the time in which an infant depends on its mother. Most of all, it takes an enormous amount of energy.

How much energy? Estimates vary, but the brain's remarkable usage of power during the infant growth surge has been the subject of a number of studies in humans, as well as comparative studies between humans and other primates. Most of these studies focus on the small set of organs that use up most of the body's energy while at rest. These organs—the heart, the liver and kidneys, the gut and the brain—are the body's energy hogs. In order to sustain human life, our bodies need to supply enough energy to satisfy the demands of these "expensive tissues"[16] and keep the organs running. The conventional measure of the body's resting energy usage is called the basal metabolic rate, or BMR. The BMR provides a floor to our energy needs, since we all need to do more than just rest. Scientists frequently draw the distinction between BMR, which is the energy we need to stay alive, and the energy required for intentional activities like moving, walking, and working.

Most of the body's energy usage through life is split pretty evenly between intentional activity and the BMR of the expensive tissues. An adult's body supplies 40 calories per kilogram per day (kcal/kg/day) with a BMR of about half that, or only 20. But infants are different; they have a much higher BMR and much less energy for extra activity. A newborn's body supplies about 110 kcal/kg/day but has to sustain a BMR of close to 100. A baby may not look as if it's doing much, but don't be fooled; its energetics are in high gear.[17]

In terms of the energy division among different types of tissue, an infant's organs are different as well. An amazing proportion of an infant's energy usage goes to its brain, both to sustain its metabolism and power its growth. Eventually, the other expensive tissues take a larger share, but not at birth. The developing brain consumes a higher share of the BMR (by one estimate it's over 80 percent at birth) than the rest of the organs combined.[18]

During the surge in infant brain growth, the energetics of the human brain are already stretched to their outer limits. During autistic brain development something gets pushed past the limit. So when we're considering the double surge in autism brain growth we need to consider just how sensitive and unprecedented this period in normal developmental really is.

Measuring brain growth in normal human development and the autism double surge raises an obvious question: Where does all the energy come from? Evolutionary biologists point to two main theories for the source of this unprecedented energy transfer.

The first theory focuses on the fact that a lot of the energy required to build a newborn's brain tissue comes from the mother during pregnancy and childbirth, by which time the brain has grown so large that it literally puts the mother's life at risk. Human childbirth is an extraordinarily unlikely proposition when compared to childbirth in the other apes for at least two reasons. Because we walk on two legs, humans require narrower pelvises than chimps; and, after our earliest human ancestors began to walk upright, their descendants began to grow larger brains. Humans, notes one expert on childbirth, "live on the knife's edge between easier births with more helpless offspring and more difficult births with greater fetal development."[19] There's really nothing else in the animal world quite like the difficulty of getting a human newborn's brain out of its mother's body.

But the mother's work doesn't stop there. A great deal of the energy for the human brain comes from the mother after pregnancy, a period when human infants "are on the ragged edge of [energy] insufficiency."[20] Lactation in humans is actually a bit shorter than in other mammals, but the period of true dependency is remarkably longer. As a result, some evolutionary biologists argue that the timing of human childbirth is quite deceptive as a marker of fetal development. Ralph Martin (the main proponent of the theory we're describing here) has argued that "for the first year of postnatal life, the human brain continues to show a fetal pattern of growth. This explains why human neonates are unusually dependent in comparison to other primates." And if human brains really show a "fetal pattern of growth" for a full year after birth, then the birth process is simply a shift in location for childbearing, not a change in gestation time. In a sense, this premature childbirth forces human mothers to play the role of a kangaroo mother, but without the pouch. "With respect to brain development," Martin concludes, "the human gestation period is really 21 months."[21]

Another remarkable thing about human mothers is that in order to make their way through this unusual period of dependency, over a year of their infant's gestation outside the womb, human mothers have to be big and strong. So strong, in fact, that there is less difference between male and female size among humans than in all of our ancestral apes. Why? It's simple: Human mothers have to hold, carry, and otherwise provide for the baby for far longer. Ralph Martin calls this gift of energy from mother to child the maternal investment theory.

But a second theory finds an energy source within the infant itself. Since one obvious cost of a large brain is that it raises the body's overall demand for energy, it would make sense to assume an infant would need a higher BMR. But this appears not to be the case. According to Leslie Aiello and Peter Wheeler (originators of the theory of brain energetics called the expensive tissue hypothesis), "There is no evidence of an increase in basal metabolism sufficient to account for the additional metabolic expenditure of the enlarged brain."

Indeed, and quite surprisingly, despite the large amounts of energy needed to power our large brains, human metabolism is not unusual in comparison to other mammals and primates.[22] But as Aeillo and Wheeler point out, the extra energy has to come from somewhere. And since most of the energy from the BMR goes to a short list of high-energy organs—the liver, the kidneys, the heart, and the gut—the list of "expensive tissues" that can balance the human energy budget is short.

Aiello and Wheeler's analysis pinpoints an organ that gives up what the brain uses in terms of energy reserves: the human gut. The human gut is more than 40 percent smaller, their analysis shows, than we'd expect for a comparable primate. "Therefore," they conclude, "the increase in mass of the human brain appears to be balanced by an almost identical reduction in the size of the gastro-intestinal tract."[23]

So if a smaller (and less functional) gut is the price we pay for our brains, how do we make do with so much less energy available for digesting our food? The main answer is that we eat better. "We could reduce our gut size to free up energy for a larger brain," Aiello theorizes, "because of a dietary change that was taking place as brain size expanded. Our ancestors were shifting from a heavily vegetarian diet, which requires a massive gut to digest plants and nuts, to a more easily digestible, nutritious diet that included meat and requires less gut tissue."[24]

This all sounds interesting, you may ask, but what does it have to do with autism? First, there is a misguided tendency among orthodox autism neurologists to draw a bright line at birth for the possible impact of environmental factors. Some scientists argue that any environmental exposure in autism occurs, indeed *can only occur*, before birth. There's little hard evidence to back up this belief, however. To be sure, some cases of autism (including Kanner's early cases) reflect "inborn disturbances," but the suggestion of a solid line between prenatal and postnatal exposures makes little sense. As we've seen here, from the perspective of the developing human brain, the event we call childbirth is a transition without biological meaning. If human gestation is really twenty-one months long, any exposure during the first twelve months after birth is effectively still "prenatal."

Second, to the extent that autism is defined by the double surge of the developing infant brain, the period after childbirth may be even more crucial as a developmental window for dangerous exposures. The most vulnerable time in brain development is the period when it's working hardest to grow, when it's perched on the "ragged edge" of oxygen and energy insufficiency.

Third, if a large proportion of the energy trade-off that fuels the remarkable surge in human brains comes from the gut, then we should not be the least bit surprised by the findings of Andrew Wakefield and John Walker-Smith. Whatever exposures push the autism brain into overdrive may also be stressing the one expensive tissue organ that has had its energy budget most drastically cut. Seen that way, it makes sense that autism, a disorder that affects the brain, would affect gut development as well.

Last, if we want to look for clues to the pathology of autism during development, perhaps the most important place to look is in the place where energy is supplied: the mitochondria.

Any discussion of the body's energy supply must eventually turn to the mitochondria. Mitochondria are called organelles, or "little organs," because they serve the cell with specialized functions in the same way one's organs serve the body. Unique among the elements that make up our cells and tissues, mitochondria have their own independent lineage: their own DNA, separate from the human genome that lies coiled inside every cell nucleus.

In keeping with their independent lineage, these little organs control their own replication and population level inside the cell, responding to the individual energy needs of specific organs. And despite being a target of active study, because mitochondria are so closely intertwined with cell development, research into their role and functioning has often fallen into the domain of stem-cell biology, a field held back for years by the Bush administration due to religious concerns. As a result, we probably know less about energy metabolism and its role in brain development than we might, but that is changing fast—in part because of autism.

The mitochondria produce energy using a process that involves a molecule known as adenosine triphosphate, or ATP, the body's own renewable energy source. As the powerhouses of the cell, mitochondria take oxygen and glucose and convert them into potential biological energy in the form of ATP, then deliver the ATP to various parts of the cell, where its energy potential is turned into usable energy.

Everything we do, from breathing to walking to thinking, is powered by these simple structures. But there are large differences in how much reserve mitochondrial capacity is available to different parts of the body. And surprisingly, relative to the other "expensive tissues," the brain is less densely populated with mitochondria. The organs with the highest density of mitochondria are the heart, liver, and kidneys, which have at least five times the density of brain mitochondria.[25]

This works out relatively well for the adult brain, which, unlike the heart, liver, and kidneys, gets a lot of rest during the day, especially while sleeping. But during infancy, the intense energy demands of infant brain growth put the brain in a vulnerable state. In addition, the other expensive tissue with relatively low mitochondrial density is the gut. And the section of the gut with the lowest mitochondrial density of all is the last part of the small intestine, the terminal ileum,[26] the heart of Crohn's disease and the area that Andrew Wakefield first described as diseased in a number of autistic patients. So when we're ranking the developing organs with the greatest sensitivity to disruptions of energy metabolism during infancy, the brain and the terminal ileum would have to rank near the top. It's a period when the interaction between the energy supplied by the mitochondria and the rapid growth and differentiation of an infant's tissues is unusually intense.

As primitive little organs, mitochondria do only one job: process energy. They depend on the rest of the cell for support and protection. Their unique DNA is more vulnerable to damage than regular nuclear DNA. They don't make the detoxifying molecule known as glutathione (GSH), so when GSH is being used up against other attacks the mitochondria can become vulnerable. They respond to even the smallest

changes in balance between molecules that either give or receive electrons (known as oxidative stress or redox imbalance).

So what happens when we introduce a toxic chemical like ethylmercury into this sensitive process? It's not hard to imagine that bad things
could happen. And we don't have to look very far for an example where
our worst fears appeared to come true. All of which brings us back to
ethylmercury, vaccines, and autism and the case of a child named Hannah Poling.

From November 9, 2007, to February 21, 2008, the U.S. government issued a remarkable pair of concessions in settlement of a case that had
been filed in vaccine court.

After a consistent period of normal development, aside from suffering
frequent ear infections, at eighteen months of age Hannah Poling received five shots against nine diseases in one visit to her pediatrician on
July 19, 2000. In short order, she began a rapid descent into autism. The
government's November 9, 2007, concession provides a description of
this regression: "According to her mother's affidavit, Hannah developed
a fever of 102.3 degrees two days after her immunizations and was lethargic, irritable, and cried for long periods of time. She exhibited intermittent, high-pitched screaming and a decreased response to stimuli.
Mrs. Poling spoke with the pediatrician, who told her that Hannah was
having a normal reaction to her immunizations. According to Hannah's
mother, this behavior continued over the next ten days, and Hannah also
began to arch her back when she cried."

Terry Poling, Hannah's mom, took her to the doctor again. "On July
31, 2000, Hannah presented to the Pediatric Center with a 101–102 degree temperature, a diminished appetite, and small red dots on her
chest. . . . Two months later, on September 26, 2000, Hannah returned
to the Pediatric Center with a temperature of 102 degrees, diarrhea,
nasal discharge, a reduced appetite, and pulling at her left ear. Two days
later, on September 28, 2000, Hannah was again seen at the Pediatric
Center because her diarrhea continued, she was congested, and her
mother reported that Hannah was crying during urination." After a
short period of improvement, things got worse. "On November 27, 2000,
Hannah was seen at the Pediatric Center with complaints of diarrhea,

vomiting, diminished energy, fever, and a rash on her cheek. At a follow-up visit, on December 14, 2000, the doctor noted that Hannah had a possible speech delay." That was the first concrete signal of autism.

Terry decided that Hannah needed a more thorough evaluation and took her to Johns Hopkins. There, "Dr. Andrew Zimmerman, a pediatric neurologist, evaluated Hannah at the Kennedy Krieger Children's Hospital Neurology Clinic, on February 8, 2001. Dr. Zimmerman reported that after Hannah's immunizations of July 19, 2000, an 'encephalopathy progressed to persistent loss of previously acquired language, eye contact, and relatedness.' He noted a disruption in Hannah's sleep patterns, persistent screaming and arching, the development of pica to foreign objects, and loose stools. Dr. Zimmerman observed that Hannah watched the fluorescent lights repeatedly during the examination and would not make eye contact. He diagnosed Hannah with 'regressive encephalopathy with features consistent with an autistic spectrum disorder, following normal development.'" A broad neurological term, an "encephalopathy" is a brain disease, often degenerative and permanent in nature.

Dr. Zimmerman's observations persuaded the government that Hannah's autism was indeed caused by her vaccines. In their November concession, the government admitted that the vaccinations Hannah received on July 19, 2000, "significantly aggravated an underlying mitochondrial disorder, which predisposed her to deficits in cellular energy metabolism, and manifested as a regressive encephalopathy with features of autism spectrum disorder."

Interestingly, this was only a partial concession. At first the government denied that Hannah's seizure disorder was related to her vaccines. But in a supplemental report in February 2008, they conceded this point, too, stating that the cause of Hannah's illness was "underlying mitochrondrial dysfunction, exacerbated by vaccine-induced fever and immune stimulation that exceeded metabolic reserves."

When the Hannah Poling concession was made public, it swept like wildfire through the autism community. Subtle markers of mitochondrial problems had been associated with autism before, but never had the connection between autism and vaccines been made so directly and publicly conceded. It was hard to understate the drama of this isolated event: the idea that vulnerability in the mitochondria, this highly sensitive bit of developmental biology, might have persuaded the government's lawyers and doctors to concede that vaccines caused a case of autism. As the concession momentarily broke through the press blockade on vaccine-autism news (Hannah and her parents gave a press conference that was broadcast on CNN and soon after appeared on *Larry King Live*), the idea that autism, vaccines, and mitochondrial biology might all be connected became a topic of intense (and continuing) interest.

Unfortunately, the legalistic language of the government settlement left more questions than answers. Did her vaccines cause autism, or something else? In what sense did Hannah really have an "underlying mitochondrial dysfunction"? An analysis of Hannah's mitochondrial DNA revealed an uncommon mutation that was present in her mother. Since her mother had no signs of mitochondrial dysfunction, was this a genetic defect or simply a random genetic variation? Finally, the language of the concession suggests precision where little is present, claiming that the nine vaccine doses that Hannah received in one day, along with 50 mcg of ethylmercury, "exceeded metabolic reserves." What exactly is a "metabolic reserve," and how were Hannah Poling's exceeded?

Given what we've learned about the vulnerability of the developing brain during its critical infant growth surge and the ragged edge of energy usage that the brain and the gut undergo during that period, can we really accept that Hannah was a single exceptional case?

Toward an Environmental Neurobiology of Autism

Even if one starts with the presumption that environmental exposures must play a role in autism neurobiology, it's extraordinarily difficult to make the connection between exposures that play out in a period of heightened vulnerability and their effect on things like brain growth, energy metabolism, and mitochondria. For while problems in the developing brain's mitochondria may help to connect the puzzle pieces on a more detailed level, the very nature of the injury process makes it difficult to observe. We can't observe much of the process in animal models, as the double surge is by definition a uniquely human event.

But we can offer some reasonable speculations for how such exposures might promote developmental injury, based on a range of recent studies. For example, accelerated brain growth is one change we are now relatively certain is part of the picture. So as the infant's brain is pressed to the outer limit of its energy resources, the cells in the brain of autistic children are likely working even harder than normal, putting more stress on the brain's energy supply system, the mitochondria. One effect, best described as pervasive rather than localized, is that connectivity across the different regions of the autistic brain suffers, especially in those functions that require coordination of brain regions that are far apart. As a result, the most "mentally integrated performances"—the skills like language, sociability, and the quest for novelty—suffer to a greater degree than functions that require less integration.

Other complex processes are probably disrupted as well. The act of recognizing faces, an act of visual perception most of us take for granted, requires unusual integration skills that many autistic people lack. Quite frequently, autistic people report difficulties in integrating the experience of a wide range of sensations, leading to unusual sensitivity to sounds, sights, smells, and tactile experiences. Not surprisingly, "sensory integration therapy" is a staple of many parents' autism recovery plan.

Psychologists have traditionally characterized autism as the discrete triad of problems: impaired social interaction and communication accompanied by restricted interests and repetitive behaviors. But when high-functioning autistic adults have written about their disability, they describe a world in which their difficulties with those "mentally integrated performances" are more of a side effect than a main feature of their disorder. Instead, they describe their problems in an almost biochemical sense: unusual ways of perceiving and processing information undergird much of the social and communication problems; and difficulties in regulating their emotions, such as anxiety, tend to create an insatiable desire for sameness.[27]

The writings of these autistic adults suggest that all of the visible manifestations of autism are surface observations: effectively emergent outcomes of something gone wrong in a developing infant's biology. This again suggests that the answers to the pervasive symptoms are best pursued in terms of observing biology at a deeper level: in terms of tissues, cells, and signaling molecules.

One influential series of papers from a group at Johns Hopkins looked at brain tissue from autistic people who passed away and donated their brain to research. What they found is best described as a subtle process of inflammation. If these changes were visible on our skin, we might call them a rash and think little of it. But a brain rash in a developing infant is far more serious business.

No one can say for sure how this inflammation develops, but it might be related to a range of biological imbalances, an echo of a complex series of events within the womb and during infancy that go on to have a range of both short- and long-term consequences.

Evidence is accumulating that two specific imbalances, each of which are connected with inflammation, might play a key role in autism; and both can be seeded quite effectively by small amounts of exposure to thimerosal and ethylmercury. Let's consider these two imbalances in turn.

First, there is increasing interest in whether children with autism show abnormalities in regulation of the oxidative status of their cells. The term "oxidative stress" has entered the common lexicon of human health without much understanding of what it means or what to do about it. Scientists who focus on this area tend to prefer the term "redox balance" to oxidative stress to reflect the fact that this balance is an intrinsic part of normal cellular regulation. *Redox* is scientific shorthand for complementary events called "reduction" and "oxidation." *Reduction* occurs when an atom's electric charge becomes more negative (and actually gains electrons); *oxidation* occurs when the electric charge becomes more positive (and a substance loses electrons); and *redox* combines the two concepts to describe the direction of change in electrical charge within a biological system.

Proper redox balance is critical to cellular function, and relatively small changes in redox balance can greatly alter the sensitivity to signaling molecules important in normal development. Nerve cells that are too oxidized are less responsive to normal signals required for their survival. Precursor cells (a term used generically to include stem cells and the dividing cells they generate that are intermediates between stem cells and differentiated cell types of a tissue) that are too oxidized may differentiate too early, or be reduced in their division for other reasons.[28]

Severe redox imbalance can lead to a situation of oxidative stress, which is seen in traumatic injury and in such degenerative diseases as Alzheimer's disease and Parkinson's disease. Oxidative stress is thought to contribute to a wide range of pathologies in all organs and at all stages of life. A rising number of scientists are focusing on the idea that redox imbalances in the human brain during critical developmental periods could alter normal cellular function in ways relevant to such diseases as autism.

One reason for this rising interest is that evidence of the occurrence of oxidative stress in children with autism has been steadily increasing. A recently published book is titled *Autism: Oxidative Stress, Inflammation and Immune Abnormalities,* and dedicated to this single subject. The book summary reports that the authors have "collect[ed] work from researchers who report on evidence indicating links between autism and a number of oxidative stress-related abnormalities such as neuroinflammation, mitochondrial dysfunction, membrane and metabolism abnormalities, and signal transduction."[29]

The second imbalance is in the signaling molecules—known as *cytokines*—that help govern our immune system. The cytokine imbalance that has been observed in children with autism would be predicted to alter function of the immune system. The brain's immune system is unique. One of the few "immunologically privileged sites" in the body, foreign tissue grafts can survive for long periods in such areas without provoking a destructive immune attack.[30] But as diseases like multiple sclerosis have shown, the brain can easily develop immune-related disease; the immune response just follows a different pattern than elsewhere in the body.

Changes in cytokine balance and redox balance may be contributory factors in autism. One analysis of abnormal head size in autism found that "larger head sizes are significantly associated with a positive history of allergic/immune disorders both in the patient and in his/her first degree relatives."[31] Since Mary Coleman's first report of autoimmune thyroid disease among parents of an early group of autism parents, numerous studies have reported increased rates of autoimmune diseases in the parents of autistic children.[32] And recent work demonstrates that these cytokine imbalances may also be found in the gut and help explain the unusual responses in autistic children to the food proteins in wheat and milk.[33]

The presence of cytokine and redox imbalances in autism raises an obvious question: How might toxic exposures like ethylmercury (most recently in the form of thimerosal) provoke autism?

There are both *immediate* and *chronic* effects of cytokine imbalance and possible toxic injuries that may well be relevant to the onset of autism. But defining exactly what *immediate* might be in the context of an environmental injury that might accumulate over days and months, and may straddle both prenatal and postnatal exposures, is difficult. Thus, there are many questions that go along with each suggested injury mechanism.

For example, increased brain size could be due to increases in cell number and/or changes in cell size—but why would either of these occur? Are precursor cells or immune cells proliferating too quickly? And what effect would cytokine imbalance and/or redox balance have on mitochondrial function?

Could exposure to thimerosal or other mercury-containing compounds contribute in immediate ways to any of the imbalances that are observed in children with autism? Despite counterclaims, the question remains a relevant one. While the press has reported that children's vaccines are now free of thimerosal, that simply isn't true.

Thimerosal *was* gradually phased out of *three* infant vaccines starting in 1999. But influenza vaccines targeted for pregnant women weren't included in the thimerosal withdrawal; these vaccines are intended for adults as well as children. As public health authorities began ramping up their efforts to mandate the flu vaccine over this same period, an entirely new source of even earlier thimerosal exposure was introduced and remains to this day.

A similar situation holds with respect to the argument that the continued rise of autism rates in combination with the advent of mercury-free infant vaccines disprove a connection between thimerosal and autism. If most flu vaccines still contain thimerosal, and these vaccines are commonly administered to pregnant women, we cannot conclude that the mercury exposure risk has been taken away, especially when multiple other mercury sources in our environment are currently on the rise.

There are several lines of scientific evidence that raise concerns about the immediate toxicity of thimerosal. For example, research presented at the Institute of Medicine meeting on autism and the environment by Mark Noble of the University of Rochester demonstrated that levels of thimerosal that seem likely to be achieved in the brains of vaccinated infants can interfere with normal growth and development of precursor cells in the developing brain. Noble and his colleagues have shown that thimerosal is as effective as methylmercury in activating cellular response pathways that lead to degradation of cell surface receptors of critical importance in normal cell division and survival. Perhaps most importantly, in the context of brain development, they found that precursor cells isolated from the developing central nervous system are more sensitive to thimerosal and methylmercury than are such differentiated cell types as neurons and astrocytes (the major support cell in the brain), with sensitivity extending down to exposure levels of 5-10 parts per billion.[34] These appear likely to be clinically relevant exposure levels, as infant monkeys exposed to thimerosal at the levels provided by the infant vaccine schedule had brain concentrations of mercury ranging from 10-20 parts per billion for prolonged periods after the injections.[35]

A second immediate effect of a potential toxic injury is premature cell death. Although there is little evidence of the widespread killing (necrosis) of cells akin to what one would expect in more acute mercury exposures, there is evidence for early cell loss in autism, especially in one of the largest and more vulnerable cell lines, the Purkinje cells of the cerebellum. Numerous laboratory studies have shown that thimerosal promotes the programmed death (apoptosis) of neuronal stem cell lines, with several of these showing that mitochondria are involved in the process.[36] Like Noble's analysis, these studies show that thimerosal has a toxic effect even at extremely low doses, with damage seen at levels even lower than five parts per billion.[37]

A third possible immediate effect of thimerosal exposure is alterations in signaling in the immune system. Vaccination itself is dependent on creating an alteration in cytokine imbalance that enhances response to the pathogen of interest. It appears that when thimerosal is administered in animal models, however, there is first a suppression and then a stimulation of the immune response.[38] In addition, a team led by Isaac Pessah of the MIND Institute also demonstrated that both immature and mature dendritic cells (immune cells involved in innate immune response) are "exquisitely sensitive" to thimerosal. Pessah's team reported that thimerosal disrupted both redox balance and other signaling channels at parts per billion (or "nanomolar") concentrations.[39]

A fourth possible outcome of toxic injury is the activation of the brain's own specialized defense system, the neuroglial cells. A Johns Hopkins research team that examined the brains of autistic cases after death reported that two kinds of these supporting cells, astrocytes (cells that support neurons) and microglia (the brain's immune cells) are activated in autism. Although it isn't yet clear whether this neuroglial activation in autism is connected to toxicant exposure, organic mercury is a well-known vehicle for activating these cells. In one series of studies on adult monkeys, low doses of methylmercury entered the brain, were "demethylated" (converted to inorganic mercury), and then trapped in the brain where the residual mercury activated the microglial cells.[40] The same team recently compared exposures of ethylmercury and thimerosal in infant monkeys and showed that the ethylmercury in thimerosal was trapped in the brain more rapidly than methylmercury, suggesting a potentially larger toxic effect.[41] Further studies are underway.

A fifth effect of thimerosal exposure is that it can also lead to depletion of cellular reserves of glutathione, a chemical that is at the center of cellular redox state regulation. Glutathione is a critical component of protection against oxidative stress and a variety of physiological stressors, including such toxins as mercury, and is critical in removing mercury from cells. Jill James of the University of Arkansas exposed neuronal stem cells to thimerosal and showed that "thimerosal neurotoxicity is associated with glutathione depletion."[42]

Finally, there is a concern as to whether thimerosal exposure could compromise mitochondrial function. Mitochondrial DNA is particularly vulnerable to oxidative stress.[43] A recent study by Mark and David Geier demonstrated that thimerosal exposure at low nanomolar concentrations provoked oxidative stress and mitochondrial dysfunction in neural stem cell lines.[44]

Would the *immediate* effects of cytokine imbalances or redox imbalances be all it takes to induce autism or is the devastation really caused by more *chronic* biological effects left behind in the wake, after the initial effect has passed? As we've seen in the history of autism's sentinel case, Donald Triplett, recovery from the worst symptoms of autism may be possible by direct intervention in immune signaling: in Donald's case a treatment for an autoimmune condition that his doctors thought was unrelated to his autism. His experience suggests that the persistent aftereffects may be just as important, if not more so, to the long-term course of the disease.

Ongoing Redox Imbalance. Although redox imbalance may well have its most disruptive effects early in life, there is also mounting evidence that oxidative stress persists for long periods after the onset of autism. Numerous studies, most notably by Jill James at the University of Arkansas[45] but supported by a host of others,[46] have demonstrated the presence of markers of oxidative stress in autistic children. There may be some genetic basis that makes autistic children vulnerable to this,[47] but there is also clear evidence that early exposure to organic mercury can have long-lasting effects as well. One recent study in mice showed that "prenatal exposure to methyl mercury affects the cerebral glutathione antioxidant systems by inducing biochemical alterations that endure even when mercury tissue levels decrease and become indistinguishable from those noted in [controls]."[48]

Ongoing Autoimmunity. There are many signs of ongoing autoimmunity in autism, long after the earliest signs of immune imbalances have passed, some of which may be a tendency passed along by the parents. A tendency toward autoimmune disease is one of the more consistent finding in all of autism[49] and one that has been observed from the very beginning. In two of Kanner's original cases, "Charles N." and "Elaine C.," doctors suspected thyroid disease and provided thyroid supplementation. Mary Coleman found a high rate of both chemical exposure and autoimmune thyroid disease in the National Autism Society parent group. In terms of the children themselves, the Johns Hopkins paper on brain tissue provides the most definitive evidence of a persistent level of immune activation in the autistic brain.[50] And following Andrew Wakefield's observation of an active bowel disease, many investigators have found markers of persistently abnormal immune signaling consistent with autoimmunity to gut tissue[51] and to sensitivity to foods like milk and wheat.[52] As with the immediate effect, ethylmercury in the form of thimerosal has been shown in multiple animal models to induce persistent autoimmune disease.[53]

Reduced Ability to Detoxify. Redox balance and the ability to sustain adequate levels of glutathione are closely connected. One of the key markers of oxidative stress is how frequently glutathione itself is oxidized. In its oxidized form, glutathione (GSH) is called "oxidized disulfide glutathione (GSSG)"; when the ratio of GSH to GSSG is lowered due to oxidative stress, the ability of the cell to detoxify itself is reduced. In several recent studies Jill James has reported evidence of lower GSH/GSSG ratios in autism,[54] indicating reduced ability to detoxify. The mechanism of damage in these studies is consistent with thimerosal exposure and closely tied to long-term mitochondrial damage.

Long-term Damage to Mitochondria. There are many unknowns in pinning down the role of mitochondria in autism. In Hannah Poling's case, the government suggested some kind of inborn defect in mitochondrial DNA. This, they implied, made her regression somehow inevitable, even as they reluctantly conceded vaccine injury. Just as likely, however, is that the lasting injury in autism is not fated by genes but rather inflicted by the exposures. In James's view, these children may be more vulnerable to the effects of redox imbalance; she argues that "because mitochondria are both the major source and primary target" of the free radicals that cause oxidative stress, the lower level of detoxification capacity that she observed within the mitochondria of autistic individuals "implies that mitochondrial antioxidant defense mechanisms are insufficient to maintain redox [balance]" and that these vulnerable individuals may be "more severely compromised with thimerosal exposure.[55] A number of recent studies have shown evidence of long-term mitochondrial dysfunction in autistic children, mostly using markers of energy metabolism. In studies of autistic populations, estimates of the rate of subtle mitochondrial dysfunction range from as low as 7 percent to up to 50 percent.[56]

In such a brief tour through these highly sensitive processes, it's not possible to develop a comprehensive picture of what the chain of cause and effect looks like. But for the first time, recent work is providing insight into the underlying biology of what we're seeing in autism: what the tissue damage is really like and how mercury (and perhaps other toxicants and chemicals) can disturb this biology at extremely low doses. As this work has progressed, thimerosal has been extensively studied and consistently shown to be capable of producing the kind of havoc we observe in autism. While many public health officials have moved to exonerate mercury in general, and thimerosal in particular, as a risk factor in autism, a steady drumbeat of science is emerging that is saying, "not so fast."

To summarize, thimerosal does all the things we're seeing in the developing brain of an autistic infant. It provokes oxidative stress; it depletes glutathione; it activates neuroglial cells; it causes premature stem cell differentiation; it induces autoimmunity; and it targets mitochondria. It does all these things at very low concentrations, similar to what a fetus or newborn might experience in the developing brain. Some of these effects are immediate, but as the exposure plays out inside the body, there are long-lasting effects. Inside the brain, we know that both common kinds of alkyl mercury can be de-alkylated (losing their methyl or ethyl parts), and once ethyl mercury converts to inorganic mercury, it can stay trapped in the brain for long periods of time; one autopsy study conducted in a victim of methylmercury poisoning two years after the event found mercury levels in the brain more than 50 times the normal levels.[57]

So if one test of a theory is that it is at least biologically plausible, we contend that thimerosal meets that standard in spades: As more research is completed, the concern over the risk of thimerosal continues to rise. But biology is not the only place where the debate of mercury in autism has taken place, there is an even more specific body of evidence on mercury exposure and autism in human populations.

The Evidence for Mercury

Beyond the persuasive lessons of history and some convincing biology, what does the current evidence on mercury and autism in populations of human beings teach us?

Public relations and controversies aside, more than any other environmental factor ever considered, the scientific evidence supports a direct role for mercury in autism. Both tissue samples and epidemiology show positive evidence for mercury's role. In both of these areas the findings have also been mixed, as the positive evidence has been replicated but not in a consistent manner. There is significantly more quiet support for mercury in tissue studies than in epidemiology, which has been more widely publicized and controversial.

Analyzing body tissue for mercury is notoriously difficult, in large part because mercury binds so quickly to tissue that it hides from most noninvasive testing. In a perfect world, one would need to trace how much mercury enters the body and where, how it is distributed in the body's tissues, which cells (and what parts of cells) it affects, and how and by what means it is excreted from the body (if ever). In the absence of a completely controlled lab environment, however, one must make do with the data available.

Although blood is an obvious place to start looking for mercury exposure, it's not a particularly good one, and most analyses of blood mercury levels in autism are uninformative. Only the most recent exposures are reflected in blood samples, since mercury exits the blood and quickly moves to other organs. Ethylmercury leaves the blood faster than methylmercury, but that doesn't mean it leaves the body quickly at all. Quite the contrary.

Despite the fact that blood is an imperfect compartment for analysis, there have been some notable findings in recent studies. Most disturbing has been work by the EPA showing that the levels of mercury in blood for women between the ages of sixteen and forty-nine are much higher than desirable.[58] By this estimate, about 8 percent of pregnant women have blood levels of mercury above the level at which harm to the fetus is possible. Most of this is organic mercury, attributed by the authors to fish consumption. In a recent analysis of the inorganic mercury levels, UCLA researcher Dan Laks found evidence of increased levels as well.[59]

Once mercury enters the body, it has to go somewhere even when it leaves one easy-to-measure compartment, such as the blood. The blood simply moves mercury around from one part of the body to another; just because mercury is not in the blood doesn't mean it has left the body.

Hair is one of the most commonly used markers for mercury exposure. In part, this is because it's one of the easiest body tissues to obtain. In fact, hair provides one of the few natural archives of childhood exposures because parents often save a lock of their child's baby hair. The conventional approach is to consider hair as a straightforward marker; the more mercury exposure, the higher the level of mercury one would expect in the hair. In many situations this can be true, and for most animals, hair is one of the primary ways that mercury gets excreted. But this is only a useful marker of mercury that has entered and then left the body, if one assumes that all humans filter and excrete mercury in the same way.

To the extent that hair provides evidence of excretion, however, it might provide clues in a different way. What if children with higher mercury in their hair, those who are capable of ridding mercury from their body, develop better, while those who can't manage an equivalent excretion are harmed? Observations of hair from autistic infants first raised this idea. A convenience sample collected starting in 2001 by a Louisiana doctor named Amy Holmes revealed that autistic children had lower levels of mercury in their first baby haircuts than did typically developing children, despite known exposures (maternal amalgams, fish diets, and vaccinations) that were the same or higher in the autism group. This was true when comparing autistic children to controls, but also when comparing children with different degrees of autism severity: the more affected the child, the lower the amount of mercury excreted in their hair.[60]

The real surprise in this data, however, was not the mercury levels of the autistic children, but the remarkably high level of mercury in the hair of normal children. In an analysis of the control children, one of us was able to demonstrate that the differences in mercury hair levels were readily explained by the children's exposures: the higher the amount of mercury exposure accumulated through the mother's amalgams, fish consumption, and the child's injected thimerosal, the higher the amount excreted in hair. The analysis showed clearly that the finding wasn't a result of random error; if anything, the study showed how hard the typically developing children's bodies were working to get rid of excess mercury.

Because of this startling finding, especially the unusually high levels of mercury in the hair of controls, this study has been harshly criticized. Critics have contended that data were simply wrong, implying false data, a fatally biased recruitment procedure, or contaminated samples. Because of the significance of the results there have also been several attempts to replicate the study. But only one followed the same approach: Jim Adams from Arizona State University collected the first baby haircuts of a group of autistic children, as Holmes had done, and compared it to controls. In his analysis, Adams found the same excretion effect as the original study, namely that "the lower level of Hg in the baby hair of children with autism indicates an altered metabolism of Hg, and may be due to a decreased ability to excrete Hg." In the Adams sample, however, the hair levels of nonautistic children were markedly lower than in the Holmes sample.[61]

Although no one but Adams collected autistic hair samples in the same way Holmes did, several other hair studies have been conducted in older autistic children. These have found quite variable results. One found nearly ten times *higher* levels of mercury in the hair of older autistic children, ranging in age from four to seven years old, in Kuwait. Although this study didn't focus much on the question of excretion during the period of onset in infancy, the findings might be consistent with the idea that these children were simply exposed to higher levels of mercury in their daily lives.[62]

One of the most prominent critical studies examined both blood and hair from a population of older Chinese children (the average age was seven). This study was led by Virginia Wong of the University of Hong Kong and found no evidence of a difference in mercury levels between autistics and controls in either blood or hair. This study was widely cited as a refutation of the mercury excretion theory.[63]

But then a few years later, two curious statisticians, Catherine DeSoto and Robert Hitlan from the University of Northern Iowa, read the paper carefully. They checked Wong's calculations and determined that the authors had made a serious statistical error. DeSoto and Hitlan shared their analysis with the journal editor who had published the study, who realized that the original article was deeply flawed and should never have passed peer review. The authors were forced to retract their finding and in the process confessed that not simply were their calculations wrong, so was most of their data, which they suggested were replete with typographical errors that explained their mistakes. As part of the journal's formal correction announcement the editor forced Wong to publish the entire spreadsheet of corrected data. On the surface, their revised calculations were now correct, and their revised data showed blood levels of mercury in autistic children that were markedly higher and arguably significant, yet the authors still refused to admit a positive finding and continued to reject any association between mercury metabolism and autism.[64]

Armed with the corrected data, DeSoto and Hitlan proceeded to re-analyze it in order to assess the Wong team's continued dismissal of a positive finding. To their surprise, DeSoto and Hitlan found clear support for the excretion argument, noting that when one examined blood and hair levels together, "the relationship between blood levels of mercury and mercury excreted in the hair is reduced for those with autism compared with nonautistic persons."[65] In other words, there was an observable impairment in mercury excretion even in these older autistic children. So although none of these results were tidy, all of them seemed to lend support, one way or another, for higher mercury exposure and/or reduced excretion in autism.

The strongest argument against the reduced excretion theory, however, came from a systematic 2004 survey that was part of the National Health and Nutrition Examination Survey (NHANES). This nationwide survey didn't look at autism at all, but rather the level of mercury in the hair of typical young children (in NHANES the youngest group surveyed was between one and five years of age). Since the high levels of mercury in the Holmes sample was so important for the reduced excretion theory, it was important to understand how valid those findings really were. In opposition to the Holmes finding, the 2004 NHANES survey found low levels in the surveyed children's hair, far lower than the results from the Holmes sample. Since the NHANES survey is a major undertaking and designed to reflect the U.S. population, the variance in results has been used to trump the Holmes data: Vaccine courts in particular have found this evidence more persuasive and have consequently rejected the Holmes analysis.[66]

But is the NHANES hair data truly comparable to that of the Holmes controls? The NHANES results didn't include just baby hair (although some of it probably was), nor did the survey require that cases and controls had received all of their thimerosal-containing vaccines on time, which was an essential requirement for inclusion in the Holmes study (although some of the hair in the NHANES study was undoubtedly from fully immunized infants). It's certainly possible that the two analyses are both correct, and that the Holmes control group simply isolated a subgroup of the population with unusually high exposure and excretion.

If that is indeed the case, then the most relevant test of the Holmes control group would be a group selected in the same way, using baby hair in infants fully vaccinated with thimerosal-containing vaccines. There aren't many such studies but there is one: The only other study that followed the same approach as Holmes, a Brazilian group that used only baby hair samples and required that all children in the sample receive a full complement of thimerosal-containing vaccines, found the same high levels Holmes found. The reported mercury levels in these typical children were even a bit *higher* than Holmes had found, 4 parts per million (ppm) versus 3.6 ppm for Holmes's controls.[67]

Given the limitations of blood and hair analyses to date, it is worth considering other tissue sources. Like hair, teeth can serve as a natural archive providing information about mercury exposures many years in the past. But unlike hair, which is an excretion path for mercury, teeth act more like an organ, and might reflect instead the elevated *retention* of mercury that goes hand in hand with reduced excretion. Since many parents keep their children's baby teeth after the period of "second dentition" has passed, the preserved teeth can provide insight into the true body burden of mercury for long periods afterward.

We've already described the use of whale and human teeth to observe mercury levels from decades or centuries past. But more recent baby tooth samples have been put to good use in studies on human health involving not mercury but lead. A legendary series of studies of inner-city children demonstrated that lead paint and lead in gasoline were dangerous to childhood development. The first author, pediatrician Herbert Needleman, was derided and attacked by industry, but ultimately, it was his analysis that proved conclusive: Children with high lead exposures invariably had unusually high lead levels in their baby teeth.

So far, there is only a single published study of mercury levels in baby teeth of autistic children. Conducted by Jim Adams at Arizona State, this study shows clear evidence of elevated mercury retention in autism: The mercury retained in the teeth of children with autism was more than twice the level of mercury in the teeth of controls.[68]

But when it comes to measuring mercury retention levels in autism, the hardest question to answer is the most obvious one: Are there elevated levels of mercury in the autistic brain? Brain tissue is guarded carefully in autism, since the opportunity to collect postmortem brain tissue from autistic people who have recently died is rare.

There is, however, one study that was performed on mercury levels in the autistic brain with a tiny sample of postmortem brain tissue. Harvard psychiatrist Elizabeth Sajdel-Sulkowska obtained a small sample of postmortem brain tissue from nineteen brains in all, nine of them autistic. Comparing the small autistic group with controls, she looked for differences between the two groups in terms of evidence of oxidative stress and mercury levels.

Despite the small samples, the results were striking. First, the evidence supported a strong relationship between mercury and a metabolic marker of oxidative stress. Second, she also observed a significant relationship between oxidative stress and autism: The oxidative stress marker was significantly elevated (by about 69 percent) in autistic brain samples. As for the direct connection between mercury and autism (as opposed to the two-step connection of mercury to oxidative stress to autism), the data were supportive but not conclusive: Mercury levels were about 68 percent higher in the autism group, but due to the sample size the increase was not statistically significant.[69]

Whether one considers the evidence in blood, hair, or brain tissue, the body of evidence suggests that mercury is often, although perhaps not exclusively, involved in causing autism. Again and again, we see the same set of simple and repeated findings: When it comes to autism and mercury, there is too much exposure, too little excretion, and too much retention.

———

Returning, then, to epidemiology, there are two areas that can inform the question of mercury exposure in autism: One focuses on the risk for autism from mercury in the general environment, the other on the risk from mercury in the form of thimerosal in vaccines. Surprisingly, perhaps, the results from the environmental mercury studies—although fewer in number—provide some of the strongest evidence implicating mercury in autism.

University of Texas scientist Ray Palmer, along with several colleagues, has found in two consecutive studies that increased exposure to mercury emissions from industrial sources, most notably coal smoke from electric power plants, is significantly associated with increased autism risk. In their first study, published in 2006, Palmer et al. found that higher emissions of mercury in a school district (after taking into account all sorts of other factors that might affect autism rates) appeared to increase autism risk.[70] In the second study from 2009, Palmer et al. refined their initial analysis. Their latest analysis shows that the closer a family lives to a major source of mercury emissions, the higher the autism rate: For every ten miles closer a family lives to a mercury source, a child's risk of autism goes up between 1 and 2 percent.[71]

Not only did Palmer et al. replicate their own findings on mercury in the Texas air, they also replicated a similar finding: In 2006 a group of researchers had looked at the levels of hazardous air pollutants in California and found roughly double the autism risk in the areas with the highest concentration of mercury in the air.[72]

What's critical to recognize about these studies is that they have little to do with all the normal routes of mercury exposure that most scientists are used to talking about. They're not about fish, fillings, or vaccines, the exposure pathways that scientists have reduced to reasonably well-defined theories of exposure and biology that they can test in their labs. As a result, scientists can't really tell us what exposure pathway we should be worried about. Are we breathing it or drinking it? Is it in the aquatic food chain or in the dust that falls on our cars? Unfortunately right now, the end-to-end modeling of the whole problem is not yet fully constructed.

As Palmer et al. point out, there's a lot of reason to be concerned about rising levels of mercury in the air from all sources. Most airborne mercury comes from coal burning, and we've seen huge increases in coal consumption during just the last few decades based on the explosive, and largely coal-fueled, growth of the Chinese economy. Mercury can come from local point sources like the ones analyzed in the Texas studies, or it can come from distant sources like Chinese power plants that launch the mercury into the upper atmosphere, where winds carry it across oceans and around the globe before it comes down to the ground level with precipitation.

While we have good reason to worry about too much carbon dioxide in the air resulting from the use of fossil fuels, we should be just as concerned about this other by-product of all that coal burning.

Under normal circumstances, epidemiology is both a blunt and sensitive instrument: blunt because the assessment of risk rarely has much validity in individual cases; sensitive because of the ability of small changes in the numbers of disease observations to swing the results of a major study. The latter problem comes into sharp relief when the study is carried out with those who have an interest in the outcome. Most famous, perhaps, has been the case of the Merck-sponsored Vioxx trial, in which three heart attacks (occurring late in the process but before the final submissions) were omitted from a study published in the *New England Journal of Medicine*.[73] Upon learning of these omissions five years after the article published, the journal slammed Merck publicly in an editorial claiming that the omissions compromised the integrity of the study.[74]

Thimerosal epidemiology has been plagued with similar problems. The connection between autism and several other neurodevelopmental disorders came up strongly significant in the first data run the CDC examined in late 1999.[75] In one analysis, the risk of autism was more than eleven times higher when comparing the group of infants with the highest exposure to thimerosal to those with no exposure. In an e-mail with the subject heading "It just won't go away" the CDC's data analyst pleaded for help from his superiors to find "an alternative explanation." In the coming weeks and months, that's exactly what happened.

The path to an alternative explanation came straight from the Vioxx playbook. The CDC's first data run included about ten cases of NDDs with thimerosal exposure levels higher than the recommended vaccine schedule. These were almost certainly due to exposures from thimerosal contained in hepatitis B immune globulin. So in the next round of analysis, in a list of excluded groups were "children that received hepatitis B immunoglobulin, as these were more likely to have high exposure and outcome levels." Poof, down came the risk numbers.

A number of other "exclusions" were made to the study group, as well as "adjustments" in the statistical models that analyzed them. By the time everything was finished and published in *Pediatrics*, the only study of autism and thimerosal done in the U.S. found no evidence of harm. Meanwhile, several other studies quickly circulated, all based on Danish data and conducted by a research team that included employees of the Danish vaccine manufacturer who manufactured the thimerosal-containing vaccines in the study. In a review of the evidence by an expert panel convened at the request of Congress, Dr. Irva Hertz-Picciotto, professor of public health at UC Davis School of Medicine and chair of the panel, told one of us that the Danish studies had serious weaknesses in their designs. These studies took on added significance due to a 2004 report issued by an Institute of Medicine (IOM) committee (funded by the CDC) that concluded, "Based on this body of evidence . . . the evidence favors rejection of a causal relationship between thimerosal-containing vaccines and autism." More than any other single finding, this IOM conclusion has been the basis for the claim that the autism-thimerosal question has been "asked and answered."[76]

But the truth of the matter is, the most honest assessment of the thimerosal epidemiology is that it has been inconclusive, with evidence and studies on both sides. In order to reach its conclusion, the IOM rejected wholesale the published body of work by the father-and-son team Mark and David Geier. With far fewer resources, and admittedly less polish, the Geiers have conducted numerous studies using only U.S. databases, including the same "vaccine safety datalink" the CDC used, and consistently come to the opposite conclusion from the CDC. From multiple angles, the Geiers have consistently found evidence that thimerosal exposure raises autism risk. More recently, a separate team of researchers from Stony Brook University has found evidence of increased autism risk due to thimerosal-containing vaccines in two separate analyses.[77]

The Geiers have readily acknowledged that they have received funding from the Autism Petitioners' Steering Committee in the U.S. vaccine court proceedings and have served as expert witnesses in vaccine compensation hearings. So in terms of interests at stake, the debate between the Geiers on one side and the CDC on the other has become an argument between the plaintiffs' and the defendants' science. In the battle of professional and public opinion, the Geiers have lost that debate and their work has largely been nullified. But in terms of the strength of the evidence, the verdict is far less clear.

In our view, the net conclusion from this epidemiological war is that despite studies on both sides of the argument, there is persuasive evidence of harm. Although one can take issue with the methods in some of the Geiers' studies, it's hard to take issue with the weight and consistency of the evidence they've accumulated. It would be rash to dismiss the thimerosal theory in light of the evidence the Geiers have put together suggesting injury.

At the same time, it would also be hasty to assume that autism is behaving like acrodynia and that the simple removal of thimerosal will eliminate every case of autism. The Geiers' data don't make that case (the increased risks due to thimerosal exposures range from 80 percent to 500 percent, but are never infinite) and don't need to be compelling. The thimerosal theory has never fully explained everything about autism. Plausibly autistic children were born before ethylmercury was invented; and one need not search long to find isolated cases of unvaccinated children with autism. If autism were more like acrodynia and less like schizophrenia, the mystery of causation would have been solved long ago. It's a complex problem that requires clear thinking and open minds.

Instead of clarity and open-minded concern, however, autism science has degenerated into a defensive and volatile conflict. In this ongoing battle, the main flash point has become the timing and role of vaccines. This has been in many ways a divisive issue, but in a search for the truth, it is also unavoidable. Unfortunately, the problem of dueling epidemiologists has led to a need to look for insight elsewhere. In this case, it proves more helpful to place a greater focus on controlled animal models. Although animal models can never address autism's double surge in human infant brains, they can provide a unique window into the mechanisms of possible vaccine injury.

Sick Monkeys

In this narrative we have seen an ebb and flow in the history of disease. The Age of Syphilis came with the "age of discovery," and penicillin subsequently solved and masked the scourge of GPI. The Age of Hysteria came and went without resolution. The role of calomel—driver of the Age of Acrodynia—was reluctantly recognized but now stands largely forgotten. Schizophrenia remains controversial, and surprisingly few have focused more attention on its meteoric rise in the nineteenth century. In the meantime, new conditions like Crohn's disease, Down syndrome, autistic congenital rubella syndrome, and autism provoke a curious and myopic impulse to accept high rates as the new normal. In the absence of a clear set of answers or a road map for action, the prevailing response of the medical profession to these tragedies has been self-congratulation: "We are doing a better job better diagnosing" has been the standard response.

To be sure, questions involving environmental causation can be complex and often contentious. Environmental causation often carries the implication of human error, even liability. Not surprisingly, powerful interests usually prefer to resist such theories to preempt the consequences if they are proven true, even if the logic and the science is strong.

And although we've attempted to show a broader sweep of the environmental arguments here, much of the current controversy in autism has coalesced around vaccination. As one would predict, the medical industry has mobilized swiftly in an attempt to nullify these arguments: The question has been "asked and answered," they say. But close inspection of the answers shows how remarkably hasty and defensive much of this work has been. In a context where dispassionate and thorough work is needed more than ever, much of what the medical industry and public health community has produced on the question of autism and vaccines has been propaganda masquerading as science.

We've made this point earlier, but it bears repeating. We are not "antivaccine"; we simply want to see the end of the autism epidemic. We support a safe vaccine program and believe that thoughtful vaccine development can be very effective in eliminating the threat of deadly diseases. The smallpox vaccine eradicated one of history's most dangerous viruses, and the rubella vaccine replaced dangerous and ineffective gamma globulin therapy while also putting an end to the ancient scourge of congenital rubella syndrome. These are examples where the benefits of the vaccine have outweighed the costs (including an adverse event risk that caused the cancelation of an effort to revive smallpox vaccination in the wake of concern over bioterrorism). But weighing costs and benefits requires dispassionate scrutiny of adverse event risk, both for individual vaccines and for their cumulative effect, and rigorous safety testing.

A very simple test goes right to the heart of the vaccine controversy: What is the difference in total health outcomes, including autism, between vaccinated and unvaccinated populations? We would argue that we've uncovered a number of natural experiments in human populations that suggests we should be seriously concerned over the ever-increasing load of childhood vaccinations, especially in the United States. At the same time, we'd argue that the right approach to what we often call the "vax/unvax" issue is not a single study but a body of science. Oddly, when it comes to doing such studies in human populations, and studying the autism levels in the Amish, the homeschooled, or philosophical objectors, vaccine industry proponents resist mightily. Conducting human vax/unvax studies in existing unvaccinated groups would be so fraught with methodological problems that they are "retrospectively impossible." As for controlled studies, they would be so burdened with permission problems that they would be "prospectively unethical." In short, the resistance to the proposal to do vax/unvax work has not only taken the attitude of "we already know the answers," but "we should not seek to know." It's pretty hard to make scientific progress in the face of this kind of epistemological nihilism.

The complexity of the vaccine safety issues is illustrated in the dual controversy over thimerosal and MMR. Each has been nominated separately as a causal factor in autism, but they might also—like the spirochete of syphilis and Van Swieten's liquor in GPI—overlap. We've suggested some ways in which thimerosal exposure by itself might provide an event toxic enough to provoke critical imbalances in a developing brain. But the three-part, live-virus dose in the thimerosal-free MMR vaccine, so frequently associated with an autistic regression, might also be a culprit. And to the extent that the early immune stimulation each can provoke might be induced in other ways, the broader expansion of the vaccine program presents yet another reasonable target for autism research. Unfortunately, the widely publicized human studies have rarely considered interactive effects.

But there is another way to deal with complexity while also working around the problem of human vax/unvax studies, and that is to conduct animal studies. These can range from cheaper and less powerful studies in mice to more expensive and persuasive studies in primates. Over the last decade, mostly with private funding or carried out by investigators outside the United States, a number of animal studies have explored some mix of the thimerosal and the vax/unvax question in depth. The results have been stunning.

The earliest investigation of the role of thimerosal in an animal model came out of Columbia University. Led by Mady Hornig of the Center for Immunopathogenesis and Infectious Diseases at Columbia's Mailman School of Public Health, a laboratory headed by Ian Lipkin, this work looked at the effect of thimerosal in a mouse model.

Hornig is a careful and meticulous researcher who has found herself caught in the swirling controversies around autism and vaccines. Hornig has made public statements on both sides of the debate. Some were made in support of the thimerosal theory; others have occurred more recently in a study of MMR.

Her MMR study, published in September 2008, failed to find evidence of measles virus in the intestinal tissue of twenty-four children with autistic regression and gastrointestinal symptoms. The findings contrasted with the results published by Wakefield in 2002, in which researchers from Ireland and the United Kingdom found measles in seventy-five of ninety-one biopsies from autistic children with GI inflammation, and in only five of seventy samples from nonautistic children. The children with autism in the 2002 study developed gastrointestinal symptoms and autistic regression after the MMR vaccine.[78]

The Hornig study was by all accounts carefully done and the reported results valid. In the press release announcing the publication, however, Hornig went further, claiming, "The work reported here eliminates the remaining support for the hypothesis that autism with GI complaints is related to MMR vaccine exposure. We found no relationship between the timing of MMR vaccine and the onset of either GI complaints or autism." In our view, this claim was an exaggeration. In her study, only five of the twenty-five children developed these symptoms after the MMR vaccine and therefore, only these five were comparable to the 2002 Wakefield study. In contrast to her public statement, her new study effectively confirmed that results from an earlier study from the laboratory of Professor John O'Leary were correct,[79] and identical to the results obtained by the participating laboratories, which included Wakefield's original collaborator, as well as the CDC and Columbia lab. Far from repudiating Wakefield's findings, it provided support for the reliability of the original analysis.

In her thimerosal model, Hornig and her lab group explored the connection between thimerosal exposure and autoimmunity that we discussed above, theorizing in a 2004 paper that "autoimmune propensity influences outcomes in mice following thimerosal challenges that mimic routine childhood immunizations." So they gave a specific breed of mice, one that is known to have a propensity to autoimmune reactions, thimerosal doses according to a schedule that was similar in terms of developmental timing and amount to the U.S. infant exposures. Then they monitored their infant mice on several dimensions, most notably behavior and brain development. In terms of behavior, the developing mice showed reduced activity and exploratory activity as well as an "exaggerated response to novelty." With respect to the brain studies, Hornig reported that the "pattern of behavioral and neuropathologic findings described here in SJL mice suggests a strain-dependent, ethylmercury-based disruption of normal programs of neural development and synaptogenesis."[80] The less susceptible mice showed little effect.

In a subsequent study, a research team at the University of California, Davis, tried to replicate Hornig's findings and found no difference between the exposed susceptible mice and controls.[81] But there were a number of differences between the designs of the two studies, so it's hard to assign significance to the discrepancy. The California study has been used in attempts to nullify Hornig's earlier paper and has received substantial attention in the United States, where criticism of Hornig's work has suggested that the California study is more reliable. What has often gone unnoticed, however, are additional attempts to replicate Hornig's study outside of the United States by researchers in Peru and Poland.

In his bestselling book *Evidence of Harm*, David Kirby saved his "final note" for a comment on the global legacy of thimerosal exposure in vaccines. In the book's closing passage, he wrote, "If thimerosal is one day proven to be a contributing factor to autism, and if U.S. made vaccines containing the preservative are now being supplied the world over, the scope of this potential tragedy becomes unthinkable. The United States, at the dawn of the twenty-first century, is not exactly the most beloved nation on earth. What if the profitable export of our vaunted medical technology has led to the poisoning of hundreds of thousands of children? What then?"[82]

One often overlooked implication of public health officials' resistance to removing thimerosal from vaccines has been to make Kirby's nightmare suggestion a reality. Vaccine manufacturers have continued to deliver thimerosal-containing vaccine formulations all over the world,[83] in effect offering a defiant double standard of mercury risk for infants from rich countries as compared to poor countries.

One of the countries where thimerosal has been retained in vaccines is Peru. This situation is a consequence of a controversial decision by the World Health Organization (WHO) and its Latin American partner the Pan American Health Organization (PAHO) to retain thimerosal as a vaccine preservative because of economic considerations. And like the United States in the early 1990s, PAHO countries like Peru have recently adopted the Hib and hepatitis B vaccines as part of their recommended childhood immunization programs. Peru also continues to use the thimerosal-containing whole-cell DPT vaccine, instead of the safer but more expensive acellular pertussis variety, DTAP.

The result of these PAHO decisions is that Peruvian children are now exposed to thimerosal in amounts that would be considered in excess of EPA guidelines in the United States. Not surprisingly, some Peruvian scientists have taken issue with this choice and have taken it upon themselves to investigate the issue. In their words: "In Peru, the authorities of the Ministry of Health (MINSA) continue using vaccines with high thimerosal content (whose multidose . . . form is, to date, used in some health establishments), noting that it has no side effects. This generated a serious challenge by the public, part of the medical community and a number of non-governmental organizations. This debate requires that begin [sic] to shed light on the investigations and take concrete steps on this issue."[84]

These Peruvian researchers published a study in the September 2007 edition of a Peruvian medical journal that has only recently been translated into English. In their study they examined the effect of thimerosal exposure on infant hamsters. They divided forty-five baby hamsters into three groups of fifteen and exposed them to three different series of injections, two of which involved no thimerosal exposure and a third that was designed to mimic the weight-adjusted ethylmercury content of the U.S. childhood immunization program in the 1990s.

The findings were stark. As the three groups of infants matured, the thimerosal-exposed hamsters showed clear signs of developmental injury due to their ethylmercury exposure. These mercury-exposed hamsters showed dramatic developmental differences in terms of body weight, brain weight, and heights, with a statistical certainty that there was a toxic effect that exceeded 99.99 percent. It should also be noted that the weight-adjusted concentration of ethylmercury received by the hamsters added up to a total dose of less than 1 microgram—an amount many times less than the 187.5 micrograms human infants received.

When the forty-five hamsters were sacrificed, the researchers compared the brain tissue of the three groups and again found dramatic differences in the thimerosal-exposed infant hamster brains. Ethylmercury produced clear injuries in the three types of brain tissue: hippocampus, cerebellum, and cerebral cortex. Furthermore, the exposed hamsters showed clear evidence of many different kinds of tissue damage, such as reduced neuron density, increased cell death, impaired myelin development, and increased inflammation. These results were also significant with a certainty of greater than 99.99 percent.[85]

Taking pains to translate their full paper into English, the Peruvian team didn't mince words. "In conclusion, thimerosal exposure, in quantities equivalent [on a weight-adjusted basis] to those of human vaccines, reduced the body weight, encephalon weight and height of postnatal hamsters in a significant way; in this way, it produced a lesser development and growth delay. Also, it produced severe neurotoxic effects at encephalon level expressing histopathological alterations at hippocampus, cerebral cortex and cerebellum levels."[86]

This hamster model doesn't stand alone. Instead, it joins a succession of animal studies demonstrating that exposing infant animals to thimerosal produces developmental brain injury. Mady Hornig's work in mice provided the template for the Peruvian group, and their hamster findings provide confirmation for Hornig's finding of thimerosal toxicity in mice.

Despite this dramatic and repeated body of evidence, public health authorities—the CDC, the WHO, the PAHO—persist in exposing the developing human brain to ethylmercury, one of the most toxic chemicals man has ever invented. These officials consider the interests of their programs—the economics of vaccine distribution in Peru, the yield of flu vaccine production in the United States, and the continued targeting of pregnant women and infants for flu shots—to carry greater weight than any countervailing evidence regarding safety. But the Peruvian researchers are clearly calling their PAHO colleagues to account for their decisions.

Meanwhile, in Poland, a group from Warsaw's Institute of Psychiatry and Neurology performed a similar replication project using rats and following Hornig's study design very closely. Like Hornig, the Warsaw group found clear differences in behavior. "The animals exposed post-natally to thimerosal," they remarked, "had noticeably impaired loco-motor activity. They were significantly slower in the open field and in water maze and exhibited more anxiety than control rats. They had markedly impaired pain reactions . . . and their social interactions were disturbed."[87] Also like Hornig, they found pronounced differences in the brains of the thimerosal-exposed rats. "The brain weights of thimerosal injected rats were significantly reduced and there were widespread mor-phological and pathological changes in several brain regions."[88] The Warsaw group came down clearly on Hornig's side of the debate in their conclusion, and echoed the hard-hitting tone of the Peruvian team.

As David Kirby points out, the rest of the world may not be quite so eager to line up behind the party line of the American medical industry.

The studies from Columbia University, Peru, and Poland were limited in two key respects. First, they focused on thimerosal by itself rather than the possible joint impact of mercury and microbes, such as those in the MMR, created when a child was exposed to thimerosal in the context of the com-plete childhood vaccination program during the 1990s. Second, the ani-mals in the study were rodents—mice, rats, and hamsters—rather than primates. But both of these problems have been addressed in a landmark research project, the results of which have only recently been made public.

In May 2008 the first research project to examine effects of the total vaccine load received by children in the 1990s found autismlike signs and symptoms in infant monkeys vaccinated the same way. The team's findings were explosive. The study was led by Andrew Wakefield and sponsored in part by Sallie Bernard. The study's principal investigator, Laura Hewitson from the University of Pittsburgh, reported developmental delays, behavior problems, and brain changes in macaque monkeys that mimic "certain neurological abnormalities of autism."[89]

These findings suggest, for the first time, that our closest animal cousins develop characteristics of autism when subjected to the same immunizations (such as the MMR shot) and vaccine formulations (such as the mercury preservative thimerosal) that American children received when autism diagnoses exploded in the 1990s.

The first publicly reported results of this research project came in both oral and poster format at the International Meeting for Autism Research in London. (Poster presentations must go through a form of peer review before they are presented at the conference; most of the findings from these posters have not yet appeared in a scientific journal.) In addition to Hewitson's oral presentation, in a related poster presentation the researchers reported in their abstract that "vaccinated animals exhibited progressively severe chronic active inflammation [in gastrointestinal tissue] whereas unexposed animals did not. We have found many significant differences in the GI tissue gene expression profiles between vaccinated and unvaccinated animals."[90]

The study found evidence of both behavioral and biological changes after the thirteen macaque monkey infants were administered proportional doses, adjusted for age, of the vaccines recommended between 1994 and 1999. Three monkeys were not given any vaccines.

"Primate development, cognition and social behavior were assessed for both vaccinated and unvaccinated infants using standardized tests developed at the Washington National Primate Research Center." MRI and PET scans looked for brain changes after administration of the MMR vaccine. And the results were startling. Vaccinated monkeys showed pronounced deficits in critical survival reflexes as well as tests of vision and learning. Brain growth patterns were different. And tests on social interactions showed a significant association between vaccine exposure and "aberrant social and non-social behaviors."[91]

———

In September 2009, more than a year after the first public discussion of this primate study, the first paper from Wakefield and Hewitson's team was published in a peer-reviewed journal. Writing in *NeuroToxicology* (and with a larger sample of unvaccinated monkeys), the authors released a limited set of results from their ongoing project, an analysis of the effect of the thimerosal-containing hepatitis B vaccine on infant reflexes. They found that a critical trio of survival reflexes, those that a newborn needs to latch on to its mother's breast, were strongly delayed in vaccinated monkeys.[92] Their findings on infant feeding problems echoed similar problems in the early Kanner cases, including those of Donald Triplett ("eating . . . has always been a problem with him"), Bridget Muncie ("she nursed very poorly") and Lee Rosenberg ("during the first days of life he did not take the breast satisfactorily").

This initial study, as we mentioned earlier, was withdrawn in February 2010 by *NeuroToxicology*, citing the judgment against Wakefield by Britain's General Medical Council involving the 1998 *Lancet* case series on developmental regression and a novel bowel syndrome. But it, too, has left a mark not so easily erased (the paper will likely reappear in another journal in late 2010), and its startling initial findings made clear that future research is needed. The direction of that research remains obvious, including publication of findings on the thimerosal-containing DTaP and Hib vaccines of the 1990s and the MMR vaccine. Later publications may include not just how the two macaque groups' observable development proceeded, but also how their gastrointestinal tracts were affected by the vaccine exposures and how their brain biology was changed. Given *NeuroToxicology*'s reversal, the main obstacle to further dissemination of the research findings appears to be publication.

For those of us who have seen more extensive results from this ambitious (and privately funded) project, there can be little doubt that the childhood vaccination program as received by these primates, one that included both MMR and thimerosal, caused harm. The rodent studies have raised similar concerns and yielded consistent findings, but in some respects have been difficult to interpret. By contrast, the results in infant monkeys were clear and conclusive.

At the same time, all of these studies have also been sharply constrained. The studies in mice, hamsters, and rats have generally used only thimerosal as opposed to thimerosal-containing vaccines. The Pittsburgh primate study used three thimerosal-containing vaccines alongside MMR, but not the entire current childhood vaccine schedule. In April 2009 an analysis by an autism parent group called Generation Rescue noted that "the vaccine schedule for children aged 5 and under has nearly tripled in

25 years. In 1983, the Centers for Disease Control recommended 10 vaccines for this age group. Today, the recommendation is 36 vaccines."[93] Hannah Poling's fateful "immune stimulation" included three thimerosal-containing vaccines (with five separate doses) alongside MMR, but also varicella and polio vaccines. Today's expanded vaccination schedule includes many vaccines added since the thimerosal-containing additions of 1990–91, including those for varicella (1995), rotavirus (1998), pneumococcus (2000), influenza (2004), and hepatitis A (2004) (the new vaccines are mostly thimerosal-free). One can only guess at this point what a primate study of this level of immune stimulation would find.

In starkest terms, the debate over exactly what kind of illness autism is has become blocked by the policies surrounding childhood vaccines. Despite strong evidence for concern, opposition remains intense to any material change in vaccine safety management. Instead, the epidemiology studies of autism and vaccines have been used to effectively reverse the 1999 decision to remove mercury from childhood vaccines. The production challenges of the influenza vaccine program have been allowed to override safety concerns, and thimerosal has been quietly resurrected as a preservative that is now actively administered via flu shots to pregnant women and infants beyond six months of age. In the meantime, rising background levels of mercury and a continuing increase in the "immune stimulation" resulting from new vaccines have corrupted the natural experiment many thought we might run on autism and thimerosal. The animal evidence is persuasive, and some might argue conclusive, but still the environmental arguments are suppressed and the medical industry continues effectively to manufacture doubt.

Sufficient but Not Necessary

Setting aside for a moment the hot-button questions of mercury and vaccines, it's worth stepping back to ask what kind of environmental insult could be driving the Age of Autism. Going back to the evidence on autism rates, we can reach a number of conclusions. First, some element of the exposures must be pervasive since, for example, the numbers within the United States have been rising across almost every state. Second, there must also be some environmental variation across geographies, because we know that the autism rates vary quite widely both between and within states.

Third, despite suggestions that autism is more prevalent in one ethnic group—at various points in the history of the disorder Jews, Japanese, European-born Americans, and Somalian immigrants have been singled out as uniquely vulnerable—autism affects multiple races and ethnics groups without favor. Fourth, to the extent that we see variations in racial or ethnic susceptibility, these differences tend to disappear as groups cross national borders, likely reflecting differences in exposures, such as vaccine policy, that are influenced by such borders. Last, whatever environmental exposures are involved in raising autism risk, their effect has been felt within a short period of time (at least in the United States and United Kingdom), affecting birth cohorts born after 1990 at dramatically higher rates. The search for candidate risk factors must necessarily favor exposures that changed rapidly in the same time period.

It's also worth reflecting a bit on how different examples of environmental disease processes might inform the investigation of potential culprits. We've reviewed a number of disease models so far that might offer up lessons for autism. Is autism an interaction of specific metals and microbes? Earlier, we showed that the combination of the syphilis spirochete and mercury treatment was needed to provoke GPI. At the same time, it appears only the spirochete was absolutely essential; arsenic treatments may also have been sufficient as part of the combination necessary to cause the disease. Despite the specificity of the disease, even here the possibility exists that alternate exposures could have been sufficient.

Alternatively, is autism a case of mercury exposure alone, one that should go away once the mercury exposures are removed? Hysteria and acrodynia both appear to fall into that category, at least as far as we know. But here as well some degree of caution is appropriate, for although mercury has been acknowledged as the primary factor in acrodynia, we certainly can't rule out the idea that some kind of microbial exposure might have served as a cofactor. We still have little idea why out of so many children exposed to mercury preparations like calomel, only a few became victims of acrodynia.

Perhaps the picture is more complex than either of these more narrowly determined models. In the case of schizophrenia, it seems clear that increasing environmental pollution has laid down a foundation for the rise of Fuller Torrey's "invisible plague," one that may be carried forward by later immune reactions to viruses or parasites. But in the case of schizophrenia, both in terms of environmental factors (lead, coal, urban living, periods of prenatal starvation) and microbial risk factors (influenza, cytomegalovirus, *Toxoplasma gondii*) there are multiple candidates that might reasonably be nominated for the microbe/metal combination.

In dealing with questions of causality in disease, medicine generally runs away from such complexity. Far more satisfying for the critical scientist is the simple standard set by Robert Koch in what has become known as Koch's postulates. In researching the cause of tuberculosis during the 1880s, he developed these postulates, a strict set of criteria for connecting a microbial exposure to the ensuing disease.[94] In Koch's formulation, establishing causation required that four conditions be met. These conditions required that the microbe be *both necessary and sufficient* to cause the disease.

So although Koch's postulates work well for simple infectious diseases like syphilis, smallpox, or the common cold, they break down when it comes to most chronic diseases and have little capacity to inform the investigations of diseases that are evoked by exposure to environmental toxins. Furthermore, when it comes to interactions between toxins and microbes occurring in the biological context of a specific host, it's clear that Koch's postulates have little relevance to the modern disease problem. For the vast bulk of industrial-age diseases we've described here, the assessment of causality has progressed relatively little since Koch's postulates and Pasteur's elaboration of germ theory in 1890.

In fact, even germ theory struggles to explain a number of diseases in which germs are necessarily involved. Paralytic polio, for example, occurs in only a small minority of polio infections; and for many years garden-variety polio was barely recognized since it was so rarely serious. At least one cofactor in paralytic polio was recognized years later. A study of Romanian polio victims in 1995 determined that peripheral nerve injury (provoked by the common Romanian practice of injecting antibiotics) dramatically increased the risk of paralytic polio after live virus vaccine exposures. The antibiotic injections created the condition for the otherwise benign virus to travel through peripheral nerves into the spinal cord and cause paralysis.[95]

GPI required a similar combination of interacting environmental factors for its effects to set in. Neither the metal nor the microbe was sufficient by itself, but together they would wreak havoc. And the list of diseases that require germs to recruit coconspirators to the job is longer than you would think. Measles, for example, is necessary to the fatal disease known as subacute sclerosing panencephalitis (SSPE), but only a minute fraction of measles cases ever provoke the disease. The risk factor (or factors) that determines the difference between a simple measles infection and SSPE remains undiscovered.

Bubonic plague, once the world's most dangerous killer, with a mortality risk that carried away a third of the human population in medieval Europe, has nearly disappeared in modernity. Although we know that improved sanitary conditions reduce the dangers of the germ that causes the Black Death, *Yersinias pestis,* we also know that the germ persists in the world. Its near disappearance as a cause of human disease remains a mystery. A group of Russian scientists, however, led by Evgeny Rotshild of the Severtsov Institute of Ecology and Evolution, think they've found a clue to this mystery. In the Siberian steppes, small rodents still fall victim to *Yersinias pestis* on occasion, but their susceptibility varies greatly depending on their foraging area. Rotshild and his colleagues have demonstrated that the behavior of the microbe varied dramatically with the local environment. Studies of variations in the metal content of plants in different areas showed that outbreaks of the disease "were associated with abnormal concentrations of certain metals in their immediate environment."[96] In other words, the germ remained deadly to rodents, but only under certain environmental conditions; without the cofactors, the conditions weren't sufficient for plague to break out. In short, in the case of microbial disease, there are many cases where the germ is *necessary but not sufficient* to provoke the disease state.

Environmental factors frequently alter the course of a disease, in ways that are almost always more confusing. In search for the equivalent of Koch's postulates, environmental disease experts have adopted their own set of standards, called the Austin Bradford Hill criteria. These criteria attempt to provide guidelines for concluding whether a certain exposure can be reliably connected to a given disease. This list of nine criteria, which channel the demanding spirit of Koch's postulates, offers useful guidance when the environmental agent is indeed playing a necessary and sufficient role. Unfortunately, the criteria have proven ill adapted for the complex challenges provided by the ages of industrial disease we have been considering here.

Perhaps because of the less determinate nature of environmental toxins, when comparing germs and toxins, there is more than just a difference in the accepted standard of causation. Whenever germs are discovered to be an essential part of a disease process, we typically attribute causation solely to the germ. We generally accept that the measles virus "causes" SSPE and the poliovirus "causes" paralysis even though we don't know why the condition turns pathogenic in some cases and not in others. By contrast, in the case of conditions where an environmental exposure is identified as a cause of a disease, instead of linking the exposure with the disease, the most frequent response is to remove the disease label from the case. Several case histories of patients who presented with symptoms of Lou Gehrig's disease (amyotrophic lateral sclerosis) have been shown with little doubt to have been suffering the effects of mercury poisoning.[97] Yet one rarely hears anyone say that "mercury causes ALS"; instead, cases that look like ALS and are tied to mercury are labeled cases of mercury poisoning, not ALS. Similar interpretations have held in the cases of congenital Minamata disease (which presents as cerebral palsy), Kawasaki disease, and Young's syndrome. This separation of the presentation from the exposure may sound logical to some, but in the process we lose a learning opportunity. What if we took more note when we could clearly connect a specific environmental factor to a specific disease, even if the exposure wasn't necessary as an explanation for every single case of the disease? Mark Noble takes a biological view of this situation when he observes, "The cell doesn't care" which toxicant it's exposed to, it only cares what signal the toxicant provides.[98] In the case of environmental exposures, there are many cases where the toxin is *sufficient but not necessary* to provoke the disease state. Unfortunately, when compared to the prevailing approach to microbes, the learning opportunities in environmental toxins are often lost.

Not all of this is an accident. Entrenched interests in the medical and manufacturing industries have frequently turned the complexity of disease causation into a propaganda tool, using the stringency of generally accepted causation standards to effectively manufacture doubt. To the extent that exposures are either not *necessary and sufficient* or not *always necessary*, there is substantial room for arguing against the role of a specific agent in disease, even if that agent can be part of the *sufficient* set of conditions to cause the disease. We have seen this strategy play out in spades in the case of autism and thimerosal: Whenever evidence supports a causal relationship, the rule is generally to "shoot the messenger"; whenever evidence emerges that goes against the strongest claim of causality, that evidence becomes a weapon to question every bit of evidence that supports a connection.

As we've said, we don't believe that exposure to ethylmercury and thimerosal are necessary to explain every case of autism and every change in the autistic brain. There are certainly unvaccinated children with autism and plausible instances of autistic children born before Morris Kharasch's invention of ethylmercury compounds. Nevertheless, we believe that thimerosal and ethylmercury are, at a minimum, sufficient in some cases of autism and almost certainly instructive as we search for the causes of a man-made epidemic. We ignore its biology and the legacy of its impact at our peril.

Mark Noble, based upon the findings in his own and other laboratories that multiple chemically diverse toxicants can converge on identical cellular pathways, has proposed that it is important to consider the application of new paradigms in epidemiological analysis. We think his insights are important enough to cite them at length:

> The simplest explanation of the disparity between current biological studies (which suggest a multiplicity of potential contributors to any particular syndrome) and epidemiological studies (which most frequently do not support association with any particular substance investigated) is that this seeming paradox is providing a meaningful indication of the relationship between toxicant exposure and disease. That is to say that, just as many different genetic mutations or polymorphisms may be sufficient to increase the likelihood of, e.g., cancer, Parkinson's disease, Alzheimer's disease, or ASD, it is also the case that *exposure to many different kinds of toxicants may be sufficient also to contribute to disease pathogenesis*. But, just as no individual genetic difference is essential to the generation of a particular syndrome, so will it also be the case that *no individual toxicant plays a necessary role in disease pathogenesis*. In this view, a large number of different potential contributors to disease pathogenesis *each may be seen as being sufficient, but no individual contributor should be seen as being necessary*. For example, ASD represents one group of neurological syndromes for which multiple environmental factors have been suggested to play a role but for which no single agent has emerged as being of central importance. . . . Epidemiological studies that are not structured in such a manner as to allow for this situation thus are seen as being intrinsically flawed.[99]

Noble sees the situation in autism as a case study of a larger problem in epidemiology. "It is impossible to overstate the implications for epidemiology of the idea that a toxicant may be sufficient but not necessary for disease pathogenesis, for what this hypothesis means is that a study that fails to demonstrate association with a particular substance cannot be taken as evidence that the substance does not contribute. It just means that such a contribution cannot be isolated sufficiently from other influences to be recognized among the other substances to which individuals in the study are exposed."[100]

In January 2008 a study was published in the *Archives of General Psychiatry* by Robert Schechter and Judy Grether with the straightforward title "Continuing Increases in Autism Reported to California's Developmental Services System." But the subtitle was the more interesting part: "Mercury in Retrograde." The meaning of this reference is made clear in the paper's conclusions. "The DDS [California Department of Developmental Services] data do not show any recent decrease in autism in California despite the exclusion of more than trace levels of thimerosal from nearly all childhood vaccines. The DDS data do not support the hypothesis that exposure to thimerosal during childhood is a primary cause of autism."[101] The paper reported an analysis of the California autism rates through the calendar year 2006—properly adjusted for age at ascertainment—that showed no sign of a decrease among three-year-olds born in 2003. Although earlier birth cohorts continued to be exposed to thimerosal-containing versions of three vaccines—hepatitis B, haemophilus influenza type B, and DTaP—by 2003 it was reasonable to expect that mercury-free versions of these vaccines had made their way into the market. If autism were to follow the model of acrodynia, one would expect the rates to fall rapidly. Sadly, they did not.

But what if, by 1931, the introduction of commercial mercury compounds was enough to create a sufficient set of conditions for a spike in autism rates among those exposed early in infancy or in utero? We believe that thimerosal and other ethylmercury products are among the most efficient ways ever created to deliver inorganic mercury to the brain. It's extremely unlikely, in our view, that all of the biological, historical, and clinical evidence implicating this toxin carries no weight.

And what if, rather than necessary, they were simply efficient? In particular, the organic mercury compound called ethylmercury thiosalicylate, aka thimerosal, does a number of things well. Thanks to Morris Kharasch's work on its chemical composition, this compound of organic mercury is water soluble, circulates readily through the bloodstream, crosses the blood-brain barrier with little difficulty, and so delivers mercury atoms many places in the body, including the brain. Ethylmercury is fat soluble, so it can cross cell membranes easily. Unlike methylmercury, ethylmercury loses its ethyl component relatively easily once inside the cell and converts to inorganic mercury. Having delivered the oxidized form of mercury to a target cell in the brain or elsewhere, thimerosal has done quite a difficult job. With relatively small amounts of starting mercury, the oxidized (and therefore reactive) form of the atom is left behind to interfere with mitochondria, provoke oxidative stress, and disrupt immune signaling for a very long time. As we've seen, once inorganic mercury enters the brain, it's meaningless to speak, as some do, of mercury's "half life" within the brain compartment. Effectively trapped inside the brain, mercury can remain there for decades, disrupting disulfide bonds of critical enzymes, altering redox signals, and leaving protective cells in a permanent state of arousal.

But just as the products of Morris Kharasch's inventive mind almost certainly can provide the sufficient exposures to cause autism, perhaps in the presence of the right combination of other immune stimulants, they may also not be necessary. Other factors—including airborne mercury from coal combustion, added immune stimulation from the continuing expansion of the childhood vaccine program, and the substitute vaccine additives such as aluminum—may have stepped in to fill the causation gap left behind by the removal of mercury from these three vaccines. In other words, these mercury products may have been sufficient to provoke autism, but they may also have had substitutes.

Even so, just as we acknowledge the importance of the ongoing rise in California autism rates, it's also critical to point out, as we've done previously, some confounding effects. As one form of thimerosal was phased out, a new form was phased in, the new exposures from influenza vaccines rising in almost perfect counterpoint to the decline in the trio being phased out. And although the total amount of exposure may have fallen, the replacement exposures come during pregnancy, when they are almost certainly more toxic.

We desperately need new models to investigate environmental toxins and their role in disease. This will require leaving Koch's postulates, and to a large degree the Austin Bradford Hill criteria, behind. As conventional epidemiology has increasingly insisted on large-scale prospective studies that by definition ignore past changes in exposures, the entire search for disease causation has careened toward a form of Know Nothingism and rendered impotent the quest for the answers in the face of industrial disease. Noble proposes at least the beginning of an answer:

> The challenges raised . . . lead directly to the central dilemma of toxicological research, which is how to make regulatory decisions when faced with incomplete data. . . .
>
> In order to offset the uncertainties created by an inability of epidemiological and pathological studies to solve the problems discussed [so far], it is necessary to strengthen the biological components of toxicology. Ideally, the goal would be to create a field of predictive toxicology.[102]

This new field, Noble argues, would use laboratory knowledge of how chemical compounds behave to guide animal studies that would then be used to predict human outcomes, guide policy, and develop treatments. We might add to Noble's agenda a renewed focus on historical epidemiology and the natural history of disease. But the building of new disciplines of predictive toxicology seems a terrific place to start.

So where are we left at the end of such a long journey through several centuries of disease? Certainly with a healthy sense of sorrow for the victims of so much medical malpractice, and a greater appreciation for burdens of diseases that are left unrecognized and undermanaged. At the same time, we can celebrate some of the greatest triumphs of modern medicine: the invention of penicillin that consigned GPI and syphilis to the dustbin of history, as well as Josef Warkany's insight that small children had no business being treated (and in some cases killed) with "mild aperients" like Steedman's Teething Powders. Meanwhile, we can welcome the passing of those Freudian theories which misassigned blame to innocent parents.

Some of these ages of disease are behind us, but schizophrenia and autism are still with us, and likely represent just the tip of an iceberg of industrial-age diseases that modern medicine has failed to engage effectively. Schizophrenia rates appear to have stabilized after many decades of increase, and numerous pharmacological treatments have emerged to contain its symptoms; still, we remain little closer to an understanding of its causes sufficient to enable its prevention. And as autism numbers are fast approaching the frequency of schizophrenia but with no comparable mechanism for management, the burden of the exploding autism population is creating an institutional problem that will rival the age of the asylum. This new generation of autistic children is fast turning into adults; they are threatening to soon become the single largest and most expensive disabled population the world has ever seen.

What will we do with all of these people?

The Train at the End of the Tunnel

In 1942 a grisly debate unfolded in the pages of the *American Journal of Psychiatry*. The main protagonist was a man named Foster Kennedy, a prominent Cornell neurologist and well-known proponent of eugenics. In a provocative essay, Kennedy argued for killing society's most severely retarded people on the basis of utilitarian logic, the greatest good for the greatest number. Kennedy wrote, "We have too many feebleminded people among us, something like 60,000, I think, in the hospitals of this country, and perhaps five times that number are outside. The idiot and the imbecile seem to me unresponsive to the care put upon them." Kennedy went on, "I believe when the defective child shall have reached the age of five years . . . that the case should be considered under law by a competent medical board." After confirming the limited future that lay ahead, he argued, "I believe it is a merciful and kindly thing to relieve that defective—often tortured and convulsed, grotesque and absurd, useless and foolish, and entirely undesirable—of the agony of living."[103]

In opposition to Kennedy's argument stood Leo Kanner. Writing his counterargument to Kennedy just a year before his landmark 1943 autism paper, as he wrote he clearly had in his mind patients as varied as Donald Triplett (Case 1) and John Trevett (Case 7). He didn't make clear where he might place autistic children in Foster Kennedy's scheme, and though he took the other side of the debate, he chose not to make his tone contentious. Like Foster Kennedy, he appealed to utilitarian concepts and suggested that some mental defectives were socially useful. But even if the remaining group was a drain on society, he argued, that didn't justify killing. "It is true," he continued, "that those of whom we spoke as absolutely deficient, the idiots and imbeciles, cannot be trained in any kind of social usefulness. Are we then justified in passing the black bottle among them? Some people have suggested just such a procedure, which they dignify with the term euthanasia."[104]

Himself a Jewish émigré, Kanner's main argument was that adopting euthanasia would make the United States little different from Nazi Germany, where he noted that "the Gestapo is now systematically bumping off the mentally deficient people of the Reich. A trustworthy German has estimated the number of 100,000."[105] This was more than just an idle issue for early figures in autism. For Hans Asperger, these issues struck much closer to home.

In the summer of 2008, we sat with Hans Asperger, Jr., in Vienna and discussed his father's work. He recounted to us how, in the midst of World War II, his father was faced with a dilemma. Hans Asperger began seeing autistic patients in Vienna at the same time Leo Kanner was seeing them in Baltimore. Unlike Kanner, however, when Asperger turned to the task of writing about his discovery, "a personality disorder already manifest in childhood which to my knowledge has not yet been described,"[106] he had more than medical concerns on his mind. Around that time, the Nazi regime had launched the so-called T4 program, the extermination program for mentally defective German citizens that marked one of the first steps toward the Holocaust.

Concerned for the children under his care, Asperger included a section in his 1944 paper on "the social value of the autistic psychopath," providing an extended case history of someone he claimed to have followed through college, a man who had once been barely functional but who then became a professor of astronomy.[107] It's a remarkable section and strange to encounter when read out of context. The case history of the astronomy professor stands out like an oddity; in the main body of his paper Asperger described only a few young children, then suddenly shifted to describe an adult he claimed to have known for many years.

Intriguingly, nearly a decade later, Asperger changed the sentence immediately following this case description. In the original 1944 version, he suggested hopefully that "this case history is by no means exceptional," but in a 1952 revision he corrected himself, saying that "this *is* a very exceptional case."[108] It might seem odd that Asperger would conjure up an optimistic case history of autism and represent it as typical, until one understands the context in which his hopeful prognosis was written. As his son made clear, Asperger deliberately exaggerated the odds of a favorable prognosis in his autistic patients. He was trying to save their lives.

Sometimes, well-meaning people ask why the increased rates matter. What good does it do to argue about whether autism rates are rising, they protest; instead, why not focus on the fact that the rates are high today? The answer is simple. If autism has always been with us, then we've already been dealing with the social cost of the problem however it has been measured or incurred. If not, if in fact we are in the epidemic growth phase of a new age of disease, then we have a different problem, one that we have not even begun to grasp. The leading edge of affected children, those born around 1990, are just now coming to the age where they would normally be leaving home, and are graduating from the special-education systems that have strained to serve them. Up to now, most of the costs of autism have been borne inside the home, by relatively young parents working in the conventional way with dependent children. Some manage well, some with great difficulty, and, in a few sad cases, the failure to cope leads to tragedy.

The reality is that we've never before seen an adult autistic population of the size that is now leaving the school system. As one autism parent put it, "We have seen the light at the end of the tunnel. And it's a train."[109]

So in a very real sense, we have a tale of two futures. If we do nothing, the numbers will continue to rise. The cost of inaction will be 3 million people with autism in the United States alone. If, on the other hand, we take collective responsibility for the problem, we can choose to end the Age of Autism and to reduce its burden in the current autism generation. That is the choice we face, between a nightmare and a dream.

EPILOGUE

THE NIGHTMARE
AND THE DREAM

The June 1943 issue of the now extinct journal The Nervous Child *carried a paper titled "Autistic Disturbances of Affective Contact"; the first 24 pages told about 11 children who had in common a pattern of behavior not previously considered in its startling uniqueness. . . . Twenty-eight years have elapsed since then. . . . The patients were between 2 and 8 years old when first seen at the Children's Psychiatric Clinic of the Johns Hopkins Hospital. What has become of them? What is their present status?*

—Leo Kanner, Follow-Up Study of 11 Autistic Children
Originally Reported in 1943, published in 1971[1]

Estimates vary, but the number of Americans today who have an autism-spectrum diagnosis—primarily autism, Asperger's, or pervasive development disorder, not otherwise specified (PDD-NOS)—is in the hundreds of thousands, the vast majority under the age of eighteen. At least forty thousand children born this year—and the next, and the next, if nothing changes—will receive the diagnosis. What will become of them? Here, we glimpse that future by updating the seven cases and families in Leo Kanner's original case series that we were able to identify. Each case begins with an excerpt from Kanner's 1971 follow-up.

John Trevett ("Herbert B."), Case 7

After a short stay at the Emma Pendleton Bradley Home in Rhode Island
and another at Twin Maples ("a school of adjustment for the problem child"
in Baltimore), he was placed by his mother with Mr. and Mrs. Moreland
who had a farm in Maryland. He seemed happy there from the beginning.
He followed the farmer around on his chores and helped him "making
things in the barn." Moreland reported in October 1950: He knows his way
around . . . and can go for miles and come back without getting lost. He
learned to cut wood, uses the power mower, rakes the lawn, sets the table
perfectly, and in his spare time works jigsaw puzzles. . . .

Occasionally he gets upset if there is a sudden change in plans. . . .
When his mother comes to visit, he gets himself absorbed and does not
come toward her. After Mr. Moreland's death, the widow opened a nursing
home for elderly people. Herbert remained with her, took the old ladies out
for walks, brought their trays to their rooms but never talked.

Herbert is now 33 years. His father wrote on January 5, 1971: "He is
with the people in Maryland. It is several years since I have seen him but I'll
take your word that he is essentially unchanged. More than anything else, he
seemed to enjoy doing jigsaw puzzles which he can do with the utmost skill."

Two men sit at opposite ends of a dining room table of a ranch house in
rural Maryland. One of them wears a large napkin as a bib. Across from
him sits another man, older, finishing his soup. In comparison to the
younger man, this man does not look impaired at all. He wears a pink
polo shirt and wire frame glasses; he could be a retired English professor.

This is John Trevett, a resident in this small, well-kept, cheerful
group home with three other men. We meet the woman who tends the
house and looks after the men; yes, she does know that he was one of the
original cases. John is no trouble, she says, as he scoops the remains of
his soup and sandwich into the wastebasket. Occasionally he will do
something odd; watering the houseplants one day, he just kept watering
and watering one plant until it overflowed. And then he kept on watering. She got after him, she said in the tone of a benevolent but no-
nonsense mother, and he didn't do it anymore.

He does not speak but he understands what is said.

He comes outside and poses with us for a picture. He does not appear to be unhappy or disturbed but he does not interact, and it is eerie and sad. This, we realize, is what autism looks like at seventy, at least for Case 7.

In 1953 John's mother, pediatrician Elizabeth Peabody, gave up her practice in Annapolis and went to Iraq to launch a well-baby outreach program for the U.S. Public Health Service, much like the Harvard project she had been part of fifteen years earlier. She described her mission in 1955 in "A Maternal Child Health Service on the Euphrates." "In our first year and a half," she wrote, "we saw 3,300 babies in 16,600 clinic visits, and 2,000 expectant mothers in 8,000 clinic visits. We immunized a large number of the 3,300 infants against diphtheria, whooping cough, tetanus, typhoid fever and smallpox."[2]

In a letter home, she wrote (the abbreviations are hers), "The obstetrical cases we get are sometimes fantastic—& tho many close calls we haven't lost a mother in the Hospital as yet. The baby-clinic is hectic—tho we limit ourselves to 1 yr & under, we have 50–75 daily and are worn out 6 days a week. An increasing no cases for well baby care now—& we try to stress the teaching aspects of pediatrics—immunizations & feeding advice. . . . It is only by showing them each step that they can understand, and they have strong superstitions and fancies which will take years to change."[3]

When she returned to the States, she joined the Public Health Service in Atlanta as director of child health services for the southeast region, continuing her lifelong commitment to disease prevention and vaccination. But this adventurous and pioneering woman's career was cut short when she developed breast cancer. She died in 1965 at the Public Health Service Hospital in Baltimore. She was fifty-nine years old.[4]

It is clear from a letter she wrote Leo Kanner not long before her death that she blamed herself or at least her marriage for her children's problems. Besides John, one child—the daughter who in infancy reversed pronouns and engaged in repetitive behaviors before seeming to blossom out after the divorce—was now a single mother to an infant following "a disastrous marriage." A second son "has cost me $450.00 monthly as he gets intensive psychiatric treatment."[5]

"Our marriage," she wrote, "seems to have produced three emotionally crippled children." Yet she bore it remarkably well. Dr. Helen Taussig, another woman medical pioneer who had helped develop the "blue baby" cardiac surgery at Hopkins, was a good friend who worked with her for two years at Hopkins and called her Betty. "Her life was not easy," Taussig wrote in a tribute upon her death. "Many would say that life had not treated her kindly, but for Betty every obstacle was a challenge to be courageously met and successfully mastered."

> A year ago she knew she had cancer. She had the comfort of knowing she had done her best for her children, and it was truly a remarkable best. She wrote me that it was 'too bad to have to leave her little grandchild so soon' but during the last months she never talked of death. One day she did say that she thought she had had 'a good life.' Those of us who knew even some of the many hardships that she faced and the difficulties that she overcame, appreciate the gallantry of her own appraisal of her life.[6]

Bridget Muncie ("Barbara K."), Case 5

Barbara was placed at the Devereux Schools in the summer of 1942 and remained there until June 1952, when she was admitted to the Springfield State Hospital (Maryland) where she is still residing. She is now 37 years old. A note written by her ward physician October 8, 1970, has this to say, "She still has the stereotyped smile, the little girl-like facial expression with a placid grin, the child-like voice when uttering her parrot-like repetitions. Whenever I pass the ward, she greets me as follows: 'Doctor, do you know I socked you once?' She then usually gets very close to the writer following her to the office. . . . She still shows a total absence of spontaneous sentence production; the same phrases are used over and over again with the same intonation. Her mind is fixed to the same subjects, which vary to some degree with the person she is communicating with. Besides all of this she is childish, impulsive, subject to temper outbursts with stamping her feet, crying loudly and upsetting other patients. Her memory is completely intact. She likes to hum some melodies monotonously; whenever she feels like it she bangs the piano with well-known songs."

At another dining room table in Maryland we sit and talk with Peter Muncie, Bridget's brother, and his wife, Mary K. Peter worked at *The*

Baltimore Sun and then spent most of his career as a writer at the World Bank. Peter is gracious but frank in telling us that he does not see a connection between our theories and Bridget's condition.

When we first identified Bridget and got in touch with him, he wrote us this account:

If I sounded shocked yesterday, I was. It was like being re-introduced to the 500-pound gorilla lurking out of sight in the room of the mind.

After I finished Dr. Kanner's write-up about 'Barbara K.' I knew that I had read it before. I don't remember where or under what circumstances, but there were a lot of "aha!" moments in rereading it. It had to have been my father who gave it to me to read.

Bridget was shipped off to Devereux when I entered kindergarten. She rarely came home, except at Christmastime when as a treat, we would share the same bed. We would chat with each other into the night anticipating Christmas as siblings would normally do. I remember visiting her at Devereux perhaps once, or, at the most, twice a year. We would have an outing at a nearby amusement park (Lenape Park it was called). Bridget and I would ride the Ferris wheel and roller coaster together; for me, if not for my parents, these outings were jolly occasions. Looking back on those times, and on those subsequent years after she was handed off to the Springfield Hospital Center (Devereux demanded a huge lump sum payment—$60,000 I think it was—for lifetime care, a sum my father could not come up with), it seems that my parents were trying to isolate me from her as if her condition might be contagious. (They would not believe that for an instant, but such is my impression.) I would see Bridget a couple of times yearly when she was at Springfield—it was a not-too-distant drive from our farm in Harford County—on her birthday and at Christmas. I vividly remember the drives back home in the wintry darkness, my mother weeping continuously, my father silent at the wheel of the car, and me scared and still in the backseat.

I really got to know Bridget well only after my father died in 1984. For decades my father saw Bridget weekly. He was a senior adviser at Springfield Hospital, mentoring and teaching young psychiatrists at the facility. (There is a building there that bears his name, the Muncie Center.) He would see Bridget after his counseling sessions. After he died, I took up the mantle, seeing Bridget one day each weekend until her death, from cancer, about ten years ago. (My mother didn't drive; she went with me and my wife on picnics with Bridget perhaps four times a year.) Even as Bridget neared the end of her life, her mind virtually gone from years of institutionalization and daily ingestion of powerful pharmaceuticals, her long-term memory was remarkable, a phenomenon observed both by me and my wife, as well as by the nurses at the hospital (who, by the way, were greatly fond of her). She remembered, for instance, the names of most of her kindergarten classmates, and she duplicated that feat in other realms. In my presence, the

nurses at the hospital would 'show off' Bridget's savant abilities, asking her questions
about names, places, and events in the distant past about which she almost invariably
could recall.

These days, I visit Bridget once a year—at our family burial plot in Harford
County. There, I commiserate with her about the shitty hand she was dealt at the time
of her birth.[7]

Lee Ruven Rosenberg ("John F."), Case 10

In December 1942, and January 1943, he had two series of predominantly
right-sided convulsions, with conjugate deviation of the eyes to the right
and transient paresis of the right arm. Neurologic examination showed no
abnormalities. His eyegrounds were normal. An EEG indicated "focal
disturbances in the left occipital region."

Dr. Hilde Bruch, who saw him in 1953, remarked on his "exuberant
emotional expression with no depth and variation and with immediate
turnoff when the other person withdraws the interest."

John died suddenly in 1966 at 29 years of age.

Jay Rosenberg is Lee's younger brother. Like his father, he is a neurologist
(Seymour Rosenberg was a neurologist-psychiatrist in the manner typical
of his day). He practices in San Diego. He's cheerful, emphatic, outgoing,
but it is clear he harbors deep scars from his childhood as the brother of
one of the original cases. They are different scars than Peter Muncie's,
because his experience is at the other end of the spectrum: His brother
was much more difficult to manage, much more physically ill, and was at
home for a much longer period of Jay's childhood, from when Jay was ten
or eleven till he was sixteen. It took a toll on his family that he remembers
vividly. Lee had drop-seizures as often as several times a day, and Jay got
used to the sound of him falling to the floor in the next room.

His father emotionally withdrew from the family and his mother was
overwhelmed—autism had decimated the emotional functioning of a
previously healthy family, the kind of dynamic that perversely came to
be seen as further confirmation of parental responsibility.

Lee had been institutionalized but, when he was about six, his parents dropped by the facility and found the guard drunk and passed out. They brought Lee home. "He had seizures—he had the worst epilepsy. As he got older, his seizures got much worse."[8] The parents reluctantly looked for another residential setting and finally found it in a group-home setting in Connecticut where the residents lived in cabins and were called campers. It was clear Jay thought that had taken far too long. "My mother was very ambivalent about placing him. She had difficult times when he came home," keeping him as long as possible. "We had to basically carry him out."

"Yes, you can have high-functioning autism," he said, but that was not his family's experience. "Nobody had any idea how to manage it. They had no drugs to manage it at the time. They couldn't manage it with behavior. I don't think it's changed a hell of a lot, that's my feeling."

Unlike Peter Muncie, who did not see a connection with mercury as a plausible factor in his sibling's case, Rosenberg did. In fact, after we outlined our research to him, he suggested developing a "poster presentation" for the American Academy of Neurology, of which he is a member.

Rosenberg believes autism is multifactorial—he is convinced his brother's case had "a strong genetic component" because of the epilepsy and the fact he was different from birth, "a failure-to-thrive baby." And although he believes the mercury association in the first cases is intriguing as a possible factor, he does not believe thimerosal from vaccines is a factor in the huge rise in autism diagnoses since 1990.

David Newcomb Speck ("Alfred L."), Case 8

He was again seen in June 1941. His parents had decided to live together. Prior to that he had been in 11 different schools. He had been kept in bed often because of colds, bronchitis, chickenpox, impetigo, and a vaguely described condition that the mother insisted was rheumatoid fever. . . .

This ended the Clinic's contact with Alfred. The mother started him out on a tour of schools and hospitals, not informing them about preceding evaluations and taking him out after a time, not disclosing the next step she planned to take. We do know that he was at the V. V. Anderson School in Stratsburg-on-Hudson, N.Y. (1948–1950); the Taylor Manor in Ellicott

City, Md. (July to October 1954); and the Philadelphia Hospital
Department for Mental and Nervous Diseases (March 3 to April 20, 1955).
Some time between the last two, he was for a time on Thorazine; then at a
"school for brain damaged children" founded by his mother in October
1954.

Alfred is now 38 years old. So far as can be determined, he is at his
mother's "school." Both at Sheppard-Pratt and Philadelphia Hospitals he
was interested in the occupational therapy materials—and did well with
them. When this was brought to the mother's attention, she decided to take
him out.

Miriam Partridge Speck's on-again, off-again relationship with her husband, John, the chemist-attorney at the Patent Office in Washington,
ended permanently when they divorced in 1966. Their marriage had
been volatile since she moved out with their newborn, David, and back
to her parents' house in Baltimore in the summer of 1932.

Her father, George Partridge, was a psychologist who got his Ph.D.
and taught at Clark University—the site of Freud's famous American
lectures in 1909. He was at Worcester, Massachusetts, at the time; perhaps he was sitting not far from Adolf Meyer to listen to the great man
speak.

In Baltimore George Partridge was the director of classification and
clinical service for the state Department of Prisons. Miriam's mother,
Emelyn Newcomb Partridge, was a psychologist as well, and the year
before David was born had written a yearlong series for *The Boston Globe*
on preschool child testing methods.

Given this milieu, it's not surprising that Miriam began taking psychology classes at Johns Hopkins after returning to Baltimore. There
was clearly tension between Leo Kanner and Miriam Partridge—"a
clinical psychologist, very obsessive and excitable, was the only parent in
the capital clinic's experience who did not allow notes to be taken when
she gave the history."[9] She pursued her own approach, opening a school
for brain-injured children. In the early days she was successful, receiving
federal grants and positive newspaper articles; in one, a Brazilian father
marveled that after a year his retarded child, whom he had come to take
home, was able to greet him in words.

But controversy appeared to follow her; there were disputes over the
start-up of two new branches of the school. She moved to Arizona and
started the Partridge Memorial Treatment Center of Arizona in Tucson;

the next year she was ignoring health department closure threats. The school was raided in 1972 and she faced eleven criminal charges that were ultimately dropped. More suits followed, and in 1972 she gave a sad interview to the local paper in which she said, "I'm old, I'm flattened out."

But between the lines it's possible to see another image of Miriam Partridge. At a time when parents were blamed for autism—by Leo Kanner, among others—and it was widely considered a hopeless diagnosis, she was looking for occupational treatments for her son, moving him from institution to institution in an urgent if impatient and imperfect search for better treatments.

In that sense, she became the first Warrior Mother, a phrase used in the autism treatment community to describe mothers who refuse to accept autism as a lifelong diagnosis or to stick to prescribed behavioral treatments, but aggressively adopt biomedical approaches, take on the medical establishment over what many of them believe to be vaccine injury, and campaign for insurance coverage and treatment programs for all affected families.

Like Warrior Mothers to come, she was also right about the cause of David's disorder—brain damage, not bad parenting or bad genes—at a time when her doctor, Leo Kanner, and the rest of the medical community were most emphatically wrong.

David Speck died in 2000, age sixty-eight, in Tucson.

"Richard M.," Case 3

The mother felt that she was no longer capable of handling him, and he was placed in a foster home with a woman who had shown a remarkable talent for dealing with difficult children. After two changes of foster homes, he was placed at a State School for Exceptional Children in his home State in May 1946. A report, dated June 23, 1954, said: "The institution accepted him as essentially a custodial problem; therefore, he was placed with a group of similar charges."

Richard is now 33 years old. In 1965, he was transferred to another institution in the same State. The Superintendent wrote on September 29, 1970: "At the time of admission, tranquilizers were pushed to the point of

toxicity. After about 3 months, he showed some awareness of his
environment and began feeding himself and going to the toilet. He is now
being maintained on Compazine, 45 milligrams t.i.d. . . . He now resides
in a cottage for older residents who can meet their own personal needs. He
responds to his name and to simple commands and there is some nonverbal communication with the cottage staff. He continues to be
withdrawn and cannot be involved in any structured activities.

Although we determined his identity as a son of Willam Dykstra and
Catherine Ritchey Miller, we were unable to find "Richard M." and
could not determine whether he is still alive.

Leo Kanner wrote there were two good outcomes in the first eleven
cases—oddly enough, the first two, "Frederick W." and "Donald T."

Frederick Creighton Wellman III ("Frederick W."), Case 2

Creighton had been placed in an institution in 1943, but he came to live
with his parents just before his father retired from the U.S. Department
of Agriculture in Puerto Rico in 1962 to become a visiting professor at
North Carolina State.

"We settled into a new home and [Frederick] did his part in it," the
Wellmans wrote Kanner. "He has become acquainted with the neighbors
and sometimes makes calls on them. We tried him out in the County Shel-
tered Workshop and Vocational Training Center. He took right to it, made
friends with the teachers, and helped with some of the trainees. Through
his relationship there, he took up bowling and he does pretty well."

Kanner's 1971 followup concluded: "In 1969 Frederick W. began
working at the National Air Pollution Administration, now part of the
Environmental Protection Agency, doing routine tasks like running a
copy machine. His boss wrote in 1970 that he 'is an outstanding em-
ployee by any standard.'"

One person who knew the Wellmans in Raleigh was Robert Aycock, the chairman of the plant pathology department whom we quoted earlier on the rise of mercury fungicides in the 1930s.

"Fred's main interest in coming to the plant pathology department at Raleigh was to summarize his 'harvest years' in the form of books, seminars, and interactions with faculty and students," Aycock told us. "He was well known by most of the Latin American graduate students and was highly thought of, not only professionally, but personally as well. Dr. Wellman had had numerous contacts in Latin America with plant pathologists who sent graduate students to North Carolina State."

My wife became acquainted with the Wellmans and we were also invited on numerous occasions into their home, which was not too far from ours. Dora was noted for being a gracious host and set a dinner table without compare; all the finest cutlery, dishes, napery, etc.—far beyond what casual friends might expect. I commented once to Dora that she need not go to all that trouble for us and she replied somewhat like this, that since eating was often a chore the least she could do was something to make the surroundings attractive.

No mention of Creighton's problems and his behavior during his early years was ever noted. Their attitude portrayed a calm acceptance of reality but also a deep love and attachment to him. They showed no embarrassment or frustration with Creighton's problems, although they would occasionally reflect with affectionate amusement on certain situations in which Creighton had been involved. The fact that Fred and Dora were devoted to each other was also quite apparent. A mutual friend remembered that it was not unusual to see Fred and Dora walk into a public gathering holding hands.

Creighton was an unusual fellow, no doubt about it. Our home was a mile or two beyond the Wellmans' and on my way home from work or shopping at nearby Ridgewood Shopping Center I often passed Creighton walking. Sometimes he would accept a ride and sometimes not. If he accepted he would usually begin immediately a conversation about some musical concert or performance that was to be held soon in Raleigh or at Duke or some other nearby place. He attended the nearby Methodist church on Ridge Road and was enraptured by the music, and his interaction there caught the eye of several members who have looked after him to some extent to this day. It was obvious that Creighton enjoyed the company of the wives in the department more than the men. My wife was a favorite and so were other wives in the department. Fred once remarked that at Christmas Creighton would present a most attractive and somewhat costly present to Dora with a much more modest gift for him.

In their late years the Wellmans sold their attractive home and moved into a retirement complex. I don't really recall how long they were there, but I do remember that Fred called me sometime after Dora's death in desperation, wanting to know what he could do to provide for Creighton, after Fred was gone. Fortunately, friends in the church and at the complex were able to work with Fred and a relative, I believe, so that care for Creighton's future was assured.[10]

In 2006 we dialed the number listed on the apartment building intercom for Creighton Wellman. The man who answered said it was the wrong number. We tried one more time, dialing carefully, and got the same man and the same answer. We followed up with a letter that received no response.

Donald Triplett ("Donald T."), Case 1

In 1942, his parents placed him on a tenant farm about 10 miles from their home. When I visited there in May 1945 [Kanner wrote in 1971], I was amazed at the wisdom of the couple who took care of him. They managed to give him goals for his stereotypes. They made him use his preoccupation with measurements by having him dig a well and report on its depth. When he kept collecting dead birds and bugs, they gave him a spot for a "graveyard" and had him put up markers; on each he wrote a first name, the type of animal as a middle name, and the farmer's last name, e.g.: "John Snail Lewis. Born, date unknown. Died, (date on which he found the animal)." When he kept counting rows of corn over and over, they had him count the rows while plowing them. On my visit, he plowed six long rows; it was remarkable how well he handled the horse and plow and turned the horse around. It was obvious that Mr. and Mrs. Lewis were very fond of him and just as obvious that they were gently firm. He attended a country school where his peculiarities were accepted and where he made good scholastic progress.

The rest of the story is contained in a letter from the mother, dated April 6, 1970:

Don is now 36 years old, a bachelor living at home with us. . . . Since receiving his A.B. degree in 1958, he has worked in the local bank as a teller. He is satisfied to remain a teller, having no real desire for promotion. . . . Other interests are Kiwanis Club (served as president one term), Jaycees, Investment Club, Secretary of Presbyterian Sunday School. He is dependable, accurate, shows originality in editing the Jaycee program information, is even-tempered but has a mind of his own. . . . He owns his second car, likes his independence. His room includes his own TV, record player, and many books. In College his major was French and he showed a particular aptitude for languages. Don is a fair bridge player but never initiates a game. Lack of initiative seems to be his most serious drawback. He takes very little part in social conversation and shows no interest in the opposite sex.

While Don is not completely normal, he has taken his place in society very well; so much better than we ever hoped for. If he can maintain status quo, I think he has adjusted sufficiently to take care of himself. For this much progress, we are truly grateful. . . . Please give Dr. Kanner our kindest regards. Tell him the couple Don lived with for 4 years, Mr. and Mrs. Lewis, are still our friends. We see them quite often. Don has never had any medication for his emotional trouble. I wish I knew what his inner feelings really are. As long as he continues as he is now, we can continue to be thankful.

We are sitting at the kitchen table of a comfortable home in Forest, Mississippi, talking to Don Triplett. This is the house his parents built in 1930; and except for the eleven months at the TB "preventorium," living on the farm with the Lewises in his early teens, and attending college, this has been his home since he was born in 1933.

Retired now at seventy-six, he is wearing a Forest Presbyterian Church T-shirt, shorts, and sneakers. When one of us visited Forest four years earlier, he was out of town—in Branson, Missouri, listening to country music. That was when we met his brother, who described his remarkable recovery after gold salts treatment for juvenile rheumatoid arthritis and said he had become a world traveler, recently touring Italy.

Constantinople was his favorite city. Now, at the kitchen table, Don Triplett tells us he has since been to Dubai to watch a golf tournament and follow Ernie Els, his favorite pro.

This is the first person diagnosed with autism? This is the sentinel case that alerted Leo Kanner to a devastating new disorder, unmistakable from early infancy, and which now is thought to affect 1 in 100 children? Talking to him does nothing to diminish our amazement. His only distinctive speech pattern is a stutter when he begins to talk. He has the sharp memory Kanner described. "I went to Baltimore three times," he recalls. "We rode on the train all three times." He remembers Leo Kanner very well, along with a female psychiatrist. "I wrote, 'What do you put on your lips?' And she put down, 'Nail polish.' I'm sure she was kidding. And I wrote 'How much do you put on there,' and she wrote, 'One quart.'"

We begin asking questions, and his answers are direct and succinct:

Q: When your parents decided to take you there [Baltimore], do you remember why that happened and what the motivation was?

A: I was just sort of different from most of the people, and she thought she would take me up there. I really don't know how she got Dr. Kanner's name. I think both my parents went.

Q: In Kanner's writing he talks about your childhood and your background. He talks about the Presbyterian Church and some of the things that were a little different about you when you were a child. Do you remember the Twenty-third Psalm and the twenty-five questions and answers of the Presbyterian catechism?

A: Yes, I did memorize the child's catechism and I did know the Twenty-third Psalm and also the Hundredth.

Q: Do you remember the catechism?

A: "Who made you? God made you. What else did God make? God made all things. Why did God make you and all things? For his own glory" . . . and so forth.

Q: Do you remember anything about your physical health when you were a child? They said that you had some feeding difficulties.

A: I did. I was a bit underweight. When I was four years old I don't think I weighed over thirty pounds.

Q: Another thing Leo Kanner mentioned was that you had arthritis as a child. How old were you then?

A: Going on fourteen. It was called rheumatoid arthritis. Dr. Hamilton was the one who gave me the gold salts [at the Campbell Clinic in Memphis].

Q: And how did that feel?

A: That got me well after about seven or eight months. But then I had another attack in 1950 and another in 1959, all in February, all three times. But I didn't have to be hospitalized for that.

Q: And that was it? You haven't had any problems since?

A: I've been feeling some joint pains but not anything like what I had when I was a child.

Q: There was a mention in some of the medical papers that when you had the gold salts therapy, all of a sudden some of the behaviors and some of the other problems got better. Do you remember that?

A: No, I don't really remember that.

Q: Did your parents say, though, that you seemed to get a lot better in terms of your relationship with the rest of the world and that sort of thing at that point?

A: Yes, as I got older, things got a whole lot better.

Q: And did they think that had something to do with it, those gold salts treatments?

A: I have a feeling it might.

Q: And the behaviors they were calling autistic, did those change most after the first one?

A: Yes, it seems like they changed.

Q: But you don't remember that kind of change taking place?

A: No, I don't remember, really.

He is not the best witness to his own recovery, of course; his parents were. That is obviously the filter through which his brother—who was six years younger and would not have clearly recalled the sequence of events himself—described the gold salts treatment that had a "miraculous" effect on his autism. Like so many clues in the original cases, this observation by the mother and father of the very first case was almost lost to history, ignored by the "experts." But it survived as an unsought treasure in the memory of a younger brother. How is *that* for serendipity?

Don Triplett takes us on a tour of his house. That is the chair where his father sat and listened to phonograph records; this is the porch where he plays his own albums, entertaining neighborhood children (favorites include Glen Campbell and Frank Sinatra). There, on the mantle, is an award from the Salvation Army—"I gave them a lot of money," he says matter-of-factly.

And everywhere there are family photographs, signs of affective contact with people both present and long gone: Beaman and Mary, the parents of whom Kanner was so suspicious; cousins and aunts and his brother and nephew; Don as an infant, at two, in high school. It is impossible to tell from the pictures, just as it is difficult at this meeting, that he was ever "different from most of the people," much less "markedly and uniquely" so, in Leo Kanner's phrase. To an attentive observer there are traces—the stutter, a lack of eye contact, little discussion of emotions, the fact he never married. But it is a far cry from inhabiting a universe of one.

⸻

We have come full circle on our journey into the history of autism, starting with Leo Kanner in Baltimore and ending here, in a small town in Mississippi, a reversed loop of the trip that brought autism to the medical world's attention.

But in a sense we were following in Leo Kanner's footsteps. His 1945 visit to Forest—seven years after "Donald T." visited the clinic, and just two years after "Autistic Disturbances" was published—shows how important Kanner considered this sentinel case. Besides that visit and Kanner's 1971 follow-up, though, interaction has been minimal; Triplett told us that he has had no direct contact with Hopkins since he saw Leo Kanner sixty-five years ago. His brother says Hopkins checks in "every decade or so."[11]

It's not as though his identity is a dark or forgotten secret; when Kanner wrote in 1979 about encountering "Donald T." for the first time, he said he was from Forest, Mississippi, and that "townspeople know him to be the first reported specimen of what many of my colleagues call 'the Kanner syndrome.'"[12] Triplett and his brother told us that a film crew from France showed up a few years ago and filmed him playing golf, and that a public television outlet in the Washington area has been in touch.

This lack of *medical* follow-up on Case 1 is symptomatic of a wider failure to investigate the natural history of autism even as it looms ever larger as the defining disorder of our time. ("Autism is currently, in our view, the most important and the fastest-evolving disorder in all of medical science and promises to remain so for the foreseeable future," says Dr. Jeffrey A. Lieberman, chairman of the department of psychiatry at Columbia University's school of medicine.)[13]

Some, if not all, of the original case records appear to have been lost; after we contacted Jay Rosenberg, he asked Hopkins for copies of anything on file for his brother, Lee ("John F."), but a thorough search turned up only a single mention that he had been seen. In the 1980s, a National Institutes of Health researcher who wanted to conduct brain scans on autistic adults contacted Kanner in search of early cases. The discoverer of autism was dying of cancer but told her how to contact a Hopkins social worker who had the case files—*in her attic*. (The NIH researcher's subsequent studies did not include any of the original eleven autistic cases.)[14] Kanner donated his papers to the American Psychiatric Association in Arlington, Virginia, but they contain no case files and precious little about autism at all; his biographical archive at Hopkins is meager, a collection mostly of newspaper clippings and speeches. The "monographic presentation" of the original case studies that he said he hoped to do remained unwritten.

Kanner's own unpublished autobiography contains five cursory pages on autism. (We read them when we visited Kanner's son, Albert, in Madison, Wisconsin.) The Johns Hopkins medical archive says it misplaced its copy of his autobiography in a recent move.

If the medical industry had been determined to obliterate the paper trail and ignore the insights available from those early cases, it could not have done a better job. But that is nothing new. On this journey we have come to see the wisdom of Josef Warkany's observation, in describing doctors' long failure to realize that pink disease was mercury poisoning, that medicine "can go forward and yet go in circles." Doctors and scientists have learned far too little from five centuries of misdiagnosed mercury poisoning in medicine; from the rising tide of pollution and its toxic effects on the most vulnerable among us; from the unsought revelations contained in the early cases of autism—and from the astonishing improvement of Case 1 after being treated for a *medical* condition.

This long nightmare of neglect and delay and denial needs to end, and our visit with Don Triplett offered a hopeful glimpse of what that day might look like. "In a few minutes," he told us as we took our leave, "I'm fixing to go out and play nine holes of golf."

ACKNOWLEDGMENTS

Any book is a journey, and this was a long one. We began over a decade ago on separate paths that ultimately converged in these pages, and it is a pleasure to thank the many people who have helped us along the way.

In 1999, Dan Olmsted began researching a prescription drug named mefloquine that appeared to have an unusual profile of side effects—including psychosis, and suicidal and homicidal impulses. In 2002, at United Press International (UPI), he and his investigative partner, Mark Benjamin, wrote a series about its impact. Soon Mark Benjamin decided to explore another controversial medical topic: Vaccines. He reported "serious problems linked to vaccines recommended by the CDC—and a web of close ties between the agency and the companies that make vaccines"; he also reported that "critics now worry about a link between vaccines and autism." Intrigued by the issue, Dan began writing a column titled "The Age of Autism." Several UPI editors backed this work strongly, sometimes in the face of resistance, and Dan especially thanks Phil Berardelli, John O'Sullivan, Martin Walker, Michael Marshall, Arnaud de Borchgrave, Russell Totten, and John Hendel.

While Dan's interest in autism was initially professional, Mark Blaxill's began in the most personal way imaginable. His younger daughter, Michaela, born in 1995, was diagnosed with autism in September 1998. Soon thereafter, and working with colleagues at SafeMinds such as Sallie Bernard, Lyn Redwood, Jim Moody, Heidi Roger, Laura Bono, Albert Enayati, Vicki Debold, Theresa Wrangham, Kelli Ann Davis, and others, he reviewed the global history of autism rates and compared them to the changing patterns of infant environmental exposures to mercury and vaccines. Meanwhile, he also began applying his training from years of experience at one of the world's top management consultancies to a statistical analysis of documents obtained from the CDC under the Freedom of Information Act and concluded the ethylmercury in childhood vaccines could indeed be contributing to an upsurge in autism cases. Along the way he authored a number of scientific papers, letters, and commentaries that were published in prominent journals.

After our paths intersected in 2004, we began comparing notes, as both of us were drawn to the natural history of the disorder and what seemed to be unanswered questions that might offer clues to its origins. For sending us in this fruitful direction, we each have several people to thank. Ed Arranga at Autism One invited Mark to give a talk on the history of autism. That led him to extend his literature review of the history of autism rates to the source document, Leo Kanner's original 1943 work, which in turn led to a fuller understanding of the roots of the earliest autism controversies, including how the "refrigerator parent" idea had been born and its malignant growth under Bruno Bettelheim; he also learned about a researcher named Mary Coleman who had clearly identified a "startling" chemical connection in the parents' occupation in families with autistic children, an important finding swept away in the surge of interest (and research funding) that began flowing from gene studies.

As Dan simultaneously read newspaper clippings and medical archives and did background interviews, he was struck by the lack of attention to the very earliest cases. Exactly who were these children and families, and what risk factors did they share? He soon realized it might be possible—as scholars had done with Freud's cases—to identify some of these first children and their families. There was also much to learn about the basics of autism, and he thanks Dr. Elizabeth Mumper for introducing him to her patients and patiently explaining the bench science that implicates mercury in autism and the biomedical treatments that might help. Lujene Clark and her late husband, Dr. Alan Clark, and Bobbie Manning were early and valued sources.

As *The Age of Autism* progressed, our separate paths combined as we began to work closely together, extending the "natural history" approach by looking for autism—or its absence—in contemporary populations. Dan's Age of Autism column explored groups with lower vaccination rates—most notably the Amish, but also a large, modern medical practice in Chicago, and the nation's homeschooled children; Dan thanks Drs. Frank Noonan, Mayer Eisenstein, and Jeff Bradstreet for their help in these investigations. We also started looking for the early cases. By early 2007, Mark and Dan had identified three of the eleven initial children described by Leo Kanner and focused deeply on "Case 2: Frederick W.," whose father had strong links to a fungicide made with ethylmercury. In 2007, the *Baltimore City Paper* ran an article Dan wrote for UPI on that case, and he thanks its editor, Lee Gardner, for publishing it in the city where autism was first identified.

As the book project took shape, we benefited from terrific research help that expanded our range of inquiry: Ralph Eckardt opened up the world of Google Books to us and worked with us as we found and examined many pre–twentieth century medical texts. He also participated in design discussions and helped us formulate our arguments on the age of industrial disease. Teresa Conrick dove deeply with us into the search for the Kanner 11. She found the Muncie family, continues to work with us on our ongoing search (we'll find Virginia S. someday!) and shares our passion for the effort. Sydney Blaxill traveled with us to Vienna and London and arranged our tour of the medical history of the cities. She brought the electron shell of the mercury atom to life for us (calling it a "hunky, slimy beast") based on her recently completed tour of high school chemistry. Then she discovered the surprising connection between the von Swietens (father Gerard and son Gottfried) and Mozart.

David Kirby, author of *Evidence of Harm* who wrote the foreword, has been a great friend and partner for many years. We thank him both for his groundbreaking work and his collaborative spirit.

Along the way, Dan made the move from UPI to the blogosphere. J. B. Handley and Kim Stagliano had started Rescue Post online, and the four of us came together and launched Age of Autism (ageofautism.com). J. B. has been both an active contributor and a fierce voice for our kids; Kim has been our day-to-day partner. Our sponsors—SafeMinds, NAA, TACA, Generation Rescue, ARI, and Lee Silsby—have helped provide a strong foundation for our ongoing investigations: Indeed, many of the ideas in this book were introduced on the blog, and our readers' responses have helped refine them. The community that has grown up around Age of Autism has carried us forward on a wave of shared energy and commitment and we are privileged to serve such a generous and engaged group. In particular we want to thank our editors, contributors, and supporters, including Katie Wright, John Stone, Jake Crosby, Julie Obradovic, Kent Heckenlively, Anne Dachel, Cathy Jameson, Jenny McCarthy, Abdulkadir Khalif, Martin Walker, Ed and Teri Arranga, Wendy Fournier, Lisa Ackerman, Becky Estepp, Steve Edelson, Jane Johnson, Barbara Loe Fisher, and Theresa Cedillo, as well as our community of commenters, too numerous to mention. We know who you are.

Our book research was aided by sources both public and private. E. Fuller Torrey graciously opened up the working papers from his book *The Invisible Plague* (and the copying machine in his office). The Small and Special Museum at Great Ormond Street in London, the Freud Archive in London, and the Pharmacology Museum at the University of

Vienna gave us access to their holdings, and their experts took the time to discuss how their material might be useful to us. We also extend our appreciation to the Special Collections Unit of the North Carolina State University Libraries, the Alan Mason Chesney Archives of the Johns Hopkins Medical Institutions, the University of Idaho Library Special Collections and Archives, the University of Maryland libraries, the National Archives, the National Library of Medicine, the New York Public Library, the National Agricultural Library, the Falls Church City Library, the Scott County, Mississippi, Library, the Maryland Room of the Enoch Pratt Free Library in Baltimore, the Library of Congress, and the Melvin Sabshin Library & Archives of the American Psychiatric Association. A good librarian is an author's best friend, and now we understand why research librarians wear old clothes—it gets dusty in there.

We received crucial translation help from Dieter Waelterman, Markus Schwickert, and Gayle DeLong. Robert Aycock, former dean of plant pathology at North Carolina State, gave us a vivid account of how toxic chemicals were used in the early days, as well as his reminiscence of Frederick L. Wellman and his family. Special thanks go to Albert Kanner and Hans Asperger Jr.

Many people have followed this path before us, often at immense sacrifice or with woefully inadequate recognition: in Britain they include Rose Kessick, Jackie Fletcher, and Andrew Wakefield, the British medical researcher now in the United States who has paid a steep price for his scientific integrity. Less controversial and outspoken but deeply committed to the truth are a number of scientists who have contributed important work on these issues: Mark Noble, Martha Herbert, Irva Hertz-Picciotto, Jill James, Tom Burbacher, Dick Deth, Isaac Pessah, Catherine DeSoto, Laura Hewitson, and the late Walter Spitzer. Also, for their research on mercury and autism, amid fierce criticism, we thank Boyd Haley and Mark and David Geier. Many doctors and clinicians have put themselves on the line to help kids, including Arthur Krigsman, Ken Bock, Brian Jepson, Jacquelyn McCandless, Woody McGinniss, Nancy O'Hara, Amy Holmes, Sid Baker, and Jon Pangborn.

Our most heartfelt thanks go out to the victims of the autism tragedy, the people whose lives were forever altered by this new scourge, and to their families—mothers, father, brothers, and sisters—whose lives have been turned upside down. Most of all, we have written this book for you.

Special thanks go to several members of the original eleven Kanner families. In Mississippi, O. B. Triplett shared stories of his family; in

Maryland, Peter Muncie wrote a moving reminiscence of his sister, Bridget ("Barbara K."), and provided childhood photos; in California, Dr. Jay Rosenberg, brother of Lee ("John F.") shared memories and sponsored a joint poster presentation with us at the American Academy of Neurology in Seattle in 2009, which posited that mercury exposure was a common factor in those early cases.

We were honored to meet Don Triplett, "Case 1," and we thank him for his hospitality and reflections on his time with Dr. Kanner and his remarkable adult life. And our visit with John Trevett ("Herbert B.") affected us deeply; he possesses a quiet dignity that we will always remember.

We have family and friends we want to acknowledge. Dan offers special thanks to his sister Rosamond Olmsted Augspuger, her husband Richard, and his sister Sara Olmsted Vana and her sons John and James; they can lay claim to the title of Biggest (and most appreciated) Fans. He also thanks his cousins Dr. Lawrence Allen and his wife Kay, Terry, Marguerite, Trevett, and Sam and Janet Allen. Thanks also to Phil and Doris Steinberg, Mimi Sutterthwaite and Susan Farmer, Beverly Crawford, Tom and Lisa Goldring, Jon and Karen Hitchings, Wyatt Weber, Carson Delmear Weber-Hansen and the late Jon Hansen, Leo Ribeiro, Alan Levinson, Becky Williams, Vi Boyer, Mary Webster, Melissa Merli, Martha Kay, Sonya and Ernesto Lopez, Dean and Denise Fulton, John and Brooke Potthast, Eric Gladen, Donna Rode, Melissa Ontiveros, Rene Mathez, Mike Worthen, Larry Kahn, Jeanne Lese, and Andrew Pogany.

The late Sue Rose, with whom Dan had a long professional bond, read the first half of the manuscript before her untimely death, and like so much else it benefited from her keen eye and compassionate heart. He thanks Peter Fenner and Michael Shandler for Nothing (they won't mind). And a fellow journalist who died too young, Bob Wilson, was a mentor in many things, including a healthy skepticism of authority.

Dan also thanks Mark Blaxill's family, and especially appreciates the serial hospitality of his indomitable wife, Elise. Mark thanks his colleagues at 3LP Advisors, who have always made sure he was asking himself the tough questions and also provided gracious support: Ralph Eckardt, Kevin Rivette, David Morland, Matt Stack, Tony Trippe, and Gerren Crochet.

We also thank our parents. Robert Olmsted was a remarkable man whose immense love of learning rubbed off to some degree (and that was more than enough). Catharine Hatfield Olmsted had a passion for good writing and good causes that her son took to heart. Sidney Blaxill served for a time as the head of an autism charity and although he never knew how autism would change his own son's life, he certainly prepared his son to become a "warrior dad." Marjorie Blaxill always hoped Mark would choose public service over a business career, and her idealism helped steel him for this challenge.

Both Dan and Mark owe a deep debt to Bernie Rimland, who encouraged Dan to believe that a nonspecialist willing to think and explore for himself could make a meaningful contribution to the autism field. Mark hopes Bernie is adequately recognized in history for forging the way in not just one, but two scientific revolutions in autism, a remarkable testimony to the intellectual depth, passion, and flexibility of the man.

Karyn Marcus, our editor at Thomas Dunne Books, gave us the gifts of her time, expertise, and commitment, providing encouragement even as she pressed us to sharpen and shape our arguments and evidence. It is commonplace to say an editor believes in a book, but her confidence and energy buoyed us all along the way. Our agent, Farley Chase, made the business of finding a publisher a pleasure.

Finally, Mark thanks his family, to whom he dedicates this book. Autism drives some families apart but it has brought the Blaxills closer. Elise is a "warrior mom" whose fight for Michaela's recovery constantly reminds him how wrong Bruno Bettelheim was; Michaela's hard work and trickster spirit gives him new motivation every day to make her future the dream rather than the nightmare.

In case it is not obvious, two of the three "Marks" in Dan's dedication are Mark Blaxill and Mark Benjamin. First and last, he is supremely grateful to Mark Milett, his steadfast partner for twenty-five years. *Domo-arigato-gozaimasu.*

APPENDIX A

NOTES ON THE TUSKEGEE STUDIES

FIRST PHASE

The initial survey was not strictly a prospective study; it was an in-depth population prevalence survey aimed at assessing "morbidity" in untreated syphilis cases.

Vonderlehr et al. (1936) found no GPI in the untreated study population at all, and no evidence of any cases in the larger syphilitic population in Macon County from which the study group was drawn.

Over time, the untreated group sought treatment on their own and by 1948, 71.8 percent of the infected population examined had received treatment of some kind (mostly "inadequate"). So as the first phase came to an end around 1950, with the majority receiving pre–penicillin era treatments in the 1930s and 1940s, the concept of a study of "untreated syphilis in the American Negro" had largely vanished.

In each examination, the investigators were intensely interested in uncovering evidence of adverse neurological results in the syphilis group. And according to all the evidence, having syphilis was never a more healthy condition than *not* having syphilis.

Still, the initial survey specifically pointed to the absence of GPI, and neither of the next two survey examinations reported any evidence of GPI, despite reporting on "pathological conditions of the nervous system" and "psychosis."

Even in the fourth survey—the 1952 autopsy study that examined one brain of a paretic, one case whose death was attributed to paresis, and one case who died of other causes and exhibited paretic symptoms—the authors commented that "the great scarcity of frank syphilitic involvement of the central nervous system and the complete absence of lesser lesions attributable to syphilis are noteworthy."

SECOND PHASE

By 1950 it had become clear that penicillin was a complete cure for syphilis. Here, the investigators faced a real moral choice: Would they offer the study

group penicillin or not? They chose not to offer penicillin to the infected men
and intensified their study.

- They redoubled their effort to find patients lost to follow-up.

- They lumped all infected patients, regardless of treatment status, back
  together in a single group, now defined as "inadequately treated."

- They intensified their publication efforts, writing six separate papers
  around the 1952 survey.

By 1952, as the frequency of "inadequate treatment" had risen, paretic patients
were reported for the first time. By 1962, it was clear that mercury injections
were common in the cases treated in the 1930s.

As many as four GPI cases were reported in the infected group, about 1
percent of the overall study population.

- Three cases (treatment status unknown) were reported in the autopsy
  study:[1]

  - One was confirmed by brain examination at autopsy.

  - One was in the autopsy group but without brain exam, and the cause
    of death was given as GPI.

  - One died of other causes but had symptoms of paresis.

  - One was reported in the group of living patients examined in 1952[2]
    and was a patient that had received "inadequate treatment."

TUSKEGEE STUDIES BIBLIOGRAPHY

First Phase Publications

1. R. A. Vonderlehr, T. Clark, O. C. Wenger and J. R. Heller. Untreated
   syphilis in the male negro: A comparative study of treated and untreated cases. *Ven Dis Inform.* 1936;17: 260–265.

2. J. R. Heller, and P. T. Bruyere. Untreated syphilis in the male Negro. II.
   Mortality during 12 years of observation. *J. Ven. Dis. Inform.* 1946;27:
   34–38.

3. A. V. Deibert and M. C. Bruyere. Untreated syphilis in the male Negro. III.
   Evidence of cardiovascular abnormalities and other forms of morbidity. *J. Ven. Dis. Inform.* 1946;27: 301–314.

4. P. J. Pesare, T. J. Bauer, and G. A. Gleeson, Untreated syphilis in the male
   Negro. Observation of abnormalities over 16 years. *Am. J. Syph, Gon,
   & Ven. Dis.* 1950;34: 201–213.

Second Phase Publications

5. E. Rivers, S. H. Schumann, L. Simpson, and S. Olansky, Twenty years of followup experience in a long-range medical study. *Public Health Reports.* 1953; 68(4): 391–395.

6. J. K. Schafer, L. J. Usilton, and G. A. Gleeson, Untreated syphilis in the male Negro; a prospective study of the effect on life expectancy. Public Health Rep. 1954;69(7):684–90.

7. S. Olansky, L. Simpson, and S. H. Schumann. Environmental factors in the Tuskegee study of untreated syphilis. Public Health Rep. 1954;69(7): 691–8.

8. J. J. Peters, J. H. Peers, S. Olansky et al. Untreated syphilis in the male Negro; pathologic findings in syphilitic and nonsyphilitic patients. *J Chronic Dis.* 1955;1(2):127–48.

9. S. H. Schuman, S. Olansky, E. Rivers et al. Untreated syphilis in the male Negro; background and current status of patients in the Tuskegee study. J Chronic Dis. 1955;2(5):543–58.

10. S. Olansky, S. H. Schuman, J. J. Peters et al. Untreated syphilis in the male Negro. X. Twenty years of clinical observation of untreated syphilitic and presumably nonsyphilitic groups. *J Chronic Dis.* 1956;4(2):177–85.

11. S. Olansky, A. Harris, J. C. Cutler, and E. V. Price. Untreated syphilis in the male Negro; twenty-two years of serologic observation in a selected syphilis study group. *AMA Arch Derm.* 1956;73(5):516–22.

12. D. H. Rockwell, A. R. Yobs, and M. B. Moore. The Tuskegee Study of Untreated Syphilis: The 30th year of observation. *Arch Intern Med.* 1964;114:792–8.

APPENDIX B

SELECTED PAPERS AND PATENTS OF THE PLANT PATHOLOGY NETWORK

SELECTED SCIENTIFIC PAPERS

- Kharasch MS and Piccard JF. 1920. Aromatic mercuri-organic derivatives. *J Am Chem Soc* 42(9): 1855–1864.

- Stieglitz J, Kharasch MS and Hanke M. 1921. Preparation of 5,5'-mercuri-bis-3-nitro-4-hydroxy-phenyl-arsonic acid. *J Am Chem Soc* 43(5):1185–1193.

- Wellman FL. 1922. Hot water and mercuric chloride treatments of some Brassica seeds and their effect on both the germination of the seeds and the viability of the fungus phoma lingam. University of Wisconsin, unpublished.

- Walker JC, Monteith J and Wellman FL. 1927. Development of three mid-season varieties of cabbage resistant to yellows. *Journ Agr Res* 35:785–809.

- Haasis FW. 1928. Germinative energy of lots of coniferous-tree seed as related to incubation temperature and to duration of incubation. *Plant Physiol* 3(4): 365–412. (Semesan treatment of pine seedlings, acknowledgment to WH Tisdale of DuPont.)

- Kharasch MS and Flenner AL. 1932. The decomposition of unsymmetrical mercuriorganic compounds: A method of establishing the relative degree of electronegativity of organic radicals. II. *J Am Chem Soc* 54(2): 674–692.

- Lindgren RM, Scheffer TC and Chapman AD. 1932. Tests of chemical treatments for control of sap stain and mold in southern lumber. *Ind Eng Chem* 25(1): 72.

- Tisdale WH and Flenner AL. 1942. Derivatives of dithiocarbamic acid as pesticides. *Ind Eng Chem* 34(4): 501–502.

• Miller WD and Maki TE. 1957. Planting pines in pocosins. *Jour For* 55(9): 559–663.

SELECTED U.S. PATENTS

• Engelmann M (DuPont). April 15, 1927. Process of producing organic mercury compounds. US Patent 1,748,331.

• Engelmann M (Bayer-Semesan). July 25, 1929. Seed disinfectant. US Patent 1,920,009.

• Kharasch MS (DuPont). August 9, 1929. Seed disinfectant composition. US Patent 1,820,001.

• Kharasch MS (DuPont). November 30, 1929. Method of making organic mercury compounds. US Patent 1,987,685.

• Engelmann M and Tisdale WH (DuPont). April 16, 1930. Wood preservation. US Patent 1,874,260.

• Engelmann M and Flenner AL (DuPont). July 28, 1932. Mercury compound and process of manufacturing. US Patent 1,993,777.

• Flenner AL, Tisdale WH, and Calcott WS (DuPont). March 30, 1934. Insecticidal spray materials. US Patent 2,044,934.

• Flenner AL and Kaufert FH (DuPont). April 7, 1939. Preservation of wood. US Patent 2,268,387.

• Flenner AL, Kaufert FH, and Salzburg PL (DuPont). April 25, 1938. Preservation of wood. US Patent 2,331,268.

ENDNOTES

EPIGRAPH

[1] Lecture, University of Lille, December 7, 1854. This and alternative translations are at www.wikiquote.org/wiki/Louis _Pasteur.

INTRODUCTION: THE SEED

[1] Judge Francis Buller, to the Jury, *Donnellan Case,* March 1781, Quoted in "Visible Proofs—Forensic Views of the Body," Exhibit at the National Library of Medicine, National Institutes of Health, 2006.

[2] Leo Kanner, "Autistic Disturbances of Affective Contact," *The Nervous Child* (April 1943), 2(3): 217–250.

[3] Leo Kanner, "Problems of Nosology and Psychodynamics of Early Infantile Autism," *American Journal of Orthopsychiatry,* 1949, 19(3): 416–26.

[4] Jeremy Veenstra-VanDerWeele and Edwin H. Cook, "Genetics of Childhood Disorders: XLVI. Autism, Part 5: Genetics of Autism," *Journal of the American Academy of Child & Adolescent Psychiatry,* 2003, 42(1): 116–188.

[5] Interview with authors, May 30, 2008.

[6] *The New Encyclopaedia: or, Universal Dictionary of Arts and Sciences,* Vol. XIV (London: Vernor, Hood, and Sharpe, and Thomas Ostell, 1807), 320.

[7] Karen Endicott, "The Trembling Edge of Science," *Dartmouth Alumni Magazine* (April 1998) www.udel.edu/OHS/ dartmouth/drtmtharticle.html.

[8] "Thimerosal in Vaccines," a joint statement of the American Academy of Pediatrics and the Public Health Service, *MMWR Morb Mortal Wkly Rep,* 1999, 48: 563–65.

[9] From *Hydrargyrum,* Latinized Greek for water and silver.

[10] Wiktionary, www.en.wiktionary.org/wiki/mercurial.

[11] John J. Putman, "Quicksilver and Slow Death," *National Geographic* (October 1972), 507–27. Photographs by Robert W. Madden.

[12] Natlie Angier, *The Canon: A Whirligig Tour of the Beautiful Basics of Science* (New York: Mariner Books, 2008), 140.

[13] Adding an average of 120 neutrons to the standard 80 protons in its nucleus gives mercury a typical atomic weight of 200.

[14] Only thallium, lead, and bismuth are heavier among nonradioactive elements.

[15] John J. Duffus, "Heavy Metals—A Meaningless Term?" *Pure Apl. Chem,* 2002, 74(5): 793–807. "The term 'heavy metal' has never been defined by an authoritative body," argues Duffus. "Over the 60 years in which it has been used in chemistry, it has been given such a wide range of meanings by different authors that it is effectively meaningless."

[16] Ralph G. Pearson, "Chemical Hardness and Density Functional Theory," *J.Chem Sci,* 2005, 117(5): 369–77.

[17] M. D. Kogan et al., "Prevalence of Parent-reported Diagnosis of Autism Spectrum Disorder among Children in the U.S.," 2007, *Pediatrics,* 2009, 124(5): 1395–403.

[18] R. M. Shavelle, D. J. Strauss, and J. Pickett, "Causes of Death in Autism," *J Autism Dev Disord,* 2001, 31(6): 569–76.

[19] Centers for Disease Control and Prevention, "In the United States, 17 percent of children have a developmental or behavioral disability such as autism, intellectual disability (also known as mental retardation), or Attention-Deficit/

Hyperactivity Disorder (ADHD). In addition, many children have delays in language or other areas." www.cdc.gov/Features/DetectAutism/.

[20]CDC, National Survey of Children's Health, 2006, "Current Asthma Prevalence Percents by Age, Sex, and Race, United States: Child, 9.3%," www.cdc.gov/asthma/asthmadata.htm.

[21]David Kirby, *Evidence of Harm—Mercury in Vaccines and the Autism Epdemic: A Medical Controversy* (New York: St. Martin's Press, 2005).

[22]Elizabeth Storie, *The Autobiography of Elizabeth Storie, a Native of Glasgow, Who Was Subjected to Much Injustice At the Hands of Some Members of the Medical, Legal and Clerical Professions.* (Glasgow: Richard Stobbs, 1859), 3, 5.

[23]Ibid., 1–2.

PART ONE
CHAPTER 1

[1]Doctors' "new awareness of just how dangerous medicine could be is usefully marked by the coining in 1860 of the phrase *primum non nocere,* 'first do no harm.' The first person to use it was Thomas Inman, who claimed (mistakenly) to be quoting Thomas Sydenham. But the phrase was quickly picked up and attributed not to Sydenham but to Hippocrates—despite the fact that Hippocrates wrote in Greek, not Latin. In reality it is an invention of 1860 and its rapid attribution to Hippocrates represents the invention of a tradition." David Wootton, *Bad Medicine—Doctors Doing Harm Since Hippocrates* (Oxford, England: Oxford University Press, 2006), 181.

[2]Edward Hooper, *The River: A Journey to the Source of HIV and AIDS* (Boston: Little, Brown and Company, 2000), 63.

[3]Randy Shilts, *And the Band Played On* (New York: Penguin Group, 1988), 3.

[4]See especially K. N. Harper et al., "On the Origin of the Treponematoses: A Phylogenetic Approach," *PLoS Negl Trop Dis,* January 15, 2008, 2(1): e148. "Our results lend support to the Columbian theory of syphilis's origin."

[5]Alfred W. Crosby, Jr., *The Columbian Exchange—Biological and Cultural Consequences of 1492* (Westport, Connecticut: Greenwood Press, 1972), 113.

[6]Deborah Hayden, *Pox—Genius, Madness, and the Mysteries of Syphilis* (New York: Basic Books, 2003), 23.

[7]Alexandri Benedetto, *Veronensis physici historiae corporus humani . . .* (1497), quoted in Claude Quetel, *The History of Syphilis* (Baltimore: The Johns Hopkins University Press, 1992), 10.

[8]Jared Diamond, *Guns, Germs, and Steel—The Fate of Human Societies* (New York: W.W. Norton & Company, 1999), 210.

[9]Hayden, *op. cit.,* 172.

[10]Emil Kraepelin, *General Paresis* (New York: The Journal of Nervous and Mental Disease, 1913), 1, 96.

[11]Ibid., 2.

[12]Ibid., 12.

[13]Ibid., 39.

[14]Ibid., 12.

[15]Ibid., 74–75.

[16]John Haslam, *Observations on Madness and Melancholy* (London: G. Hayden, 1809), 260.

[17]Leo Kanner, "Citation Classic—Autistic Disturbances of Affective Contact," *Current Contents,* 1979, 25:14. www.garfield.library.upenn.edu/classics1979/A1979HZ31800001.pdf.

[18]Kraepelin, *op. cit.,* 160, 161.

[19]Ibid., 163–164.

[20]"Syphilis among the Indians is very common, according to the statements of a great number of authors, and it is very frequently, almost proverbially, said by people living near Indian reservations that the great majority of the members of the red race have syphilis." G. S. Adams and Leo Kanner, "General Paralysis Among the North American Indians—A Contribution to Racial Psychiatry," *American Journal of Psychiatry,*1926, 83: 125–33.

[21]Leo Kanner, unpublished autobiography, Archives of the Leo Kanner Collection, courtesy Melvin Sabshin Library &

Archives, American Psychiatric Association.

[22] Adams and Kanner, *op. cit.*

[23] Ibid.

[24] Leo Kanner, unpublished autobiography.

[25] Adams and Kanner, *op. cit.*

[26] Thomas W. Salmon, "General Paralysis as a Public Health Problem," *American Journal of Insanity*, 1914, 71: 41–50.

[27] Adams and Kanner, *op. cit.*

[28] Kraepelin, *op. cit., General Paresis*, 140–141.

[29] E. Kringlen, "A History of Norwegian Psychiatry, *Hist Psychiatry*, September 2004, 15 (59 Pt. 3), 259–83.

[30] Kraepelin, *op. cit.*, 159.

[31] *Dr. Buchan's Domestic Medicine* (Newcastle, England: K. Anderson, 1812), 583–4.

[32] Meriwether Lewis and William Clark, *The History of the Lewis and Clark Expedition, Volume 2*, edited by Elliott Cous (New York: Dover Publications, 1892), 780.

[33] Interview with authors, May 2007.

[34] George Cheever Shattuck, "Lesions of Syphilis in American Indians," *American Journal of Tropical Medicine*, 1938, s1–18 (5): 577–586.

[35] Elisabeth Stawicki, "A Haunting Legacy—Canton Insane Asylum for American Indians," Dec. 9, 1997, www.rootsweb .ancestry.com/~sdlincol/hiawatha.htm.

[36] Cellini, *Autobiography*, I. 28. Cited in *Diseases of Workers* by Bernardino Ramazzini, 1713. Translated by Wilmer Cave Wright. (The University of Chicago Press. Chicago: 1940).

[37] Andrew Mathias, *The Mercurial Disease—An Inquiry into the History and Nature of the Disease Produced in the Human Constitution By the Use of Mercury, with Observations on Its Connexion with the Lues Venera* (London: Printed for J. Callow, Medical Bookseller, 1811), 18–19.

[38] Ibid., ii–iii.

[39] Ramazzini, *op. cit., Diseases of Workers*, 44–45.

[40] Henri Dujardin-Beaumetz, *Clinical Therapeutics—Lectures in Practical Medicine, Delivered in the Hospital St. Antoine, Paris, France,* translated by E. P. Hurd (Detroit: George S. Davis, 1885), 311.

[41] John Emsley, *The Elements of Murder—A History of Poison* (New York: Oxford Universtiy Press, 2005), 71–72.

[42] D. R. De Horne, *Exposition raisonee des differentes methods d'administrer le mercure dans les maladies veneriennes, precede de l'examen des preservatifs* (Paris, 1779). Cited in Quetel, *op. cit., The History of Syphilis*, 85.

[43] Robert Spaethling, *Mozart's Letters, Mozart's Life.* (New York: W.W. Norton & Company, 2000), 69.

[44] Ibid., 430.

[45] Otto Erich Deutsch, *Mozart: A Documentary Biography,* translated by Eric Blom, Peter Branscombe, and Jeremy Noble (Stanford, California: Stanford University Press, 1966), 396.

[46] H. C. Robbins Landon, *1791: Mozart's Last Year* (New York: Thames and Hudson, 1999), 180.

[47] Mozart's first biographer, Franz Niemachek, wrote in German: *Schon in Prag kränkelte und medizinierte Mozart unaufhörlich; seine Farbe war blaß und die Miene traurig, obschon sich sein munterer Humor in der Gesellschaft seiner Freunde doch oft noch in fröhlichem Scherz ergoß.* This phrase has been translated into English in diverse ways. Two typical examples show how slight changes can alter the meaning significantly. From Helen Mautner's translation: "While he was in Prague Mozart became ill and was continually receiving medical attention. He was pale and his expression was sad, although his good humour was often shown in merry jest with his friends." Now, the same phrase from Robert Davies's translation reads: "In Prague Mozart fell ill and dosed himself ceaselessly; his colour was pale and his countenance sad, although his merry sense of humour often bubbled into jesting in the company of his friends." We asked Dieter Walterman, a professional German-English translator, to give us an independent reading. "It's definitely not passive in German," Walterman told us. "Mozart was treating/medicating himself."

[48] Franz Xaver Niemetschek, *Mozart—The First Biography,* translated by Helen Mautner (New York: Berghahn Books, 2007), 33.

[49] Landon, *op. cit., 1791: Mozart's Last Year,* 179.

[50]*The Oxford English Dictionary,* Second edition, CD-Rom Version 3.0 (Oxford, England: Oxford University Press, 2002).

[51]Anton Neumayr, *Music & Medicine—Haydn, Mozart, Beethoven, Schubert* (Bloomington, Illinois: Medi-Ed Express, 1994), 198.

[52]Peter I. Davies, "Mozart's Illnesses and Death—2, The Last Year's and Mozart's Fatal Illness," *The Musical Times,* 1984, 125; 1700: 554–61.

[53]"Pork Chop Killed Mozart," BBC News, June 11, 2001, "Mozart's symptoms, including a fever, rash, limb pain, and swelling, match those brought on by trichinosis, according to Dr. Jan V. Hirschmann of Seattle's Puget Sound Veterans Affairs Medical Center. www.news.bbc.co.uk/2/hi/entertainment/1382537.stm.

[54]Neumayr, *op. cit.,* 188–89.

[55]Landon, *op. cit., 1791: Mozart's Last Year,* 156.

[56]*Collected Essays of Albert Borowitz—Crimes Gone By,* Legal Studies Forum 2005, 29 (2): "Locked in interesting combat with the medical authorities attributing Mozart's death to disease is a substantial body of modern physicians who would support Mozart's own suspicion by declaring that he was indeed poisoned. These doctors, including Dieter Kerner and Gunther Duda of Germany, believe that the poison administered was mercury, which attacks the kidneys and produces much the same diagnostic picture as that presented by the final stages of a natural kidney failure." www.tarlton.law.utexas.edu/lpop/etext/lsf/29-2/salieri.html.

[57]*Gunn's Domestic Medicine, Or, Poor Man's Friend in the Hours of Affliction, Pain, and Sickness.* (New York: C. M. Saxton, Barker & Co., 1860), 432.

[58]E. Esquirol, quoting "Dr. Conolly," in *Mental Maladies: Treatise on Insanity,* translated by E. K. Hunt. (Philadelphia: Lea and Blanchard, 1845), 443.

[59]Ibid., quoting "Doct. Bell, Superintendent of the McLean Asylum, Charlestown, Massachusetts," 444.

[60]Ibid., 439.

[61]George Lewin, *The Treatment of Syphilis With Subcutaneous Sublimate Injections,* translated by Carl Proegler and E. H. Gale (Philadelphia: Lindsay and Blakeston, 1872), vii–viii.

[62]Kraepelin, *op. cit., General Paresis,* 150.

[63]Esquirol, *op. cit.,* 41.

[64]Quetel, *op. cit., The History of Syphilis,* 162–163.

[65]E. Mattauschek and A. Pilcz, "Zweite Mitteilung über 4134 Katamnestisch Verfolgte Falle von Luetisher Infektion, *Ztschr. f. d. ges. Neurol. u. Psychiat,* 1913, Orig. 15, 608.

[66]J. Aebly, "Kritisch-statistische Untersuchungen zur Lues—Metalues—Frage, nebst Bemerkungen über die Anwendung der Statischen Methode in der Medizin," *Arch f. Psyhiatr,* 1920, 61: 693.

[67]Moore, cited in Trygve Gjestland, "The Oslo Study of Untreated Syphilis: An Epidemiological Investigation of the Natural Course of Syphlitic Infection Based Upon a Re-study of the Boeck-Brunsgaard Material," *Acta Derm Venereol,* 35 (Suppl 34).

[68]In *The History of Syphilis,* Quetel cites a 34.7 percent rate of GPI in the 1870s in the patient population at Charenton, France, which specialized in admitting such cases (p. 161). Fred Osview, Richard Munich, and Richard L. Munich, in *Principles of Inpatient Psychiatry* (Philadelphia: Lippincott Williams & Wilkins, 2009) write that "100 years ago, as many as 20% of patients in psychiatric hospitals were there because of the ravages of general paresis of the insane" (p. 82).

[69]Esbern Lomholt, "Another Re-Study of the Boeck-Bruusgaard-Gjestland Material," *Acta-Dermato-Venereologica,* 1957, 37(1): 37–49.

[70]Joseph Earle Moore, *The Modern Treatment of Syphilis* (Baltimore: Charles C. Thomas, 1942), 75.

[71]Ibid., 155.

[72]E. Bruusgaard, "Ueber das Schicksal der Nicht Specifisch Behandelten Luetiker" [The Fate of Syphilitics Who are not Given Specific Treatment], *Arch Dermat und Syph [Archive fur Dermatologie und Syphilis],* 1929, 157: 309–32.

[73]Ernest L. Zimmerman, "A Comparative Study of Syphilis in Whites and in Negroes," *Arch. Dermat. & Syphil,* 1921, 4: 75–88.

[74]R. A. Vonderlehr, et al., "Untreated Syphilis in the Male Negro: A Comparative Study of Treated and Untreated Cases," *Journal of Venereal Disease Information,* 1936, 17: 260–65.

[75]Sidney Olansky, Lloyd Simpson, and Stanley H. Schuman, "Environmental Factors in the Tuskegee Study of Untreated Syphilis," *Public Health Reports,* 1954, 69 (7): 691–98.

[76]Vonderlehr, *op. cit.*

[77]Ibid.

[78]Olansky et. al., *op. cit.*

[79]Stanley H. Schuman, Sidney Olansky, Eunice Rivers, C. A. Smith, and Dorothy S. Rambo, "Untreated Syphilis in the Male Negro—Background and Current Status of Patients in the Tuskegee Study," *Journal of Chronic Diseases,* 1955, 2 (5): 543–58.

[80]Ibid.

[81]J. Sartin and H. Perry, "From Mercury to Malaria to Penicillin: The History of the Treatment of Syphilis at the Mayo Clinic," 1916–1955, *Journal of the American Academy of Dermatology,* 1995, 32 (2 Pt. 1): 255–61.

[82]J. Nielsen, "Follow-up of Syphilitics: Late Manifestations in 467 Male Patients with Early Syphilis Followed for 29–36 Years," *Acta Derm Venereol,* 1950, 30 (6): 507–12.

[83]Trygve Gjestland, "The Oslo Study of Untreated Syphilis: An Epidemiologic Investigation of the Natural Course of Syphilitic Infection Based upon a Re-study of the Boeck-Brunsgaard Material," *Acta Derm Venereol,* 1955, 35 (Suppl 34): 3–368.

[84]Esbern Lomholt, *op. cit.,* "Another Re-Study of the Boeck-Bruusgaard-Gjestland Material."

CHAPTER 2

[1]Sigmund Freud, Three Essays on the Theory of Sexuality (1905). *The Standard Edition of the Complete Psychological Works of Sigmund Freud, Volume VII,* James Strachey, editor (London: The Hogarth Press, 1953), 123–246.

[2]Sigmund Freud, *Dora—An Analysis of A Case of Hysteria* (New York: Touchstone, 1997), 12.

[3]Ibid., 13.

[4]Ibid.

[5]Peter Gay, editor, *The Freud Reader* (London: W.W. Norton & Company, Limited, 1989), 173.

[6]Freud, *op. cit., Dora—An Analysis of A Case of Hysteria,* 14.

[7]Ibid.

[8]Sigmund Freud and Josef Breuer, "Fraulein Elisabeth Von R.," *Studies in Hysteria,* translated by Nikola Luckhurst (London: Penguin Books, 2004), 148.

[9]The use of the word *hysterical* in the nineteenth century eerily presages the term *emotional* to describe parents of autistic children—mostly mothers—who believed their children were vaccine damaged, subtly implying women were more easily swayed by feelings than by science.

[10]Freud, *op. cit., Dora—An Analysis of A Case of Hysteria,* 15.

[11]Ibid. Freud does not give the year of Philipp Bauer's syphilis treatment, but it coincides with Dora's symptoms: he had a detached retina when Dora was "about 10. . . . Some two years later," Freud treated Philipp Bauer with the "energetic course" of syphilis medicine. "When [Dora] was about 12," Freud writes without making any connection, "she began to suffer from hemicranial headaches in the nature of a migraine, and from attacks of nervous coughing."

[12]Ibid., 49.

[13]Ibid., 41.

[14]Ibid., 22–23.

[15]Benedict Carey, "Psychoanalytic Therapy Wins Backing—Though Endangered as Passé, It Can Be Effective," *The New York Times,* Oct. 1, 2009, A20.

[16]George H. Pollock, "Anna O.: Insight, Hindsight, and Foresight," *Anna O.: Fourteen Contemporary Reinterpretations,* Max Rosenbaum and Melvin Muroff, editors (New York: The Free Press, 1984), 32.

[17]Freud, *op. cit., Dora—An Analysis of A Case of Hysteria,* 25.

[18]Ibid., 26.

[19]Camille-Henry Hischmann, *Intoxications et Hystérie* (Paris: 1888).

[20]The Freud Library, 1554–1938: Title List, August C. Long Health Sciences Library, Columbia University, www.library
.cpmc.columbia.edu/hsl/archives/findingaids/freudtitles.html.

[21]Joseph Lister, "On a New Method of Treating Compound Fractures, Abscesses, Etc., with Observations on the
Conditions of Suppuration," *The Lancet,* 1867, 1: 326–29, 357–59, 387–89, 507–09; 2: 95–6.

—"On the Antiseptic Principle in the Practice of Surgery." *The Lancet,* 1867: 2: 353–56, 668–69.

[22]Robert Koch, *Ueber Desinfection, Mitteilungen aus dem Kaiserlichen Gesundheitsamt,* 1881, 1: 234–82.

[23]Joseph Lister, "An Address on Corrosive Sublimate as a Surgical Dressing; delivered at the opening meeting of the
Medical Society of London, Monday, October 20, 1884," *The British Medical Journal,* October 25, 1884, 803–07.

[24]Sigmund Freud, "Über Coca: Centralblatt für die Ges," *Therapie 2,* 1884, 289–314.

[25]Sigmund Freud, "Paris Report," *Standard Edition, Volume I* (London: Vintage, 2001), 8.

[26]A.R.G. Owen, *Hysteria, Hypnosis and Healing—The Work of J. M. Charcot* (New York: Garrett Publications, 1971), 29–38.

[27]Peter D. Kramer, *Freud—Inventor of the Modern Mind* (New York: HarperCollins Publishers, 2006), 37.

[28]Axel Munthe, *The Story of San Michele* (London: John Murray Publishers Ltd., 2004), 214.

[29]Jean-Martin Charcot, *Clinical Lectures on Diseases of the Nervous System Delivered at The Infirmary of La Salpêtrière,*
Volume III, translated by Thomas Savill (London: The New Sydenham Society, 1889).

[30]Ibid., Figures 13, 16, 18, 22–25, 62, 63, 83.

[31]Ibid., Figures 14, 45, 55–61, 64, 65–73, 78, 84–86.

[32]Ibid., Figures 17, 19, 21, 80–82.

[33]Charcot, *op. cit.,* "Appendix I: A Case of Hystero-traumatic Paraplegia Supervening on a Street Accident," 374.

[34]Richard Webster, "Freud, Charcot and Hysteria: Lost in the Labyrinth," from Webster's volume in the Weidenfield
Great Philosophers Series, *Freud* (2003), www.richardwebster.net/freudandcharcot.html.

[35]Charcot, *op. cit.,* Volume II, 199.

[36]Charcot, *op. cit.,* Volume III, 425.

[37]Ibid., Volume III, 232–33.

[38]Paul D. Blanc, *How Everyday Toxins Make People Sick—Toxins at Home and in the Workplace* (Berkeley: University
of California Press, 2006), 147–48.

[39]Francis Xavier Dercum, *A Text-Book on Nervous Diseases* (Philadelphia: Dornan Printer, 1895), 282.

[40]Ibid.

[41]"Observation of a Severe Case of Hemi-Anesthesia in a Hysterical Male," *Standard Edition, Volume* 1, 25–31. Original
citation: *Wien. Med. Wochenschr,* December 4, 1886 (1674–6). Königstein, Ibid., December 11.

[42]Josef Breuer, "Fraulein Anna O.," *Studies in Hysteria, 42.*

[43]Ibid., 27.

[44]Ibid., 28–31.

[45]Ibid., 30.

[46]Eli Lilly Material Data Safety Sheet for Thimerosal, www.scribd.com/doc/23383798/Eli-Lilly-Material-Data-Safety
-Sheet-for-Thimerosal.

[47]Patricia A. D'Itri and Frank M. D'Itri, *Mercury Contamination: A Human Tragedy* (New York: John Wiley & Sons, 1967), 186.

[48]Alice Hamilton, *Industrial Poisons in the United States* (New York: Macmillan, 1925), 243.

[49]Ibid., 242–243.

[50]Robert Storrs, "On Paralysis from the Effects of Mercury as a Medicine," *Provincial Journal,* 1847.

[51]H. H. Hoppe, "Male Hysteria—A Paper Read Before the Academy of Medicine, May 8, 1893," *The Cincinnati
Lancet-Clinic: A Weekly Journal of Medicine and Surgery,* Volume 69, 621.

[52]J. Breuer and S. Freud, "On the Psychical Mechanism of Hysterical Phenomena," *Standard Edition, Volume II,* Studies
in Hysteria, 1–17.

[53]Freud, *op. cit.,* "Fraulein Elisabeth Von R.," 139–40.

[54]Ibid., 144.

[55]Ibid., 148.

[56]Ibid., 149.

[57]Ibid., 152.

[58]Ibid., 156.

[59]Freud and Breuer, op. cit., "Theoretical Issues," *Studies in Hysteria,* 234.

[60]Freud, *op. cit.,* "Fraulein Elisabeth Von R.," 165–6.

[61]Ibid., 166.

[62]"Acute pneumonitis [inflammation of lung tissue] due to mercury vapor, while less common than systemic mercury poisoning, is by no means rare. Young children appear to be especially vulnerable. . . . [Four workers] showed signs of pulmonary irritation: cough, rales, and fever; along with tightness of the chest," writes Leonard J. Goldwater in *Mercury: A History of Quicksilver* (Baltimore: York Press, 1972), 159, 160.

[63]DiagnosisPro www.en.diagnosispro.com/.

[64]Sigmund Freud, "From the History of an Infantile Neurosis [The Wolfman]," *The 'Wolfman' and Other Cases* (New York: Penguin Books, 2003), 282.

[65]Karin Obholzer, *The Wolf-Man Sixty Years Later—Conversations with Freud's Patient,* translated by Michael Snow (London: Routledge & Kegan Paul Ltd., 1982).

[66]Ibid., 46–7.

[67]Freud, *op. cit., The 'Wolfman' and Other Cases,* 274.

[68]Ibid., 274.

[69]Obholzer, *op. cit.,* 48.

[70]Leo Kanner, "In Defense of the Parent," *The New York Times Magazine,* February 4, 1940, 100.

[71]Leo Kanner, *In Defense of Mothers* (Springfield, Illinois: Charles C. Thomas, 1941), 131.

CHAPTER 3

[1]Duncan Leys and Kenneth Cameron, "A Psychiatric Study of Six Cases of Infantile Acrodynia," *British Medical Journal,* 1952, 1:191–193.

[2]Leo Kanner, unpublished autobiography.

[3]Leo Kanner, "Folklore of the Teeth" (New York: The Macmillan Company, 1928).

[4]Ibid.

[5]Ibid., 27.

[6]Ibid., 33.

[7]Ibid.

[8]Ibid., xi.

[9]Leo Kanner, unpublished autobiography.

[10]Wootton, *op. cit., Bad Medicine: Doctors Doing Harm Since Hippocrates,* 26.

[11]Ibid., 7.

[12]Ibid., 21.

[13]Alfred Stille, *Therapeutics and Materia Medica: A Systematic Treatise on the Action and Uses of Medicinal Agents, Including Their Description and History,* Volume II (Philadelphia: Collins, 1860), 790–93.

[14]Thomas Dover, "The Ancient Physician's Legacy," 6th Edition, 1742, in *Thomas Dover's Life and Legacy,* edited and introduced by Kenneth Dewhurst (Metuchen, New Jersey: The Scarecrow Press, 1974), 138.

[15]Kenneth Dewhurst, *The Quicksilver Doctor—The Life and Times of Thomas Dover, Physician and Adventurer* (Bristol, England: John Wright & Sons Ltd., 1957), 156.

[16]Stille, *op. cit.,* 789.

[17]Benjamin Rush, *An Account of the Bilious Yellow Fever as It Appeared in Philadelphia in the Year 1798* (Philadelphia: Printed by Thomas Dobson, 1794).

[18]Ibid.

[19]Robert L. North, "Benjamin Rush, MD: Assassin or Beloved Healer?" *BUMC Proceedings* 2000:13; 45–9.

[20]www.civilwarhome.com/casualties.htm.

[21]Harris L. Coulter, *Divided Legacy: A History of the Schism in Medical Thought,* Vol. 3 (Washington, D.C.: Wehawken Book Co., 1975), 72–3; cited in Jennifer Schmid, "Beautiful Black Poison—The History of Calomel as Medicine in America," *Wise Traditions in Food, Farming and the Healing Art* (2008), 9(2), 17–31.

[22]George M. Beard, *"A Practical Treatise on Nervous Exhaustion (Neurasthenia)—Its Symptoms, Nature, Sequences, Treatment"* (New York: William Wood & Co., 1880), 9.

[23]Ibid., 51.

[24]Charles Rocaz, *Pink Disease (Infantile Acrodynia)* (London: Martin Hopkinson Ltd., 1933).

[25]W. P. Logan, "Mortality from Pink Disease in 1923–47," *The Lancet.* April 9, 1949, 1(6554): 608.

[26]Rocaz, *op. cit.,* 131.

[27]Ibid., 1.

[28]Ibid., 2.

[29]Ibid., 6.

[30]Ibid., 36.

[31]Ibid., p. 28–30.

[32]Josef Warkany and Donald M. Hubbard, "Mercury in the Urine of Children with Acrodynia," *The Lancet,* May 29, 1948, 1(6509): 829.

[33]Warkany and Hubbard, "Adverse Mercurial Reactions in the Form of Acrodynia and Related Conditions," *Am J Dis Child,* March 1951, 81(3): 335–73.

[34]Donald M. Hubbard, "Determination of Mercury in Urine—A Photometric Method Using a New Reagent, Di-Beta-Naphthythiocarbazone," *Ind. Eng. Chem. Anal. Ed.,* 1940, 12(12): 768–71.

[35]Jacob Cholak and Donald M. Hubbard, "Microdetermination of Mercury in Biological Material," *Ind. Eng. Chem. Anal. Ed.,* 1946, 18(2): 149–15.

[36]Warkany and Hubbard, *op.cit.,* "Adverse Mercurial Reactions in the Form of Acrodynia and Related Conditions.

[37]Donald Cheek, "Pink Disease (Infantile Acrodynia)," *The Journal of Pediatrics,* 1953, 42(2): 239–60.

[38]Leys and Cameron, *op. cit.,* "A Psychiatric Study of Six Cases of Infantile Acrodynia."

[39]*Hints to Mothers on the Treatment of their Children—From Teething to Teens,* Eighteenth Edition (London: John Steedman & Co., undated).

[40]Ibid., 72–3.

[41]A 1930 Merck monograph, "Syphilis—Symptomatology Diagnosis and Modern Approved Treatment for the General Practitioner," noted that mercury had taken second place to the arsphenamines but discussed both mercury rubs and injections; describing Mercury Intramuscularly, "Soluble and insoluble salts are used, differing in their action, dosage, and the relation between the dosage and absorption" (p. 27). Thus Van Swieten's liquor survived into its third century as an approved treatment for syphilis.

[42]"John Steedman & Co., Walworth—127 Years of Pharmaceutical Control," *The Pharmaceutical Journal,* November 18, 1939.

[43]Ibid.

[44]Harold Kalter, "Josef Warkany 1902–1992," *Teratology* 48: 1–3, 1993.

[45]Warkany and Hubbard, *op. cit.,* "Mercury in the Urine of Children with Acrodynia."

[46]"Dr. Hirschmann said that in houses where he had had cases of acrodynia, he practically always found that the household had been attacked by influenza." S. Heymann, "Three cases of acrodynia (Pink disease)," *South African Medical Journal,* 1932, 1: 638.

[47]D. Young, "Surgical Treatment of Male Infertility," *J. Rerp Fertil* 1970, 23, 541–2.

[48]W. F. Hendry, R. P. A'Hern, and P. J. Cole, "Was Young's syndrome caused by exposure to mercury in childhood?" *British Medical Journal,* 1993, 307: 1578–82.

[49]N. Shibuya, K. Shibuya, H. Kato, and M. Yanagisawa, "Kawasaki Disease Before Kawasaki at Tokyo University Hospital," *Pediatrics,* August 2002, 110(2 Pt 1): e17.

[50]J. P. Orlowski and R. D. Mercer, "Urine Mercury Levels in Kawasaki Disease," *Pediatrics,* 1980, 66(4): 633–6.

[51]J. Mutter and D. Yeter, "Kawasaki's Disease, Acrodynia, and Mercury," *Curr Med Chem,* 2008, 15(28): 3000–10, Review.

[52]Heather Thiele, Founder, Pink Disease Support Group, 2005, www.lammag.com/reviewsLammagQUECKSILBER.htm.

[53]J. Warkany, "Acrodynia: Postmortem of a Disease," *Am J Dis Child,* 112 (1966), 147–56.

CHAPTER 4

[1]Peter Thorsheim, *Inventing Pollution: Coal, Smoke, and Culture in Britain since 1800* (Athens: Ohio University Press, 2006), 1.

[2]R. Eide, G. B. Wesenberg, and G. Fosse, "Mercury in Primary Teeth in Preindustrial Norway," *Scand J Dent Res,* February 1993,101(1): 1–4.

[3]Helene M. Tvinnereim, Rune Eide, and Gisle Fosse, "Mercury in Primary Teeth from Contemporary Norwegian Children," University of Bergen, Norway, October 2003. www.mercurypoisoningproject.org/pdf/oct2003primaryteeth.pdf.

[4]P. M. Outridge, K. A. Hobson, and J. M. Savelle, "Changes in Mercury and Cadmium Concentrations and the Feeding Behaviour of Beluga (Delphinapterus leucas) near Somerset Island, Canada, During the 20th Century," *Sci Total Environ,* November 1, 2005, 350(1–3): 106–18.

[5]Achim Steiner, United Nations under-secretary general and Environment Program Executive Director, "Mercury Pollution Harms Millions—and Action on Curbing Its Use Is Overdue," *The Guardian,* February 13, 2009, www.guardian.co.uk/environment/2009/feb/13/pollution-waste.

[6]John Evelyn, *Fumifugium: Or the Inconvenience of the Aer and Smoake of London Dissipated Together With some Remedies humbly proposed by John Evelyn Esq; To His Sacred Majestie, and To the Parliament now Assembled,* First Published in 1661 and Reprinted by the National Society of Clean Air (London), 1961, 11–12.

[7]Ibid., 18.

[8]Paul F. Schuster, David P. Krabbenhoft, David L. Naftz et al., "Atmospheric Mercury Deposition during the Last 270 Years: A Glacial Ice Core Record of Natural and Anthropogenic Sources," *Environ. Sci. Technol.* 2002, 36:2303–2310; H. Biester, R. Bindler, A. Martinez-Cortizas; D. R. Engstrom, "Modeling the Past Atmospheric Deposition of Mercury Using Natural Archives," *Environ Sci Technol,* 2007, 41(14): 4851–60.

[9]Biester, Ibid., 2007.

[10]Ibid.

[11]Laurie Garrett and Jane C. S. Long, "2008 Beijing Olympic Games: Cutting through China's Smoke," *Los Angeles Times,* October 7, 2007.

[12]Jim Yardley, "Chinese Dam Projects Criticized for Their Human Costs," *The New York Times,* November 19, 2007.

[13]John Myers, "Mercury Rising in Minnesota Fish," *Duluth News Tribune,* February 17, 2009.

[14]Friedrich Engels, *The Condition of the Working Class in England* (Oxford, England: Oxford University Press, 1999).

[15]James Phillips Kay, *The Moral and Physical Conditions of the Working Classes Employed in the Cotton Manufacture in Manchester* (London: James Ridgway, 1832), 10.

[16]Engels, *op. cit.,* 72.

[17]Ibid., Engels cites: Factories' Enquiry Commission's Reports, 3rd Volume, 118.

[18]Ibid., 118–19.

[19]E. Fuller Torrey, M.D., and Judy Miller, *The Invisible Plague—The Rise of Mental Illness from 1750 to the Present* (New Brunswick, New Jersey: Rutgers University Press, 2001), 345.

[20]Haslam, *op. cit., Observations on Madness and Melancholy,* v.

[21]George Cheyne, *The English Malady: Or, A Treatise of Nervous Diseases of All Kinds, as Spleen, Vapours, Lowness of Spirits, Hypochondriacal, and Hysterical Distempers* (London: G. Strahan in Cornhill, and J. Leake at Bath, 1833), ii.

[22]Torrey, *op. cit.,* 113.

[23]Ibid., 154–56.

[24]Ibid., 328.

[25]Ibid., 330–3.

[26]R. H. Yolken and E. F. Torrey, "Are Some Cases of Psychosis Caused by Microbial Agents? A Review of the Evidence," *Mol Psychiatry,* 2008, 13(5): 470–9.

[27]A. S. Brown, M. D. Begg, S. Gravenstein et al., "Serologic Evidence of Prenatal Influenza in the Etiology of Schizophrenia," *Arch Gen Psychiatry,* 2004, 61(8): 774–80.

[28]M. G. Opler, S. L. Buka, J. Groeger et al., "Prenatal Exposure to Lead, Delta-aminolevulinic Acid, and Schizophrenia: Further Evidence," *Environ Health Perspect,* 2008, 116(11): 1586–90.

[29]John McGrath and James Scott, "Urban Birth Risk and Schizophrenia: A Worrying Example of Epidemiology Where the Data Are Stronger Than the Hypotheses," *Epidemiologica e Psichiatrica Sociale,* 2006, 15(4): 243–46.

[30]George Frederic Still, "Rheumatism," *Common Disorders and Diseases of Childhood* (London: Henry Frowde and Hodder & Stoughton, 1920), 409–85.

[31]George Frederic Still, "The Goulstonian Lectures on Some Abnormal Psychical Conditions in Children," *The Lancet,* 1902, 1:1008–12.

[32]Haslam, *op. cit., Observations on Madness and Melancholy,* 185–87.

[33]Ibid., 188–91.

[34]J. Langdon H. Down, "Observations on an Ethnic Classification of Idiots," *London Hospital Reports,* 3: 1886, 259–62.

[35]J. Langdon H. Down, "On Some of the Mental Affections of Childhood and Youth," J & A Churchill, 1887.

[36]D. A. Treffert, "Dr. J. Langdon Down and Developmental Disorders," 2004. Wisconsin Medical Society. www .wisconsinmedicalsociety.org/savant_syndrome/savant_articles/doctor_down.

[37]Down, *op. cit.,* 1887.

[38]Treffert, *op. cit.,* 2004.

[39]Down, *op. cit.,* 14.

[40]Ibid., 15.

[41]Ibid., 9.

[42]Ibid., 10.

[43]Down focused at length on the teeth and mouth, both in this publication and two others, one in 1862 in *The Lancet* which he called "The Condition of the Mouth in Idiocy," the other a speech he delivered in 1872 called "The Teeth and Mouth in Mental Development." It is hard not to wonder whether this kind of study in the 1860s led doctors to overmanage the processes of dentition and provide teething powder as a medical intervention.

[44]Treffert, *op. cit.,* 2004.

[45]Alessandro Castriota-Scanderbeg and B. Dallapiccolla, "Mental Retardation, X-Linked, Associated with FRA Xq27.3," *Abnormal Skeletal Phenotypes* (Berlin: Springer Berlin Heidelberg, 2005), 757.

[46]L. Kent et al., "Comorbidity of Autistic Spectrum Disorders in Children with Down Syndrome," *Developmental Medicine and Child Neurology,* 1999, 41: 153–58.

[47]Down, *op. cit.,* "Observeration on an Ethnic Classification of Idiots."

[48]Down, *op. cit.,* "On Some of the Mental Affections of Childhood and Youth," 66.

[49]A. E. Mirkinson, "Is Down's Syndrome a Modern Disease?" *The Lancet,* June 13, 1968.

[50]E. Peter Volpe, "Is Down Syndrome a Modern Disease?" *Perspectives in Biology and Medicine,* Spring 1986, 29(3 Pt 1): 423–36.

[51]Ibid.

[52]Down, *op. cit.,* "Observations on an Ethnic Classification of Idiots."

[53]Henry Maudsley, "Is Insanity on the Increase?" *British Medical Journal 1* (1872) 36–39, in Torrey and Miller, *op. cit.,* 80.

[54]"Copy of the Special Report of the Commissioners in Lunacy to the Lord Chancellor on the Alleged Increase of Insanity" (London: Eyre and Spottiswood, 1897), 28.

[55]Torrey and Miller, *op. cit., The Invisible Plague—The Rise of Mental Illness from 1750 to the Present,* 330.

[56]Leo Kanner, *A History of the Care and Study of the Mentally Retarded* (Springfield, Illinois: Charles C. Thomas, 1964), 99.

[57]Ibid., 100.

CHAPTER 5

[1]"Better Grain Yields With New Improved Ceresan," leaflet from Bayer-Semesan Company, Wilmington, Delaware, undated; Frederick L. Wellman papers, MC 347, Special Collections Research Center, North Carolina State University Libraries, Raleigh, North Carolina.

[2]"Morris Selig Kharasch 1895–1957, A Biographical Memoir by Frank H. Westheimer" (Washington, D.C.: National Academy of Sciences, 1960), 123–52.

[3]"Gas Offense in the United States—A Record Achievement," *The Journal of Industrial and Engineering Chemistry,* January 1919.

[4]Julius Stieglitz, "Chemists and the Country's Crisis," *The Journal of Industrial and Engineering Chemistry,* 9 (March 1917), 224.

[5]Quoted in record of The Board of Trustees, University of Chicago, J. Spencer Dickerson, Secretary, "These two expressions are contained in a letter of Mr. Gerald L. Wendt . . ."

[6]Julius Stieglitz, Morris Kharasch, and Martin Hanke, "Preparation of 5,5'-Mercuri-Bis-3-Nitro-4-Hydroxy-Phenyl-Arsonic Acid," *Journal of the American Chemical Society,* 1921, 43(5): 1185–93.

[7]Morris S. Kharasch and Jean F. Piccard, "Aromatic Mercuri-Organic Derivatives," *Journal of the American Chemical Society,* 1920, 42(9): 1855–64.

[8]Morris S. Kharasch and Lyman Chalkley, Jr., "Mercuri-Organic Derivatives: II. Nitrobenzene Mercury Compounds; an Indirect Method of Mercurizing Organic Compounds," *Journal of the American Chemical Society,* 1920, 43(1–6): 607–12.

[9]*The New York Times,* April 11, 1952.

[10]Ibid., October 11, 1957.

[11]United States Patent and Trademark Office Trademarks Database. Filing date May 13, 1929, for Ceresan.

[12]Benjamin Koehler, "Seed Treatments for the Control of Certain Seed Diseases of Wheat, Oats, Barley," *University of Illinois Agricultural Experiment Station, Bulletin 420* (Urbana, Illinois: 1935).

[13]Ibid.

[14]Robert Aycock, personal communication.

[15]*op. cit.,* "Better Grain Yields with New Improved Ceresan," Wellman Archive.

[16]R. M. Lindgren, T. C. Scheffer, and A. D. Chapman, "Tests of Chemical Treatments for Control of Sap-Stain and Mold in Southern Lumber," *Industrial and Engineering Chemistry,* 1933, 25(1): 72–5.

[17]Philip C. Wakely, "A Biassed [sic] History of the Southern Forest Experiment Station Through 1933," published by the Southern Forest Experiment Station.

[18]Waldemar Kaempffert, "Experiments With Deadly War Gases Result in Compounds That Will Save Many Lives," *The New York Times,* March 3, 1946, E9.

[19]Rachel Carson, *Silent Spring* (New York: Mariner Books, 2002), 80.

[20]Ibid., 16, 17.

[21]Patent U.S. 1672615.

[22]"Serum Averts Diphtheria – Behring Has Now Made Treatment Preventive as Well as Curative," *The New York Times,* December 7, 1913.

[23]Ibid.

[24]W. Atkinson, J. Hamborsky, L. McIntyre, S. Wolfe, eds. (2007), *Diphtheria*. In: *Epidemiology and Prevention of Vaccine-Preventable Diseases* (*The Pink Book*, 10th ed.), Washington D.C.: Public Health Foundation. pp. 59–70. Cited in Wikipedia – Diptheria. www.wikipedia.org/wiki/Diphtheria#cite_note-Pinkbook-4.

[25]"City Starte Drive to End Diphtheria—Wynne Opens Campaign at the Bellevue Yorkville Center as 3 Infants Get Injections—44 Stations Open Today—All Parents Urged to Bring Young Children in for Free Immunization Treatments," *The New York Times,* January 19, 1929.

[26]"Diphtheria Deaths Rise," *The New York Times,* May 16, 1932.

[27]"Diphtheria Toxoid Announced By Parran—Agent for Use With Children Under 10 is Held to Be More Effective Than Toxin-Antitoxin," *The New York Times,* May 16, 1932.

[28]"Toxoid Instead of Toxin-Antitoxin," Weekly Bulletin, New York City Department of Health 21 (48:377): December 3, 1932.

[29]"Report of the Health Department—1931," Baltimore, Maryland, 69. The report notes: "On October 1 the Bureau of Child Welfare began the use of diphtheria toxoid exclusively in all their clinics."

[30]Cynthia Crossen, "How Elixir Deaths Led U.S. to Require Proof of New Drugs' Safety," *The Wall Street Journal,* October 3, 2005.

[31]H. M. Powell and W. A. Jamieson, "Merthiolate As a Germicide," *American Journal of Hygiene,* 1931, 13: 296–310.

[32]Augustus Wadsworth, James J. Quigley, and Gretchen R. Sickles, "The Purification and Concentration of Diphtheria Toxoid," *J Exp Med,* 1932, 4: 815–28.

[33]Donald Hunter, Richard R. Bomford, and Dorothy S. Russell, "Poisoning by Methyl Mercury Compounds," *QJM,* 1940, 9: 193–226.

[34]Ake Swensson and Ulf Ulfvarson, "Toxicology of Organic Mercury Compounds Used as Fungicides," *Occup Health Rev,* 1963 (15): 5–11.

[35]K. Borg, H. Wanntorp, K. Erne, and E. Hanko, "Alkyl Mercury Poisoning in Terrestrial Sweden Wildlife," *Viltrevy,* January 1, 1960, 6(4): 301–79.

[36]S. Jensen and A. Jernelov, "Biological Methylation of Mercury in Aquatic Organisms," *Nature,* 1969, 223: 753–54.

[37]Laman Amin-Zaki, M. A. Majeed, Michael R. Greenwood et al., "Methylmercury Poisoning in the Iraqi Suckling Infant: A Longitudinal Study over Five Years," *Journal of Applied Toxicology,* 1981, 1(4): 210–14.

[38]Lionel K. A. Derban, "Outbreak of Food Poisoning Due to Alkyl-Mercury Fungicide On Sountern Ghana State Farm," *Arch Environ Health,* 1974, 28: 49–52.

[39]Y. Takizawa, "Studies on the Niigata Episode of Minamata Disease Outbreak: Investigation of Causative Agents of Organic Mercury Poisoning in the District along the River Agano," *Acta Med Biol* (Niigata),1970, 17(4): 293–7.

[40]Ibid.

[41]Y. Takizawa et al., "Studies on the Cause of the Niigata Episode of Minamata Disease Outbreak," *Acta Med Biol* (Niigata), 1972, 19(3): 193–206.

[42]Y. Hoshino, H. Kumashiro, Y. Yashima et al., "The Epidemiological Study of Autism in Fukushima-ken," *Folia Psychiatr Neurol Jpn,* 1982, 36(2): 115–24.

[43]Ibid.

[44]Frederick L. Wellman papers, NCSU.

[45]Frederick L. Wellman, "Hot Water and Mercuric Chloride Treatments of Some Brassica Seeds and Their Effect Both on the Germination of Seeds and the Viability of the Fungus Phoma Lingam," graduate paper written at University of Wisconsin, dated Spring 1922, Wellman papers, NCSU.

[46]Wellman resume, 14.

[47]Memorabilia folder, Wellman papers, NCSU.

[48]Public Health Statement for Mercury, Agency for Toxic Substances and Disease Registry, Department of Health and Human Services, March 1999. www.atsdr.cdc.gov/toxprofiles/phs46.html.

[49]C. Kay-Scott (Frederick Creighton Wellman), *Life Is Too Short, An Autobiography* (New York: J. B. Lippincott Company, 1943).

[50]Frederick L. Wellman, *Plant Diseases–An Introduction For the Layman* (Garden City, New York: The Natural History Press, 1971), 5.

[51]Leo Kanner, "Autistic Disturbances of Affective Contact," *The Nervous Child* (April 1943).

PART TWO

CHAPTER 6

[1] Leo Kanner, *op. cit.,* "Autistic Disturbances of Affective Contact."

[2] Wendell Muncie, *Psychobiology and Psychiatry* (St. Louis: The C.V. Mosby Company, 1939), 9.

[3] Ibid., 24.

[4] Ibid., xvii.

[5] Harold C. Stuart, M.D., and Staff, "Studies from the Center for Research in Child Health and Development, School of Public Health, Harvard University. I. The Center, the Group Under Observation, Sources of Information, and Studies in Progress," Monographs of the Society for Research in Child Development, Volume IV, No. 1 (Serial No. 20), published by Society for Research in Child Development, National Research Council, Washington, D.C., 1939.

[6] Augustus S. Rose, Laurence D. Trevett, Joseph A. Hindle et al., "Penicillin Treatment of Neurosyphilis—Preliminary Report of Seventy Cases followed from Four to Twelve Months," *American Journal of Syphilis, Gonorrhea, and Venereal Diseases,* 29(5): September 1945.

[7] William J. French, "Place of Maternal and Child Health Services in a Generalized Program in a Health Unit," *American Journal of Public Health,* May 1941, 31(5): 465–70. French writes, "The latter part of 1939 the Children's Bureau of the Department of Labor inquired whether the Anne Arundel County Health Department would be interested in adding delivery and pediatric services to our program."

[8] *Annapolis Capitol,* April 16, 1947, 5.

[9] Kanner, *op. cit.,* "Autistic Disturbances of Affective Contact," 231.

[10] Information on the Triplett family is from interviews with Don and O. B. Triplett and Leo Kanner's case study in *Autistic Disturbances.*

[11] Interview with O. B. Triplett.

[12] Leo Kanner, *op. cit.,* "Citation Classic."

[13] Kanner, *op. cit.*

[14] Leo Kanner letter to Ernest Harms, January 19, 1942, in APA archives.

[15] Leo Kanner, "Editor's Introduction," *The Nervous Child,* 1943, (2)2: 216.

[16] "Wisconsin Pathogen—Issued Occasionally from the Plant Pathology Department of the University of Wisconsin, Madison," Feb. 15, 1930.

[17] "Science: Du Pont vs. Pests," *Time* magazine, April 19, 1937.

[18] L. R. Jones, J. C. Walker, and W. B. Tisdale, "Fusarium Resistant Cabbage," *Research Bulletin* 48, Agricultural Experiment Station of the University of Wisconsin, November 190.

[19] Ernest E. Hubert, "The Protection of Jointed Wood Products Against Decay and Stain," *The University of Ohio Bulletin* (Moscow, Idaho: 1934), 29(5): 3–36.

[20] Ibid.

[21] Ibid.

[22] Kanner, *op. cit.,* "Autistic Disturbances of Affective Contact."

[23] William D. Miller and T. E. Maki, "Planting Pines in Pocosins," *Journal of Forestry,* September 1937.

[24] Maki cited in "Biassed History," p. 123, "T. E. Maki (generally 'Waldy,' but still 'Tenyo' to a few old friends) is now Hoffman [sic] Distinguished Professor of Forest Management and head of the Department of Silviculture, School of Forestry, at North Carolina College."

[25] U.S. Census, 1930.

[26] Mary C. Schwab, "Krebs, Mitchell Share History of Bienville Lumber Co.," *The Scott County Times,* April 13, 2005, 5B.

[27] Southern Forest Experiment Station, Annual Report, 1933, 37.

[28] Report of the [Baltimore] Health Department, 1933, p. 107, "On January first a new educational project in the form of a special greeting card was inaugurated," sent to infants' families when they turned six months—about 33 cards a day. David Speck, by then living in Baltimore with his mother, would have been just over 6 months old on January 1.

[29]Ibid., 108.

[30]"Elizabeth Fee, "Partners in Community Health: The Baltimore City Health Department, the Johns Hopkins School of Hygiene and Public Health, and the Eastern Health District, 1932–1992," *Maryland Medical Journal*, 1993, 42(8): 735–44.

[31]"Baltimore Experiment in Public Health Work," *The Baltimore Sun*, Ocotober 23, 1938, quoted in Fee, "Partners in Community Health."

[32]P. C. Bucy and W. S. Muncie, "Neuroepithelioma of the Cerebellum," *American Journal of Pathology*, 1929, 5(2): 157–70.

[33]Kanner, *op. cit.*, "Autistic Disturbances of Affective Contact."

[34]Ibid.

[35]W. Freeman, T. C. Fong, and S. J. Rosenberg, "The Diathermy Treatment of Dementia Paralytica: Microscopic Changes in Treated Cases, *Journal of the American Medical Association*, 1933, 100(22): 1749–53.

[36]W. K. Stewart et al., "Urinary Mercury Excretion and Proteinuria in Pathology Laboratory Staff," *British Journal of Industrial Medicine*, 1977, 34: 26–31.

[37]Interview with authors, August 12, 2005, Forest, Mississippi.

[38]William Fowler, "State Diphtheria Immunization Requirements—Comparative Analysis of Statutes and Health Department Regulations," *Public Health Reports*, 1942, 57(10).

[39]Kanner, *op. cit.*, "Autistic Disturbances of Affective Contact."

[40]Louise Despert to Leo Kanner, undated letter, APA archives.

[41]Louise Despert to Leo Kanner, July 12, 1943, letter, APA archives.

[42]Leo Kanner to Louise Despert, July 15, 1943, letter, APA archives.

[43]Ibid.

[44]Kanner, *op. cit.*, "Autistic Disturbances of Affective Contact."

[45]"By these criteria, the human childhood stage of life spans the time from about 3 to 7 years of age," Barry Bogin, "Evolutionary Hypotheses for Human Childhood," *Yearbook of Physical Anthropology* (1997), 40: 63–89.

[46]R. A. Q. Lay, "Schizophrenia-Like Psychoses in Young Children," *Journal of Mental Science*, 1938, 84: 105–33.

[47]Darold A. Treffert, "Dr. J. Landon Down and Developmental Disorders," www.wisconsinmedicalsociety.org/savant_syndrome/savant_articles/doctor_down.

[48]Lorna Wing, "The History of Ideas on Autism: Legends, Myths, and Reality," *Autism*, 1997, (1)1: 13–23.

[49]Roy Richard Grinker, *Unstrange Minds—Remapping the World of Autism* (New York: Basic Books, 2007), 52.

[50]Kanner, *op. cit.*

[51]George C. Darr and Frederic G. Worden, "Case Report Twenty-Eight Years After an Infantile Autistic Disorder," *The American Journal of Orthopsychiatry*, July 1951, 21(3): 559–70.

[52]Kanner, *op. cit.*, "Autistic Disturbances of Affective Contact."

[53]L. Witmer, "Orthogenic Cases, XIV-Don: A Curable Case of Arrested Development Due to a Fear Psychoses the Result of Shock in a Three Year Old Infant [sic]," *Psychol Clinic*, 1919–22, 13, 97–111.

[54]Mitzi Waltz and Paul Shattock, "Autistic Disorder in Nineteenth-century London—Three Case Reports," *Autism: The International Journal of Research and Practice*, March 2004, 8(1): 7–20.

[55]Nicole Simon, "Kasper Hauser's Recovery and Autopsy: A Perspective on Neurological and Sociological Requirements for Language Development," *Journal of Autism and Childhood Schizophrenia*, 1978, 8(2): 209–17.

[56]Ibid.

[57]Harlan Lane, *The Wild Boy of Aveyron* (Cambridge, Massachusetts: Harvard University Press, 1976), 176.

[58]Ibid., 177.

[59]Ibid., 178.

[60]*The Animal Kingdom or Zoological System of the Celebrated Sir Charles Linnaeus*, trans. with additions by Robert Kerr, 1792, cited in Michael Newtown, *Savage Girls and Wild Boys, a History of Feral Children* (New York: Picador, 2002), 38.

[61]Bernard Rimland, written statement on behalf of the Autism Research Institute.

[62]Hans Asperger, " 'Autistic Psychopathy' in Childhood," 1944. Translated and annotated in Uta Frith, editor, *Autism and Asperger Syndrome* (Cambridge, England: Cambridge University Press: 1991), 37–92.

[63]Ibid.

[64]Roy Richard Grinker, *op. cit., Unstrange Minds—Remapping the World of Autism* (New York: Basic Books, 2007), 57, 58.

[65]Charles N. Leach, Claus Jensen, and Georg Poch, "Diphtheria Immunization with a Single Injection of Highly Purified Formol-Toxoid and Al(Oh)3," *The Journal of Clinical and Laboratory Medicine,* 1935, 20(5): 451–59.

[66]Kanner, *op. cit.,* "Autistic Disturbances of Affective Contact," 2002.

[67]Interview with O. B. Triplett, Forest, Mississippi, August 12, 2005.

[68]Leon Eisenberg, "The Autistic Child in Adolescence," *The American Journal of Psychiatry,* 1956, 112: 607–12.

[69]Leo Kanner, "Follow-Up Study of 11 Autistic Children Originally Reported in 1943," *J Autism Child Schizophr,* 1971, 1: 119–45.

[70]Adams and Kanner, *op. cit.,* "General Paralysis Among the North American Indians—A Contribution to Racial Psychiatry," 1926.

[71]Kanner, Citation Classic.

[72]Robert K. Merton and Elinor Barber, *The Travels and Adventures of Serendipity* (Princeton, New Jersey: Princeton University Press, 2004), 174.

CHAPTER 7

[1]E. Fuller Torrey, *Freudian Fraud—The Malignant Effect of Freud's Theory on American Culture and Thought* (Bethesda, Maryland: Lucas Books, 1992), 257.

[2]D. A. Van Krevelen, *Early Infantile Autism, Z. f. Kinderpsychiat,* 1952, 19: 91–7, cited in Rimland, "Infantile Autism."

[3]Van Krevelen, personal communication, January 7, 1963, in Rimland, "Infantile Autism," 37.

[4]Para-acetylaminebenzoate, also called deaner, is "a precursor of acetylcholine which is essential to the transmission of impulses between neurons." Frederick Lemere and James A. Laseter, "Deanol (Deaner): A New Cerebral Stimulant for the Treatment of Neurasthenia and Mild Depression—A Preliminary Report," *American Journal of Psychiatry,* 1958, 114: 655–56.

[5]Kanner, *op. cit.,* "Autistic Disturbances of Affective Contact."

[6]Leo Kanner, "Irrelevant and Metaphorical Language in Early Infantile Autism," 1946. *American Journal of Psychiatry,* 1994, 151(6 Suppl): 161–4.

[7]Ibid.

[8]Leo Kanner, "Problems of Nosology and Psychodynamics of Early Infantile Autism," *American Journal of Orthopsychiatry,* 1949, 19(3): 416–26.

[9]Ibid.

[10]Leo Kanner, "Emotional Interference with Intellectual Functioning," *Am J Ment Defic,* 1952, 56(4): 701–7.

[11]Leo Kanner and Leon Eisenberg, "Early Infantile Autism, 1943–55," *Psychiatr Res Rep Am Psychiatr Assoc.* 1957, (7): 55–6.

[12]Leo Kanner, "To What Extent Is Early Infantile Autism Determined by Constitutional Inadequacies?" *Res Publ Assoc Res Nerv Ment Dis,* 1954, 33: 378–85.

[13]Kanner and Eisenberg, "Early Infantile Autism," 1943–1955.

[14]Leo Kanner and L. I. Lesser, *Early Infantile Autism, Pediatr Clin North Am* 1958, 5(3): 711–30.

[15]Kanner and Eisenberg, "Early Infantile Autism," 1943–1955.

[16]Leo Kanner, "The Specificity of Early Infantile Autism," *Acta Paedopsychiatrica* 1958, 25: 108–13.

[17]Victor Lotter, "Epidemiology of Autistic Conditions in Young Children, I. Prevalence," *Social Psychiatry Research Unit,* 1966,1: 124–37.

[18]D. A.Treffert, personal communication, July 2, 2009.

[19]D. A. Treffert, personal communication, July 2, 2009.

[20]E. Fuller Torrey, Stephen P. Hersh, and Kinne D. McCabe, "Early Childhood Psychosis and Bleeding during Pregnancy—A Prospective Study of Gravid Women and Their Offspring," *Journal of Autism and Childhood Schizophrenia,* 1975, (5)4: 287–97.

[21]M. F. Blaxill, "What's Going On? The Question of Time Trends in Autism," *Public Health Rep,* Nov-Dec 2004, 119(6): 536–51.

[22]V. J. Lotter, "Childhood Autism in Africa," *Child Psychol Psychiatry,* July 1978, 19(3): 231–44.

[23]C. I . Longe, "Four Cases of Infantile Autism in Nigerian Children," *African Journal of Psychiatry,* 1976, 2: 161–75.

[24]M. Dhadphale, M. G. Lukwago, and M. Gajjar, "Infantile Autism in Kenya," *Indian J Pediatr,* Jan–Feb 1982, 49(396): 145–8.

[25]Quoted in Edward Dolnick, *Madness on the Couch*—Blaming the Victim in the Heyday of Psychoanalysis," (New York: Simon & Schuster, 1981), 216.

[26]Richard Pollak, *The Creation of Dr. B.—A Biography of Bruno Bettelheim* (New York: Touchstone Books, 1977), 25.

[27]Bruno Bettelheim, "Schizophrenia as a Reaction to Extreme Situations," *The American Journal of Orthopsychiatry,* 1956, 26(3): 507–18.

[28]Bruno Bettelheim, *The Empty Fortress—Infantile Autism and the Birth of the Self* (New York: The Free Press, 1967), 65.

[29]Pollak, *op. cit.*

[30]Bruno Bettelheim, "Joey: A 'Mechanical Boy,' " *Scientific American,* 1959, 200: 116–27. Adapted in *The Empty Fortress.*

[31]Ibid., 238–39.

[32]Ibid., 242.

[33]Ibid., 66.

[34]Mary Coleman and Bernard Rimland, "Familial Autism," *The Autistic Syndromes,* Mary Coleman, editor (Amsterdam, The Netherlands: North-Holland Publishing Company, 1976), 175–82.

[35]Lucille Wiedel and Mary Coleman, "The Autistic and Control Population of This Study—Demographic, Historical and Attitudinal Data," *The Autistic Syndromes,* 15.

[36]Ibid.

[37]Thomas Felicetti, "Parents of Autistic Children: Some Notes on a Chemical Connection," *Milieu Therapy,* 1981, 1: 13–16.

[38]Dan Olmsted, "The Age of Autism: Something Wicked—1," United Press International, August 16, 2006.

[39]Christopher Gillberg and Mary Coleman, *The Biology of the Autistic Syndromes,* 3rd Edition (Cambridge, England: Cambridge University Press, 2000), 108.

[40]C. Swan, A. L. Tostevin, B. Moore et al., "Congenital Defects in Infants Following Infectious Diseases During Pregnancy," *Med J,* August 1943, 2: 201–10.

[41]R. C. Beswick, R. Warner, and J. Warkany, "Congenital Anomalies Following Maternal Rubella," *Am J Dis Child,* 1949, 78(3): 334–48.

[42]"Congenital Cataract Following German Measles in the Mother," *The Medical Journal of Australia,* December 6, 1941. "The series is so striking," the journal editors wrote, "and the sight of the children is so seriously affected that the facts must be made known without undue delay to the general body of the medical profession."

[43]H. O. Lancaster, "Deafness as an Epidemic Disease in Australia: A Note on Census and Institutional Data," *British Medical Journal,* 1951, 2(4745): 1429–32.

[44]E. S. Levine, "Psychoeducational Study of Children Born Deaf Following Maternal Rubella in Pregnancy, *AMA Am J Dis Child,* 1951, 81(5): 627–35. B. H. Kirman, "Rubella as a Cause of Mental Deficiency," *The Lancet,* 1955, 26;269(6900): 1113–5. R. Lundstrom and S. Ahnsjo, "Mental Development Following Maternal Rubella: A Follow-up Study of Children Born in 1951–1952," *Acta Paediatr Suppl,* 1962, 135: 153–9.

[45]Levine, op cit; M. A. Menser, L. Dods, and J. D. Harley, "A Twenty-Five-Year Follow-up of Congenital Rubella," *The Lancet,* 1967, 23;2 (7530): 1347–50. M. D. Sheridan, "Final Report of a Prospective Study of Children Whose Mothers Had Rubella in Early Pregnancy," *British Medical Journal,* 1964, 2(5408): 536–9.

[46]Menser, *op. cit.* E. D. McIntosh and M. A. Menser, "A Fifty-year Follow-up of Congenital Rubella," *The Lancet,* August 15, 1992, 340(8816): 414–5. J. M. Forrest and F. M. Turnbull et al., "Gregg's Congenital Rubella Patients 60 Years Later, *Med J Aust,* 2002, 177(11-12): 664–7.

[47]D. M. Bindon, "Make-a-Picture Story Test Findings for Rubella Deaf Children," *Journal of Abnormal Psychology,* July 1957, 55(1): 38–42. Sheridan, *op. cit.*

[48]J. T. Grayson and R. H. Watten, "Epidemic Rubella in Taiwan, 1957–1958. III. Gamma Globulin in the Prevention of Rubella," *New England Journal of Medicine,* December 1959, 3; 261: 1145–50.

[49]Janet B. Hardy, "Fetal Consequences of Maternal Viral Infections in Pregnancy," *Arch Otolaryngol,* 1973, 98(4): 218–27.

[50]M. M. Desmond, G. S. Wilson, J. L. Melnick et al., "Congenital Rubella Encephalitis: Course and Early Sequelae, *Journal of Pediatrics,* 1967, 71(3): 311–31.

[51]S. Chess, "Autism in Children with Congenital Rubella, *J Autism Child Schizophr,* 1971, 1(1): 33–47.

[52]L. Z. Cooper and S. Krugman, "Clinical Manifestations of Postnatal and Congenital Rubella, *Arch Ophthalmol,* 1967, 77(4): 434–9.

[53]F. R. Lock, H. B. Gatling, C. H. Mauzy, and H. B. Wells, "Incidence of Anomalous Development Following Maternal Rubella: Effect of Clinical Infection or Exposure and Treatment with Gamma Globulin," *Am J Obstet Gynecol,* March 1961, 81: 451–64.

[54]Jennifer M. Best, Carlos Castillo-Solorzano, John S. Spika et al., "Reducing the Global Burden of Congenital Rubella Syndrome," report of the World Health Organization steering committee on research related to measles and rubella vaccines and vaccination, June 2004.

[55]Salah Al-Awaidy, Ulla K. Griffiths, Hosammudin Mohammed Nwar et al., "Costs of Congenital Rubella Syndrome (CRS) in Oman: Evidence Based on Long-term Follow-up of 43 Children," *Vaccine,* 2006, 24: 6437–45.

[56]Tatiana M. Lanzieri, Maria S. Parise, Marilda M. Siqueira et al., "Incidence, Clinical Features, and Estimated Costs of Congenital Rubella Syndrome After a Large Rubella Outbreak in Recife, Brazil, 1999–2000, *Journal of Pediatric Infectious Disease,* 2004, 23: 1116–22.

[57]Robert C. Beswick, Robert Warner, and Josef F. Warkany, "Congenital Anomalies Following Maternal Rubella, *Am J Dis Child,* 1949, 78(3): 334–48.

[58]Bernard Rimland, *Infantile Autism—The Syndrome and Its Implications for a Neural Theory of Behavior* (Englewood Cliffs, N. J.: Prentice Hall, 1964).

[59]Edward Dolnick, *op. cit., Madness on the Couch,* 221.

[60]Ibid., 219.

[61]Rimland, *op. cit.,* 60.

[62]Ibid., 62.

[63]Leo Kanner, S. Spafford Ackerly Lecture, May 16, 1972, 9–10.

[64]Ibid., 9.

[65]Bruno Bettelheim, "Where Self Begins," *The New York Times,* February 12, 1967, 243.

[66]"In Brief," *The New York Times,* February 26, 1967, BR23.

[67]Eliot Fremont-Smith, "Children Without an 'I,'" *The New York Times,* March 10, 1967, 37.

[68]"For Summer Reading," *The New York Times,* June 4, 1967.

[69]Bernard Rimland, Letter to the Editor, *The New York Times,* March 12, 1967, 241.

[70]"Mr. Leo Kanner accepts a citation presented during N.S.A.C.'s Annual Meeting July 17–19, 1969 (Transcribed from a tape recording)," courtesy Stephen Edelson, Autism Research Institute.

[71]Rimland, *op. cit., Infantile Autism—The Syndrome and Its Implications for a Neural Theory of Behavior,* 54.

[72]Coleman and Rimland, *op. cit.,* "Familial Autism," 176.

[73]S. Folstein and M. Rutter, "Infantile Autism: A Genetic Study of 21 Twin Pairs," *J Child Psychol Psychiatry,* September 1977, 18(4): 297–321.

[74]Ibid.

[75]E. R. Ritvo, B. J. Freeman, A. Mason-Brothers et al., "Concordance for the Syndrome of Autism in 40 Pairs of Afflicted Twins," *American Journal of Psychiatry,* January 1985, 142(1): 74–7.

[76]Jay Joseph, *The Missing Gene—Psychiatry, Heredity, and the Fruitless Search for Genes* (Algora Publishing, 2006), 160.

[77]S. E. Folstein and J. Piven, "Etiology of Autism: Genetic Influences," *Pediatrics*, May 1991, 87(5 Pt 2): 767–73.

[78]S. Steffenburg et al., "A Twin Study of Autism in Denmark, Finland, Iceland, Norway, and Sweden," *J Child Psychol Psychiatry*, May 1989, 30(3): 405–16.

[79]A. Bailey et al., "Autism as a Strongly Genetic Disorder: Evidence from a British Twin Study," *Psychol Med*, January 1995, 25(1): 63–77.

[80]Steffenberg, *op. cit.*

[81]Joseph, *op. cit., The Missing Gene*, 162-163

[82]Bailey et al., *op. cit.*

[83]Hiroko Taniai, Takeshi Nishiyama, Taishi Miyachi et al., "Influences on the Broad Spectrum of Autism: Study of Proband-Ascertained Twins," *American Journal of Medical Genetics Part B (Neuropsychiatric Genetics)* 147B:844–849 (2008).

[84]Michael Rutter, "Biological Implications of Gene-Environment Interaction," *Journal of Abnormal Child Psychology*, DOI 10.1007/s10802-008-9256-2.

CHAPTER 8

[1]Irva Hertz-Picciotto quoted by Marla Cone in "Autism Epidemic Not Caused by Shifts in Diagnoses; Environmental Factors Likely," *Environmental Health News*, January 9, 2009. www.environmentalhealthnews.org/ehs/news/autism-and-environment.

[2]CDC Surveillance and Research Studies in Autism and Other Developmental Disabilities, September 21, 2004, North Shore Autism Support Center Conference, Danvers, Massachusetts.

[3]Bobbie Gallagher, interview with authors, December 8, 2007.

[4]Linda A. Johnson, "U.S. Investigates Possible Autism Cluster," The Associated Press, January 19, 1999.

[5]Agency for Toxic Substances and Disease Registry, Department of Health and Human Services, Public Health Assessment, Brick Township Investigation, November 19, 2000, prepared by Superfund Site Assessment Branch, Division of Health Assessment and Consultation, Agency for Toxic Substances and Disease Registry, www.atsdr.cdc.gov/HAC/pha/brick/bti_toc.html.

[6]J. Bertrand et al., "Prevalence of Autism in a United States Population: The Brick Township, New Jersey, Investigation," *Pediatrics*, 2001, 108: 1155–61.

[7]California Department of Developmental Services (1999), "Changes in the Population of Persons with Autism and Pervasive Developmental Disorders in California's Developmental Services System: 1987 through 1998," A Report to the Legislature, Department of Developmental Services, Sacramento, California.

[8]E. Fombonne, "Is There an Epidemic of Autism?" *Pediatrics*, 2001, 107: 411–13.

[9]Ibid.

[10]R. S. Byrd et al., "Report to the Legislature on the Principal Findings from the Epidemiology of Autism in California: A Comprehensive Pilot Study," Davis (CA): MIND Institute, October 17, 2002.

[11]California Department of Developmental Services, "Autistic Spectrum Disorders: Changes in the California Caseload, an Update: 1999 through 2002," Sacramento: California Health and Human Services Agency, Department of Developmental Services, 2003.

[12]L. A. Croen et al., "The Changing Prevalence of Autism in California," *Journal of Autism and Developmental Disorders*, 2002, 32: 207–15.

[13]Eric Fombonne, Editorial Commentary, *Journal of Autism and Developmental Disorders*, 2002, 32(3): 151–52.

[14]Mark F. Blaxill, David S. Baskin, and Walter O. Spitzer, Commentary: Blaxill, Baskin, and Spitzer on Croen et al. (2002), "The Changing Prevalence of Autism in California," *Journal of Autism and Developmental Disorders*, 2003, 33(2).

[15]L. A. Croen and J. K. Grether, Response: A Response to Blaxill, Baskin, and Spitzer on Croen et al. (2002), "The Changing Prevalence of Autism in California," *Journal of Autism and Developmental Disorders,* 2003, 33: 227–9.

[16]J. G. Gurney et al., "Analysis of Prevalence Trends of Autism Spectrum Disorder in Minnesota," *Arch Pediatr Adolesc Med,* 2003, 157: 622–7.

[17]C. J. Newschaffer, M. D. Falb, and J. G. Gurney, "National Autism Prevalence Trends from United States Special Education Data, *Pediatrics,* March 2005, 115(3): e277–82.

[18]H. Jick, J. A. Kaye, and C. Black, "Changes in Risk of Autism in the U.K. for Birth Cohorts 1990–1998," *Epidemiology,* 2003, 14(5): 630–2.

[19]M. F. Blaxill, "Study Fails to Establish Diagnostic Substitution as a Factor in Increased Rate of Autism," *Pharmacotherapy,* 2004, 24(6): 812–3, author reply, 813–5.

[20]W. J. Barbaresi, et al., "The Incidence of Autism in Olmsted County, Minnesota, 1976–1997: Results from a Population-based Study," *Arch Pediatr Adolesc Med,* 2005, 159(1): 37–44.

[21]Blaxill, *op. cit.,* "What's Going On?"

[22]F. R. Volkmar, A. Klin, and D. J. Cohen, "Diagnosis and Classification of Autism and Related Conditions: Consensus and Issues," in D. J. Cohen and F. R. Volkmar, editors, *Handbook of Autism and Pervasive Developmental Disorders,* 2nd ed. (New York: John Wiley and Sons, 1997), 5–40.

[23]Byrd et al., Report to the Legislature.

[24]M. F. Blaxill, "Any Changes in Prevalence of Autism Must Be Determined," *BMJ,* February 2002, 324(7332): 296.

[25]L. Burd et al., "A Prevalence Methodology for Mental Illness and Developmental Disorders in Rural and Frontier Settings," *Int J Circumpolar Health,* 2000, 59: 74–86.

[26]C. Gillberg, S. Steffenburg, and H. Schaumann, "Is Autism More Common Now Than Ten Years Ago?" *British Journal of Psychiatry,* 1991, 158: 403–9.

[27]H. L. Chang et al., "Screening for Autism Spectrum Disorder in Adult Psychiatric Outpatients in a Clinic in Taiwan," *Gen Hosp Psychiatry,* 2003, 25(4): 284–8.

[28]L. Nylander and C. Gillberg, "Screening for Autism Spectrum Disorders in Adult Psychiatric Out-patients: A Preliminary Report," *Acta Psychiatr Scand,* 2001, 103(6): 428–34.

[29]S. K. Katusic et al., "Case Definition in Epidemiologic Studies of AD/HD," *Ann Epidemiol,* 2005, 15(6): 430–7.

[30]Carl Haub, "How Many People Have Ever Lived on Earth?" *Population Today,* February 1995, www.prb.org/Articles/2002/HowManyPeopleHaveEverLivedonEarth.aspx.

[31]Gillberg et al., *op. cit.,* "Is Autism More Common Now?"

[32]C. Gillberg, H. Schaumann, and I. C. Gillberg, "Autism in Immigrants: Children Born in Sweden to Mothers Born in Uganda," *J Intellect Disabil Res,* 1995, 39 (Pt 2): 141–4. I. C. Gillberg and C. Gillberg, "Autism in Immigrants: A Population-based Study from Swedish Rural and Urban Areas," *J Intellect Disabil Res,* 1996, 40 (Pt 1): 24–31.

[33]C. Gillberg, H. Schaumann, and I. C. Gillberg, "Autism in Immigrants: Children Born in Sweden to Mothers Born in Uganda," *J Intellect Disabil Res,* 1995, 39 (Pt 2): 141–4.

[34]M. Barnevik-Olsson, C. Gillberg, and E. Fernell, "Prevalence of Autism in Children Born to Somali Parents Living in Sweden: A Brief Report," *Dev Med Child Neurol,* 2008, 50(8): 598–601.

[35]Mark F. Blaxill, "Out of Africa and Into Autism: More Evidence Illuminates the Somali Anomaly in Minnesota," Age of Autism, November 24, 2008, www.ageofautism.com/2008/11/out-of-africa-a.html.

[36]Dan Olmsted, "The Age of Autism: The Amish Anomaly," United Press International, April 19, 2005.

[37]Dan Olmsted, "The Age of Autism: 1 in 15,000 Amish," United Press International, June 8, 2005.

[38]Dan Olmsted, "The Age of Autism: Witness," United Press International, May 10, 2005.

[39]Ken Reibel, "Autism and the Amish," *Autism News Beat,* January 30, 2008, www.autism-news-beat.com/archives/29.

[40]Author interview with family, August 9, 2007.

[41]Centers for Disease Control and Prevention, "Congenital Rubella Syndrome Among the Amish, 1991–1992," *MMWR Weekly,* 1992, 41(26); 468–469, 475–476.

[42]Julie Gerberding at CDC Media Briefing, July 19, 2005, Washington, D.C.

[43]111th Congress, 1st Session, "A Bill to Direct the Secretary of Health and Human Services to Conduct or Support a Comprehensive Study Comparing Total Health Outcomes, Including Risk of Autism, in Vaccinated Populations in the United States with Such Outcomes in Unvaccinated Populations in the United States, and for Other Purposes," www.maloney.house.gov/documents/health/mercury/111_vaccine%20study%20bill.pdf.

[44]Jeffrey Bradstreet, quoted by Dan Olmsted, "The Age of Autism: Homeschooled," United Press International, June 28, 2005.

[45]Mayer Eisenstein, Autism One Conference, Chicago, May 24, 2009.

[46]W. R. Kates et al., "Neuroanatomic Variation in Monozygotic Twin Pairs Discordant for the Narrow Phenotype for Autism," *American Journal of Psychiatry,* 2004, 161(3): 539–46.

[47]L. A. Croen, J. K. Grether, and J. Hallmayer, "A Population-based Study of Autism Among Twins in California," IMFAR, Orlando, Florida, November 2002: 69.

[48]Taniai et al., *op. cit.,* "Influences on the Broad Spectrum of Autism: Study of Proband-Ascertained Twins."

[49]D. A. Greenberg, S. E. Hodge, J. Sowinski, and D. Nicoll, "Excess of Twins Among Affected Sibling Pairs with Autism: Implications for the Etiology of Autism," *Am J Hum Genet,* 2001, 69(5): 1062–7. C. Betancur, M. Leboyer, and C. Gillberg, "Increased Rate of Twins Among Affected Sibling Pairs with Autism," *Am J Hum Genet,* 2002, 70(5): 1381–3.

[50]J. N. Constantino and R. D. Todd, "Autistic Traits in the General Population: A Twin Study," *Arch Gen Psychiatry,* 2003, 60(5): 524–30.

[51]Testimony of Jeana Smith before the U.S. House of Representatives Government Reform Committee, April 6, 2000.

[52]Diane Powell, personal communication.

[53]Kim Stewart, personal communication.

CHAPTER 9

[1]Thomas S. Kuhn, *The Structure of Scientific Revolutions,* 2nd Edition, Enlarged (Chicago: University of Chicago Press, 1970), 77.

[2]*Shorter Oxford English Dictionary Sixth Edition* (Oxford, England: Oxford University Press, 2002, 2007). A word "formed by Horace Walpole after the title of a fairy tale, *The Three Princes of Serendip,* the heroes of which 'were always making discoveries, by accidents and sagacity, of things they were not in quest of.' "

[3]Kanner, Citation Classic.

[4]Lecture, University of Lille, December 7, 1854. This and alternative translations are at www.wikiquote.org/wiki/Louis_Pasteur.

[5]T. K. Dalziel, "Chronic Interstitial Colitis," *British Medical Journal,* 1913, 2: 1068–70.

[6]Burrill B. Crohn, Leon Ginzburg, and Gordon D. Oppenheimer, "Regional Ileitis," *Journal American Medical Association,* 1932, 99: 1323–9.

[7]Burrill B. Crohn and Harry Yarnis, *Regional Ileitis,* 2nd edition (New York: Grune & Stratton, 1958), v.

[8]"The worldwide increase of Crohn's disease during the 20th century and its greater frequency in industrialized countries over underdeveloped countries suggest environmental precipitating factors (microbial agents, food additives, industrial pollutants, etc.) not unique to any particular geographic area or to any ethnic group, interacting with an incompletely defined abnormality of the gastrointestinal tract (epithelial permeability, overreacting epithelium) and a genetically determined vulnerability to external agents," J. B. Kirsner, "Crohn's Disease: Yesterday, Today, and Tomorrow," *Gastroenterology,* 1997, 112(3): 1028–30.

[9]"The apparent rise in incidence of Crohn's disease cannot be explained by changes in diagnostic criteria, interval between symptom onset and hospital admission, inter-regional or national referral patterns or the population base." Also, "The results of this study . . . have serious implications for both doctors and patients," J. R. Barton, Sandra Gillon, and Anne Ferguson, "Incidence of Inflammatory Bowel Disease in Scottish Children Between 1968 and 1983, Marginal Fall in Ulcerative Colitis, Three-fold Rise in Crohn's Disease," *Gut,* 1989, 30(5): 18–22.

[10]John Walker-Smith and Simon Murch, *Diseases of the Small Intestine in Childhood,* 4th Edition (Oxford, England: Isis Medical Media, 1999), 300–1.

[11]One popular theory held that paratuberculosis, a relative of tuberculosis, was the infectious agent. Intestinal tuberculosis infection was among the handful of similar diseases typically excluded in the process of differential diagnosis that pinpointed a Crohn's disease case. More importantly, paratuberculosis infection had been identified as the specific cause of a cattle infection known as Johne's disease. The pathogenesis of Johne's disease in cattle strongly resembles that of Crohn's in humans. Logically enough, a large number of investigators were exploring (and continue to explore) the connection between paratuberculosis and Crohn's. But there were numerous questions about the paratuberculosis theory and substantial evidence against it, so theories about other infectious agents emerged around the same time, including measles. Measles virus is a relative of rinderpest, a viral cause of intestinal disease in cattle and also a cause of an identified form of persistent measles infection in humans (subacute sclerosing panencephalitis, or SSPE).

[12]They screened tissue, for example, for herpes virus DNA and used plastic resin casts to reveal the structure of the network of blood vessels in diseased patients. John Walker-Smith was so impressed by these images that he put one of them on the cover of his textbook.

[13]Andrew J. Wakefield, R. M. Pittilo, R. Sim et al., "Evidence of Persistent Measles Virus Infection in Crohn's Disease," *J Med Virol,* 1993, 39(4): 345–53.

[14]Anders Ekbom, H. O., Adami, C. G., Helmick et al., "Perinatal Risk Factors for Inflammatory Bowel Disease: A Case-control Study," *American Journal of Epidemiology,* 1990, 132(6): 1111–9.

[15]Anders Ekbom, Andrew J. Wakefield, M. Zack et al., "Perinatal Measles Infection and Subsequent Crohn's Disease," *The Lancet,* 1994, 344(8921): 508–10.

[16]Anders Ekbom, P. Daszak, W. Kraaz, and A. J. Wakefield, "Crohn's Disease After In-utero Measles Virus Exposure," *The Lancet,* 1996, 348(9026): 515–7.

[17]N. P. Thompson, Scott M. Montgomery, Roy E. Pounder, and Andrew J. Wakefield, "Is Measles Vaccination a Risk Factor for Inflammatory Bowel Disease?" *The Lancet,* 1995, 345(8957): 1071–4.

[18]Ironically, while Bettelheim's theory reviled the mother; it offered a ray of hope for the child: remove the mother, take him from the family home to a therapeutic milieu and a better life.

[19]Walker-Smith was in transition to the Royal Free from St. Bart's during this period, which created some delays in the treatment process. Walker-Smith's initial consultation with William Kessick came before his move to the Royal Free, but wasn't very extensive. After his move there, he began working with William and with other children more intensively.

[20]One "having symbolic significance . . . marking a beginning." *Shorter Oxford English Dictionary,* Sixth Edition (Oxford, England: Oxford University Press, 2002, 2007).

[21]Andrew J. Wakefield, Simon H. Murch, A. Anthony et al., "Ileal-lymphoid-nodular Hyperplasia, Non-specific Colitis, and Pervasive Developmental Disorder in Children," *The Lancet,* 1998, 351(9103): 637–41.

[22]The official body was called the Legal Aid Board. Not every child in *The Lancet* case series had approached the LAB, and none of them had done so at the point of referral. But over time, most of them became involved.

[23]William R. Long, "On Second Looking into the Case of Dr. Andrew J. Wakefield," *The Autism File,* March 2009.

[24]The literature on autoimmunity and bowel disease in autism is vast. The following is a sample of some of the most powerful evidence supporting Wakefield's finding of a novel pathology in autistic subjects. F. Balzola et al., "Panenteric IBD-like Disease in a Patient with Regressive Autism Shown for the First Time by Wireless Capsule Enteroscopy: Another Piece in the Jig-saw of the Gut-brain Syndrome?" *American Journal of Gastroenterology,* 2005, 100(4): 979–981. L. Gonzalez, K. Lopez, D. Navarro et al., "Endoscopic and Histological Characteristics of the Digestive Mucosa in Autistic Children with Gastro-Intestinal Symptoms," *Arch Venez Pueric Pediatr,* 2005, 69: 19–25. F. Balzola et al., "Autistic Enterocolitis: Confirmation of a New Inflammatory Bowel Disease in an Italian Cohort of Patients," *Gastroenterology,* 2005, 128(Suppl. 2); A-303. S. Walker, K. Hepner, J. Segal, and A. Krigsman, "Persistent Ileal Measles Virus in a Large Cohort of Regressive Autistic Children with Ileocolitis and Lymphonodular Hyperplasia: Revisitation of an Earlier Study" [IMFAR May 2007]. Paul Ashwood and Andrew J. Wakefield, "Immune Activation of Peripheral Blood and Mucosal CD3+ Lymphocyte Cytokine Profiles in Children with Autism and Gastrointestinal Symptoms," *Journal of Neuroimmunology,* 2006, 173(1-2): 126–34. Andrew J. Wakefield, Paul Ashwood, K. Limb, and A. Anthony, "The Significance of Ileo-colonic Lymphoid Nodular Hyperplasia in Children with Autistic Spectrum Disorder," *Eur J Gastroenterol Hepato,* 2005,17(8): 827–36. Paul Ashwood, A. Anthony, F. Torrente, and Andrew J.

Wakefield, "Spontaneous Mucosal Lymphocyte Cytokine Profiles in Children with Autism and Gastrointestinal Symptoms: Mucosal Immune Activation and Reduced Counter Regulatory Interleukin-10," *J Clin Immunol*, 2004, 24(6): 664–73. Paul Ashwood, A. Anthony, A. A. Pellicer et al., "Intestinal Lymphocyte Populations in Children with Regressive Autism: Evidence for Extensive Mucosal Immunopathology," *Journal of Clinical Immunology*, 2003, 23(6): 504–17. F. Torrente, Paul Ashwood, R. Day et al., "Small Intestinal Enteropathy with Epithelial IgG and Complement Deposition in Children with Regressive Autism," *Mol Psychiatry*, 2002, 7(4): 375–82, 334. F. Torrente, A. Anthony, R. B. Heuschkel et al., "Focal-enhanced Gastritis in Regressive Autism with Features Distinct from Crohn's and Helicobacter Pylori Gastritis," *Am J Gastroenterol*, 2004, 99(4): 598–605. R. L. Furlano et al., "Colonic CD8 and Gamma Delta T-cell Infiltration with Epithelial Damage in Children with Autism," *Journal of Pediatrics*, March 2001, 138(3): 366–72.

[25]O. Ivar Lovaas, "Behavioral Treatment and Normal Educational and Intellectual Functioning in Young Autistic Children," *J Consult Clin Psychol*, 1987, 55(1): 3–9.

[26]J. J. McEachin, T. Smith, and O. Ivar Lovaas, "Long-term Outcome for Children with Autism Who Received Early Intensive Behavioral Treatment," *Am J Ment Retard*, 1993, 97(4): 359–72.

[27]"Uproar Over a Little-known Preservative, Thimerosal, Jostles U.S. Hepatitis B Vaccination Policy," *Hepatitis Control Report*, 1999, 4(2).

[28]Centers for Disease Control and Prevention (CDC), "Thimerosal in Vaccines: A Joint Statement of the American Academy of Pediatrics and the Public Health Service," *Morb Mortal Wkly Rep*, 1999, 48(26): 563–5.

[29]J. A. Lowell, S. Burgess, S. Shenoy et al., "Mercury Poisoning Associated with High-dose Hepatitis-B Immune Globulin Administration After Liver Transplantation for Chronic Hepatitis B," *Liver Transpl Surg*, 1996, 2(6): 475–8.

[30]Sallie Bernard, Albert Enayati, Lyn Redwood et al., "Autism: A Novel Form of Mercury Poisoning," *Med Hypotheses*, 2001, 56(4): 462–71.

[31]Myron Levin, " '91 Memo Warned of Mercury in Shots," *Los Angeles Times*, February 8, 2005.

[32]Thomas Verstraeten, Robert L. Davis, Frank DeStefano et al., Vaccine Safety Datalink Team, "Safety of Thimerosal-containing Vaccines: A Two-phased Study of Computerized Health Maintenance Organization Databases," *Pediatrics*, 2003, 112(5): 1039–48.

[33]Mady Hornig, D. Chian, and W. Ian Lipkin, "Neurotoxic Effects of Postnatal Thimerosal are Mouse Strain Dependent," *Mol Psychiatry*. 2004, 9(9): 833–45.

[34]Thomas M. Burbacher, D. D. Shen, N. Liberato et al., "Comparison of Blood and Brain Mercury Levels in Infant Monkeys Exposed to Methylmercury or Vaccines Containing Thimerosal," *Environ Health Perspect*, 2005, 113(8): 1015–21.

[35]David Kirby, *op. cit., Evidence of Harm.*

[36]Robert F. Kennedy Jr., "Deadly Immunity," *Rolling Stone*, June 20, 2005.

[37]Gardiner Harris and Anahad O'Connor, "On Autism's Cause, It's Parents vs. Research," *The New York Times*, June 25, 2005.

[38]David Kirby, personal communication, November 22, 2005.

[39]Martha R. Herbert, "Autism: A Brain Disorder, or a Disorder that Affects the Brain?" *Clinical Neuropsychiatry*, 2005, 2(6): 354–379.

[40]Wakefield, et al. *op. cit.,* "The Significance of Ileo-colonic Lymphoid Nodular Hyperplasia in Children with Autistic Spectrum Disorder."

[41]One study reported a connection between HOX genes and autism, J. L. Ingram, C. J. Stodgell, S. L. Hyman et al., "Discovery of Allelic Variants of HOXA1 and HOXB1: Genetic Susceptibility to Autism Spectrum Disorders," *Teratology*, 2000, 62(6): 393–405. Subsequent studies failed to replicate the finding, J. Li, H. K. Tabor, L. Nguyen et al., "Lack of Association Between HoxA1 and HoxB1 Gene Variants and Autism in 110 Multiplex Families," *Am J Med Genet*, 2002, 114(1): 24–30. L. Gallagher, Z. Hawi, G. Kearney et al., "No Association Between Allelic Variants of HOXA1/HOXB1 and Autism," *Am J Med Genet B Neuropsychiatr Genet*, 2004, 124B(1): 64–7. B. Devlin, P. Bennett, E. H. Cook Jr., et al., "Collaborative Programs of Excellence in Autism (CPEA) Genetics Network. No evidence for Linkage of Liability to Autism to HOXA1 in a Sample from the CPEA Network," *Am J Med Genet*, 2002, 8;114(6): 667–72.

[42]For a recent negative study, see N. Ramoz, J. G. Reichert, T. E. Corwin, C. J. Smith et al., "Lack of Evidence for Association of the Serotonin Transporter Gene SLC6A4 with Autism," *Biol Psychiatry*, 2006, 60(2): 186–91. For a

description (overly optimistic, in our view) of the conflicting findings in the serotonin transporter gene, see B. Devlin, E. H. Cook Jr., H. Coon et al., "CPEA Genetics Network. Autism and the Serotonin Transporter: The Long and Short of It," *Mol Psychiatry*, 2005, 10(12): 1110–6.

[43]For a general discussion of the "hot spot" of copy number variation on chromosome 16p11 see E. E. Eichler and A. W. Zimmerman, "A Hot Spot of Genetic Instability in Autism," *New England Journal of Medicine*, 2008, 358(7): 737–9. For the study behind it see, L. A. Weiss, Y. Shen, J. M. Korn et al., Autism Consortium. "Association Between Microdeletion and Microduplication at 16p11.2 and Autism," *New England Journal of Medicine*, 2008, 358(7): 667–75.

[44]A "suggestive linkage" on chromosome 11p12 was reported in Autism Genome Project Consortium, "Mapping Autism Risk Loci Using Genetic Linkage and Chromosomal Rearrangements," *Nat Genet*, 2007, 39(3): 319–28.

[45]The first claim of a "common genetic variant" in an autism gene was reported in K. Wang, H. Zhang, D. Ma et al., "Common Genetic Variants on 5p14.1 Associate with Autism Spectrum Disorders," *Nature*, 2009, 459(7246): 528–33.

[46]The "hot spot" finding reported by the Harvard group in February 2008 was contradicted by a study published in May 2009 by the Children's Hospital of Philadelphia (CHOP), J. T. Glessner, K. Wang, G. Cai et al., "Autism Genome-wide Copy Number Variation Reveals Ubiquitin and Neuronal Genes," *Nature*, 2009, 459(7246): 569–73. The CHOP group, reporting no differences on 16p11 between cases and controls, said "We observed a similar frequency of deletions and duplications of the 16p11.2 locus in the ASD cases (~0.3%) as previously reported; however the CNV frequency in the control subjects at this locus was also comparable to that of the cases." The CHOP finding of a common inherited autism gene on chromosome 5p14 (which itself failed to confirm the "suggestive linkage" on chromosome 11p12 reported in 2007 by the Autism Genome Project Consortium) was subsequently contradicted by the Harvard group, see L. A. Weiss and D. E. Arking et al., Gene Discovery Project of Johns Hopkins & the Autism Consortium, "A Genome-wide Linkage and Association Scan Reveals Novel Loci for Autism," *Nature*, October 8, 2009, 461(7265): 802–8. While CHOP claimed that 65% of autism cases displayed the common genetic variant (as compared to 61% of controls), the Harvard group reported the opposite, saying, "During review of this manuscript, another genome-wide association study was published which identified significant association to SNPs on chromosome 5p14. Although there was significant overlap between study samples, each of these scans contained a large set of unique families, so we sought to evaluate independent evidence of the top SNP (rs4307059) reported at 5p14 . . . [W]e observed no support for association at this locus..[and instead found a gene transmission frequency] in favour of the minor allele, a trend in the opposite direction as reported."

[47]Paul Offit, *Autism's False Prophets* (New York: Columbia University Press, 2008).

[48]Karl R. Popper, "The Problem of Demarcation" (1974), in David W. Miller, editor, *Popper Selections* (Princeton: Princeton University Press, 1985).

[49]Authors' calculations. The cumulative infant mercury dose through 24 months of age (weight adjusted, on a per kilogram basis) was 38 µg/kg in the 1990s. The cumulative exposure for an average infant exposed to mercury through influenza vaccines (including in utero exposures) is now 33.7µg/kg. The latter figure is biased in two ways: although we know that organic mercury concentrates in the fetus, it is overstated by excluding the maternal weight in the calculation; it is understated relative to the 1990s calculations because the mercury exposure comes earlier in neurological development.

[50]In the case of the MMR, this would include 2 different doses of 3 different vaccines—measles, mumps, and rubella—in one product, the MMR II.

[51]Robert Schechter and Judith K. Grether, "Continuing Increases in Autism Reported to California's Developmental Services System: Mercury in Retrograde," *Arch Gen Psychiatry*, 2008, 65(1): 19–24. In this study, the observed sample was limited, only three-year-olds born in 2003 would have fallen outside the period in which thimerosal-containing vaccines were in use, but the autism rate in three-year-olds went up in children born in 2003.

[52]John Stone, "The 64 Billion Dollar a Year Question for Simon Baron-Cohen, Ben Goldacre, Fiona Fox, and Autism Speaks UK," *Age of Autism*, April 21, 2009.

[53]Simon Baron-Cohen, Fiona J. Scott, C. Allison et al., "Prevalence of Autism-spectrum Conditions: UK School-based Population Study." *British Journal of Psychiatry*, 2009, 194(6): 500–9.

[54]Autism and Developmental Disabilities Monitoring Network Surveillance Year 2000 Principal Investigators; Centers for Disease Control and Prevention. "Prevalence of Autism Spectrum Disorders—Autism and Developmental Disabilities Monitoring Network, Six Sites, United States, 2000," *MMWR Surveill Summ*, 2007, 56(1): 1–11. Autism and

Developmental Disabilities Monitoring Network Surveillance Year 2002 Principal Investigators; Centers for Disease Control and Prevention. "Prevalence of Autism Spectrum Disorders—Autism and Developmental Disabilities Monitoring Network, 14 sites, United States, 2002," *MMWR Surveill Summ,* 2007, 56(1): 12–28.

CHAPTER 10

[1]Terence W. Deacon, *The Symbolic Species: The Co-evolution of Language and the Brain* (New York: W.W. Norton & Co. 1997), 23.

[2]Wendell Muncie, *Psychobiology and Psychiatry* (St. Louis: The C.V. Mosby Company, 1939), 24.

[3]T. W. Deacon, "What Makes the Human Brain Different?" *Annual Review of Anthropology,* 1997, 26: 337–57.

[4]J. DeSilva and J. Lesnik, "Chimpanzee Neonatal Brain Size: Implications for Brain Growth in Homo Erectus," *Journal of Human Evolution,* 2006, 51: 207–212.

[5]A. S. Dekaban and D. Sadowsky, "Changes in Brain Weights During the Span of Human Life: Relation of Brain Weights to Body Heights and Body Weights," *Ann Neurol,* 1978, 4: 345–56.

[6]Barry Bogin, "Evolutionary Hypotheses for Human Childhood," *Yearbook of Physical Anthropology,* 1997, 40: 63–89.

[7]Dekaban and Sadowsky, *op. cit.,* 1978.

[8]Bogin, *op. cit.,* 1997.

[9]Dekaban and Sadowsky, *op. cit.,* 1978.

[10]C. R. Gale, F. J. O'Callaghan, K. M. Godfrey et al., "Critical Periods of Brain Growth and Cognitive Function in Children," *Brain,* 2004, 127: 321–9.

[11]C. R. Gale and F. J. O'Callaghan et al., Avon Longitudinal Study of Parents and Children Study Team, "The Influence of Head Growth in Fetal Life, Infancy, and Childhood on Intelligence at the Ages of 4 and 8 Years," *Pediatrics,* 2006, 118(4): 1486–92.

[12]Martha R. Herbert, "Large Brains in Autism: The Challenge of Pervasive Abnormality," *Neuroscientist,* 2005, 11(5): 417–40.

[13]E. Courchesne, K. Pierce, C. M. Schumann et al., "Mapping Early Brain Development in Autism," *Neuron,* 2007, 56(2): 399–413.

[14]Y. A. Dementieva, D. D. Vance, S. L. Donnelly et al., "Accelerated Head Growth in Early Development of Individuals with Autism," *Pediatric Neurology,* 2005, 32(2): 102–8.

[15]Herbert, *op. cit.,* 2005.

[16]Leslie C. Aiello and Peter Wheeler, "The Expensive-tissue Hypothesis: The Brain and the Digestive System in Human and Primate Evolution," *Current Anthropology,* 1995, 36(2): 199–221.

[17]Malcolm A. Holliday, "Body Composition and Energy Needs During Growth," in F. Falkner and J. M. Tanner editors, *Human Growth: A Comprehensive Treatise,* 2nd edition (New York: Plenum Pres, 1986), 101–17.

[18]Ibid.

[19]William H. Thomas, *What Are Old People For? How Elders Will Save the World* (Acton, Massachusetts: VanderWyk & Burnham, 2004), 52.

[20]H. T. Epstein, "Possible Metabolic Constraints on Human Brain Weight at Birth," *Am J. Phys. Anthrop,* 2005, 39: 135–5.

[21]R. D. Martin, "Human Reproduction: A Comparative Background for Medical Hypotheses," *Journal of Reproductive Immunology,* 2003, 59: 111–35.

[22]W. R. Leonard and M. L. Robertson, "On Diet, Energy Metabolism, and Brain Size in Human Evolution," *Current Anthropology,* 1996, 37(11): 125–9.

[23]Aiello and Wheeler, *op. cit.,* "The Expensive-tissue Hypothesis: The Brain and Digestive System in Human and Primate Evolution," 1995.

[24]A. Gibbons, "Solving the Brain's Energy Crisis," *Science,* 1998, 280(5368): 1345–7.

[25]P. L. Else and A. J. Hulbert, "Mammals: An Allometric Study of Metabolism at Tissue and Mitochondrial Level," *Am J Physiol Regulatory Integrative Comp Physiol,"* 1985, 248: 415–21.

[26]W. Qian, M. Nishikawa, A.M. Haque et al., "Mitochondrial Density Determines the Cellular Sensitivity to Cisplatin-induced Cell Death," *Am Journal of Physiol Cell Phsyiol,* 2005, 289(6): 1466–75.

[27]B. Chamak, B. Bonniau, E. Jaunay, and D. Cohen, "What Can We Learn About Autism from Autistic Persons?" *Psychother Psychosom,* 2008, 77(5): 271–9.

[28]Mark Noble, "Redox Modulation of Cellular Function: Cellular and Mechanistic Analyses" Presentation to the Workshop on Autism and the Environment: Challenges and Opportunites for Research, Institute of Medicine, April 18, 2007, www.iom.edu/~/media/Files/Activity%20Files/Research/NeuroForum/Noblefinal04_16_07.ashx accessed June 24, 2007.

[29]Abha Chauhan, Ved Chauhan, and Ted Brown, editors, *Autism: Oxidative Stress, Inflammation and Immune Abnormalities* (Florida: CRC Press, 2009).

[30]Charles A. Janeway, Paul Travers, and Mark Walport, *Immunobiology: The Immune System in Health and Disease*, 4th edition (New York: Garland Publishing, 1999), 525.

[31]R. Sacco, R. Militerni, A. Frolli et al., "Clinical, Morphological, and Biochemical Correlates of Head Circumference in Autism," *Biol Psychiatry,* 2007, 62(9): 1038–47.

[32]Several studies have reported on the relationship between familial autoimmunity and autism. These include, A. M. Comi, A. W. Zimmerman, V. H. Frye et al., "Familial Clustering of Autoimmune Disorders and Evaluation of Medical Risk Factors in Autism," *J Child Neurol*, 1999, 14(6): 388–94. T. L. Sweeten, S. L. Bowyer, D. J. Posey et al., "Increased Prevalence of Familial Autoimmunity in Probands with Pervasive Developmental Disorders," *Pediatrics,* 2003, 112(5): e420. L. A. Croen, J. K. Grether, C. K. Yoshida et al., "Maternal Autoimmune Diseases, Asthma and Allergies, and Childhood Autism Spectrum Disorders: A Case-Control Study," *Arch Pediatr Adolesc Med,* 2005, 159(2): 151–7. H. O. Atladóttir, M. G. Pedersen, P. Thorsen et al., "Association of Family History of Autoimmune Diseases and Autism Spectrum Disorders," *Pediatrics,* 2009, 124(2): 687–94.

[33]H. Jyonouchi, L. Geng, A. Ruby et al., "Evaluation of an Association Between Gastrointestinal Symptoms and Cytokine Production Against Common Dietary Proteins in Children with Autism Spectrum Disorders," *Journal of Pediatrics,* 2005, 146(5): 605–10.

[34]Noble 2007. In his IOM presentation, Noble provided data showing that thimerosal exposure reduced the survival of neuroglial precursor cells at concentrations in the range of 20–50 nanomolar, which is equivalent to 4–10 parts per billion.

[35]Burbacher et al., *op. cit.,* "Comparison of Blood and Brain Mercury Levels in Infant Monkeys Exposed to Methylmercury or Vaccines Containing Thimerosal," 2005.

[36]M. L. Humphrey, M. P. Cole, J. C. Pendergrass, and K. K. Kiningham, "Mitochondrial Mediated Thimerosal-induced Apoptosis in a Human Neuroblastoma Cell Line (SK-N-SH)," *Neurotoxicology,* 2005, 26(3): 407–16. L. Yel, L. E. Brown, K. Su et al., "Thimerosal Induces Neuronal Cell Apoptosis by Causing Cytochrome and Apoptosis-inducing Factor Release from Mitochondria," *Int J Mol Med,* 2005, 16(6): 971–7.

[37]See D. K. Parran, A. Barker, and M. Ehrich, "Effects of Thimerosal on NGF Signal Transduction and Cell Death in Neuroblastoma Cells," *Toxicol Sci,* 2005, 86(1): 132–40. Toxic effects were observed at concentrations of 10–100 nanomolar.

[38]S. Havarinasab and P. Hultman, "Organic Mercury Compounds and Autoimmunity," *Autoimmun Rev,* 2005, 4(5): 270–5.

[39]S. R. Goth, R. A. Chu, J. P. Gregg et al., "Uncoupling of ATP-mediated Calcium Signaling and Dysregulated Interleukin-6 Secretion in Dendritic Cells by Nanomolar Thimerosal," *Environ Health Perspect,* 2006, 114(7): 1083–91. Toxic effects were observed at concentrations of 20–40 nanomolar.

[40]J. S. Charleston, R. P. Bolender, N. K. Mottet et al., "Increases in the Number of Reactive Glia in the Visual Cortex of Macaca Fascicularis Following Subclinical Long-term Methyl Mercury Exposure," *Toxicol Appl Pharmacol,* 1994, 129(2): 196–206.

[41]Burbacher et al., *op. cit.,* "Comparison of Blood and Brain Mercury Levels in Infant Monkeys Exposed to Methylmercury or Vaccines Containing Thimerosal," 2005.

[42]S. J. James, W. Slikker, S. Melnyk et al., "Thimerosal Neurotoxicity is Associated with Glutathione Depletion: Protection with Glutathione Precursors," *Neurotoxicology.* 2005; 26(1):1–8.

[43]F. M. Yakes and B. Van Houten, "Mitochondrial DNA Damage Is More Extensive and Persists Longer Than Nuclear DNA Damage in Human Cells Following Oxidative Stress," *Proc Natl Acad Sci U.S.A.,* 1997, 94(2): 514–9.

[44]D. A. Geier, P. G. King, and M. R. Geier, "Mitochondrial Dysfunction, Impaired Oxidative-reduction Activity, Degeneration, and Death in Human Neuronal and Fetal Cells Induced by Low-level Exposure to Thimerosal and Other Metal Compounds," *Toxicological & Environmental Chemistry,* 2009, 91(4): 735–49.

[45]S. J. James, P. Cutler, S. Melnyk et al., "Metabolic Biomarkers of Increased Oxidative Stress and Impaired Methylation Capacity in Children with Autism," *Am J Clin Nutr,* 2004, 80(6): 1611–7. S. J. James, S. Melnyk, S. Jernigan et al., "Metabolic Endophenotype and Related Genotypes are Associated with Oxidative Stress in Children with Autism," *Am J Med Genet B Neuropsychiatr Genet,* 2006, 141B(8): 947–56.

[46]A. Chauhan, V. Chauhan, W. T. Brown, and I. Cohen, "Oxidative Stress in Autism: Increased Lipid Peroxidation and Reduced Serum Levels of Ceruloplasmin and Transferrin—The Antioxidant Proteins," *Life Sci,* 2004, 75(21): 2539–49. S. Söğüt, S. S. Zoroğlu, H. Ozyurt et al., "Changes in Nitric Oxide Levels and Antioxidant Enzyme Activities May Have a Role in the Pathophysiological Mechanisms Involved in Autism," *Clin Chim Acta,* 2003, 331(1–2): 111–7. S. S. Zoroğlu, M. Yürekli, and I. Meram et al., "Pathophysiological Role of Nitric Oxide and Adrenomedullin in Autism," *Cell Biochem Funct,* 2003, 21(1): 55–60. S. S. Zoroglu, F. Armutcu, S. Ozen et al., "Increased Oxidative Stress and Altered Activities of Erythrocyte Free Radical Scavenging Enzymes in Autism," *Eur Arch Psychiatry Clin Neurosci,* 2004, 254(3): 143–7. X. Ming, T. P. Stein, M. Brimacombe et al., "Increased Excretion of a Lipid Peroxidation Biomarker in Autism," *Prostaglandins Leukot Essent Fatty Acids,* 2005, 73(5): 379–84. J. K. Kern and A. M. Jones, "Evidence of Toxicity, Oxidative Stress, and Neuronal Insult in Autism," *J Toxicol Environ Health B Crit Rev,* 2006, 9(6): 485–99. T. L. Sweeten, D. J. Posey, S. Shankar, and C. J. McDougle, "High Nitric Oxide Production in Autistic Disorder: A Possible Role for Interferon-gamma," *Biol Psychiatry,* 2004, 15;55(4): 434–7.

[47]S. J. James, S. Melnyk, S. Jernigan et al., "Metabolic Endophenotype and Related Genotypes are Associated with Oxidative Stress in Children with Autism," *Am J Med Genet B Neuropsychiatr Genet,* 2006, 141B(8): 947–56.

[48]J. Stringari, A. K. Nunes, J. L. Franco et al., "Prenatal Methylmercury Exposure Hampers Glutathione Antioxidant System Ontogenesis and Causes Long-lasting Oxidative Stress in the Mouse Brain," *Toxicol Appl Pharmacol,* 2008, 227(1): 147–54.

[49]See above and Comi et al., *op. cit.,* "Familial Clustering of Autoimmune Disorders and Evaluation of Medical Risk Factors in Autism," 1999. Sweeten et al., *op. cit.,* "Increased Prevalence of Familial Autoimmunity in Probands with Pervasive Developmental Disorders," 2003. Croen et al., *op. cit.,* "Maternal Autoimmune Diseases, Asthma and Allergies, and Childhood Autism Spectrum Disorders: A Case-control Study," 2005. Sacco et al., *op. cit.,* "Clinical Morphological, and Biochemical Correlates of Head Circumference in Autism," 2007.

[50]D. L. Vargas, C. Nascimbene, C. Krishnan et al., "Neuroglial Activation and Neuroinflammation in the Brain of Patients with Autism," *Ann Neurol,* 2005, 57(1): 67–81.

[51]P. Ashwood, A. J. Wakefield, "Immune Activation of Peripheral Blood and Mucosal CD3+ Lymphocyte Cytokine Profiles in Children with Autism and Gastrointestinal Symptoms," *Journal of Neuroimmunology,* 2006, 173(1-2): 126–34. R. I. Furlano, A. Anthony, R. Day et al., "Colonic CD8 and Gamma Delta T-cell Infiltration with Epithelial Damage in Children with Autism," *Journal of Pediatrics,* 2001, 138(3): 366–72. P. Ashwood, A. Anthony, A. A. Pellicer et al., "Intestinal Lymphocyte Populations in Children with Regressive Autism: Evidence for Extensive Mucosal Immunopathology," *Journal of Clinical Immunology,* 2003, 23(6): 504–17. P. Ashwood, A. Anthony, F. Torrente, and A. J. Wakefield, "Spontaneous Mucosal Lymphocyte Cytokine Profiles in Children with Autism and Gastrointestinal Symptoms: Mucosal Immune Activation and Reduced Counter Regulatory Interleukin-10," *Journal of Clinical Immunology,* 2004, 24(6): 664–73. F. Torrente, P. Ashwood, R. Day et al., "Small Intestinal Enteropathy with Epithelial IgG and Complement Deposition in Children with Regressive Autism," *Mol Psychiatry,* 2002, 7(4): 375–82, 334.

[52]H. Jyonouchi, L. Geng, A. Ruby et al., "Evaluation of an Association Between Gastrointestinal Symptoms and Cytokine Production Against Common Dietary Proteins in Children with Autism Spectrum Disorders," *Journal of Pediatrics,* 2005, 146(5): 605–10. H. Jyonouchi, S. Sun, and N. Itokazu, "Innate Immunity Associated with Inflammatory Responses and Cytokine Production Against Common Dietary Proteins in Patients with Autism Spectrum Disorder," *Neuropsychobiology,* 2002, 46(2): 76–84. A. Vojdani, A. W. Campbell, E. Anyanwu et al., "Antibodies to Neuron-specific Antigens in Children with Autism: Possible Cross-reaction with Encephalitogenic Proteins from Milk, Chlamydia Pneumoniae and Streptococcus Group A. *Journal of Neuroimmunology,* 2002, 129(1–2): 168–77.

[53]S. Havarinasab, and P. Hultman, "Alteration of the Spontaneous Systemic Autoimmune Disease in (NZB x NZW)F1 Mice by Treatment with Thimerosal (ethyl mercury), *Toxicol Appl Pharmacol,* 2006, 214(1): 43–54. S. Havarinasab, B. Häggqvist, E. Björn et al., "Immunosuppressive and Autoimmune Effects of Thimerosal in Mice," *Toxicol Appl Pharmacol,* 2005, 204(2): 109–21. S. Havarinasab, L. Lambertsson, J. Qvarnström, and P. Hultman, "Dose-response Study of Thimerosal-induced Murine Systemic Autoimmunity," *Toxicol Appl Pharmacol,* 2004, 194(2): 169–79.

[54]S. J. James, S. Rose, S. Melnyk et al., "Cellular and Mitochondrial Glutathione Redox Imbalance in Lymphoblastoid Cells Derived from Children with Autism," *FASEB J*, 2009, 23(8): 2374–83. S. J. James, S. Melnyk, G. Fuchs et al., "Efficacy of Methylcobalamin and Folinic Acid Treatment on Glutathione Redox Status in Children with Autism," *Am J Clin Nutr*, 2009, 89(1): 425–30. S. J. James, P. Cutler, S. Melnyk et al., "Metabolic Biomarkers of Increased Oxidative Stress and Impaired Methylation Capacity in Children with Autism," *Am J Clin Nutr*, 2004, 80(6): 1611–7.

[55]S. J. James, S. Rose, and S. Melnyk et al., "Cellular and Mitochondrial Glutathione Redox Imbalance in Lymphoblastoid Cells Derived from Children with Autism," *FASEB J*, 2009, 23(8): 2374–83.

[56]See G. Oliveira, A. Ataíde, C. Marques et al., "Epidemiology of Autism Spectrum Disorder in Portugal: Prevalence, Clinical Characterization, and Medical Conditions," *Dev Med Child Neurol*, 2007, 49(10): 726–33. C. Correia, A. M. Coutinho, L. Diogo et al., "Brief Report: High Frequency of Biochemical Markers for Mitochondrial Dysfunction in Autism: No Association with the Mitochondrial Aspartate/Glutamate Carrier SLC25A12 Gene," *J Autism Dev Disord*, 2006, 36(8): 1137–40. J. S. Poling, R. E. Frye, J. Shoffner, and A. W. Zimmermann, "Developmental Regression and Mitochondrial Dysfunction in a Child with Autism," *J Child Neurol*, 2006, 21(2): 170–2.

[57]L. E. Davis, M. Kornfeld, H. S. Mooney et al., "Methylmercury Poisoning: Long-term Clinical, Radiological, Toxicological, and Pathological Studies of an Affected Family," *Ann Neurol*, 1994, 35(6): 680–8.

[58]S. E. Schober, T. H. Sinks, R. L. Jones et al., "Blood Mercury Levels in U.S. Children and Women of Childbearing Age, 1999–2000," *JAMA*, 2003, 289(13): 1667–74.

[59]D. R. Laks, "Assessment of Chronic Mercury Exposure Within the U.S. Population, National Health and Nutrition Examination Survey, 1999–2006," *Biometals*, August 21, 2009. [Epub ahead of print]

[60]A. S. Holmes, M. F. Blaxill, and B. E. Haley, "Reduced Levels of Mercury in First Baby Haircuts of Autistic Children," *Int J Toxicol*, 2003, 22(4): 277–85.

[61]J. B. Adams, J. Romdalvik, K. E. Levine, and L. W. Hu, "Mercury in First-cut Baby Hair of Children with Autism Versus Typically-developing Children," *Toxicological & Environmental Chemistry*," 2008, 90(4): 739–753.

[62]A. Fido, S. Al-Saad, "Toxic Trace Elements in the Hair of Children with Autism," *Autism*, 2005, 9(3): 290–8.

[63]P. Ip, V. Wong, M. Ho et al., "Mercury Exposure in Children with Autistic Spectrum Disorder: Case-control Study," *Journal of Child Neurology*, 2004, 19(6): 431–4.

[64]Ibid., Erratum in *Journal of Child Neurology*, 2007, 22(11): 1324.

[65]M. C. Desoto, and R. T. Hitlan, "Blood Levels of Mercury are Related to Diagnosis of Autism: A Reanalysis of an Important Data Set," *Journal of Child Neurology*, 2007, 22(11): 1308–11.

[66]M. A. McDowell, C. F. Dillon, and J. Osterloh et al., "Hair Mercury Levels in U.S. Children and Women of Childbearing Age: Reference Range Data from NHANES 1999–2000," *Environ Health Perspect*, 2004, 112(11): 1165–71.

[67]R. C. Marques, J. G. Dórea, M. F. Fonseca, W. R. Bastos, and O. Malm, "Hair Mercury in Breast-fed Infants Exposed to Thimerosal-preserved Vaccines," *Eur J Pediatr*, 2007, 166(9): 935–41.

[68]J. B. Adams, J. Romdalvik, V. M. Ramanujam, and M. S. Legator, "Mercury, Lead, and Zinc in Baby Teeth of Children with Autism Versus Controls," *J Toxicol Environ Health A*, 2007, 70(12): 1046–51.

[69]E. M. Sajdel-Sulkowski, B. Lipinski, H. Windom et al., "Oxidative Stress in Autism: Elevated Cerebellar 3-nitrotyrosine Levels," *American Journal of Biochemistry and Biotechnology*, 2008, 4(2): 73–84.

[70]R. F. Palmer, S. Blanchard, Z. Stein et al., "Environmental Mercury Release, Special Education Rates, and Autism Disorder: An Ecological Study of Texas," *Health Place*, 2006, 12(2): 203–9.

[71]R. F. Palmer, S. Blanchard, and R. Wood, "Proximity to Point Sources of Environmental Mercury Release as a Predictor of Autism Prevalence," *Health Place*, 2009, 15(1): 18–24.

[72]G. C. Windham, L. Zhang, R. Gunier et al., "Autism Spectrum Disorders in Relation to Distribution of Hazardous Air Pollutants in the San Francisco Bay Area," *Environ Health Perspect*, 2006, 114(9): 1438–44.

[73]C. Bombardier, L. Laine, A. Reicin et al., VIGOR Study Group, "Comparison of Upper Gastrointestinal Toxicity of Rofecoxib and Naproxen in Patients with Rheumatoid Arthritis," *New England Journal of Medicine*, 2000, 343(21): 1520–8, 2 p following 1528.

[74]G. D. Curfman, S. Morrissey, and J. M Drazen, Expression of concern: Bombardier et al., "Comparison of Upper Gastrointestinal Toxicity of Rofecoxib and Naproxen in Patients with Rheumatoid Arthritis," *New England Journal of Medicine*, 2000, 343: 1520–8. *New England Journal of Medicine*, 2005, 353(26): 2813–4.

[75]Kirby, *op. cit., Evidence of Harm—Mercury in Vaccines and the Autism Epidemic: A Medical Controversy*, 407–9.

[76]Institute of Medicine, Committee on Immunization Safety, *Immunization Safety Review: Vaccines and Autism* (Washington, D.C.: National Academics Press, 2004).

[77]C. M. Gallagher and M. S. Goodman, "Hepatitis B Triple Series Vaccine and Developmental Disability in U.S. Children Aged 1–9 Years," *Toxicological & Environmental Chemistry*, 2008, 90(5): 997–1008. C. M. Gallagher and M. S. Goodman, "Hepatitis B Vaccination of Male Neonates and Autism, *Annals of Epidemiology*, 2009, 19(9): 659.

[78]M. Hornig, T. Briese, T. Buie et al., "Lack of Association Between Measles Virus Vaccine and Autism with Enteropathy: A Case-control Study," *PLoS One*, 2008, 3(9): e3140.

[79]V. Uhlmann, C. M. Martin, O. Sheils et al., "Potential Viral Pathogenic Mechanism for new Variant Inflammatory Bowel Disease," *Mol Pathol*, 2002, 55(2): 84–90.

[80]M. Hornig, D. Chian, and W. I. Lipkin, "Neurotoxic Effects of Postnatal Thimerosal are Mouse Strain Dependent," *Mol Psychiatry*, 2004, 9(9): 833–45.

[81]R. F. Berman, I. N. Pessah, P. R. Mouton et al., "Low-level Neonatal Thimerosal Exposure: Further Evaluation of Altered Neurotoxic Potential in SJL Mice," *Toxicol Sci*, 2008, 101(2): 294–309.

[82]Kirby, *op. cit., Evidence of Harm*, 418.

[83]J. G. Dórea, R. C. Marques, and K. G. Brandão, "Neonate Exposure to Thimerosal Mercury from Hepatitis B Vaccines," *Am J Perinatol*, 2009, 26(7): 523–7.

[84]J. Laurente, F. Remuzgo, B. Valos et al., "Neurotoxic Effects of Thimerosal at Vaccines Doses on the Encephalon and Development in 7-day-old Hamsters," *An. Fac. Med*, 2007, 68(3): 222–237.

[85]Ibid.

[86]Ibid.

[87]M. Olczak, M Duszczyk, P. Mierzejewski, and M. D. Majewska, "Neonatal Administration of a Vaccine Preservative, Thimerosal, Produces Lasting Impairment of Nociception and Apparent Activation of Opioid System in Rats," *Brain Res*, 2009, 1301: 143–51.

[88]Ibid.

[89]Hewitson et al., IMFAR 08.

[90]Ibid.

[91]Ibid.

[92]L. Hewitson, L. A. Houser, C. Stott et al., "Delayed Acquisition of Neonatal Reflexes in Newborn Primates Receiving a Thimerosal-containing Hepatitis B Vaccine: Influence of Gestational Age and Birth Weight," *NeuroToxicology*, October 2, 2009. [Epub ahead of print]

[93]Generation Rescue, "Autism and Vaccines Around the World: Vaccine Schedules, Autism Rates, and Under 5 Mortality," April 2009/www.generationrescue.org/documents/SPECIAL%20REPORT%20AUTISM%202.pdf. Accessed December 18, 2009.

[94]Robert Koch Biography, "The Nobel Prize in Physiology or Medicine: 1905," www.nobelprize.org/nobel_prizes/medicine/laureates/1905/koch-bio.html. Accessed December 18, 2009.

[95]P. M. Strebel, N. Ion-Nedelcu, A. L. Baughman et al., "Intramuscular Injections Within 30 Days of Immunization with Oral Poliovirus Vaccine—A Risk Factor for Vaccine-associated Paralytic Poliomyelitis," *New England Journal of Medicine*, 1995, 332(8): 500–6.

[96]E. Rotshild, "Infectious Disease as Viewed by a Naturalist," *The Open Country*, 2001, 3: 46–62.

[97]For example, see C. R. Adams, D. K. Ziegler, and J. T. Lin, "Mercury Intoxication Simulating Amyotrophic Lateral Sclerosis, *Journal of the American Medical Association*, 1983, 5; 250(5): 642–3. T. E. Barber, "Inorganic Mercury Intoxication Reminiscent of Amyotrophic Lateral Sclerosis," *J Occup Med*, 1978, 20(10): 667–9. A. D. Kantarjian, "A Syndrome Clinically Resembling Amyotrophic Lateral Sclerosis Following Chronic Mercurialism," *Neurology*, 1961, 11: 639–44. Beyond case studies like this, there is a modest amount of literature on the connection between ALS and mercury exposure, much of it from Japan, with a common finding of increased risk of ALS resulting from mercury exposure.

[98]Mark Noble, manuscript in preparation.

[99]Ibid.

[100]Ibid.

[101]R. Schechter and J. K. Grether, "Continuing Increases in Autism Reported to California's Developmental Services system: Mercury in Retrograde," *Arch Gen Psychiatry,* 2008, 65(1): 19–24.

[102]Mark Noble, manuscript in preparation.

[103]F. Kennedy, "The Problem of Social Control of the Congenital Defective: Education, Sterilization, Euthanasia," *American Journal of Psychiatry,* 1942, 99: 13–16.

[104]Leo Kanner, "Exoneration of the Feeble-minded," *American Journal of Psychiatry,* 1942, 99: 17–22.

[105]Mark Noble, personal communication.

[106]Hans Asperger, *op. cit.,* " 'Autistic Psychopathy' in Childhood."

[107]Ibid.

[108]Ibid.

[109]Scott Bono, personal communication.

EPILOGUE

[1]Leo Kanner, *op. cit.,* Follow-Up Study.

[2]Elizabeth Peabody Trevett, "A Maternal and Child-health Service on the Euphrates, *Children* 1955, 2(2): 56–62.

[3]Elizabeth Peabody Trevett Biofile, Personal correspondence, Courtesy of The Alan Mason Chesney Medical Archives of The Johns Hopkins Medical Institutions.

[4]Elizabeth Peabody Trevett Biofile.

[5]Leo Kanner, Follow-Up Study.

[6]Helen Taussig, memorial tribute, Elizabeth Peabody Trevett Biofile.

[7]Peter Muncie, personal communication.

[8]Jay Rosenberg, interview with authors, Dec. 22, 2008, Montreal, Canada.

[9]Leo Kanner, *op. cit.,* "Autistic Disturbances of Affective Contact."

[10]Robert Aycock, personal communication.

[11]O. B. Triplett III, interview with authors, August 12, 2005, Forest Mississippi.

[12]Kanner, *op. cit.,* Citation Classic.

[13]Jeffrey A. Lieberman at New York State Assembly public hearing on autism, March 8, 2007. Albany, New York. www.youtube.com/watch?v=A4w87pQTvjw&feature=related.

[14]J. M. Rumsey, N. C. Andreasen, J. L. Rapoport, "Thought, Language, Communication, and Affective Flattening in Autistic Adults," *Arch Gen Psychiatry,* 1986, 43(8): 771–7. J. M. Rumsey, R. Duara, C. Grady et al., "Brain Metabolism in Autism—Resting Cerebral Glucose Utilization Rates as Measured with Position Emission Tomography," *Arch Gen Psychiatry,* 1985, 42(5): 448–55.

APPENDIX A

[1]J. J. Peters, J. H. Peers, S. Olansky et al., "Untreated Syphilis in the Male Negro; Pathologic findings in Syphilitic and Nonsyphlitic Patients," *J Chronic Dis,* 1955, 1(2), 127–48.

[2]S. Olansky, Sh. H. Schuman, J. J. Peters et al., "Untreated Syphilis in the Male Negro: Twenty Years of Clinical Observation of Untreated Syphilitic and Presumably Nonsyphilitic Groups," *J Chronic Dis,* 1956, 4(2): 177–85.

INDEX